# Education and Development in East Asia

REFERENCE BOOKS IN INTERNATIONAL EDUCATION
VOLUME 31
GARLAND REFERENCE LIBRARY OF SOCIAL SCIENCE
VOLUME 942

# Education and Development in East Asia

Edited by
Paul Morris
Anthony Sweeting

Garland Publishing, Inc.
New York and London
1995

**Library of Congress Cataloging-in-Publication Data**

Education and development in East Asia / edited by Paul Morris, Anthony Sweeting.
p. cm. — (Garland reference library of social science ; vol. 942. Reference books in international education ; vol. 31)
Includes bibliographical references and index.
ISBN 0-8153-1598-8 (alk. paper)
1. Education—Economic aspects—East Asia. 2. Economic development—Effect of education on. I. Morris, Paul, 1946– II. Sweeting, Anthony. III. Series: Garland reference library of social science ; v. 942. IV. Series: Garland reference library of social science. Reference books in international education ; vol. 31.
LC66.5.E18E38 1995
338.4'7370'95—dc20 95-1545
CIP

Printed on acid-free, 250-year-life paper
Manufactured in the United States of America

# Contents

# Series Editor's Foreword

This series of scholarly works in comparative and international education has grown well beyond the initial conception of a collection of reference books. Although retaining its original purpose of providing a resource to scholars, students, and a variety of other professionals who need to understand the role played by education in various societies or regions of the world, it also strives to provide up-to-date information on a wide variety of selected educational issues, problems, and experiments within an international context.

Contributors to this series are well-known scholars who have devoted their professional lives to the study of their specialization. Without exception these men and women possess an intimate understanding of the subject of their research and writing. Without exception they have not only studied their subject in dusty archives, but they have also lived and traveled widely in their quest for knowledge. In short, they are "experts" in the best sense of that often overused word.

In our increasingly interdependent world, it is now widely understood that it is a matter of survival that we not only understand better what makes other societies tick, but that we also make a serious effort to understand how others, be they Japanese, German or Chilean, attempt to solve the same kinds of educational problems that we face in North America. As the late George Z.F. Bereday wrote: "[E]ducation is a mirror held against the face of a people. Nations may put on blustering shows of strength to conceal public weakness, erect grand façades to conceal shabby backyards, and profess peace while secretly arming for conquest, but how they take care of their children tells unerringly who they are" (*Comparative Methods in Education*, New York: Holt, Rinehart & Winston, 1964, p. 5).

Perhaps equally important, however, is the valuable perspective that studying another education system (or its problems) provides us in understanding our own system (or its problems). To step outside our own limited experience and our commonly held assumptions about schools and learning in order to look back at our system in contrast to another places it in a very different light. To learn, for example, how the Soviet Union or Belgium handles the education of a multilingual society; how the French provide for the funding of public education; or how the Japanese control admissions into their universities enables us to understand that there are alternatives to our own familiar way of doing things. Not that we can often "borrow" directly from other societies; indeed, educational arrangements are inevitably a reflection of deeply rooted political, economic, and cultural factors that are unique to a society. But a conscious recognition that there are other ways of doing things can serve to open our minds and provoke our imaginations in ways that can result in new approaches that we would not have otherwise considered.

Since this series is intended to be a useful research tool, the editor and contributors welcome suggestions for future volumes as well as ways in which this series can be improved.

*Edward R. Beauchamp*
*University of Hawaii*

# Preface

After the Second World War, the East Asian region was among the poorest of the world. Characterized by high levels of illiteracy and ravaged by the aftermath of wars and civil wars, the region's prospects were not viewed with optimism. It was countries in Africa and Latin America that were thought to be on the threshold of rapid development. That scenario proved illusory. From 1965 to 1990, the twenty-three economies of East Asia grew faster than all other regions of the world, and most of this was a consequence of the growth in Japan, Hong Kong, Singapore, South Korea, Taiwan, Malaysia, China, Indonesia, and Thailand. The first seven of these countries,* along with Macau, are the subject of this volume. Those countries have grown more than twice as fast as the rest of East Asia, five times as fast as Latin America and South Asia and five times faster than sub-Saharan Africa. Further, this growth has been achieved along with an improvement in the distribution of income and of other measures of human welfare.

Attempts to explain the reasons for this success have spawned a number of studies which have identified a range of critical factors. When development in its broadest sense occurs, it involves improvements in various phenomena, including the provision and quality of education. It encourages analysts to focus on positive correlations between development and different variables (for example, physical or human capital) which may be viewed as both a source and a manifestation of development. As this latter point suggests, however, this situation also makes it difficult to disentangle the causes from the effects of development.

Our concern in this volume is to examine the specific role that formal education has played in the process of development. Our perspective is

*We use the term "country" throughout this volume for ease of expression and comparison. We recognize that, in constitutional terms, Hong Kong and Macau are not normally referred to in this way.

not a technical one, designed solely to measure the relationship between inputs and outputs. These have emphasized education's role as a source of growth but do not tell the entire story. We analyze education's role with reference to its links with the economic, social and political domains in the postwar period. We hope to demonstrate both the changing nature of education's role within the countries and the varied nature of its role across the countries.

The book is organized as follows: chapter 1 provides an introduction which briefly describes the extent of development in East Asia and distinguishes the main perspectives used to explain the role of education in development. Chapters 2–9 analyze the role education played in the development of eight countries in East Asia. The order of these chapters follows the chronology of rapid development. We thus start with Japan and end with the People's Republic of China. The final chapter compares the country-specific analyses and identifies the common and diverse features across them.

# 1 Education and Development

## An Introduction

*Paul Morris*

### Preface

We are concerned in this chapter with examining the obviously complex, intertwined and often symbiotic relationships between formal education and the various dimensions which can be used to classify development within a society. We use the term "development" in its broad sense, which encompasses not only improvements in living standards, but the introduction of new technologies and of social and institutional transformations. These include: the substitution of subsistence by exchange activities, increased urbanization, the increasing emphasis on forms of social differentiation based on criteria related to achievement rather than ascription, and the emergence of the nation-state as the basis for the political system. Thus while economic *growth* can occur as a result of an increase in GDP, whether or not this constitutes *development* will depend on whether there are associated structural changes in such other dimensions as the political and social. While we are, therefore, concerned with more than the purely economic aspects of development, we recognise that such development lies at the core of changes in other areas. Just as education affects aspects of development, so it is itself a reflection of and is influenced by the social, economic and political context in which it operates. Thus, we are also concerned with the impact of development on education.

The contributors to this volume examine the role education has played in eight societies in East Asia. Those societies are diverse in terms of their size, ethnic mix, economic structure and political system. They range from the small city states of Singapore, Hong Kong and Macau to the world's most populous nation, the People's Republic of China. In political terms they include the colonies of Hong Kong and Macau, the world's last remaining ostensibly communist superpower and the products of incomplete civil wars—Taiwan and South Korea. To varying degrees in each of the societies, government has performed a different role. This has ranged from tight control by the Communist Party in the PRC, the highly interventionist role of the governments in South Korea, Taiwan and Singapore (despite ostensibly democratic frameworks), to the relatively non-interventionist governments of Hong Kong and Macau which tend to provide only what cannot be provided by the private sector. Despite these differences, the respective governments, perhaps with the exception of the PRC, have linked their own survival and legitimacy to economic success.

## Development in East Asia

Japan's growth can be traced back to the Meiji Restoration in the late nineteenth century. By 1960, it was the most affluent society in Asia. This growth was emulated—though in a shorter time period—by a group of countries variously referred to as the Asian "Tigers" or "Dragons" or NICs (Hong Kong, South Korea, Taiwan and Singapore). Since 1980, China, Malaysia, Indonesia and Thailand have also begun to grow rapidly.

Table 1 provides data on a range of key social and economic indicators for the eight East Asian economies which are subsequently analyzed in this book. It also provides data on two economically less successful Asian countries, India and the Philippines. It can be seen that Japan and the four Asian tigers have achieved a high level of economic growth and of per capita GDP. In contrast the more recent rapidly growing Asian economies such as China, Malaysia and Macau have achieved impressive rates of growth but the level of GDP per capita is still low compared with the former group.

The extent, speed and unanticipated nature of this development needs underlining. In 1960 Japan had a per capita GDP which was one-eighth of that of the United States. In that year South Korea's GDP was the same as Sudan's while Taiwan's was the same as that of Zaire. The economic prospects of Asia were not viewed with optimism (Myrdal, 1968) and it was anticipated that the Philippines would be the country in Asia most likely to attain rapid economic growth.

From 1960 to 1990, several Asian economies (excluding the Philippines) have grown more rapidly and more consistently than any other group of economies in the world. Their average annual growth rate in this period was 5.5% and currently Hong Kong and Singapore have a higher per capita GDP than many OECD countries. Macau is often ignored in analyses of East Asia but it deserves to be included as one of the rapidly growing Asian economies. Its record has been impressive (7.7% from 1982 to 1988 and 5% in 1993), and in the latter year its GDP per capita was higher than that of Taiwan and about the same as that of New Zealand.

Table 1. Key Indicators of Selected Asian Economies

| | *Population 1991 (Millions)* | *Population Growth Rate % 1980–91* | *GDP per Head, US$, 1993* | *GNP Real Growth Rate %, 1980–91* | *Gini Coefficient* 1980–91* | *Literacy Rate, % 1990* | *Female Labor Force (% of Total) 1989* | *Secondary School Enrollment (% of Age Group) 1991* | *Primary School Enrollment (% of Age Group) 1991* | *Tertiary Enrollment Students per 10,000 Population 1990* | *Public Expenditure on Education as a % of GNP 1991* |
|---|---|---|---|---|---|---|---|---|---|---|---|
| China | 1,150 | 1.5 | 360 | 9.4 | | 73 | 43 | 48 | 132 | 190 | 2.3 |
| Hong Kong | 6 | 1.4 | 16,382 | 6.9 | 0.39 | 90 | 45 | 90 | 106 | 1,410 | 3.0 |
| Japan | 123 | 0.5 | 27,326 | 4.3 | 0.30 | 99 | 38 | 96 | 102 | 2,328 | 5.8 |
| Malaysia | 18 | 2.6 | 2,965 | 5.6 | 0.42 | 78 | 35 | 59 | 102 | 680 | 6.9 |
| Macau | 0.47 | 3.5 | 11,300 | | | 61 | | 70 | 95 | NA | 0.7 |
| Singapore | 3 | 2.1 | 15,200 | 7.1 | 0.41 | 88 | 32 | 69 | 115 | 963 | 3.4 |
| Taiwan | 20 | 1.9 | 10,215 | 7.9 | 0.30 | 90 | 45 | 95 | 101 | 3,792 | 5.45 |
| South Korea | 43 | 1.1 | 6,635 | 10.0 | 0.34 | 96 | 34 | 87 | 104 | 3,899 | 3.6 |
| India | 865 | 2.1 | 310 | 5.5 | | 48 | 25 | 44 | 98 | NA | 3.5 |
| Philippines | 61 | 2.4 | 835 | 1.2 | | 90 | 31 | 73 | 106 | 2,738 | 2.9 |

Sources: World Bank; UN, *Economist, World Education Report* 1993.
* A measure of income distribution. A ratio of 1 indicates a very uneven distribution of income.

The comparative pace of development is instructive. It took Britain 58 years to double real per capita income from 1780. The United States achieved the same result in the 47 years from 1839; Japan did it in 34 years from 1900 and South Korea took 11 years from 1966. Thus, the later a country has industrialized, the faster it has grown, and most of the countries which have developed rapidly in the post-war period have been in East Asia. This rapid economic growth has been accompanied by significant shifts in other, less precise, indicators of development especially in Japan and the four Asian Dragons. Infant mortality rates, family size, life expectancy, population growth rates, income distribution and political stability have all improved markedly over the last three decades in both absolute and relative terms. Further, in most of the societies we examine strong nation states have emerged and in some of them the political system has become increasingly pluralistic and tolerant of diversity.

## Education and Development: Alternative Approaches

Prior to analysing the various potential roles of education in the process of development, it is necessary to try to place these within a more general explanatory framework. Two very broad approaches to explaining development can be identified (Berger, 1990). The first focuses on those structural and institutional factors seen as critical for development. These have been identified as vital to development and include: free economic markets or managed markets, export-oriented trade policies and efficient, honest bureaucracies, investment in physical and human capital, and strong and purposeful governments. The degree of government intervention in decisions relating to these structural features has been a key issue on which analysts have differed. Some have argued that East Asia's success was a result of a low level of government involvement (Chen, 1979; Wolf, 1988) and others (Wade, 1990) view government's role as more critical, but characterized by a tendency to support adjustments consistent with the nature of the market.

In contrast, a second, more social psychological approach focuses more on those values and attitudes which are perceived to be prerequisites for development. Explanations which focus on the role of Confucianism in East Asia (Hung, 1989; Rozman, 1991), the Protestant ethic in Northern Europe (Weber, 1952) and the need for achievement (McClelland, 1961) are examples of the sorts of attitudes and values which have been identified as consistent with, and supportive of, development.

Both of these two broad approaches and specific explanations consistent with them can marshall evidence to verify their propositions because the reasons for development are extremely complex and because different societies have achieved that goal through the interaction of different forces and strategies. For example, in terms of structural factors, Singapore has clearly benefited from the strongly directive role of the government and its location at the center of South East Asian trade. Hong Kong has benefited from a low level of government intervention and from its role as a gateway to China, which has allowed it to emerge as a regional center for finance and entrepôt trade. Macau has also benefited from a low level of government intervention and its location near Hong Kong, which has allowed it to develop a thriving gambling sector. South Korea's growth has been based on huge government-sponsored industrial conglomerates, while those of Taiwan, Hong Kong and Macau have relied more on small and medium-sized firms.

Most of these societies have to varying degrees protected their industries from overseas competition and pursued export-oriented policies. This of course was only possible because the markets of North America and, to a lesser extent, Europe were open. As the World Bank (1993) comments in its substantial analysis of "the East Asian success story":

> We found that the diversity of experience, the variety of institutions, and the great variation in policies among the high-performing Asian economies means that there is no East Asian model of rapid growth with equity. Rather, each of the eight economies we studied used various combinations of policies at different times to perform the functions for rapid growth. . . . Most of the policies that they used reflected sound economic fundamentals. . . .

This book is premised on the assumption that the role of education in the process of development has also varied markedly across different East Asian societies in ways which defy simple or singular explanations.

The broad distinction outlined above can be applied to an analysis of the specific role of education in the process of development. Education can be interpreted as one of the social structures which needs to be provided as a basis for development, or it can be perceived as a vehicle for transmitting those values and attitudes supportive of development. Clearly these two approaches are not mutually exclusive, but they have their roots in different academic disciplines, economics dominating the first approach and the second emerging from sociology, history, psychology and anthropology. This separation has tended to result in a limited cross-fertilization of ideas and a tendency to promote explanations from the framework of a single discipline. As Foster (1982) comments:

> the effect of enhanced educational inputs upon economic outputs must be seen within a broader historical and sociological perspective which attempts to examine the problematic relationship between education and development in the widest sense.

In what follows we examine in more detail those key relationships which are posited between education and development. Firstly we analyze that relationship from the perspective of economists who view education as an investment in human capital that makes a direct contribution to economic growth. Subsequently we look at other analyses which have seen education as one of the contributing factors to development, thereby playing more of an indirect role in the relationship.

## Education and Development: The Economic Perspective

Economists have, not surprisingly, focused on the relationship between education and the economy through analyses of the returns to the individual and society of investment in education. This concern of economists with human capital creation is usually associated with the work of Schultz (1961), but it is important to recognize two rather different analytic traditions (Sobel, 1978; Foster, 1982). An early approach which had its heyday in the 1960s was concerned with human resource development and was exemplified by the work of Harbison and Myers (1964). It emphasized the critical role of education in economic development by generating a series of correlations between educational measures and other complex indicators of development. This resulted in a rather simplistic set of propositions about the role of education in development. For example it emphasized the role of tertiary and secondary education as compared to primary education and tended to view all levels of education as mere steps toward tertiary education. It also served to emphasize the key role of specialist technical and vocational education and of manpower planning. This approach was supported by studies of growth accounting. These attempted to identify the extent to which economic growth could be explained by changes in the number of hours worked and by capital inputs. The remaining unexplained element was attributed to the increased education of the workforce. Thus Denison (1962), for example, argued that between 1930 and 1960, 23% of the increased output of the United States could not be accounted for by changes in labour and capital. He concluded that this residual factor was largely due to the increased education of the workforce.

This kind of approach did nothing more than correlate sets of variables without attempting to analyse either the degree of causality between them or estimating the relative efficiency of investment in education. To demonstrate a correlation between education and various indicators of development at any point in time is not equivalent to showing that the relationship is causal nor does it suggest any directions for policy. What is obvious is that more developed societies do spend more on education than less developed societies and educated employees earn more than the less educated. The problem, however, is one of cause and effect. Notwithstanding these limitations, the general appeal for greater investment in education, especially at the tertiary and technical levels, was attractive to policy makers often trying to create or bolster up a nation state after decolonization. In many cases, it led to a gross misallocation of resources as money was poured into expanding tertiary and technical education, in an attempt to produce the high level manpower who would support economic development (Ahmad and Blaug, 1973).

A second approach emerged from more orthodox neo-classical economic analysis. It was concerned with questions of both internal and external efficiency. The former relates to the efficiency of schools in using different mixes of educational inputs to achieve improvements in student outcomes and is less central to the concerns of this chapter. The latter is of more central concern as it focuses on education's ability to meet broader societal goals. The critical question was whether investment in education could produce higher private and social returns than the alternatives available—such as investment in physical capital. A large number of rate of return studies were summarized by Psacharopoulos (1973 and 1981) and his main conclusions were: the returns on educational investment were higher in less developed than in more developed countries; the private and social rates of return were highest at the primary level; the rates of return were greater than those obtained from investing in physical capital; and the returns to general education were higher than those for technical and vocational types of training. The difficulties inherent in these calculations were analyzed in detail by Blaug (1976). Foremost among them is the extent to which higher earnings are evidence of greater productivity or whether educational qualifications are a proxy indicator of different ability levels, social class differences, or merely a device to screen persons who will hold higher paid jobs. In essence, rate of return analysis is premised on the assumption that labor markets are free and operate in the way described by neo-classical economic theory, which assumes that higher wages are a function of higher productivity. The nature of the labor market in many countries, such as China, is clearly not congruent with those assumptions. These findings are in direct contradiction to the policy implications of the human resource development approach, which emphasized the importance of tertiary education, especially that which produced technical and scientific graduates.

Economists who have focused on questions of efficiency, as opposed to manpower planning, have performed a useful service in two major respects. Firstly they have in a general sense highlighted the importance of education. In a more specific sense, they have demonstrated that returns to education may diminish and that the returns to education vary at different levels of development. Within the realms of academic discourse, the methodological and policy limitations of attempts to measure the relationship between economic growth and education have been recognized. Despite this, as becomes evident in some of the subsequent chapters, human capital theory has been used by policy makers to support the belief that investment in education is both a necessary and primary source of development. It has also been used to justify educational provision being linked to the economy's labor needs through a process of manpower planning. Adams (1977) described these interpretations of human capital theory as "one of the most romantic tales of the century." The most influential funding agency, the World Bank, was described as adopting a view of education's role in development as one which is "no less than a celebration of human capital theory which results in generalized appeals for increased expenditures on education reminiscent of the 1960s" (Jones, 1992). More recent publications (e.g., World Bank, 1991b and 1993) do, however, adopt a more cautious note and have recognised the policy implications of the analyses of rates of return which do not support generalized appeals for investment reminiscent of the 1960s.

The rapid development of the Asian economies specifically has been harnessed as evidence to support the critical role of education in development. Investment in education is described in broad and unqualified terms as having been a crucial factor in this process. For example *The Economist* states:

> . . . the last lesson is probably the most important: investing in Education pays in spades. The tiger's single biggest source of comparative advantage is their well-educated workers. (*Economist,* November 16, 1991b)

and,

> Investing in education is to the 1990's what nationalisation was to the 1940's and privatization to the 1980's—the universal panacea of the day. Right wingers value education partly because it promises to

make labour markets more efficient, left wingers partly because it gives a respectable role for state activism. . . . They are right. (ibid.)

The IMF comment that:

> one lesson from the past is that the economies—such as Japan and South Korea—which committed themselves to education and training made great strides in both human development and economic growth. (IMF World Development Report 1991)

The precise way in which formal education has contributed to improving productivity specifically or to development generally is still unclear and not amenable to solely economic analysis. Thus, while economists have provided a plausible argument as to the role of education in economic development, they have not really demonstrated what exactly it is that schools do to make people more productive. Education has in effect been treated as a black box the contents of which were not directly amenable to conventional economic analysis. It has also not addressed what has been described as the putative spillover effects which may contribute to development. In the next section we examine those which might arise from formal education.

Finally, at the risk of ignoring our earlier caveats and attempting to generalise, there are some common threads evident with regard to the economic aspects of education in the Asian societies which we analyze. The level of public investment in schooling in most of the Asian countries we examine has not, with the exception of Japan, been high compared with that of many other countries. In 1989 the average proportion of GDP spent on education by East Asian countries was 3.7% compared with 3.6% for developing countries and about 5.8% for the OECD countries. However, this crude indicator masks two important considerations, highlighted in the World Bank study (1993). Firstly, in many countries, the level of private expenditure on education was substantial in the early phase of educational expansion. Parents often paid for education, especially tertiary education. Secondly, each of the societies experienced rapid declines in their population growth rates. This allowed the level of expenditure per pupil to increase as the size of school populations declined.

## Education and Development: Other Explanations

In this section we examine briefly the insights into the relationship between education and development which have emerged from, respectively, history, sociology, psychology and politics. While historical studies have analyzed the relationship between economic development and education, other disciplines have examined education's role with regard to prerequisites for development such as modernization, social cohesion and a stable polity.

The direct role of education as an agent for promoting economic growth has been questioned at an empirical level by historical analyses. If education plays a critical role, then one would expect to see a pattern of expanding educational provision prior to or in parallel with the process of rapid growth and industrialization. However, economic historians provide limited evidence to support such a scenario. The modernization of Japan during the Meiji Restoration is a notable exception for it is seen to have been heavily dependent on educational reforms which climaxed in the early introduction of compulsory schooling. However, the industrialization of Northern Europe and the United States is not widely viewed as closely linked to educational provision. For example, the first industrial country, England, was the laggard in terms of the public provision of education.

Other countries which were the first to develop sophisticated public systems of mass education, like France and Germany, waited over a century for industrialization. Prussia legislated for compulsory schooling to age 14 in 1826. England achieved similar provision in 1921. Green's (1990) summary of the evidence is worth quoting at length:

> We can summarize the relationship between educational development and the technical requirements of industrial growth as follows. Firstly, in no country does it appear that secular changes in educational provision were determined exclusively or even primarily by narrowly economic or technical factors. Secondly, even where economic change did call for an educational response, schools did not, in general, respond either aptly or promptly. Thirdly, what educational responses there were varied considerably from nation to nation and bear no close correlation with chronology of industrial advance. . . . the role of purely economic factors . . . seems to have been a surprisingly limited one.

Clearly the role of education in a modern technological society which competes within a global market will not necessarily be the same as it was in the early stages of industrialization in Western societies during the eighteenth and nineteenth centuries. The rapidly growing societies of Asia achieved economic growth initially through the production of low value products which were relatively labor intensive. The level of technology of the production process and the level of skills required of labor were relatively low. This stage was, however, shortlived as the societies diversified quickly in terms of products, markets and technology. This consideration only serves to highlight the need for evidence, rather than assertion, as to the role of education, and for a recognition that its role might vary between countries and at different stages of economic development. A similar skepticism toward education's role as a key for development emerged from studies of developing countries. For example Feinberg (1975) argued that education was only effective if a country had industrialized. Aran et al. (1972) asserted that education would not "produce results compatible with effective modernization." Other studies (Colclough, 1982) have queried the evidence associating increases in the provision of primary education with subsequent economic change. Bock (1982) asserted education "cannot empirically be shown to deliver predicted improvement in either national or individual well being."

Sociologists argue that education has contributed to a change in people's beliefs, values and behaviors and that these have been conducive to development. The term *modernization* was used to describe those adjustments which accompanied economic development. Inkeles argued that more developed societies displayed attitudes and beliefs more "modern" than those of less developed societies. The values which were associated with modernization were thus derived from those thought to prevail in the West and included: participation, communality, punctuality, observance of abstract rules, objectivity and cooperation. Education was seen as the institution which could transform a traditional society into one with modern Western values. Modernization theory therefore provided a positive and optimistic view of education's role which paralleled and reinforced that provided by interpretations of human capital theory. McClelland (1961) presented the classic psychological formulation of this relationship. He argued that more developed societies had a greater proportion of people with a personality trait which he termed the "need for achievement."

There is a strong empirical link between various proxy indicators of modernization and the level of development of a society. Holsinger (1974), for example, concluded with reference to Brazilia that: "for any child in Brazil, the longer he is exposed to formal schooling, the higher will be his modernity score. . . . If a nation had no other resource than its schools, it could expect some modernization of its pre-adult population to occur." The education of women has specifically been associated with improvements in child health and reduced fertility.

There are a number of critiques (Fågerlind and Saha, 1989) of these perspectives and it is not appropriate to repeat them in detail here. Two critical points worth noting are Ward's (1974) assertion that: "the systems of education now to be found in the developing countries still resemble those that preceded them. They have expanded more than they have changed." With regard to the situation in East Asia, an analysis of the nature of their school curricula (Marsh and Morris, 1991) would support Ward's contention. While the formal curriculum has changed, the implemented curriculum, especially the patterns of teaching and learning, were seen to reflect long-standing and essentially traditional values. Similarly, the comparison of the pedagogical practices and values held by teachers and pupils in Asian and Western societies reveals major differences (Holloway, 1988; Hamilton et al., 1989). Secondly, the indicators of modernization used by researchers includes items which are themselves the result of exposure to Western styles of education. Inevitably, then, more education is associated with higher levels of modernization.

The relationship between education and social cohesion was highlighted early on by Durkheim (1977). He saw changes in education following and reflecting changes in society. His concern was that major economic change would result in social disorder and conflict. The solution was for societies to develop what he termed a collective morality which would encourage social solidarity and cohesion. It was a key role of the state to pursue this goal and education was one of the primary means for achieving it.

> Society can only exist if there exists among its members a sufficient degree of homogeneity. Education perpetuates and reinforces this homogeneity by fixing in the child, from the beginning, the essential similarities that collective life demands.

This view of education was in direct contrast to that which was prevalent in England where the need to encourage individuality was stressed and it was posited that the common good was best maximized by each individual pursuing his own self-interest.

Many of the societies we analyze have pursued educational policies which would seem to be wholly consistent with Durkheim's formulation. Schools are expected to maintain social cohesion through the promotion of both a strong sense of national identity and a belief in the prevailing national ideology. In Malaysia this is embodied in the doctrine of the *Rukunegara* (Maimunah and Lewin, 1991). In Indonesia the national ideology is termed *Pancasila* (Thomas, 1991). These are actively promoted through the formal and informal school curriculum. In other societies the ideology has shifted with major political shifts as was the case in China which moved from promoting Maoist dogma in the Cultural Revolution to a more recent emphasis on the Four Modernizations. Hong Kong was until recently notable for the apolitical role of schooling and the prevalence of a doctrine of self interest which has been termed "utilitarianistic familism" (Lau, 1982). In Singapore there has been a tension between the desire to promote a modern technological society which is embodied in the "New Economic Order" and to retain the traditional values of a Confucian society. Similarly, at the level of classroom interaction, evidence suggests a strong emphasis in Asian societies on promoting communal values and group cohesion, which is in marked contrast to the individualistic focus in the West.

Education's role as an agency for maintaining social cohesion is also compatible with those explanations that have focused on Confucianism to explain Asia's economic success. Schools are portrayed as a key agency in promoting a set of values (diligence, thrift, respect for authority, communality, filial piety) that are viewed as Confucian and conducive to development. Clearly schools do mirror and reinforce the prevailing value systems in society. However, whether we can assign a critical role to a specific set of values is problematic as those values are defined in a way which reflects those attributes one is trying to explain. Further, and more fundamentally, the impact of Confucianism does not fit well with the evidence. As Vogel (1991) comments, it cannot explain the slow development of Asian societies in the 1950s, why the heartland of Confucianism (the PRC) was a relative late developer, and why societies at the fringes of the Confucian core, that had their origins in an agricultural/peasant culture, such as Hong Kong, Singapore and South Korea, were among the star performers. Also, it cannot easily be used to explain the cases of Malaysia and Thailand, where Islam and Buddhism have been the predominant value systems. Vogel does, however, identify a cluster of institutions and attitudes which he terms "Industrial Neo-Confucianism" as contributors to the Asian success story. These are: the emergence of a meritocratic elite within the bureaucracy, a highly competitive examination system, a focus on the group rather than the individual, and the prevalence of the goal of self-improvement. Education served to reinforce those values generally. Specifically it provided the highly competitive and selective environment which revolved around the examination system. He argues that the emergence of school systems oriented to examination success contributed to the decline of feudalism, and encouraged both learning and disciplined work habits desirable to employers.

Where a country's population has comprised a mixture of ethnic and religious groups, as in Singapore and Malaysia, this has placed a premium on the school curriculum promoting a strong sense of a unified national identity. As will become apparent in the chapters which follow, a major motive for expanding education has in some societies derived from a desire to promote social cohesion and consensus where the potential for ethnic and political conflict exists.

Education's ability to serve as a vehicle for national integration is, however, problematic. As a United Nations document (1964) commented:

> . . . in many developing countries there is a kind of cleavage, or rather apparent divorce between scientists, technicians and educated people, on the one hand, and society in general on the other.

Education can also be a source of conflict and divisiveness when it serves to select unfairly and segregate people, especially those from different ethnic, linguistic, religious or regional backgrounds as was the case in sub-Saharan Africa. There is also the potential that if educational provision expands at a faster rate than the economy, the result is a pool of well-educated unemployed who can serve as a focus of political discontent and destabilization. Political instability is not conducive to economic growth, especially when firms operate on a global rather than a national basis. Finally, the recent re-emergence of religious and ethnic differences in central Europe following the collapse of Communism provides a salutary reminder of the strength of influences other than schools on a people's sense of identity.

A more critical perspective of education's role in maintaining social cohesion views it as an appendage of the economic system which primarily serves to reinforce, legitimate and reproduce prevailing social inequalities (Bowles and Gintis, 1976). That structure essentially embodies two classes—the owners of capital and the proletariat. Dependency theory extends this analysis to a global context. Affluent Western societies are placed in the role of the owners of capital who exploit poorer countries through patterns of trade and aid. Thus, less developed societies are the result of dependency on and exploitation by richer countries. Formal education is seen largely in terms of its role in maintaining and perpetuating that relationship.

Economic development has also been associated with the emergence of political systems that allow an orderly transfer of power and low levels of political violence. The expansion of schooling is thought to contribute to this as evidence indicates (a) a link between higher levels of access to education and more democratic political attitudes, and (b) low levels of violence and an orderly transfer of power are evident in countries with higher levels of access to education. It is, however, unclear whether education is a determining or determined factor. It is also clear that (a) development is often accompanied by instability and violence, and (b) education does not necessarily result in greater allegiance or commitment to the nation state. The effectiveness of schools' attempts to promote civic values has also been questioned by Torney et al. (1975), who cite the strong influence of other agencies, such as the mass media and the inherent contradiction between the values of a hierarchical and non-participative school system and democratic values.

Historical evidence on the link between education and democracy shows a mixed pattern. In the United States, the provision of education was explicitly linked to the goal of promoting democracy and a unified national ideology. In contrast, in Europe, England and France were amongst the earliest to develop democratic political systems but were slow to expand educational opportunities. Ironically it was the less democratic and authoritarian German states which had the most well-developed educational systems. This itself was a reflection of education's political role—it was in Germany seen as a vehicle for maintaining an authoritarian society and it has been described by Taylor (1982) as a "gigantic engine of conquest." Similarly in Japan, especially during the inter-war period, schools were a key institution for promoting militarism and ultra-nationalism. But the influence of education on developing aspects of political socialization associated with democracy are less easily demonstrated.

There is ample evidence of the impact of politics on education as schools are used by the state to promote the prevailing political ideology to varying degrees of explicitness which range from political indoctrination to socialization. The nature of the political system is also important in determining the process of schooling. Bronfenbrenner's (1974) study showed that schooling in the United States reflects a competitive and individualist orientation suited to the needs of a capitalist system. In contrast, Russian schools had a more collective and less individualistic orientation geared to life in a socialist system.

Another aspect of the relationship between education and the political domain has focused on its role in producing political elites (Wilkinson, 1969) but studies in this area have not demonstrated any systematic variation between educational provision and the formation of political elites.

Green (1990) provides probably the most comprehensive theoretical account of the differential patterns of growth of educational systems with regard to the political domain. He argues that the development of systems of mass education are best understood with reference to the process of state formation. Thus, for example, where the state emerges strongly as a result of an external threat (Prussia) or revolution (France), then the expansion of educational systems receives high priority as a vehicle for consolidating the role of the state and national consciousness. In contrast, the very late development of mass schooling in Britain and the absence of a unified national system of education is seen to be the result of the laissez faire role of the state. Green summarizes his analysis in terms which have parallels with those of Durkheim.

> The major impetus for the creation of national education systems lay in the need to provide the state with trained administrators, engineers and military personnel; to spread dominant national cultures and inculcate popular national ideologies of nationhood; and so to forge the political and cultural unity of burgeoning nation states and cement the ideological hegemony of their dominant classes.

Green's analysis has obvious parallels in East Asia where both the nature and role of the state are in many societies of relatively recent origin. Similarly, many of the societies were born of relatively recent conflicts and there is in some a perception of a continued external threat (e.g., South Korea and Taiwan). In terms of explaining the role of education in development this perspective would view formal education as a key institution not in promoting democratic political values, but in legitimating the government's role and in maintaining the stability of an essentially authoritarian state.

In different degrees, the political systems that prevailed in East Asia were largely authoritarian. The quest for a more democratic system in Taiwan, South Korea and Hong Kong is a relatively recent phenomenon. Even in Japan, the democratic process had until recently had little impact on the running of the economy by the bureaucracy. The link between an authoritarian state and development has focused on two factors. First, it can allow the state singlemindedly to pursue developmental goals without concern for short term political considerations. Second, the absence of democracy is associated with a lower propensity for "rent seeking behavior"—seeking a profit in ways which do not contribute to the output of goods and services. Consequently, there is less need for the government to seek consensus by using resources to satisfy the needs of groups who have the potential to derail government policy.

## Conclusion

What emerges clearly from this brief introduction to the role of education in development is primarily that there is an abundance of propositions which suggest significant relationships between schooling and various aspects of development. We have distinguished these in terms of two broad approaches, one which focuses on structural and institutional factors and the other which focuses on values and culture. The former has been dominated by economic explanations which view education as an investment in human capital. These explanations have yielded important insights but they have tended to ignore the complex social and political contexts within which development occurs.

We hope to demonstrate the nature of the complex, diffuse and varied role which education has played in East Asian societies. In terms of complexity we focus on education's link with the social and political dimensions which have received relatively scant attention compared with the economic dimension. In terms of variety, it is necessary to tolerate a degree of ambiguity as education's role has varied markedly across East Asian societies. Further, a full understanding requires that we recognize that the relationship is not confined to national boundaries. Societies can benefit from educational reforms and provision which are offered in other countries. The key question which all of our country-chapter authors have been asked to address is how has education interacted in the widest sense with the development of the society on which they focus. This has the potential to allow us to move beyond the more deterministic and partial relationships posited by human capital theory.

# 2 JAPAN

*Wing On Lee*

## INTRODUCTION

Japan's post-war economic and technological developments have attracted much interest, especially in terms of research designed to identify factors explaining Japan's success. Education has been regarded as one of the most significant factors. For example, Vogel (1979) suggests that Japan's educational development is an integral part of its post-war successes. Similarly, Reischauer (1977, p. 167; 1988, pp. 186, 295) makes it clear that Japan's high literacy rates and excellent educational standards are the major factors contributing to the country's economic and technological advancement. The World Development Report (World Bank, 1980b, pp. 37–39) also suggests that Japan's outstanding rates of growth could not have been achieved without early mass literacy and numeracy, which (together with land reform, more advanced education and good economic management) contributed to increased agricultural productivity, to the expansion of labor-intensive manufacturing and exports, and to their remarkable ability to adapt to changes in technology and world demand.

Within Japan, the belief that educational development has made a direct contribution to economic and technological development is particularly evident. For example, the Japanese National Commission for UNESCO (1966, pp. 8–11) argued that education has played a stronger role than any other factors in the industrialization of the country, especially in respect to the supply of qualified labor in the earlier period of industrialization, and the training of leaders in the later period, after the take-off. However, despite the prevalence of such a view, how precisely education causes economic and technological development is still not sufficiently clear. This chapter aims to explore the relationships between education and development in the case of Japan. First, following an outline of the historical, political and demographical background, it analyzes Japan's post-war economic development, industrial and technological development, and educational development. Against this background, it shows particularly how educational development has been closely associated with economic and technological development, both in terms of government policy and in terms of the development of technical education. The second part of this chapter depicts a picture seemingly contradictory to that portrayed earlier. It argues that policy emphasis can be quite different from implementation. It points out the assumption of a direct causal linkage between education and economic and technological development can be quite simplistic. On the one hand, there are certainly some other significant factors which can better explain Japan's economic and technological development. On the other hand, when looking at the link between education and development, it is also important to look at its indirect contribution in terms of reinforcing a kind of social ethos favorable to development. The conclusion of this chapter stresses the importance of this socio-cultural perspective on education's role in explaining Japan's development, although it also cautiously points out the limitations of this perspective.

## Background

### *History and Politics*

Japan was subject to strong influences from China and Korea in its early period. For example, Japan imported Confucianism and Buddhism from both countries, and established the system of laws and government organization based on the Chinese model. However, later Japan developed its own distinct culture. *Bushido*, for instance, was developed during the period of Kamakura in the late twelfth century. It embodied the ideals of Japanese chivalry and the spirit of *samurai* fortitude. Toward the end of the sixteenth century, Tokugawa Ieyasu established the Tokugawa Shogunate, leading to the establishment of a feudalistic system. This involved a strong system of central control with each region under the rule of an individual lord (*daimyo*).

Japan came into contact with the West for the first time in the mid-sixteenth century. Japan's first reaction was to ban Christianity and impose a closed-door policy. By the end of the eighteenth century, Japan came under increasing pressure to open its ports to foreign traders. The era of the Meiji Restoration in the nineteenth century inaugurated a period of modernization. This opened up the country to Occidental science, technology and civilization. The Meiji modernization established rapid industrialization and the establishment of modern political institutions.

For Japan, the first half of the twentieth century was marked by two major wars. After its defeat in World War II, Japan entered into seven years of occupation by foreign forces, under substantial American influence. The political system was significantly democratized. Today's Japan has a parliamentary system, with five major political parties. For most of the time, post-war Japan has been ruled by the Liberal-Democratic party. Recent discontent toward the Conservative government because of corruption and the unwillingness of the government to reform the political structure has led to its loss of power in the parliament. However, in the main, there has been a lack of struggle for political rights among people, despite the existence of a democratic system. Moreover, Japanese politics has been referred to as "money politics," because the government is closely intertwined with the business sector. For this reason, it is alleged that the real rulers of the country are the business people.

The government is highly bureaucratic and adopts a centralized model for its administration. A high degree of centralized control is also evident in the educational system. Since the fifties, the Conservative government has tried to increase the power of the Ministry of Education in the supervision of local schools, curricula and textbooks, despite strong opposition (Richardson, 1974, pp. 231–2, 241–3).

### *Geography and Population*

Japan comprises four major islands—Hokkaido, Honshu, Shikoku, and Kyushu—and about 3,900 adjacent small islands. Their combined area is 377,765 square kilometers—slightly larger than Italy and Malaysia and smaller than Morocco. The country is well known to be poor in physical resources, and consequently it lacks nearly all vital minerals for industry. Hence it has to import over 99% of the petroleum products and over 83% of copper. However, the country has a relatively large population. Japan has experienced a substantial growth in population over the past five decades. In 1990, the country's population was 123.6 million, comprising about 2.3% of the world population, making Japan the seventh most populous country in the world. However, population growth has been slow in recent years. In 1989, the rate was as low as 0.3% . There has also been a remarkable growth in the size of urban population. In 1920, urban dwellers comprised only 18% of the total population. The proportion rose to 38% in 1940, 40% in 1970, and 43% in 1985. Japan's overall population density is about 332 persons per square kilometer, but the population density is much higher in the major cities. For example, there are 3,627 persons per square kilometer in Tokyo, 2,143 persons per square kilometer in Osaka, and 1,111 persons per square kilometer in Nagoya (*Facts and Figures*, 1985, p. 22; Statistics Bureau, 1991, p. 21). In terms of ethnicity and language, the country is rather homogeneous. "Foreigners" comprise less than 10% of the total population, the majority of whom are Koreans and Chinese. Many of these are integrated into the society in terms of culture and language.

## Economic Development

Japan's economic miracle took shape in the early sixties when industrial production increased enormously. During that decade, the annual growth in GNP averaged 10% (Boltho, 1975, p. 8). In 1965, Japan joined the exclusive $100 billion–GNP nations, and it began to accumulate a trade surplus (Kojima, 1977, p. 13; Burks, 1981, p. 171). Over the period 1945–1976, the economy increased 55-fold (Johnson, 1982, p. 6). The growth rate of the economy has been above that of the Western European countries and the USA since 1973. In 1980, Japan's GNP stood at $1,035.8 billion—40% of that of the United States. In 1983, its GNP constituted about 10% of the world's GNP, and both its GNP and its national income ranked second in the free world, next to the USA, and ahead of Western European countries (*Statistical Survey*, 1982, p. 73; Statistics Bureau, 1985, p. 27).

Consequently Japan's role and influence in the world economy has increased remarkably. In terms of foreign investment, Japan's total investment in Asia increased ten-fold during 1970–78, from $780 million to $1,688 million (Kojima, 1983, p. 114). Moreover, it has become one of the largest foreign aid donors in the world, and in 1983, it ranked third as a foreign aid donor with $3.76 billion, following the United States ($7.99 billion) and France ($3.82 billion) (Shibagaki, 1987, p. 212). In 1988, Japan became the world's second largest aid donor with $9.1 billion with only the United States exceeding its contributors (Waterhouse, 1989, p. 65).

Manufacturing, commerce and services are the three major sectors of employment. These sectors comprise roughly equal parts of the labor force in Japan: 23.7% in the manufacturing sector, 23% in the commercial sector and 20.5% in the services sector (1985 figures; Yano Tsuneta Kinenkai, 1991, p. 90).

While the general living standard of the society has improved, there are still large numbers of people living in hardship (see Fukutake, 1981, pp. 84–5). The "social wage" or social welfare which can help to alleviate their difficulties is low. This has contributed to a high incidence of saving. In 1982, the Japanese saved 11.4% of their disposable income. One of the major reasons for saving relates to educational expenses. Although primary and junior secondary education in Japan is free and compulsory, most parents send their children to "cram schools" (*juku* and *yobiko*) which charge high tuition fees (Patrick, 1976, p. 15; Nairai, 1983, p. 13; Statistics Bureau, 1983, p. 115).

### Industrial and Technological Development

Japan's history of industrialization can be traced back to the eighteenth century when the "first industrial revolution" took place. Emphasis at this stage was placed on the mechanization of light industries such as spinning and textiles. The "second industrial revolution" took place in the nineteenth century, which was characterized by the development of heavy industries such as steel, petrochemicals, household appliances and car industries (Kumon, 1986, p. 3). The "third industrial revolution" seems to be taking place now in the twentieth century, and involves transforming the country into a society of high technology, represented by robots, numerically controlled machine tools, computers, semiconductors, telecommunications equipment and medical electronics (Masuda, 1986, p. 5). This new industrial revolution has inaugurated the new age of "softnomics" and "software-ization" ("Softnomics," 1986, p. 10; Kumon, 1986, p. 3) in Japan, and transformed the society into an information or post-industrial society (Morley, 1974, p. 8; Burks, 1981, p. 171).

The initial stage of modernization was represented by assimilation and adaptation of technical ideas originating in the West, thus making Japan a well-known imitator. However, with continuing emphasis on technological innovations, it has gradually shed its "copycat" image. For example, in 1981, Japanese applications for new patents comprised 13% of all applications submitted in the United States and about 10% of applications in Germany, England and France, whilst American applications comprised only 4.7% in Japan (Duke, 1986, p. 6). Moreover Japan is able to take the lead in high-tech exports particularly in fiber optics for telecommunications, gallium arsenide memory chips for superfast computers, numerically-controlled machine tools and robots, and computer disk-drives, printers and magnetic storage media (Valery, 1986, p. 7).

Japan's pace of technological development seems to be synchronized with its emphasis on Research and Development (R&D). Expenditure for R&D increased at an annual rate of 8% during fiscal 1985–90, and amounted to Y13,078 billion, or the equivalent of 3% of GNP for fiscal 1990 (Statistics Bureau, 1992, p. 139). MITI, the Ministry of International Trade and Industry, has played a significant role in shaping long-term planning strategies, enhancing development of the "next generation industries," and sponsoring national research and development programs. Much research work is conducted by MITI–operated industrial laboratories in cooperation with private bodies, such as the Nomura and Mitsubishi research institutes, and the universities (Hofheinz and Calder, 1982, pp. 149–55; Smith, 1985, p. 19). The establishment of science cities has also provided the development of R&D within the country. In 1980 there were 43 government research institutes, two universities and many private institutes operating in the Tsukuba Science City (Hofheinz and Calder, 1982, p. 151; Gregory, 1985, pp. 43–50; Smith, 1985, pp. 10–1).

## Educational Development

With the policy of modernization that started early in the nineteenth century, Japan made an effort to expand educational access. Enrollment and literacy records before the war were impressive. Primary school attendance rose from 28% in 1873 to over 50% in 1883; and it was found that 43% of boys and 15% of girls were literate in 1874 (Kobayashi, 1986, p. 13; White, 1987, p. 50). In 1907, compulsory education was extended to six years, and school attendance reached 98% by that year. Universal and compulsory primary schooling was achieved thirty years before the war. At the secondary level, in 1905, there were places for only 4.3% of the relevant age group, but the percentage rose to 19.9 in 1915 (MOE, Japan, 1963, p. 30). Post-war enrollment and literacy rates were even more impressive. As shown in Table 1, the enrollment rates at the primary and junior secondary levels have been nearly 100% since 1948. The enrollment rates at the senior secondary level have increased steadily since 1955 to 95.4% in 1991. With successful universalization of primary and secondary education, Japan achieved a literacy rate of 98% as early as in 1960, and it is virtually 100% today (UNESCO, 1972, p. 116; White, 1987, p. 64). At the higher education level, the pre-war enrollment rates were only 1% and 3% of the appropriate age group in 1915 and 1935 respectively. However, the rate increased from 10% in 1954 to 36.3% in 1991. The success in increasing the enrollment rates was made possible with the expansion of the private sector. The private sector's contribution to the expansion of higher education is particularly conspicuous, but its significance in the secondary education level is also notable. By the late eighties, the private sector accounted for 76% of university enrollments and 28% of secondary enrollments (James and Benjamin, 1987, p. 471).

Education has undergone many major reforms since the Meiji modernization. Under the 1872 Fundamental Code of Education as a part of the modernization policy, the modern system of primary, secondary and university education was established. This was usually regarded as the First Educational Reform in Japan. Under the new school system, there were three stages of education: primary school, middle school and university. With the successful implementation of four years of compulsory primary education, 91% of boys and 72% of girls of primary school age were enrolled in schools in 1900. In 1907, the period of compulsory education was further extended to six years (Cowen and McLean, 1984, p. 243). Generally speaking, Japan's pre-war educational system was characterized by a multi-track structure. Pupils could continue education through different tracks beyond compulsory education. This included the academic track, the normal school track, the technical track, the youth track, or the girls' track. The existence of the multi-track system inevitably led to inequalities of educational opportunity based on sex, residence, wealth and other factors, making the system highly selective and elitist. However, this also meant that many of those who wished to pursue education beyond the compulsory level could get access to some type of schooling (Anderson, 1975, pp. 52–8).

TABLE 1. Enrollment Rates and Proportion of Students Going on to Higher Levels of Education in Japan (1948–1991)

| *Year* | *Kindergarten* | *Primary* | *Lower Secondary* | *Higher Ed* | *% Going on to Upper Secondary* | *% Going on to Higher Ed* | *% Going on to Grad School* |
|---|---|---|---|---|---|---|---|
| 1948 | 7.3 | 99.64 | 99.27 | — | — | — | — |
| 1950 | 8.9 | 99.64 | 99.20 | — | 42.5 | — | — |
| 1955 | 20.1 | 99.77 | 99.92 | 10.1 | 51.5 | 18.4 | — |
| 1960 | 28.7 | 99.82 | 99.93 | 10.3 | 57.7 | 17.2 | — |
| 1965 | 41.3 | 99.81 | 99.91 | 17.0 | 70.7 | 25.4 | 4.2 |
| 1970 | 53.8 | 99.83 | 99.89 | 23.6 | 82.1 | 24.2 | 4.4 |
| 1975 | 63.5 | 99.91 | 99.91 | 37.8 | 91.9 | 34.2 | 4.3 |
| 1980 | 64.4 | 99.98 | 99.98 | 37.4 | 94.2 | 31.9 | 3.9 |
| 1985 | 63.7 | 99.99 | 99.99 | 37.6 | 94.1 | 30.5 | 5.5 |
| 1990 | 64.0 | 99.99 | 99.99 | 36.3 | 95.1 | 30.6 | 6.4 |
| 1991 | 64.1 | 99.99 | 99.99 | 37.7 | 95.4 | 31.7 | 6.7 |

Source: MOE, 1992, pp. 15–16.

The conclusion of World War II marked the initiation of the Second Educational Reform. During the period of Occupation, 1945–52, Japan's education underwent radical change. The Supreme Commander for the Allied Powers issued a directive to the Japanese government concerning the demilitarization and democratization of all aspects of government, including education. In March 1946, a United States Education Mission was invited to visit

Japan to advise on measures for educational reform. In April, the Mission submitted a policy guide to the Occupation authority and the Japanese government. In the main, the guiding principles of the educational reform were democracy, freedom, decentralization, mass education, diversity and internationalism in place of fascism, control, centralization, elite education, uniformity and parochial nationalism. More specifically, members of the Mission advised a comprehensive reform of education—the new goals of education were to pursue liberalism and individualism, and the curriculum was to be revised to meet such a change. They also recommended the adoption of *Romaji* (Romanization) for the Japanese language, the establishment of publicly elected education commissions, the adoption of a single-track schooling system, and a reform of the teacher training system (Aso and Amano, 1983, pp. 62–3). This proposed shift within the educational system from control to freedom and from centralization to decentralization was a radical one for the Japanese. In March 1947, the first and most important post-war legislative reform of education, the Fundamental Law of Education, was promulgated, replacing the 1890 Imperial Rescript on Education. The main features of Japan's post-war educational system were thereby established:

> As the initial reactor for a chain for reforms, the Fundamental Law of Education brought about the decentralization of public education, the establishment of the 6–3–3–4 school system, reorientation of curricula, courses of study, textbooks and teaching methods, and total reorganization of educational administration in this country. (MOE, 1969, p. 16)

In addition to the Fundamental Law, there were other significant educational establishments introduced between the late forties and the sixties. These included (1) the promulgation of a number of education laws concerning social education, private schools, and subsidies for compulsory education; (2) the establishment of the Central Council for Education; and (3) several revisions of the National Courses of Study for primary schools, junior secondary schools and senior secondary schools.

The Central Council for Education set forth Japan's Third Educational Reform by submitting a report, *Basic Guidelines for the Reform of Education*, to the Minister of Education in 1971. The report called for:

1. standardization of school curricula from the primary to the senior secondary levels, but diversification of the senior secondary curricula to encourage individual development,

2. expansion of special education,
3. increase of teachers' salaries,
4. substantiation of the private schools subsidy scheme, and
5. more flexibility and diversification in the higher educational system.

The eighties saw the advent of further reform proposals. The Nakasone government considered that a major reform of education was necessary to enable Japan to meet the needs and challenges of the twenty-first century. The prime minister established an Ad Hoc Council on Educational Reform in 1984. The council (which was later renamed the National Council) submitted a total of four reports from 1985 to 1987. In these reports, it urged a basic and comprehensive reorganization of the educational system, suggested strategies for educational reform involving families, schools and society as a whole, and called attention to a lifelong learning system. It also put forward eight principles as guidelines for educational reform:

1. emphasis on individuality,
2. emphasis on basics,
3. fostering of creativity and independent thought and expression,
4. greater opportunity for choice in education,
5. cultivation of a more humanistic educational environment,
6. lifelong learning,
7. internationalization, and
8. adjustment to the information society. (Provisional Council, 1985, p. 4)

Post-war educational reforms in Japan showed two major characteristics. First, they were directly addressed to the changing nature of the economy and society. For example, the number of jobs requiring a high level of knowledge and skill increased as a result of technological development. This led to an expansion of senior secondary and higher education, and this resulted in a revision of the school curricula, and changes to allow for flexibility and diversity in higher education. Second, invariably, several reform proposals addressed the problems of rigidity, uniformity and centralization in the educational system. This reflected that the educational system was still firmly controlled by the central government, from the establishment of schools, curricula and textbooks to staff qualifications and training. The reiteration of the need for flexibility and diversification also reflected that there was basically little change resulting from the various reform proposals (see Aso and Amano, 1983, pp. 91–92).

## Education for Economic and Technological Development

Throughout the post-war period, the need for technical education has been central to a range of policy initiatives, as it has been considered vital for supporting industrial development, which is the key to the country's economic development. The policy initiatives designed to improve the link between education and the needs of the economy included:

1. The promulgation of the Industrial Education Promotion Law in 1951, in order to "to nurse a just and proper belief among the people toward labor, give them practical knowledge concerning industry, and develop their ability to design and create" (cited by Kobayashi, 1986, p. 90).
2. The promulgation of the Science Education Promotion Law in 1953 to promote science teaching in primary, middle and high schools (Kobayashi, 1986, pp. 90–1).
3. The revision of the school curriculum in 1958, devoting more time to science and mathematics and upgrading the contents of these subjects.
4. The establishment of a new system of higher technical colleges in 1962, which assigned a substantial proportion of its new programs for secondary schools and universities for the improvement of facilities for science and technology courses (Cummings, 1980, pp. 59–60).
5. The publication of the 1962 White Paper on Japan's Growth and Education, which recommended an extension of higher education in response to progress in science and technology, the expansion of technical courses in senior secondary education, and the coordination and consolidation of the entire system of scientific research (MOE, 1963, pp. 1–8, 136–7).
6. The publication of the 1963 Report on Objectives and Measures for Developing Human Capabilities and the 1966 Report on the Expansion and Development of Senior Secondary Education, both of which advocated a widely diversified educational system for enhancing vocational education, the expansion of curricula for technical high schools, and the training of leaders and professionals for an industrial society (Kobayashi, 1986, pp. 93–5).
7. The formulation of the Economic and Social Development Plan 1967–71 to promote large-scale research and the setting up of long-term policies for the establishment of vocational education centers, diversification of senior secondary education for teaching general culture, training specialist workers and higher-level scientists and researchers, the expansion of five-year technical colleges, and the establishment of a qualifying examination system and a skill-appraising system (Economic Planning Agency, 1967, pp. 111–5).
8. The formulation of the New Economic and Social Development Plan

1970–75, which again stressed education as a foundation for the balanced development of the economy and society, and recommended the expansion and improvement of teaching of science and engineering in higher education, improving the capability for technological innovation in the country (Economic Planning Agency, 1970, pp. 64–85; cf. Kobayashi, 1986, pp. 105–6).

9. The submission of four educational reports by the Ad Hoc Council on Education in the eighties, which recommended diversification of curricula in technical colleges, the promotion of basic research in universities, the increase of government funds for scientific research in the most advanced areas (National Council, 1986, pp. 7–8, 27–30).

## Links between Education and Economic and Technological Development

As revealed in the above discussion, Japan has experienced tremendous development in its economy, technology and education since its modernization. In the course of modernization, education has undoubtedly been seen as an institution for promoting technological and economic development. From the reports and development of policies as cited above, it seems that there has been an assumption of a triadic relationship between technological development, economic development and education. That is, reports on economic development constantly called for technological development and educational development. Similarly, reports on technological development are argued on the basis of economic development, and they also called for the development of education, particularly technical education. Further, educational reforms were primarily justified with reference to the need for enhancing economic and technological development. Hence it is assumed that education is basic to the country's technological advancement and economic development. Such a relationship among the three is well expressed in the 1962 White Paper on Education:

> [T]he expansion and raising of the level of education is the prerequisite of socio-economic development. Meanwhile, in the industrially developed countries, such human factors as scientific creativeness, technological talents, laborer's skill and the abilities to use completely all available resources, have been recognized as affecting economic development as well as physical capital and the labor force. . . . In this context, the viewpoint of regarding education as an investment should be more emphasized. (MOE, 1963, p. 7)

The Economic Council has also pointed out strongly that "economic competition among nations is a technical competition, and technical competition has become an educational competition" (cited by Shimahara, 1979, p. 133). However, while the relationship between education and economic and technological development seems to have been taken for granted and also to have presented a major influence on policy, further considerations reveal a number of issues and complexities concerning the nature of that relationship.

First, despite the fact that there were many reforms and policies promoting technological development, there is also evidence that they were not successfully implemented because there are still many complaints, especially from employers and industrialists. For example, in 1952, the Japanese Federation of Employers' Associations (*Nikkei-ren*) published a document on Re-examining the New Education System. It raised the need for the diversification of high school curricula by introducing more vocational courses and a higher degree of professionalization within universities to better meet the needs of industry. In 1956, *Nikkei-ren* published another report on Technical Education for the Needs of the New Era. It strongly criticized the educational system on the grounds that on the one hand it paid too little attention to the importance of technical education and on the other hand it emphasized the university tradition which placed most emphasis on law and liberal arts:

> Japan carried out a reform of the school system after the war, but little attention was paid to the importance of technical education. At universities, the custom of placing too great importance upon law and the liberal arts compared with natural science and engineering has not yet been rectified, while the effort to promote scientific and vocational education in the course of compulsory education is still far from satisfactory. (cited by Aso and Amano, 1983, p. 79)

Similar complaints were also made by the Economic Council: "Despite the fact that education is well developed, there is no sufficient readiness to train these talented human resources and to offer unique educational programmes. But a dynamic age of technological innovation requires human resources of high competence. . . " (cited by Shimahara, 1979, p. 135). It is also worth noting that measures for improving technical education were not initiated by the Ministry of Education, but in most cases were made as a response to criticism by the industrial sector. This is evidenced by the fact that many of the reports were prepared by organizations other than the Ministry of Education, such as the *Nikkei-ren*, the Economic Planning Agency, Economic Council, etc. *Nikkei-ren's* concern can be further evidenced by the relatively small ratio of students taking scientific, technical and vocational courses. As shown in Figures 1 and 2, the proportion of upper secondary students taking general academic courses was 74.1 in 1991, while the proportion taking technical courses was 8.7. At the university level, humanities and social sciences students accounted for 55.2%, while science and engineering students accounted for 23% only. A similar picture can also be seen in junior colleges.

FIGURE 1. Percentage Distribution of Upper Secondary School Students by Type of Course, as of May 1991

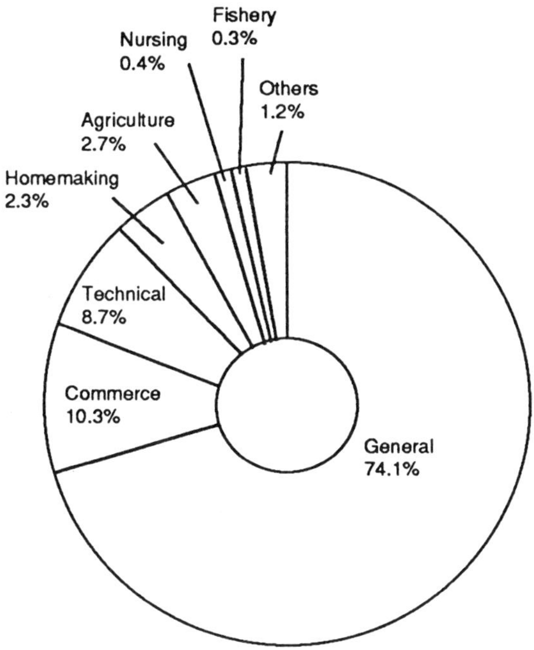


Source: MOE, 1992, p. 20.

The proportion of students involved in science and technology research is much higher at the postgraduate level. However, their direct contribution to technological advancement is uncertain, as much of the research has been done by the government and the industrial sector. Government departments and industry recruit the graduates of the prestigious universities and then provide the equivalent of in-house postgraduate training (Stephens, 1991, p. 127).

FIGURE 2. Percentage Distribution of University and Junior College Students by Major Field of Study, as of May 1991

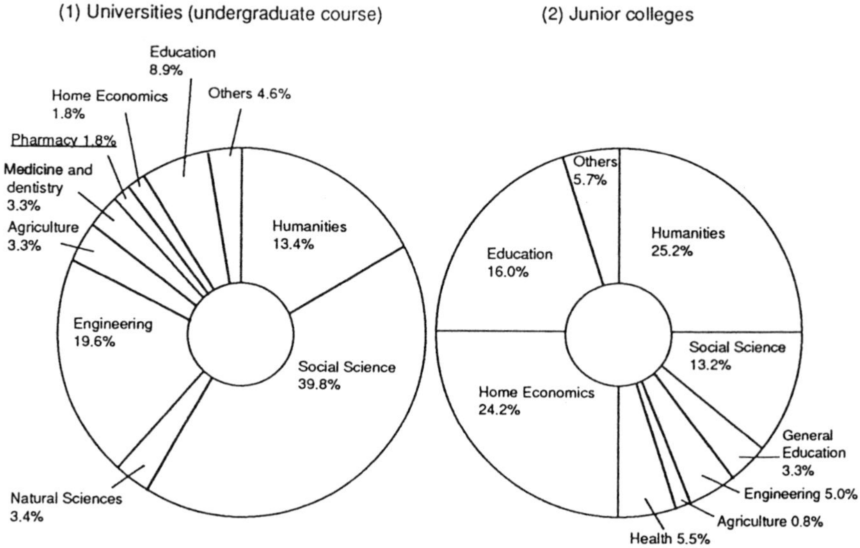


Source: MOE, 1992, pp. 20–21.

There are also problems with Japan's technical education. As elsewhere, technical education, even when expanding, is not considered to be within the mainstream of academic education in Japan. It still represents only a small part of education, and enjoys a low status. In 1990, there were only 62 technical colleges in contrast to 507 universities and 593 junior colleges (Statistics Bureau, 1991, p. 130). According to Von Kopp's (1985, pp. 122–3) analysis of technical education in the seventies in Japan, a large pool of industrial workers actually came from the mainstream of schooling, as nearly 40% of all senior secondary school graduates entered industry. Although there exist some polytechnical components and vocational tracks in schools, the main emphasis is on general education. This can be seen from the decreased proportion of vocational courses in technical schools which dropped from 40% in the 1970s to only 25% today (MOE, 1992, pp. 299–300). Moreover, the Japanese educational system has neither stressed knowledge of the technical side of production nor promoted what Von Kopp termed "the technological mind," which he argues is essential for industrial production.

Thirdly, in contrast to the general view that education is a primary factor in economic development via technological development, Shimahara (1979, p. 50) argues that post-war economic growth has not been a result of the dynamic development of higher education, but the direction of influence was precisely the opposite. Structural changes in the economy were brought about by social conditions outside the educational system, namely, the dissolution of the *zaibatsu* (i.e., giant family trusts), land reform, the formation of labor unions, etc. Rapid post-war economic growth was indeed stimulated by the renovation of industries and equipment destroyed in the war, the importation of technical knowledge, and the Korean War. These conditions created the demand for large numbers of graduates, which led to the expansion of higher education in Japan. However, the rapid expansion of higher education has created numerous problems, such as insufficient funding for the higher institutions for research and facilities, and the difficulty of maintaining the quality of higher education, especially in the private sector.

### Alternative Explanations for Japan's Economic and Technological Development

Shimahara's assertion that Japan's economic development should be accounted for in terms of social and political conditions rather than education is worth noting. In addition to the factors that Shimahara has pointed out, there are studies suggesting other alternative explanations for Japan's post-war rapid economic and technological development.

First, in addition to the favorable social conditions for its economic development, other aspects of the economic structure also help to partly explain Japan's post-war economic successes. For example, the extensive use of subcontracting in manufacturing allows specialization in production and rapid response toward changing needs of the market. Moreover, under a system of managerial, production-orientated capitalism rather than a shareholder-dominated form of capitalism, corporations have obtained a very high proportion of their capital in the form of bank loans rather than equity. Corporate managements therefore could look to long-term developments which might in the long run compensate a short-to-medium-term drain on resources (Dore, 1987, pp. 13–4).

Second, post-war international relationships also offered a favorable environment for Japan's economic growth. For example, Japan's economic growth in the sixties was greatly boosted by easy access to Western markets, notably that of the United States, while its own market maintained a certain degree of protectionism. Although protectionism has been declining, especially recently, it was important when Japan was building up key industries to a point where they were competitive in international terms. Japan's relationship with the United States has been central to its post-war economic development. The economy began to grow in the fifties with America's participation in the Korean War, as American spending in Japan was substantial. Moreover, as Japan's defense budget has been limited to the level of 1% of GDP, in comparison with other countries which spend 6% (e.g., the United States) to 10% (e.g., the former Soviet Union and China), Japan could make use of a sizable amount of money for more productive investment, which was essential for its economic development (Stephens, 1991, pp. 118–9).

Third, within Japan, it is important to note that a large part of technological development is attributed to the contribution of the industrial sector. For example, while the Tsukuba Science City was a national project, the newly established Kansai Science City is privately funded (Stephens, 1991, p. 128). In terms of R&D expenditure, companies accounted for over 60% in the 1980s (Smith, 1985, p. 13), and in 1990 the proportion rose to 70.9% in 1990, followed by universities and colleges, 17.6%, and research institutes, 11.6% (Statistics Bureau, 1992, p. 139). Japan's strength in applied research and weakness in basic research further illustrates the dominance of the industrial sector and the lack of influence of the education sector in R&D (see Vogel, 1987, p. 13; Reischauer, 1988, p. 200).

Fourth, the bulk of industrial training and research is provided by industry itself. For example, Toyota itself has a training staff of 130 providing a variety of training programs. Various programs are offered at different levels to new recruits. Smaller firms also offer their own training programs whether independently or in cooperation with other small companies, and they can obtain subsidies from the government (Cantor, 1985, p. 73). There are also other organizations providing other kinds of systematic training. For example, the Japan Productivity Centre conducts research in productivity and provides senior management education, the Institute of Business Administration and Management conducts seminars on recent development and provides one- or two-year courses for individual managers, the Japan Management Association holds many seminars in various fields, the Nippon Office Management Association offers training in office management such as punch card systems and systems engineering courses, the Japan Management School offers management training, the Union of Japanese Scientists and Engineers Inc. provides training of engineers and technicians, the Japanese Standards Association conducts quality control training, and the Sales Promotion Bureau provides marketing and sales training, and so forth (Tawara, 1968, pp. 196–7). Japanese firms always look for young people of high caliber in general and not necessarily in the technical field, and provide them with further on-the-job training for their specific needs. Hence training has become a regular feature of industrial life in Japan, even after graduation. Generally speaking, firms invest about 5% of their annual sales turnover on training staff. On-the-job training is not limited to induction; retraining and the upgrading of skills are seen as equally important. Moreover, Japanese industrial firms not only provide training for upgrading staff, but they play an important role in research and development as well (Smith, 1985, p. 16).

The fifth explanation refers to Japan's cultural characteristics. For example, the society's emphasis on effort rather than intelligence or ability has allowed the possibility of success for nearly every member of society, and this serves as a prime motivating factor for people to work hard. The adoption of a highly selective and competitive examination system further reinforces this characteristic. Moreover, the existence of a strong sense of group loyalty (and group competition) has become an important factor for employees to treat their company as a family-like organization, and devote their efforts to the success of the company. The prevalence of a highly developed national consciousness that penetrates to the lowest levels of the society has also been an essential factor for mobilizing everyone to work in order to foster the country's economic and technological development (see Vogel, 1987, pp. 15–6). And it is the educational system which contributes most to fostering and reinforcing these cultural traits in Japan. These considerations will be elaborated in the next section.

## Education and Social Development

The socializing role of education has always been strong in Japan. A paramount characteristic of the educational system is the fostering of a strong sense of national identity. This is best expressed in the 1890 Imperial Rescript on Education, which stated that education in Japan should aim at fostering Confucian ethics and national identity (Passin, 1965, p. 258). Before the war, such an emphasis had fostered nationalism or "ultra-nationalism." After the war, Japan was cautious of such ultra-nationalism. However, this has by no means lessened its emphasis on national consciousness albeit of a less militaristic form. As Vogel (1987, p. 15) has observed, the Japanese have a highly developed national consciousness that penetrates the lowest levels of the society, and this is "something that comes partly from education, from getting trained from kindergarten and grade school on up about national priorities."

A second characteristic of Japanese education is that it reinforces the significance of diligence. This is manifest in the promotion of the spirit of *gambare*, which means persistence, perseverance or doing one's best (Singleton, 1990, p. 10). The spirit of *gambare* is a marked characteristic of the Japanese society, and is very much emphasized in schools. Concerning this, Duke (1986, p. 122) says:

> Throughout the lifetime of the Japanese they are surrounded, encouraged, and motivated by the spirit of *gambare*. It begins in the home. The school takes it up from the first day the child enters the classroom. It continues through graduation. The company then thrives on it. It engulfs every facet of society. It is employed in work, study, and even at play and leisure. *Gambare* is integral to being Japanese.

A third characteristic of Japanese schooling is the fostering of group spirit. As LeVine and White (1986, p. 103) remark, schools in Japan socialize children into the "motivating group": an individual is encouraged to see himself or herself as part of a group—actually not "*just* part of the group," but identified by self-enhancing membership which brings out the best of the person's potential. Therefore, desirable qualities promoted in school are those that reinforce team membership. The school values accomplishment as a group and the coordinated commitment of effort by everyone (cf. White, 1987, p. 43). This sense of collective identity is a manifestation of another aspect of *gambare,* which is a major component of competition, particularly group competition. It is the basic rallying cry for nearly every group in Japanese society. In the process of exerting effort, the goals of each participant must be pursued through a collective effort. "*Gambare*" has become a sort of exhortation, not only encouraging oneself to work hard, but also encouraging the other group members. When a child disappoints, the teacher will challenge him/her to *gambare*, not just to persevere to accomplish a goal but to exert every effort toward keeping that child "running full speed" in any endeavor in order not to let his/her group down. To succeed, all must *gambare* together (Duke, 1986; Singleton, 1990).

A fourth characteristic of Japanese schooling is the fostering of a sense of egalitarianism and the spirit of meritocracy. When identifying the social reasons for people valuing education in Japan, LeVine and White (1986, pp. 110–111) stress that egalitarianism and meritocracy are significant factors. Cummings (1980, pp. 16–35) points out that Japanese post-war education has brought about an egalitarian transformation in the society. The official curriculum is rich in egalitarian and participatory themes. For example, the

Course of Study of the primary six texts places emphasis on an egalitarian sense of the division of labor in society, and a large proportion of the description is devoted to identifying the contributions of wholesale and retail shopkeepers, farmers and food processors, foresters, fishermen, blue-collar workers, firemen, policemen, etc., while leaving high-status occupations such as doctors and government officials conspicuously untouched. The significance of participatory democracy and the contribution of the people's role in shaping local government decisions are also stressed in the Course of Study (Cummings, 1982, p. 26).

Moreover, it is worth noting that effort rather than innate intelligence is emphasized in Japan's education system, fostering a very specific type of meritocracy. A basic premise of Japanese maternal teaching strategies is that children are born with no particular innate abilities but all have a chance at developing them through environmental influences and the engagement of effort on their and their mother's part (LeVine and White, 1986, p. 119). Nowadays Japanese children are educated until the age of 15, or throughout the nine years of compulsory schooling, wholly in mixed-ability classes in mixed-ability schools (Dore, 1987, p. 205). It is also noteworthy that nearly every Japanese student (over 90%) continues his or her education beyond compulsory schooling to the senior secondary level of education. Although the basic motivation for proceeding to senior secondary schooling is that students are eventually rated according to their performance in senior secondary schools, the fact that nearly everyone proceeds suggests that not many Japanese students like to consider themselves as inferior in intelligence or ability.

## Conclusion

The phenomenal growth of Japan has attracted much research, especially in identifying factors for such growth. It is commonly believed in Japan that education serves as a causal factor for Japan's economic and technological development. This is exemplified in many of the reports which have emphasized the significance of investing in education to meet the manpower needs of the country. While education has been widely seen as essential in supporting a country's development, further analysis suggests that there exist certain complexities and uncertainties, if we are to establish a causal relationship. Apart from the fact that the emphasis in education is mainly academic in Japan, which is not directly relevant to its technological and economic development, it is also clear that Japan's educational expansion, especially of higher education, has been primarily supported by its growing economy, and has responded to the shifts in the economy.

The contribution of education seems to have been more fundamental in reinforcing and sustaining a cultural system which is conducive to development, namely, fostering national consciousness, group spirit, perseverance, egalitarianism, meritocracy, and so forth. Von Kopp (1985, p. 126) stresses the need for a cultural perspective to understand an educational system which does not cultivate the "technological mind" and yet can achieve technological advancement. LeVine and White (1986, p. 1226) also point out that the success of Japanese education has been achieved through means very different from the West. This makes the Japanese case unique, and its implications go beyond education to broader questions of cultural conditions.

However, there are problems with the cultural model of explanation. First, it easily creates a tendency to look for an "advanced" culture, the concept of which has been challenged severely and regarded as simplistic. For example, when the Western countries developed into advanced industrial economies, such variables as the Protestant ethic, modern values and civic culture were seen as the aspects of culture correlated with economic and technological advancement. With remarkable East Asian successes, explanations have recently shifted to Confucian ethics. This suggests how relativistic cultural explanations can be. Benedict has rightly posed a classical challenge to the assumption that one culture can be "higher" than another. She posits that there are both good sides and dark sides in all cultures, and that all cultures should be respected (Benedict, 1961; cf. Langness, 1987, p. 108). Second, adopting a cultural explanation suggests that every case is unique, and therefore it is difficult to generalize principles of development. The best we can achieve is that under certain circumstances, particular cultural traits serve as contributive factors for development. However, the same may not be true for the other nations. An example is that while Confucian ethics have been conveniently identified as a contributing factor for development in the East Asian countries, there are certainly other Asian countries possessing a Confucian tradition which have not experienced such development, and some that have developed that are not Confucian (e.g., Thailand). It is worth noting that underdevelopment in China in the nineteenth and early twentieth centuries was attributed to the influence of the Confucian tradition (Peck, 1971, pp. 43–4). Wright (1957, pp. 7–10) bluntly asserted that the "requirements of modernization ran counter to the requirements of Confucian stability." In his discussion on the possibility of identifying an East Asian model of success, Berger distinguishes between two models, namely, the "culturalist" model and the "institutionalist" model. While the culturalist model looks for cultural explanations of success, the institutionalist model looks for economic policies and practices independent of who implements the policies and practices. Berger further points out that the institutionalist model is a model transferable to other countries, but the culturalist model is not, as it makes no sense, for example, to suggest to Arabs or Latin Americans that they should adopt Confucian ethics (Berger, 1990, p. 9). Third, despite an awareness of how Japanese education fosters cultural and social traits conducive to development, there are doubts now emerging about how successful contemporary Japanese schools are in the process of socialization. There are increasing concerns that the younger generation of Japan is no longer upholding traditional Japanese values. In regard to this, the 1984 White Paper complained that:

> Japanese youth is pampered, over-sexed, over-fed, money-grabbing, self-interested, introverted, apathetic, lazy and lacking in the sense of responsibility that has traditionally characterized Japanese society. And perhaps not surprisingly, most of this is attributed to the Western culture that has poisoned the old values. (cited by Parkins, 1985)

The National Council on Educational Reform (1986, p. 4) also described the present condition of education as "an educational wasteland," and argues that the country is experiencing a crisis of "desolation in education" the symptoms of which include bullying, school violence, and excessive competition in examinations. While competition is a part of Japan's educational system, bullying and school violence are certainly not something taught in schools but conformity is. This suggests that Japan's schools are subject to other social influences, such as the increasing affluence in society, despite their attempt to transmit traditional values; and the role of schools is not static, as it changes with wider developments.

All this suggests that Japan's educational development is to be understood in terms of the country's economic and social development. There are certainly factors other than education to be considered, such as the economic structure of the society, international relationships, and the cultural factors which can serve as positive or negative forces of development. These factors may explain more about Japan's development than education alone, as education primarily functions as a means of conserving existing social and cultural norms, and at best develops as a response to social change, rather than a leading force. It has, however, performed an important role in reinforcing those social values which might have been supportive of development.

# 3 Hong Kong

*Anthony Sweeting*

## Introduction

It is a cliché to declare that Hong Kong is unique. As other chapters in this book clearly demonstrate, in several important respects it is also untrue. Like the seven other East Asian societies investigated, Hong Kong is an export-oriented market economy. Like them, it is noted for the industriousness of its workers and the enterprise of its entrepreneurs. Like them, it has acquired economic strength mainly since the end of the Second World War.

Hong Kong is, however, a very special case. It represents one of the greatest success stories of the second half of the twentieth century, a triumph for hard work, adaptability and good sense over very limited natural advantages, an absence of good-neighborliness and a scarcity of international goodwill. And yet there is another, seamier, side to its image as perceived in and by the rest of the world, a side underscored with allegations about shoddy products, sweated labor and, particularly, the exploitation of children and young women.[1] Thus, the chorus of comments about Hong Kong in the last years of its colonial existence encompasses the encomiums of such economists as Milton Friedman, in general harmony with the periodic respect of *The Economist.* The chorus also contains the counterpoint of cheap jibes from the envious, the resentful, and the ignorant. Both the praise and the prejudice frequently point to assumptions about how the success of the economy is linked with the characteristics of the education provided. Occasionally, such comments point to the possible connections among what are considered to be retarded political development, a lack of community spirit and educational shortcomings. The main purpose of this chapter is to investigate these supposed links. Evidence will be presented and interpreted about the contributions which education has made to all major aspects of development—economic, political and social—and about the contributions which development has made to education.

The special case of Hong Kong becomes clearer when one recognizes four major ways in which it is different from most or all of the seven other East Asian societies examined in this book. First, although Hong Kong shares its export-oriented market economy aspects with the other seven, on the whole, as Milton Friedman emphasized, its government adopted laissez-faire policies much more wholeheartedly than the others ever did.[2] Indeed, in the post-World War II period, policies of the governments of Japan, Singapore, South Korea, Taiwan, Malaysia, and the People's Republic of China approximate *dirigisme* more closely. In Philip Foster's view, something resembling a "Concordat" was reached between the Administration and the Business Sector in Hong Kong, with senior civil servants, like a latter-day Louis-Philippe, sending out a clear message to businessmen, industrialists, and financiers—"Enrichez-vous!"[3] Second, not only did the Hong Kong government give a free hand to business, for much of the time it also refrained from taking a very active part in education. In many of the other East Asian societies, the state played a significant role in the direct provision of schooling, in the manipulation of both educational and employment opportunities, and in curricular initiatives. This did not happen to anything like the same extent in Hong Kong. Third, unlike the other societies,[4] Hong Kong was not a nation-state. It was a colony. Policy makers did not need to seek a regular mandate from the public. Individually, they did not need to cater to a constituency. They might, therefore, be able to take a longer-term and territory-wide view. Moreover, Hong Kong was a very special sort of colony. Its rationale was commercial and strategic. It was not concerned with the settlement of population from the "home country" and, because a large and significant part of its territory was leased, it harbored few, if any, pretensions toward permanence. Thus, a concordat between administrators and businessmen in the interests of material returns made sense. Fourth, Hong Kong remained very closely linked—economically, socially, and politically—with China. The size and pace of influxes of population from China depended on natural calamities, economic hardships, and political disturbances on the mainland, but there was never a sign that the influxes would cease during Hong Kong's colonial existence. Post-war development in Hong Kong was facilitated by the import of high quality human capital from China. At first, the import was stimulated by the Sino-Japanese War; later it was stimulated by the Chinese Civil War and its outcome. It might appear that Taiwan and Macau benefited in similar ways from the import of the same sort of human capital. In the case of Taiwan, however, the incoming population became the new master class, disrupting, if not destroying, much of the native Taiwanese political, social, and economic structures. In the case of Macau, the influx did not happen to the same extent as it did in Hong Kong, and did not consist of the same quality.

A major thesis of this chapter is that Hong Kong's post-war development is best understood in relation to these four "special" factors. It is appropriate, therefore, that we begin more detailed investigation by considering aspects of its particular setting.

*Setting*

Geographically, Hong Kong is situated at the edge of the Pearl River Delta, about 150 kilometers from the city of Guangzhou in Southern China. It comprises islands, a peninsula, its hinterland, and land reclaimed from the sea. Its climate is tropical and it is within the "typhoon belt" of the South China Sea. High humidity and intermittent natural (and man-made) disasters raise personal temperatures, pressures, and anxieties, though in the latter part of the twentieth century these have been mollified for many people by modern technology.

Constitutionally, Hong Kong resumed the status of a British Crown Colony[5] in 1945. It is expected to remain one until midnight on June 30, 1997, after which sovereignty over the territory will revert to China. This makes it an unusual, but still not a unique, case. Most former colonies undergoing a period of transition move toward self-government and then independence. A few, however, like Goa, East Timor, and in the future Macau and possibly Gibraltar, are reabsorbed into the largest political entity in their vicinity, on the questionable grounds that this represents a return to their origins. In real operational terms, Hong Kong achieved something approaching effective, if not titular, decolonization quite early in the post-war period. This was largely the outcome of Britain's own decline and, in particular, its failure to help Hong Kong over its "problem of people."[6] It may also have been partly influenced by the way the economy of the colony has so patently out-performed that of its metropole. In the later twentieth century, metaphorically Britain could scarcely afford the cost of second-hand pipes. Its own domestic problems ensured it could no longer act as paymaster of pipers. It could not realistically expect, therefore, to call the tune.

According to all conventional indicators of macroeconomic development, the post-World War II period has been for Hong Kong a time of great change and almost unrelieved progress and success (Ho, 1993). As Lloyd George (1992, p. 57) notes, "in the past forty years, Hong Kong has been transformed from a small British trading port into the third largest international financial and trading centre in the world." *The Economist* (December 25, 1993–January 7, 1994, p. 73), commenting on its own findings about economic indicators and its detection of a general trend for rich countries to have experienced sluggish growth over the past decade when compared with newly industrializing countries, points out that "the exception is Hong Kong, which has both a high average income of $18,520 (well ahead of Britain's $16,340) and one of the fastest growth rates [at 6.3% for 1983–92]."

Socially, Hong Kong is a fascinating, but problematic admixture (but rarely amalgam)—of races, of cultures, of lifestyles. Throughout the post-war period, over 97% of its population have been ethnic Chinese and, of these, about 90% Cantonese. This has meant that the *lingua franca* has been neither English nor Putonghua (Mandarin), but Cantonese, a situation attended by some advantages in colloquial liveliness, but also by problems, past, present and future, in connection with social, economic and political relations (Chen, 1989; So, 1992). In respect of population composition, then, Hong Kong might be considered practically mono-cultural. However, within the predominant Chinese culture, numerous divisions have operated, concerning place of origin, social class, dialect or accent, length of residence, degree of urbanization versus degree of traditionalism and level of cosmopolitanism versus level of parochialism. The non-Chinese elements of the population have sometimes exercised an influence on economic, political, social and cultural development disproportionate to their numbers. However, although some of them would claim a "sense of belonging" to Hong Kong, few, except possibly the Eurasians, can confidently feel it.[7] At all times during the post-war period, significant numbers of people have been planning to leave the territory. This has been especially true of the ethnic Chinese and increasingly true since the Sino-British Agreement of 1984 confirmed that Hong Kong's future was as part of China. It makes increasing sense to discuss the "internationalization of the population and the globalization of families" (Kwong, 1993). Many families from Hong Kong have, in effect, developed a "trans-national" (or post-national) identity.

In many respects, Hong Kong, like man in general, is not an island (even plus peninsula, hinterland, and reclaimed land) entire of itself. Instead, it is subject to a whole range of exogenous forces. Concerning most aspects of life, the main influence from outside its present borders comes from its nearest neighbor and possessor-designate, the People's Republic of China. Other influences include, of course, that of its constitutional "superior," the United Kingdom. When Hong Kong people consider going, or actually go, to live overseas, especially in the United States of America, Canada and Australia, these places also gain in influence over family members left in Hong Kong. Trading partners, sources of overseas investment, and places for recreation and relaxation from the pressures of life in Hong Kong, such as Japan, the Philippines, Indonesia, Malaysia and Singapore, also wield influence, as does the European Community and the United Nations.

A similar medley of influences affected the development of education in Hong Kong. For much of its recorded history, there has naturally been a "Chinese" stream of education, at first traditional, later in various more modern guises. From 1843, this was supplemented by a numerically smaller, but, in terms of the prospects of new employment openings, highly significant "Anglo-Chinese" stream, in which a Western-style education was delivered to local students (the vast majority being Chinese) through the medium of the English language. From the early twentieth century, there has also been a very small "English" stream, catering at first for the children of British employees who could not afford or did not want to send their children "home" for education. In origin even earlier, but in its latest forms more recently, there developed an "international" stream of education, with various schools preparing the children of expatriates in the curriculum of, and for higher or further education in, their home countries. Until the end of the Second World War, the vast majority of local schools were more or less pale imitations of their models, usually from abroad (including China). It was only in the post-war period that something approaching an autochthonous system of schooling developed (Luk, 1991; Sweeting, 1993). Even then, however, there has been much criticism of the quality of education, with most critics focusing on allegations about excessively academic curricula, low levels of creativity, the lack of initiative in students and teachers, and the dead hand of over-frequent and highly competitive formal examinations. On the other hand, various successes have been claimed for education in Hong Kong. In particular, its students' achievements in mathematics and in science subjects have been cited as evidence of successful instruction and/or successful learning (Holbrook, 1990). In general, there has been considerable admiration for, and some envy of, the work ethic manifested by so many of the Hong Kong students who have attended educational courses abroad. Furthermore, a similar dichotomy to that concerning traditionalism and modernism in society at large has affected education. The traditional respect for academic scholarship persists. However, it is accompanied by an admiration of the self-made person, a more modern and pragmatic valuation of effective action.

Hong Kong qualifies clearly as a post-industrial society. It certainly makes use of sophisticated technology, especially as related to communications. We have noted that it might also be considered to be post-nationalist, especially in the sense that many families resident in Hong Kong either have other members who are nationals of foreign countries or intend to send one or more of their members to a foreign country in the near future. Most visitors will recognize that, over the past half-century, it has been constantly de-constructing and re-constructing itself, both in architectural and in more conceptual terms. In all these respects as well as via its pragmatic eclecticism, Hong Kong is probably the most eligible candidate for the title of the world's first post-modern society.

### *General Observations on Human Capital Theory, Manpower Planning, and Culturalist Explanations of Successful Development*

As the Introduction to this book and several of the other chapters emphasize, a widespread assumption since the 1960s is that the investment of (mainly) public money in "human capital" enhancement is the surest way to bring about economic development. The early human capital theorists (e.g., Schultz and Becker) suggested that those aspects of economic development which could not be explained in other ways must be the result of education or investment in human capital, the "residual factor." They encouraged a focus on studies estimating the contribution of education to economic growth and, in particular, measuring the rates of return to schooling. Often this was posited on a study of earnings distribution which was correlated with duration of schooling. Early studies emphasized that rates of return to basic, primary schooling were particularly high. They shared, however, one of the general features of the whole school of thought: education was regarded as a "black box." The important considerations were inputs and outputs, not what actually happened in the process of education itself.

In about the same period, confidence developed in the efficacy of manpower planning by central governments. Another assumption gained credence: that systematic manpower needs predictions indicate how technical education and vocational training will optimize the rates of return on investment in human capital. In the days of decolonization, post-colonization, and, in some places, neo-colonization, the message purveyed by the developed (often ex-colonialist) powers to the developing (often ex-colonized) countries was simple: you will only be able to start to catch up if you become fiscally sober and if you devote large proportions of public investment (including newly contracted loans) into specialized forms of education. Their assumption was that there is a direct, linear and causal relationship between investment in education, especially the higher reaches of technical and technological education, and national development. Receptive ears listened to this reasoning in the developing countries themselves. The fact that post-colonial realities offered lucrative and prestigious opportunities for a small number of highly educated specialists from the new nation in question added to the motive force for generous investment in higher and technically or professionally oriented education. Especially in the 1960s, numerous new nations in Africa and the Pacific followed this line, influenced by both exogenous and endogenous forces of the types identified above. Governments in these new nations tended to become interventionist. The emotive justification was usually anti-colonialist and, selectively, pro-nationalist. The outcome, however, was very rarely indeed economic development or even political stability. Thus, human capital theory, married to manpower planning and as applied by politicians and other policy makers, had largely disappointing results in terms of economic development. This was at least partly because investment in human capital was rarely accompanied by or integrated with changes to the structure of the economy. As we will see, Hong Kong's experience was very different.

An alternative set of explanations for economic progress emphasizes culturalist factors. Here, the reasoning appears to have been influenced more by the discipline of sociology than by economics. Some efforts to explain the success of Japan and the "Little Dragons" (e.g., Hofheinz and Calder, 1982; Morishima, 1982; Dore, 1987 and 1988; Tai, 1989) have, therefore, focused on the Confucian Ethic, which is believed to have fuelled and motivated both labor and management. Diligence ranks highly among Confucian values. The reciprocal nature of relationships such as ruler–ruled, parent–children and employer–employee is certainly emphasized. In these senses, vestiges of the Confucian tradition in Hong Kong have contributed to its economic strength. As Vogel (1991) points out, however, numerous societies have achieved industrial transformation without the help of a Confucian subtext and some countries with such "help" are relatively late on the industrial scene. In the case of Hong Kong, Confucian traditions and values retain some force, but they exist within a pluralistic, eclectic and quite materialistic culture.

Hong Kong has witnessed dramatic economic development in the second half of the twentieth century. This has included continued development even when much of the developed world suffered from recession and much of the rest of the developing world from poverty and demoralization. For most of the time, Hong Kong experienced political stability, if only slow and, according to several observers, belated political development toward democratization. By identifying the main trends which have operated in the case of post-war Hong Kong and by focusing attention on the macro and the micro aspects of development, one should be able to find data which will both illuminate and challenge common and possibly simplistic assumptions.

## Main Trends and Their Linkages

To begin with, it is worth seeking an overview of post-war development in Hong Kong. It is possible, for example, to conceive of the relationships relevant to development of the educational system along "triadic" lines, similar to those suggested by Fågerlind and Saha (1989). Figure 1, below, provides a general framework for the exploration of relationships between educational policy, social change, and political and economic development. It also offers a rationale for the structure of much of the remainder of the present chapter. In the search for conceptual clarity, both this diagram and Figure 2 obscure the extent of overlapping and "fuzzy" influences.

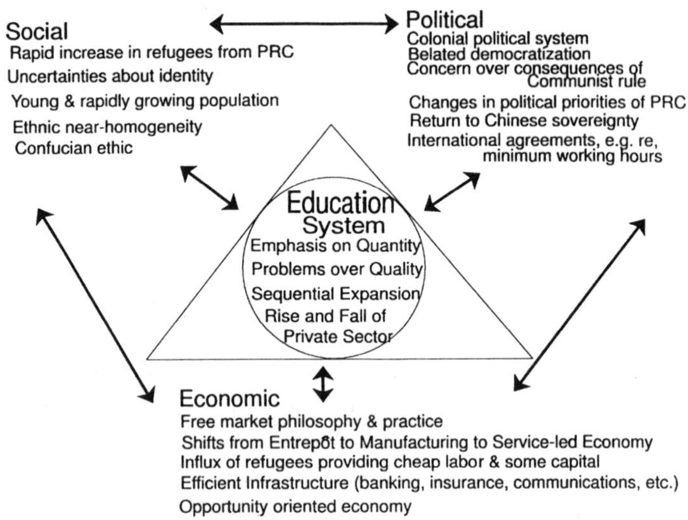


Figure 1. A Triadic Framework

Figure 2 presents four timelines, permitting cross references between developments in the economy, political developments, social developments, and changes in educational practice and policy.

With a reminder that, in reality, post-war development in Hong Kong was neither as conceptually tidy nor as chronologically discrete as Figure 2 suggests, it would be worth turning to an examination of each of the components of this complex set of interrelationships.

### *Economic Development*

Over the last two decades, Hong Kong has been one of the most successful economies in the world. The gross domestic product (at constant market

| | Economic | Political | Social | Educational |
|---|---|---|---|---|
| 95 | *DIVERSIFICATION:* | *BELATED DEMOCRATIZATION* | *HONG KONG IDENTITY* | *EFFORTS TO PLAN* |
| | *SERVICES & MANUFACTURING* | | | *Focus on Tertiary level* |
| | | *Onset of Party Politics* | *Growth of the Middle Class* | *Problems over Quality & over Services for Non-Mainstream Pupils* |
| | *Financial Center* | *Importance of 1997 Factor* | *Consumerism* | |
| 85 | *Use of High Technology* | *Some Disenchantment with China and with the UK* | *Yuppification* | *Continued Decline of Private Sector* |
| | *Links with China's Modernization* | | *Pressure Group Activity* | *Politicization* |
| | | | *Media Mentality* | *TOWARD A POLICY* |
| | | *BUREAUCRATIC OLIGARCHY* | *Brain Drain* | *Focus on Secondary Schooling* |
| 75 | *MANUFACTURING* | | *Social Problems* | *Mass Education* |
| | | | *UNCERTAINTIES* | *Problems of Administration* |
| | *Rapid Expansion* | *Positive Non-Interventionism & Centralilized Populism* | | *Beginning of Decline of Private Sector* |
| 65 | *Industrialization* | *A-Politicization* | | *Beginning of Expansion of Technical Education* |
| | *Increase in Female Participation in the Workforce* | *Leadership Problems* | *Refugee Mentality* | *RECONSTRUCTION & EXPANSION* |
| | *Important part played by Immigrant Labor and Capital* | *Growth of Pressure-Groups* | *Disturbances* | |
| 55 | | *Importance of Non-formal Politics* | *Transience* | *Focus on Primary Schooling* |
| | *Relatively Small-Scale Businesses and Factories* | | *Focus on Livelihood* | *Highly Selective & Elitist* |
| | | | *Doubts over Identity* | *Growth of Private Sector* |
| | *RECONSTRUCTION* | | | |
| 45 | *Entrepôt* | *RECONSTRUCTION* | *RECOVERY* | |

FIGURE 2. The Chronology of Development in Post-War Hong Kong

prices) increased at an average annual rate of 8% from 1978 to 1989 and the average annual increase of real per capita income was 6%, the fourth highest in the world. In 1990, the per capita GDP at constant (1980) prices was equivalent to $5,909, the highest in Asia outside Japan. The level of unemployment has remained very low. How did this situation arise? And what connections, if any, did the reasons for economic success have with education?

In late 1945, the economy began to recover from the Japanese occupation which had resulted in a massive outflow of population and a rundown of the entrepôt economy. From an entrepôt center, Hong Kong became a major manufacturer and exporter of goods in its own right. By 1959, the entrepôt trade had declined. Only 30% of total exports were re-exports and 70% were goods manufactured in Hong Kong. This was the exact opposite of the situation in 1953. By the end of the 1950s, Hong Kong's secondary industries had become established and were growing fast. The first major industry was textiles but other industries soon developed. As might be expected, there were multiple causes for this major economic shift. Some stemmed from exogenous forces. The flight of factory owners and other capitalists from the Shanghai region of China to Hong Kong during the Chinese Civil War was particularly significant (Wong, 1988), as was the outbreak of the Korean War in 1952 and the two embargoes on trade with China, which, almost overnight, crippled Hong Kong's entrepôt services. Endogenous forces also played a part, however. The willingness of Hong Kong families not only to put aside some of their earnings into savings but also to invest these savings in small, often family-based, industrial ventures[8] was a key factor. The readiness of both long-term Hong Kong residents and the refugee-newcomers to work long hours in difficult conditions was another. The relatively high participation rate of women in the labor force was a third.

By 1970, over 30% of GDP and 47% of employment arose from the manufacturing sector. Soon after, another major economic shift of emphasis took place. Since 1975, Hong Kong has retained a strong industrial sector, but has also developed into a major financial and commercial center. By 1981, 2.0% of the working population were involved in the primary sector (down from 8.1% in 1961), 49.8% in the secondary sector (up from 48.9% in 1961), and 46.8% in the tertiary sector (up from 41.6 in 1961). By 1991, the percentages were 0.8, 36.7 and 62.2, respectively (Government of Hong Kong, 1993b). The diversification of the economy was clearly recognized to be important and to merit encouragement (Government of Hong Kong, 1979; Sung, 1991). At the outset, at least, it was primarily the result of China's increased involvement in international trade after the end of the "Cultural Revolution."

Accompanying this trend was the gradual change from a transient to a more settled, mainly indigenous population, very high levels of female employment, especially in the manufacturing sector of the economy, and, certainly from the 1960s, increasing affluence. Chart 1 graphically illustrates the effects of these trends on gross domestic product.

The first obvious message is one of general macroeconomic growth. The impact of this macroeconomic growth as increasing affluence for individuals in Hong Kong, even allowing for inflation, is indicated by a comparison of the two sets of data. The general similarity of the curves in Chart 1 suggests that the rewards of economic success were reasonably fairly distributed among the population, a conclusion ratified by a recent World Bank publication.[9] In both cases, there were hiccoughs in the general growth pattern, the first in the mid-1970s, caused largely by the short-term effects of the running-down and end of the Vietnam War, the second in the mid-1980s,

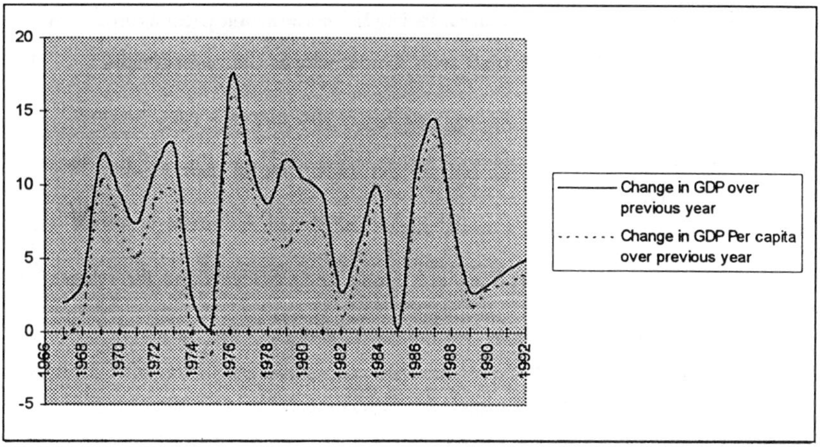


CHART 1. Change in GDP and GDP Per Capita at Constant 1980 Prices

Source: Census and Statistics Department: Estimates of Gross Domestic Product, 1966–92

caused mainly by the knock-on effects of widespread recession. In both cases, the brief pause was followed by renewed growth, although in the eighties this was more immediately noticeable in terms of GDP and slower in terms of *per capita* GDP. The generally healthy growth rates at a time of structural shifts in the economy indicate that growth was accompanied by successful economic development.

## LINKS WITH EDUCATION

Together, these factors created a much higher public demand for kindergarten and primary education. Initially, this demand was met in the main by increased provision of school places in the private sector. From the mid-1940s the government responded to the pressures in three main ways: its own school building program in the primary, if not the kindergarten sector; offering interest-free loans and favorable consideration over building sites to voluntary (mainly religious) associations; and, more grudgingly, similar assistance to selected private schools. It was, however, the private sector which grew most rapidly and by the mid-1970s was providing all the kindergarten places, about 15% of the primary school places, and about 70%

of all secondary school places. In 1971, free, universal and compulsory primary education was achieved. The inevitable extension of demand to secondary education resulted at first in the rapid growth of private secondary schools. Though the quality of these new schools varied, they served a ready market in what was basically a meritocratic system (Luk, 1990). To increase enrollments and make feasible its new target of nine years of subsidized education for all (i.e., six years of primary schooling plus three of junior secondary), in 1974 the government adopted the expedient of "buying" a large number of places in private schools. As soon as possible, however, it was intended that all secondary places should be provided in public sector schools and the basic trend of the 1980s was an expansion of the aided sector and the attenuation of the bought places scheme.

Chart 2, below, shows clearly both the rise of the private sector in the 1960s and its renewed lease of life with the bought places scheme of the late seventies. It also shows the decline of the private sector in the eighties and nineties. In general, one might conclude, however, that, especially during the critical periods of structural change to the economy (i.e, in the late 1940s/early 1950s and again in the 1970s), Hong Kong's ability to develop a reasonably efficient and equitable educational system was largely because the government took little direct part. Chart 3 shows the relative proportions of the total expenditure of *public* funds on the different levels of edu-

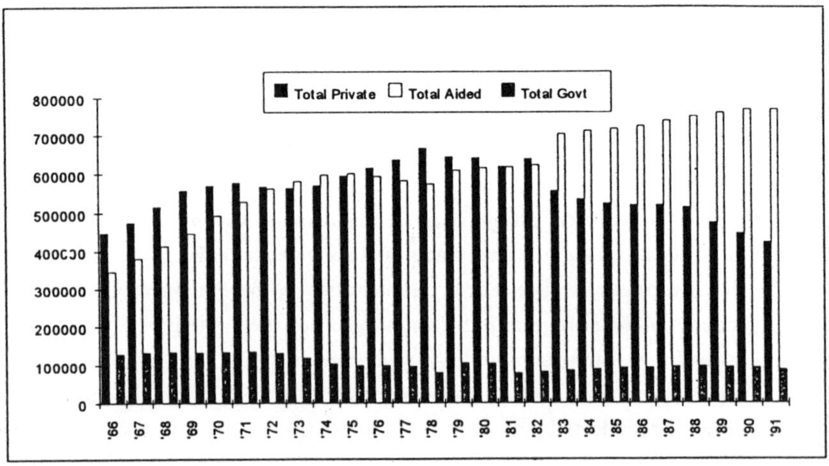


CHART 2. Total School Enrollments, 1965–1991, by Method of Financing

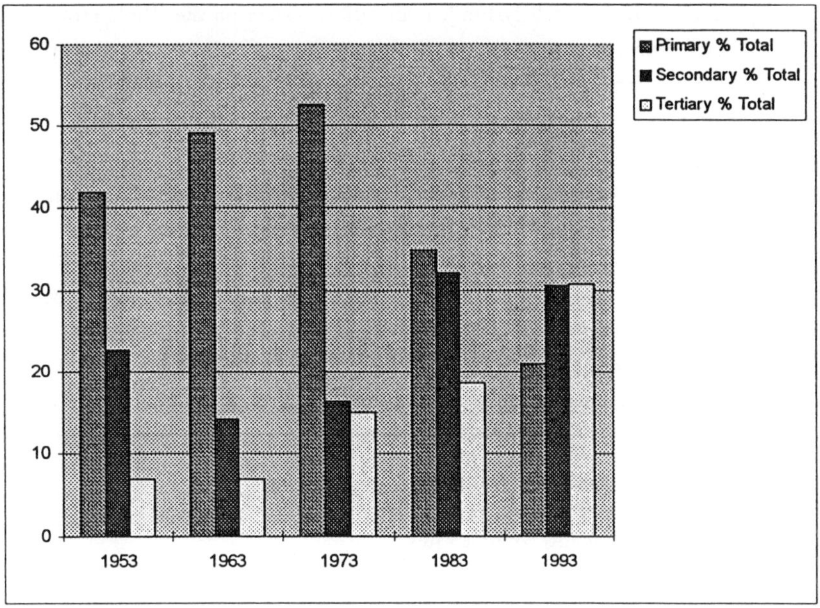


CHART 3. Proportion of the Total Public Expenditure on Education Devoted to Different Levels of Education

cation at five points in time over the past four decades. If government subsidizing of the voluntary associations and its helping of the private sector is added to its own direct maintenance of schools, it becomes obvious that, over time, the priorities for expansion changed. As can be clearly seen, Hong Kong did not make the mistake of spending a disproportionate amount of public funds on specialist secondary and tertiary education during the early phase of economic development. Indeed, during the late 1940s and 1950s, the government deliberately held back the expansion of both secondary and tertiary education in order to focus on the expansion of primary education. Similarly, in the late 1970s and 1980s, the government restricted opportunities for tertiary education within the territory, concentrating instead on the expansion of secondary education.

On the whole, the period from 1945 to about 1971 saw what might best be characterized as a minimalist approach to educational planning being overtaken by events and pre-empted by crisis intervention. Immediately after 1945, the publicly funded education system on the whole replicated key features of the pre-war period (Sweeting and Morris, 1993).[10] It was highly selective and elitist, providing the relatively small public and international sectors of the economy with the bilingual manpower they required. As Charts 2 and 4 illustrate, however, interesting new trends concerning the management of schools and their operation began to develop in the post-war period.

Early post-war expansion of schooling was very largely achieved through the private sector. By the 1960s, the subsidized sector was beginning to catch up in terms of total enrollments. By the mid-1980s, it had overtaken the private sector, which in recent years has continued to decline. Schools directly provided and maintained by the government have never catered to a large proportion of the student population, but have been intended instead to serve as models and as ways of offering some children and young people from the lower socioeconomic levels reasonably efficient education at reasonably low-fee rates.

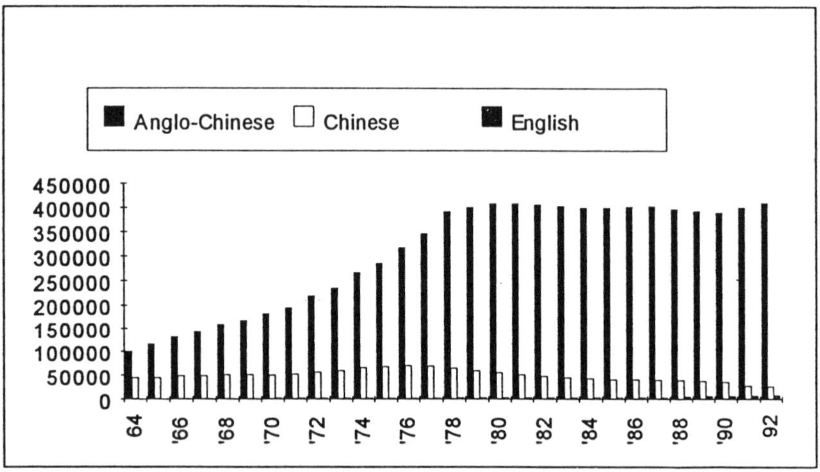


CHART 4. Secondary School Enrollment by Language Type

At the secondary school level, Chinese medium education expanded rapidly in the earlier part of the post-war period. However, students from Chinese middle schools had no ready access to tertiary education in Hong Kong, a problem made all the sharper by the fact that, for many, the customary alternative—tertiary education in China—became a less attractive and less feasible option.[11] The result was that school-leavers from Chinese medium schools were strongly directed towards the sector of the economy which revolved around small family businesses. Thus, the absence of tertiary educational opportunities meant that many competent Chinese middle school leavers went directly into family businesses as a way of pursuing their personal aspirations while sublimating any academic ambitions. Some of them now own the most successful of Hong Kong's economic enterprises.

Several factors brought change to the educational situation, resulting in the massive expansion of primary education in the 1950s and 1960s, secondary education in the 1970s and 1980s, and tertiary education in the 1990s. Prime among these was demography, with Hong Kong's population increasing dramatically from an estimated 600,000 in 1945 to about 1.9 million in 1949, about 2.5 million in 1955, 4.3 million in 1974, and 5.8 million in 1992. The initial growth of population was the result of the post-war immigration from China of (mainly) young persons. This augmented the general post-war "baby-boom" and the result was a population structure skewed at first to the younger age-bands. Population pressures increased the *demand* for educational opportunities. In Hong Kong, as Chart 2 affirms, the government was prepared, albeit reluctantly at times and only until it felt it could afford something better, to permit a very significant portion of the *supply* of educational opportunities at each level of schooling to be provided by private operators who were interested in cutting costs in order to maximize profits.

In the case of primary education, it was the Seven Year Plan of 1954–61 which enabled the public sector to overtake the private sector. In the case of secondary education, reliance on the private sector lasted well into the 1970s and was partly prolonged by the use of the "Bought Places Scheme" in the later 1970s to ensure the achievement of the target of free and universal junior secondary education at a time of temporary economic downturn. In the case of tertiary education, early post-war efforts to satisfy the increasing demand for places was largely satisfied by the private "Chinese Post-Secondary Colleges" (Cramer, 1959; To, 1965). The University of Hong Kong's seven-year development plan of 1959–66 and the establishment of the Chinese University of Hong Kong in 1963, however, heralded the expansion of the "public sector" and this trend was strongly reinforced by the opening of the Hong Kong Polytechnic in 1971, the City Polytechnic of Hong Kong in 1989, the Hong Kong University of Science and Technology in 1990, and by the extension of the ambit of Hong Kong's Universities and Polytechnics Grants Council (UPGC) during the 1980s to include both Lingnan

College and the Hong Kong Baptist College.

Generally, the secondary school expansion reflected the earlier structure, with an emphasis on academic rather than vocational schooling. In 1969, only about 4% of all secondary students attended vocational or technical schools. By 1979, the figure was 6.23% and in September 1989, the figure was 8.96%. The main change in secondary school provision since the 1960s involved the decline of the Chinese medium sector. Parents and pupils preferred to opt for schools that, at least, officially, provided English medium instruction because this was perceived as offering greater opportunities for tertiary education, employment, and, an increasingly important factor since the mid-1980s, emigration. The establishment of the Chinese University of Hong Kong (CUHK) in 1963, though designed to provide tertiary opportunities for Chinese middle school leavers, failed to arrest the decline of this sector.

The rising aspirations of the population, together with their increasing affluence and the continued growth of secondary schooling, created demands for an expanded tertiary sector. The establishment of CUHK, the Hong Kong Polytechnic in 1973, the City Polytechnic of Hong Kong in 1984, the Open Learning Institute (OLI) in 1989, and the Hong Kong University of Science and Technology (HKUST) in 1991 were the main official concessions to this pressure.[12] The White Paper of 1978, however, with its repercussions on practical policy for most of the 1980s, put a check on expansion at the tertiary level because of anxieties about over-educated unemployment (Government of Hong Kong, 1978) and it was not until 1989 that a dramatic shift in policy was announced and implemented. Similar factors, especially reinforced by the high participation rate of young women in the labor force, stimulated demands for an expanded and improved pre-primary sector. The main official concessions to this pressure were the Green Paper of 1980, the White Paper of 1981, the introduction and upgrading of subsidies to poorer parents in order to help them send their young children to pre-schools while father and mother went out to work, together with promises about and, eventually, limited action in, the field of teacher education at the pre-school level. Over the whole period, the proportion of total public expenditure devoted to education fluctuated between little more than 10% and about 20%, the highest figures occurring most recently. As comparisons between Chart 5 below and Chart 1 above will indicate, there was not an immediate and direct link between economic performance and the level of educational "investment." However, the fact that public expenditure on education remained relatively high (in comparison both with expenditure on other concerns within the territory and with expenditure on education by other governments) and was accompanied by significant private expenditure on education (both in relation to the supply of school places by private school operators and in relation to the payment of school fees) not only enabled education itself to continue its development, but also contributed as a facilitating factor to economic development.[13]

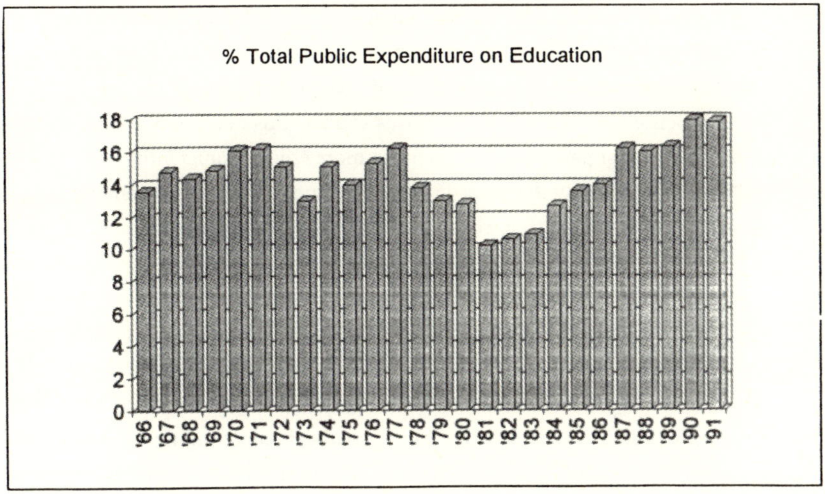


CHART 5. Proportion of Total Public Expenditure Devoted to Education

On the whole, then, education in post-war Hong Kong has been characterized by three major features. These are:

- *Expansion.* At any one time, some level of schooling provision was growing. This was in marked contrast to many of the developed societies of the West. It presented opportunities, especially for the employment and promotion of young teachers. It also reinforced existing tendencies to focus on quantitative matters at the expense of quality in education.
- *Sequential.* The first major growth area was primary schooling, which provided the main focus of the attentions and efforts of policy makers from 1945 to 1971. The second was secondary education, which began to receive greater attention in the 1970s. Toward the end of the 1970s, pre-school education began to attract increased publicity and some, relatively limited, action. However, the third major area which entered an expansionist phase was tertiary education. At the end of the 1980s, decisions were taken to reverse

the 1978 White Paper policy to hold back expansion lest Hong Kong face the problems of over-educated unemployment and a discontented as well as underemployed intelligentsia, which, it was noted, had caused problems in other societies.[14] In October 1989, the government announced its intention to increase the number of tertiary education places within Hong Kong to 18% of the age cohort, where they had represented about 2% of the cohort in 1978.[15]

- *The private sector* acquired huge operational importance, especially in the early stages of each growth phase. This was not, however, accompanied by high social status. In the case of each growth phase, efforts were made to dispense with the private sector as soon as this became a feasible policy option (at least partly by absorbing the more efficient units into an expanded "aided" sector). By the early 1990s, opportunities for private enterprise, at any level of education except the pre-schools, were becoming increasingly limited.

The overall picture which emerges is that of an educational system which is responding, often after a time-lag, to the pressures placed on it by varied economic and demographic changes. The success of the economy has permitted the government to respond positively, encouraging increased educational provision. However, the key structural shifts in the economy from an entrepôt to manufacturing base and then to a service-plus-manufacturing base were not preceded by any major structural changes to the educational system. Schooling has focused on the traditional academic disciplines, technical and vocational education remaining a very small sector until the mid-1970s.

The expansion of the polytechnics and the technical institutes occurred at the very time when the economy was moving away from a reliance on its manufacturing sector, although it is true that the later manufacturers used more advanced technologies. Similarly, the massive expansion of tertiary education opportunities is occurring over a decade after the beginning of the resurgence of the tertiary sector of the economy. The key role has been undertaken by the economy, although political and social factors also played their part in shaping educational change and were in turn influenced by it. To use a metaphor popular in human capital theory, if education has to any extent been an engine of growth in Hong Kong it has not been a very finely tuned one, being mainly applied to the basic task of producing an amenable and trainable workforce with acceptable quotients of literacy and numeracy. In fact, it makes more sense to accept that economic development has fueled educational change. The fueling has not been without fits and starts. At times, the less than smooth drive towards economic and educational change has been affected by trends in political development.

### *Political Development*

In one important sense, the most conspicuous feature of Hong Kong's political life in the post-war period has been the *lack* of development. Constitutionally, it has remained a colony. Operationally, for most, if not all, of the period, its economic progress has been achieved within a polity headed by a bureaucracy allied to an oligarchy. If "political development" is considered to be synonymous with participatory democracy, then one needs to emphasize that Hong Kong's has been arrested, or at least retarded. Until the past decade, there have been very few demands for a representative form of government and none for political independence. Most people in Hong Kong seemed more interested in making money. The few who did make waves, like some students or other leaders of pressure groups, gained little public support and were often associated with movements and ideas originating outside the territory. In this sense, the Hong Kong colonial government, which was not normally an oppressive regime, was rarely challenged. When it was, it tended to respond through ad hoc concessions, some concerning educational provision.

At both the macro and the micro levels, political development in Hong Kong since the end of the Second World War has been chiefly concerned with the survival and future status of Hong Kong. In retrospect, it appears to have passed through three distinct periods:

1. the re-establishment (and rehabilitation) of British rule over Hong Kong, with promises of constitutional reform (circa 1945 to circa 1949) and efforts to restore the essentials of the pre-war education system;
2. "counter-Communist activities," the "shelving" of constitutional reform, and the attempted apoliticization of education (circa 1949 to the early 1980s);
3. efforts to reach agreement about the future of Hong Kong with the People's Republic of China, "convergence," and the politicization of education (early 1980s to the present).

The first period was concerned, naturally enough, with the resumption of sovereignty over the territory after the defeat of the Japanese. In China, in Britain, in the United States, and in Hong Kong itself, doubts were expressed during the war about whether the British should re-occupy the territory or whether the rightful new rulers should be the Chinese Nationalist allies of the United States (Chan, 1990). Once it was generally accepted that Britain had regained Hong Kong, officials in Hong Kong and in Britain made some efforts to *reconstrue*, not merely to *reconstruct* the colonial situation. The constitutional proposals for reform were closely connected with the name of Sir Mark Young, briefly pre-war governor of Hong Kong, more recently prisoner-of-war of the Japanese, and, from May 1, 1946, the first post-war civilian governor of Hong Kong. They included plans to expand representative and participatory democracy, especially by means of direct elections for a Municipal Council which was intended to assume important responsibilities, including the provision of education. These plans were, however, overtaken by events, especially by the increasingly obvious triumph of the Communist forces over the Nationalist forces in the Chinese Civil War and the new threats this seemed to portend for the continued survival of Hong Kong in its colonial state. The eventual failure (or, at least, "shelving") of attempts at constitutional reform in the early 1950s sprang from the government's perception of susceptibility, together with the less than wholehearted support by senior officials and established political figures (Tsang, 1988). This failure occurred at the very time when other areas of the world, including significant parts of Asia, were experiencing or were being prepared for decolonization. In Hong Kong, for many people decolonization did not appear to be an attractive option. In the first post-war years, it was not even supported by Communists because the prospect of a strengthened Guomindang, allied with the United States and eager to escalate Cold War tensions into more heated confrontation, did not please. By early 1949, the Chinese Communists were gaining the upper hand in the Civil War and were beginning to be perceived as the main threat to the continued existence of Hong Kong as a colony.

The second period, starting at this time, lasted in effect until the early 1980s, though one can detect some signs of change before then. The Hong Kong and British governments, supported by a relatively small Chinese and Eurasian elite in Hong Kong, reacted to the perceived threats from Communist forces by emasculating plans for political reform on the grounds that the circumstances were now not appropriate for participatory democracy with its prospect of demagoguery, by enacting quite draconian legislation against political organizations, trade unions, and other "associations" which might pose a direct challenge to the legitimacy of colonial rule, and by arranging "counter-Communist activities" within the public and private sectors of education.

The third period was formally signaled by the announcement in 1982 of the commencement of negotiations with the People's Republic of China about the future of Hong Kong. Certainly from 1984, with the signing of the Sino-British Joint Declaration on the Future of Hong Kong, the trend toward a new politicization of Hong Kong life went into full flood. The most obvious symptoms of this development were renewed, but belated, attempts to bring about a greater element of participatory and representative democracy to Hong Kong. The introduction of indirectly elected and, later, directly elected members (in addition to the *ex officio* members and the appointed members) to the Legislative Council had significant effects on the relations between that council and its constitutional superior, the Executive Council. Until this time, the normally overlapping membership of the two councils enabled the governors and their leading officials to secure compliance with their policies through the influence of those Executive Councillors who were also Legislative Councillors or those Legislative Councillors who were ambitious either to become Executive Councillors or at least to merit an extension of their term of office as Legislative Councillors. However, elections, whether indirect or direct, meant that members would pay more attention to their constituencies than to the blandishments of officials. When combined with the second main feature of this period, the growth of party-politics, the introduction especially of direct elections (in 1991) and the overwhelming success of one of the new political parties, the United Democrats of Hong Kong, led eventually to the formal separation of the membership of the Legislative and Executive Councils. This ploy, introduced by the new governor, Mr. Chris Patten, soon after his assumption of office in 1992, enabled him to avoid appointing to the highest government council[16] local politicians who had clearly become *persona non grata* with the leaders of the People's Republic of China. It also ensured that Executive Council members' influence over the ideas and activities of Legislative Councillors was radically reduced.

### Links with Education

Efforts to reconstrue the colonial situation in the first year or two after the end of the Japanese occupation were paralleled by similar efforts to create a "brave new world" in education. Soon, however, the focus on restoration and short-term remedies to immediate problems led to conflict between the visionary and the pragmatic. A typical issue centred on the freedom or control of schools run by voluntary associations and private concerns (Sweeting, 1993).

On the whole, in the second phase of political development, the forces favoring control won. The "counter-Communist" activities mentioned above as typical of the second phase included amending the Education Ordinance in order to strengthen the discretionary powers of the Director of Education to de-register schools, school managers, principals and teachers; the actual closure of some schools and their replacement by government-controlled ones; the establishment of a "Special Bureau" within the Education Department with powers to inspect schools for political activities and to arrange curricular and extracurricular activities which might inoculate students against communism; and the tightening of centralized control over the curriculum and curricular materials, especially textbooks (Sweeting, 1993). In general, however, and especially in the Cold War climate of the time, the most significant "political" development which affected schooling in Hong Kong during this second phase comprised attempts to apoliticize the curriculum. Such attempts were compatible with rule by a colonialist government of limited popular support. They were also closely linked with anxiety about the impact of political activity within Hong Kong on the sensitivities of leaders in China. In this sense, they can trace their provenance at least as far back as the late nineteenth century when the headmaster of the premier government school in Hong Kong declared that he was "averse to any instruction in Chinese history which would expose us to the charge of being the nursery for Revolutionists on the [Chinese] continent" (Sweeting, 1991a).

One effect of post–World War II attempts at apoliticization, especially to the extent that they reinforced already existing tendencies to purvey exhortations, platitudes and non-controversial information in the name of "civic education," was a quite noticeable lack of popular, substantial and skillful local leaders in the formal political arenas. In the less formal arenas, however, political temperatures and tempers were often high, especially as influenced by the Cultural Revolution in China (Choi, 1990; Sweeting and Morris, 1993; Sweeting, 1995). Indeed, with the relatively sudden emergence of numerous pressure groups in the 1970s and especially their utilization of the mass media, the latter part of the decade qualifies to be considered as a transition-phase into the third period.

With regard to education, the most publicly obvious impact of the new politicization trend during the third phase was on curriculum matters, especially in the direction of providing detailed information about the political, economic, and social structure of the People's Republic of China (Morris, 1988). The fact that, even under the system of indirect elections, the teachers comprised the largest of all "special constituencies," ensured that the views of the teachers' representative on the Legislative Council received much publicity from the mass media. Eventually, administrators conceded to that figure representation on the major advisory committees conceded to that figure representation on the major advisory committees concerning education—first, the Board of Education and, later, the Education Commission, despite apparent misgivings, especially about the effect of this appointment on the confidentiality of business. All local politicians, whether directly or indirectly elected to the Legislative Council, were well aware of the intense interest that members of the public show in educational issues. Consequently, debates on these issues tended to be fiery and the chances of officially sponsored policies being rejected or radically revised became greater than at any other time in Hong Kong's history—or, probably, at any time in its future.

If one takes an overview of the three periods, one might claim that, politically, Hong Kong came of age after the Second World War. This is not to say that it developed a sophisticated form of electoral politics. Such is only now beginning to exist. But it is to say that, in a period of widespread decolonization, Hong Kong assumed a *de facto* independence from its metropole, Britain. The same period witnessed a gradually increasing *de-Anglocentrification* and eventually, a *localization*, of the curriculum, especially in such subject areas as history, geography, and economic and public affairs (Morris, 1988). As noted in the introduction to this chapter, the Hong Kong education system began to develop elements of autochthony in the period which followed the Second World War. This has direct links with an important international trend concerning, especially, curricular focus and control. On the whole, until the 1960s and 1970s, most colonial societies were content to accept the advantages of mass production and simply undertake to examine the relatively few students who proceeded to upper secondary and tertiary education on syllabi prepared in and for the metropole. Students in the British colonies in Africa, the Pacific, the Caribbean and Asia, for example, all studied British history, English literature and even UK-oriented science. They were examined under syllabi and regulations issued by the major British Examinations Boards, such as the Cambridge, Oxford and Cambridge, and London Examinations Boards.

With the onset of decolonization, especially in the 1960s and 1970s, local examinations boards were set up in the former colonies. They tended to make major changes to the focus of the examination syllabi. Thus, in East Africa, African history replaced a detailed study of Walpole or the Tudors and Stuarts. An African orientation to geography and economics and even science replaced an Anglo-centric one. In Hong Kong, similar changes occurred, though, in effect, with something of a time-lag. Following the dissolution of the Examination Division in the government's Education Department, the "Hong Kong Examinations Authority," an autonomous public examinations body, was formally established on August 1, 1977. It was made responsible for the three current major school examinations—the Hong Kong Certificate of Education (from 1978), the Higher Level Examination, previously run by the Chinese University of Hong Kong at the end of Form 6 [Grade 11] (from 1979), and the Advanced Level Examination previously run by the University of Hong Kong at the end of Form 7 [Grade 12] (from 1980), together with all examinations that might be subsequently introduced (Education Department Annual Summary, 1977–8). In the formal sense, this Hong Kong change was in the mainstream of the general decolonizing trend. Operationally, however, for some time it made little difference. Initially, the Director of Education was the chairman of the Examinations Authority, presiding over the transitional period of three years. Most curriculum changes remained UK-inspired, with the earlier adoption of integrated science assuming almost cargo-cult proportions and the ongoing attempts to "promote" integrated social studies having little grass-roots support (Wong, 1992). Although there was some de-Anglocentrification of the history, geography, and economics and public affairs curricula in the 1970s, the main *localization* of curricula began to take place only after the Joint Sino-British Agreement on the Future of Hong Kong in 1984 and it accelerated after the June 4, 1989 "incident" in Tiananmen Square (Sweeting, 1990b).

A result of Hong Kong's colonial status has been the essentially tenuous but symbiotic relationship between the government and the populace (Sweeting, 1983). The government has been tolerated by the population for three main reasons: the alternative to colonial government was not independence but control by the ruling party in China; the growth of the economy has allowed people to focus on the task of making their livelihood; and, generally, especially in the earlier part of the post-war period, the Hong Kong government had little direct impact on the day-to-day activities of individuals and their families. A consequence of the low level of government legitimacy has been a sensitivity to crises which were considered capable of escalating into threats to the status quo. Thus, the response to the demand for, at first, primary, and then, secondary school places, like the reactions to the riots of 1966 and 1967 and other "crises of legitimacy" (Scott, 1989), reflects a desire by the government to satisfy those social expectations which appeared congruous with its own survival. In this sense, education was treated more as a "political good" than an "economic good." Under pressure, the Hong Kong government was prepared to offer the public expanded educational opportunities. Unlike ancient Roman governments, it relied on schooling and the chances this provided for higher earnings, rather than on bread and circuses, to distract or defuse opposition and discontent.

Neither political nor educational development ran smoothly in the post-war period. Both were affected by exogenous as well as endogenous forces. Politically, the most significant extraneous influences were the Cold War, the Chinese Civil War, the outbreak of the Korean War, the decline of Britain as an imperial power, the Cultural Revolution, and the increased pace of modernization in China (Sweeting, 1993). Educationally, the most conspicuous outcome was enormous quantitative expansion which permitted a change-over from the elitist system of the past to something resembling a meritocratic mass education system. This was part of a more general expansion of the scope of government concern, the same period witnessing a massive expansion of the public sector in housing. Politically, Hong Kong's continued relationship with the United Kingdom and a recognition by senior civil servants of the need to present an acceptable image in international circles increased sensitivity about international agreements, such as those concerning the minimum working age and the achievement of universal and compulsory primary education. The most dramatic exogenous factors, however, resulted from changes in the priorities of the People's Republic of China (PRC). This was particularly true of the Cultural Revolution and, later, of the revival of the "Open Door Policy" in the interests of modernization under Deng Xiao Ping from the late 1970s onward.

As far as endogenous forces were concerned, probably the most significant in the post-war period as a whole was the fact that Hong Kong is not in operational terms ruled by a government constitutionally responsible to the public of Hong Kong. It is ruled by a bureaucracy, responsible at the highest levels to the British Crown. Until 1992, even the highest authority in Hong Kong, the governor, was a civil servant, a former staff member of the British Foreign and Commonwealth Office. Legally, the Hong Kong "government" was defined as the "Governor-in-Council," which meant that the governor was normally expected to rule in accordance with the wishes of the Executive Council of Hong Kong, which comprised a small number of officials, whose votes were at the disposal of the governor, and a similar, but slightly larger number of unofficials, appointed by the governor for a limited term (Davies and Roberts, 1990). Operationally, the "government" meant, for most members of the public, the civil service departments and, in the latter decades, the "policy branches" of the Secretariat. Especially after the riots and disturbances of the late 1960s, the fact that the government was not *responsible* to the Hong Kong public actually made it highly *responsive* to that source of opinion. In particular, from the seventies onward, the government became very sensitive to the possibility of challenges from the young intelligentsia. The forms of *centralized populism* identified below, which became most apparent from the 1970s onward and which operated in counterpoint not only with "positive non-interventionism" but also, more exceptionally, with heavy-handed attempts at suppression,[17] are directly related to these phenomena. On about the same time-scale and for similar reasons, such a heightened concern for public relations developed that the mass media and "media-friendly" officials began to assume greater importance than the substance of their messages warranted. In the last decade and a half this process has escalated. It may be seen in the use made of leaks and of press conferences by the Board of Education and, after 1983, the Education Commission. It received a new boost recently from the appointment of a skillful politician as governor in place of a career diplomat. During the past decade especially, it has led, in the field of education, as in other fields, to marked discrepancies between policy formulation, policy dissemination, and policy implementation, with the last-named often proving to be a disappointment to those supportive of the rhetoric behind the first. Indeed, in the educational field, as attested to by the limited and slow implementation of the Direct Subsidy Scheme and Target Oriented Curricula,[18] the under-resourcing and over-working of the Curriculum Development Institute, several honorific and/or China-influenced appointments to positions of prestige and influence, and, in general, the decline in credibility of the Education Commission, Hong Kong appears to be adopting the obverse of a famous Maoist doctrine. In Hong Kong's case, too often it is proving to be a matter of "one step forward, two steps backward." This phenomenon, like so many others in post-war educational policy and practice, is an outcome of anxiety about China's reactions. Contrary to current preoccupations and assumptions, the nexus between the politics and schooling in Hong Kong was not democracy. It was Chinese nationalism.

### *Social Development*

Social trends in post-war Hong Kong were intra-community reflections of the major demographic, economic, and political factors which shaped post-war Hong Kong. Most of them are similar to those which have been detected in other modern, technologically sophisticated societies. In other words, in this respect, too, Hong Kong is not unique. One might note trends toward nuclear families and the increasing number of single-parent families, toward relatively small-space housing, often in large housing estates, toward dietary sufficiency (and, sometimes, a surfeit of convenience foods), toward the ubiquity of television sets and the proliferation of video cameras, fax machines, computers, portable telephones and other means of local and international communication,[19] toward greater facility for travel within Hong Kong, within its broader region and internationally, and toward the sorts of environmental problems which many other large cities also experience.

Probably the single most distinctive social force that has affected post-war Hong Kong and has had an impact through each of the three phases outlined in Figure 2 is what has elsewhere been termed *transitization* (Sweeting, 1991b). For much of its colonial history, Hong Kong served as a temporary workplace, bolt-hole from economic or political disaster, or stepping stone toward a new home. Consequently, it engendered little loyalty. The short recovery phase after the Japanese occupation and the period which followed included a renewed influx of refugees, many of whom expected to remain only briefly in the territory and some of whom actually did move on. It was in this second period especially that the Hong Kong government shaped and sought to control an educational system which catered for the new population and, whatever its faults or weaknesses, offered opportunities for achieved status to people who, on the whole, lacked ascribed status. Government officials did this in sometimes uneasy partnership with voluntary (mainly religious) associations and making use of a private sector about which they harboured doubts. Concern about the level of fees and the provision of scholarships, fee-exemption schemes, student loans and transport subsidies shows an acceptance of responsibility for social equity. Despite and partly because of the strains and frailties of the education system which emerged—its intense competitiveness and selectivity, its deliberate efforts to avoid overt political messages, its formal expository teaching styles, its hidden curriculum of credentialism for the sake of meritocracy—it contributed to social cohesiveness and even to the gradual emergence of a Hong Kong identity.

### Links with Education

Among the social attitudes which have changed, largely to accommodate transitization, its moderation, especially in the 1970s, and its re-emergence in a new guise after the Sino-British Agreement on the Future of Hong Kong, are those which relate to various specific aspects of education. These changes and their educational connotations have only indirect connections with the economic development of the territory.

In the case of female education, for example, the cruder, more quantitative indicators show that unequal opportunities between the sexes have gradually been rectified. Gender stereotypes are still reflected, however, in enrollments for further and tertiary education courses and in the actual implementation of curricula, as well as in television commercials. Responses to the recent Green Paper on *Equality of Opportunity for Women and Men* (Government of Hong Kong, 1993a) testify that there is little optimism about the generation of critical approaches by teachers and courses among students towards discrimination against women.

With early childhood education, sheer economic necessity has produced exponential increase in the demand for and supply of places. However, the government has, to date, refused to moderate its official stance that pre-schooling is unnecessary and, therefore, need not be supported generously from the public purse. It is now facing pressure in this field on several fronts. The largest teachers' trade union (the Professional Teachers' Union, or PTU), whose chairman is also the representative of the educational "Special Constituency" on the Legislative Council, is campaigning in favor of salary increases for pre-school teachers as a precondition of any further reform. Connected with this is the support, again especially from the PTU, for the whole field of early childhood education to receive government subsidies so that the private operators will be able to afford higher salaries for the teachers. Third, one of the voluntary organizations formed to coordinate the field of pre-school education, the Hong Kong Council of Early Childhood Education and Services (CECES) has commissioned a report which emphasizes that priority should be given to extending and improving teacher education (Ebbeck, 1993).

Sex education has witnessed major moves toward official blessing. These include the appointment of a representative of the Family Planning Association to the Curriculum Development Council and numerous public service broadcasts on radio and television. Such moves have, however, been unable to prevent an increase in the incidence of sexual abuse, including rape and incest, and of sexually transmitted diseases.

In the case of physical education, the status of the curriculum area has been enhanced by more generous funding, especially from non-government sources, such as the Jockey Club, and by the increasing fashionability of, and public interest in, Sports Science. Cultural education experienced a similar boost in the post-war period, from similar sources and with a similar increase in public acceptability as well as participation (typified since the mid-1970s by the annual Hong Kong Arts Festival and its "fringe," and, from the early 1980s, by the training and performances provided by the Academy of Performing Arts).

Technical and technological education has overcome, at least ostensibly, its earlier pejorative image (when it was associated with the training of the criminally inclined), partly through private funding, partly through government espousal. Indeed, it has become associated in some minds with desirable aspects of modernism and postmodernism. The Hong Kong University of Science and Technology has benefited from this and been able to draw on generous funds from the public and private purses.

As noted above, with political and moral education, new political forces provide new motives for exhortations, most recently about the need for convergence with China. They have, however, so far provided little evidence of new approaches within the educational process focusing on participatory skills and critical attitudes.

Environmental Education has certainly begun to have a proselytizing impact in Hong Kong, especially as practiced by voluntary groups such as the Conservancy Association, the World Wildlife Fund for Nature, and the Friends of the Earth. Despite the establishment of an Environmental Pollution Advisory Committee (EPCOM), it has yet to make major inroads into the practices of Hong Kong firms.

As noted in the previous section, one can detect the emergence of a type of *centralized populism* in counterpoint to "positive non-interventionism," especially in the Maclehose years.[20] Typical manifestations of this more interventionist stance by government include the various PR-style campaigns (e.g., Keep Hong Kong Clean; Fight Violent Crime, Walk for a Million, etc.), at a time when the economy was beginning to diversify and when the Cultural Revolution in China and riots, the Chinese Language Movement, the Students' Movement, and the Certificated Masters' Dispute at home began to pose new threats to the government's legitimacy. The main unanswered questions are whether centralized populism can engender or provoke initiatives at the grass-roots level and whether, in process terms, education has done anything to equip and qualify the people of Hong Kong to take initiatives. If "utilitarianistic familism," as identified by S.K. Lau (1982), remains a norm in the mainstream of Hong Kong society, other questions about the sense of Hong Kong "identity" become even more significant.

In the most recent period, economic diversification, accompanied by a reinvigorated emphasis on the China trade, has coexisted with belated democratization and politicization but renewed tensions in relations with the People's Republic, the emergence of a Hong Kong identity and of a popular culture which is essentially "middle of the road," and, in the field of education, variably successful efforts to plan. Movements in the direction of manpower planning have certainly occurred. At the macro level, they were most conspicuous in the (unpublished) Topley Report on Post-Secondary and Technical Education of 1981 and, especially, with the publication by the Education and Manpower Branch of *A Statistical Projection of Manpower Requirements and Supply for Hong Kong* (Government of Hong Kong, 1990). The Topley Report, however, was never published and was effectively overtaken by the pressure group-sensitive report of the Visiting Panel (1982), entitled *A Perspective on Education in Hong Kong.*

The Education and Manpower Branch's *Statistical Projection* has been used to support the initially more modest proposals for tertiary education expansion, then the more ambitious proposals of the autumn of 1989, and finally the revised targets of 1992. The reasons for the variations seemed to be related at least as much to political factors as to manpower considerations. At the more specific level, the recent track record for rational planning based on manpower predictions is not an impressive one. A case in point is the planning of facilities for degree courses in dentistry, which, by effectively ignoring the factor of overseas trained dentists flocking into Hong Kong, has within a few years contributed to an oversupply of trained dentists in the territory.

As education and other concerns have become increasingly open to debate in the increasingly politicized public forum, policy makers have tended to become very aware of the importance of public relations and to adopt PR techniques to promote images and facilitate compliance. These frequently make use of the rhetoric of human capital theory and assume the efficacy of manpower planning. On occasions, they adopt Orwellian "newspeak" or unannounced changes of definitions to create the appearance of an orderly and planned achievement of rational objectives.[21]

One important outcome is the noticeable decline in the "potency" of the major advisory boards, which, in the earlier periods, had exercised a very significant role in policy making. In the educational field, this has been true of the Board of Education for several years. The emasculation trend now also appears to include the Education Commission. By late 1993, two resignations cast a spotlight of doubt on the efficacy of the Education Commission itself. Although Dr. Paul Morris and Professor Arthur Li resigned officially because of the lack of progress achieved in the area of pre-school education, the comments which they made about the commission becoming a "talking shop" directed toward technical or trivial matters rather than substantive policy issues seemed to strike a responsive chord, at least with the mass media. It reverberated with earlier criticism (Cheng, 1991) and suggested that the Education Commission was the latest example of the trend toward the enfeeblement of advisory bodies and their use as mere (and frequently ineffectual) PR-style window-dressing. This seemed particularly worrying in relation to post-1997 prospects. The replacement of Morris and

Li by three new members—one from The University of Hong Kong, one lay-member from a well-known family and one associated closely with the pre-school field—seemed designed to allay suspicions.

On the other hand, the interaction between the increasingly politicized public forum and the more secretive committee rooms in which policy matters are scrutinized has stimulated and helped shape efforts to reform the curriculum. In some cases, such as civic education and the long-awaited "bridging programmes" to enable students to switch from one medium of instruction to the other, the results seem more cosmetic than real. In others, such as the sixth form curriculum, opportunities provided by the decision to introduce a new, "broadening" level of study, the "Advanced Supplementary" level, were taken to bring about much-needed changes to the mainstream "Advanced Level" curricula. Significantly, perhaps, in many of these cases, the reforms included increasing the Hong Kong-centerd aspects of the curriculum[22] (Sweeting, 1990b).

## Conclusions

The toleration of apparent ambiguities and inconsistencies in explanations of the links between education and development is congruous with the postmodernistic aspects of Hong Kong's post-war situation. Thus, a chaos theory–oriented approach should apply, openly acknowledging the possibility that the operation of similar factors in similar circumstances can lead to a bewildering array of outcomes, some with almost fractal properties.

Key aspects of the links between education and development in Hong Kong include the simple fact that the existence of a reasonably literate and numerate workforce, most of whom had received general and basic schooling, contributed as a factor conducive to Hong Kong's "economic miracle." That the actual quality of education in Hong Kong for much of the post-war period has been very questionable is not necessarily a paradox. It could be argued, for example, that the earlier schooling experiences of many workers—in poor conditions of study, with unimaginative and incompetent teaching, excessively academic and formal curricula, largely irrelevant to the pupils' eventual employment, highly selective and ruthlessly competitive, but dubiously reliable or valid examinations, and inadequate learning and teaching resources—actually served to prepare them for adult life as workers. At least, it might have raised their boredom threshold and made them amenable to assembly-line techniques. Moroever, many aspects were accurate reflections of Hong Kong society.

Another simple fact is that public expenditure on education, though not massive, was, especially in the earlier part of the post-war period, when the foundations for Hong Kong's economic success were laid, utilized largely to finance the expansion of primary education. Public funds were not applied in a grossly disproportionate way, as happened in many developing countries in Africa, Latin America and the Pacific, to higher education and to narrowly specialized technical, technological or professional/vocational education. No assumption is made here of foresight on the part of Hong Kong's education policy makers. All that is being claimed is that the effect of their practical policy was to produce large numbers of generally educated workers who were open to on-the-job training, career switching and other means of manpower enhancement. Those individuals who did proceed to secondary and tertiary educational opportunities were (and are) duly rewarded. The more recent expansion of places at university, polytechnic and technical institute levels has, so far, been more than justified by employment opportunities and earlier anxieties about over-educated under-employment appear now to have been misplaced.

With regard to the more general relationship between the economy and education, Hong Kong's experience endorses Tyack's (1967) assertion that educational change has followed rather than preceded major structural changes in the economy. Thus, post-war industrialization was followed by the expansion of first primary and then secondary education. The growth of a thriving tertiary sector since 1975 preceded by a decade the growth of the tertiary education sector. Further, throughout the period, technical and vocational education have constituted a very small sector of educational provision and the growth of this sector occurred during the period when the manufacturing sector declined in importance. Overall, schooling has concentrated on providing a highly academic curriculum which reflects the traditional range of academic disciplines. Therefore, the idea that the process of education directly results in economic growth is problematic. Clearly, while higher levels of education are associated with higher levels of income, we cannot infer from this that investment in education will necessarily cause economic growth. Hong Kong's experience suggests that major structural shifts in the economy were not initiated by educational developments. However, the latter played a role in supporting and facilitating those shifts. Education certainly made a major contribution to the shift from low to high value manufacturing in the 1970s, for example, and, over the whole of the post-war period, in the provision of a literate and adaptable workforce. In the sense that the early phases of each of the sequential expansions of schooling (primary, secondary, tertiary) were made possible by a reliance on the private sector, educational growth reflected that of the economy.

The impact of economic development on educational policy (or even educational practice unsanctioned by policy) is much more difficult to establish because the links are much more tenuous. Hong Kong data suggest that such links are rarely direct, linear and causal. This is where chaos theory has relevance. Data provided in the charts above, as well as the accompanying interpretations, narratives and analyses, suggest that the growth and development of the economy was an enabling factor, only very rarely a causal one. The relationship between education and politics has been relatively direct and explicit. Education has been sensitive to political influences, but Hong Kong's status as a colony which did not have the prospect of attaining political independence placed a premium on the conscious pursuit of a school curriculum which strived to avoid political issues. This goal was pursued effectively until the mid-1980s. It ensured that the Hong Kong government's own status was not threatened, that a society which comprised mainly refugees from China could focus on their own economic advancement and that the political leaders of the People's Republic of China were not embarrassed by the activities in Hong Kong of groups sympathetic to the Guomindang. Since the public recognition of Hong Kong's return to Chinese sovereignty in 1997, education has been rapidly harnessed to achieve a range of political goals, including providing students with detailed information about the People's Republic of China in order to prepare them for the future. Education, then, is highly sensitive to and influenced by the changing political realities which have affected Hong Kong. Whilst the overriding motive of the government has been to minimize any threat to its status, this has operated in parallel with the attempts to avoid offending the sensibilities of political leaders in the PRC. Interpretations of Hong Kong's educational policy premised on the existence of a colonialist conspiracy to subjugate the natives and to promote the interests of the colonial power are based upon an over-rating of farsightedness and skills of the administrators. Ad hoc responses to perceived doubts about its legitimacy certainly played a significant part in education policy making at the macro level. As we have seen, at the micro level, the rice-bowl has been a much more forcefully motivating factor than the ballot box.

As mentioned earlier, some accounts of Hong Kong's post-war miracle make much of the "Confucian ethic," which, it is argued, imbues most Hong Kong workers and managers, providing them with a sense of purpose and of responsibility. Through an emphasis on reciprocal relationships (father/son, husband/wife, employer/employee, ruler/ruled, etc.), the Confucian ethic is argued to be socially cohesive and, also, economically stabilizing. There is certainly an element of truth in these claims, though, equally certainly, they do not constitute sufficient conditions for Hong Kong's successes. Indeed, there are enough ironies and inconsistencies in this position to suggest that the Confucian ethic was not even a necessary condition for Hong Kong's successes. As Vogel (1991) points out, it was precisely the Confucian ethic, which was cited as a major cause for East Asia's relative backwardness in earlier periods—specifically the disdain for manual labor and the general conservatism that Confucianism was deemed to comprise. Whatever are the actual components of the Confucian ethic, it has taken a long time to work its wonders for the economy in its place of origin, China. With regard specifically to Hong Kong, one should recognize that the Confucian ethic co-exists with the rather more transcendental Taoist and Buddhist approaches as well as with a wide range of Protestant and Catholic attitudes to the basic factors of production, not to mention the widely acknowledged pragmatism of residents of the territory.

Perhaps more relevant to Hong Kong's post-war development than any of the virtues attributable to the Confucian ethic is the indubitable contribution made by the *work ethic.* The widespread willingness to devote considerable effort and persistence to work is a feature not only of the labor force, but also of many managers. Moreover, a similar characteristic has been detected in the field of education about numerous Hong Kong students. The provenance of the Hong Kong work ethic is not easy to establish. It may, indeed, be connected with Confucian traditions. Probably, it is more immediately linked with the "refugee mentality" which saw pulling oneself up by one's bootstraps as an urgent necessity and viewed all "rags to riches" stories not with envy but as cases meriting emulation. It may also relate to a more fundamental aspect of Chinese popular culture. This is the tendency for parents (mothers, especially) to over-indulge their children (sons, especially) in their early years, up to the "age of reason" or *tung chi* (at about 7 years old) in expectation of reciprocal treatment when the parents are old (Ho, 1986; Bond, 1991). Once *tung chi* is attained, the children (and the adults they grow into) are expected to devote all their energies to school work, chores, and, later, their gainful employment in order to be in a position to support their parents, which, in turn, would earn respect and admiration for the whole family. In this respect as in others, Hong Kong was and is not unique. The same attitudes and customs appear to have been influential in post-war Taiwan and very similar ones in Japan,[23] with some commentators assuming a connection to the economic successes of those countries. On the other hand, the same attitudes and customs had affected pre-war Hong Kong, pre-war China, and, though moderated by loyalty to the

Communist party, to early post-war China. In none of these cases was economic development of the level or types experienced by post-war Hong Kong apparent or even latent. To the extent that these attitudes and social customs really did influence the practices of Hong Kong workers in the post-war period, and to the extent that the attitudes and customs were spread by an important non-formal educational agency, the family, a link between education in its broadest sense and development in its economic sense may be a close one. No doubt, the "yuppification" of Hong Kong's middle classes was partly the result of the influence of non-formal education and contributed to the strengthening of the service sector of the economy. The economy itself, however, remains largely export driven.

However flat-footed a conclusion it may seem, in Hong Kong's case education, especially as organized through formal schooling, did not and does not determine development. Development did not and does not determine education. In relation to development, education was certainly not the horse; nor, however, was it merely the cart. As we have seen, the links between education and development are many and complex. They are also intricately fascinating. The relations between them are symbiotic, mutually supportive, but they are not uni-linear. This chapter provides evidence to suggest that, for Hong Kong and, by extension, for every society, in an important sense, they are special and distinctive, if not unique.

## Notes

1. These allegations have more substance when applied, as in other societies, to the early stages of industrialization.

2. Macau is a possible exception to this generalization, but here, at least in the first few post-war decades, the lack of government activity appears to be more the result of negligence than of deliberate economic policy.

3. Personal communication from Professor Philip Foster to the present author, January 30, 1994.

4. Except, again, Macau. However, the fact that Hong Kong was a British colony within a colonializing culture which accepted indirect rule further distinguished it from Macau, with its links to Portugal and traditions of much more direct, if not always efficient and energetic, rule.

5. For an interesting discussion of "the unreformed colonial state" of Hong Kong, see Ian Scott, *Political Change and the Crisis of Legitimacy in Hong Kong*, Hong Kong, Oxford University Press, 1989, pp. 39–80.

6. This expression was first used publicly by C.G. Hamilton in Chapter 1, *Hong Kong Annual Report, 1956*.

7. It is only recently that "belonger" status (gained after seven years of residence in Hong Kong) was replaced by a "right to land" in non–Hong Kong-issued passports. Eurasians, some Indians and some Europeans consider Hong Kong to be their home, but very few have been granted the three asterisks on their identity cards which would qualify them for automatic entry/exit rights for China and Macau which ethnic Chinese resident in Hong Kong gain.

8. Such small-scale "industrial" and commercial undertakings included the

private sector of education in Hong Kong, where, metaphorically, assembly-line techniques and sweated labour conditions operated to cater for growing demand and, thus, to maximize profits.

9. World Bank, *The East Asian Miracle: Economic Growth and Public Policy*, Washington, D.C., World Bank, September 1993, Summary, pp. 3–4.

10. This was the immediate post-war development. Largely because of exogenous forces, the education system of Hong Kong not only rose from the ashes of the Japanese occupation, it also became *A Phoenix Transformed*. See Sweeting (1993) pp. 239–40.

11. This was closely related to the tense relations between Hong Kong and China immediately before and after the establishment of the People's Republic in October 1949 and also to the outbreak of the Korean War in 1950 and the official "closing" of the frontier between Hong Kong and China. The last-named development had more symbolic than practical effect. The Hong Kong authorities were unable at the time to prevent Chinese entering the territory or leaving it. Personal preferences, however, ensured that only a few Hong Kong residents wished their children to receive higher education in China during the 1950s. See the Keswick *Report on Higher Education* (1952) and Sweeting, "The Reconstruction of Education in Post-War Hong Kong" (1989), pp. 901–924.

12. Together (eventually) with a significant change in the proportion of the government's education budget devoted to tertiary education. See Chart 3, above.

13. As well as to political stability. See discussion below. For an interesting discussion of demographic and educational expenditure data, with inferences derived about the role of government policy, implications for social mobility, and findings about the significance of the mother's educational attainment level, see David Post, "Educational Attainment and the Role of the State in Hong Kong," *Comparative Education Review*, 37, 3, 1993, pp. 240–262.

14. Government of Hong Kong White Paper on *The Development of Senior Secondary and Tertiary Education* (October 1978), para. 3.4, p. 4.

15. Governor's speech at the Opening of the Legislative Council, Hong Kong, October 1989; see also P. Morris, J.A.G. McClelland, and Leung Yat Ming, "Higher Education in Hong Kong: The Context of and Rationale for Rapid Expansion," *Higher Education*, 27, 1994, pp. 125–140.

16. The Executive Council is responsible for the preparation of all legislation and, ultimately, for all (non-emergency) policy making in Hong Kong. See Norman Miners, "Constitution and Administration," in *The Other Hong Kong Report, 1993*, Hong Kong, Chinese University Press, 1993, pp. 1–5.

17. E.g., the initial reactions to the Precious Blood Golden Jubilee Secondary School dispute, when senior officials accused schoolgirls from a Catholic convent school and some of their teachers of being Trotskyite dissidents. See Sweeting and Morris (1993), pp. 209–211. The slogan "positive non-interventionism" was given wide currency by Sir Philip Hadon-Cave, a forceful Finance Secretary and, eventually, Chief Secretary, in Hong Kong in the 1970s. It is, of course, a latter-day term for the *laissez-faire* attitudes and policies so much admired by Milton Friedman.

18. The Direct Subsidy Scheme is a proposal to offer subsidized or private schools greater autonomy over fees, recruitment of students, curricula and administration, together with limited subsidies. Target Oriented Curricula, influenced by the British National Curriculum, seeks to identify criterion-based assessment targets and to involve teachers in their achievement and measurement.

19. At the time this chapter was written, there appeared to be a distinct possibility of dissonance and divergence (rather than congruence and convergence) between recent Hong Kong trends and prevailing official Chinese attitudes, the Chinese government's decision to control and limit the installation of satellite TV antennae being a case in point.

20. The "Maclehose years" were 1971–1982. They witnessed increasing pros-

perity, more attention to social welfare and greater self-confidence within Hong Kong.

21. One example of this type of disingenuousness occurred in the mid- and late 1970s, when, in order to present the impression that the new targets for the expansion of junior secondary education were capable of being achieved without problems over teacher supply, the definition of "qualified graduate teacher" was changed to mean a person who was qualified as a graduate but not necessarily as a teacher. More recently, the prerequisites for entry into the Colleges of Education have been lowered in order to ensure a reasonable number of applicants at a time when many young people were either leaving Hong Kong for other countries or taking up more lucrative employment opportunities outside teaching in Hong Kong made available at least partly because of the outflow of young professionals to other countries.

22. This is particularly true of history, geography and liberal studies.

23. The retrospective reciprocation motives behind traditional Chinese socialization practices and the concepts of *amae-a* and *ganbaru* in Japan appear to share in fundamental essentials, for example, despite efforts to establish the uniqueness of the Japanese concepts, e.g., in Doi Takeo, *The Anatomy of Dependence [Amae no kõzõ]*, Tokyo, Kodansha America Inc., 1973.

# 4 SINGAPORE

*Saravanan Gopinathan*

## INTRODUCTION

The republic of Singapore sits at the southern tip of Malaysia, just north of Indonesia. It is a small island, about 42 km by 22 km with a population of just under three million. However, a successful tourist image has resulted in it attracting about five and a half million tourists yearly. It is a plural society with the population distributed as follows: Chinese 77%; Malays 14%; Indian 7%; and 2% others, and the vertical cleavages of race, language, religion and culture have not been quite eroded by four decades of effort to integrate the population. It is well urbanized, with about 50% of total land area judged to be "built up." It is still a young nation with a median age of the resident population at 30.2 years. The literacy rate is an enviable 90.7%, with those literate in two or more languages reaching 46% in 1990. Its political structure resembles Westminster-type parliamentary democracy, though it has recently amended the constitution to create an executive presidency. Political culture in Singapore was and is dominated by Lee Kuan Yew, Singapore's prime minister for almost four decades and currently a senior minister in the cabinet.

## DEVELOPMENT CHALLENGES

Like all developing ex-colonial states Singapore faced, upon the onset of limited self-government in 1956 and later full independence in 1965, the twin challenges of creating a cohesive and robust sense of nationhood, and economic growth. Unlike Hong Kong, for instance, Singapore, through a liberal colonial policy of promoting immigration from South Asia and China had all the hallmarks of a plural society at the beginning of the twentieth century. British colonial policy, more correctly the lack of such, particularly in education, resulted in a strengthening, both of ethnic identity as well as close links with original homelands. The emergence of separate streams of education led to vertical cleavages, and the limited availability of English medium education split communities on the basis of language as well; even today the English- and non-English-educated occupy different spheres in political and social life (Wilson, 1978; Gopinathan, 1994). The experiences and frustrated ambitions of the Chinese-educated resulted in hostility and anti-government activities in the interwar years. The challenge of the fifties was to pacify and incorporate the non-English-educated and plant the seeds for an emergent Singapore identity. Even Singapore's viability as a cohesive nation-state was in doubt and the British were only prepared to hand over power within the context of a wider, non-Communist, non-Chinese-dominated Malaysia, which was eventually created in 1963. Two years later, Singapore was ejected from Malaysia and began the task of nation-building anew.

Economic challenges too threatened the fragile state. Singapore had survived, and indeed prospered, as part of the British trading and military empire. Many aspects of the economy were overly dependent upon the British, yet others were underdeveloped, and rapid population growth in the fifties and sixties threatened to overwhelm resources. Britain's sudden decision to withdraw its military forces and to devalue sterling in the early seventies underlined further the need for a wide base for the economy (Lim Chong Yah, 1983, 1989; Chia Siow Yue, 1989).

## Political and Social Development

The major strategies adopted by nationalist leaders in the fifties and sixties to cope with the political and social development challenge could be set out as follows:

- that Singapore would be a non-Communist parliamentary democracy,
- that equal rights, respect and opportunity would be offered to all ethnic groups,
- that national-level social institutions would work to reduce communalism and foster a national identity, and
- that economic growth would be promoted via an industrialization strategy based on labor-intensive, export-oriented manufacturing industries.

One major act of enfranchisement, stemming from the Rendel Committee's constitutional proposals, was automatic registration which expanded the voting population from 75,000 to 300,000, including a large number of the non-English-educated. Self-government was attained in 1959 and the first general election was held that year. A referendum on merger held in 1962 gave approval to Singapore's incorporation into Malaysia in

September 1963. But the merger was short-lived, and Singapore became fully independent in 1965. (Yeo Kim Wah, 1973; Shee Poon Kim, 1985, Chan Heng Chee, 1989).

One principal commitment in the mid-fifties which had educational implications was the concept of "equality of treatment." In linguistic terms this meant the acceptance of English, Chinese, Malay and Tamil as official languages. The 1956 All Party Report on Chinese Education, set up to examine the problems of Chinese education, came up with wide-ranging recommendations. These included unifying the English and non-English medium schools into a single system which in turn set the stage for the evolution of a national system; to set out the rationale and aims of a bilingual policy; to commit the government to supporting and improving non-English medium schools; and the indigenization of textbooks to create a "Malayan identity." Though the last quarter century has witnessed many refinements of policy and practice, the basic principles of the Report continue to underpin the present education system.

## Economic Development

What has caught the international community's eye has been the spectacular economic growth that Singapore has posted in the last twenty years. The GDP in 1990/91 stood at S$69,076 (million); per capita indigenous GNP at current market prices reached S$20,031 in 1991 compared to S$2761 in 1971. Official foreign reserves stood at S$55.8 billion. The economy grew by 10% a year from 1978 to 1982; in 1990, despite the Gulf War the estimated growth rate was 8.3%. Singapore's savings rate at 47% of GDP is said to be the highest in the world.[1] The government has invested heavily in infrastructure and so the growth of the economy has been reflected in a rise in the standard of living; everywhere there is evidence of good quality subsidized public housing, the transportation network which includes a recently completed mass rapid transit system is excellent, the telecommunication network is world class, the port has, like the airport, been extensively modernized, and both rank among the most efficient in the world.

The figures cited above indicate the outcome or the result of economic growth. Another way of viewing the transformation of the economy is to examine structural changes in the economy that reflect shifts in inter-sectoral growth. It has been noted that at the beginning of the industrialization process in Singapore, the nation had only a small agricultural sector and some sophisticated industries which required advanced technical skills such as food processing, petroleum refining, maintenance and repair of engineering and transport equipment; in addition it had a well-developed commercial port and a British naval base at the north of the island, both serviced by competent workforces. Singapore also, at the beginning of its industrialization phase, had a developed commerce and trade infrastructure since it enjoyed premier status in the region as an entrepôt center. As Table 1 shows, in 1960 the primary sector contributed 3.8% to GDP while manufacturing and commerce contributed 16.6 and 24.6%, respectively. Construction contributed a relatively low 5.3% to GDP. Indicative of the undeveloped nature of the economy GDP per capita stood at S$1,482. Unemployment stood at 14%.

TABLE 1. Growth and Development in the Singapore Economy

| *Years/Sectors* | *1960* | *1970* | *1980* | *1990/1* |
|---|---|---|---|---|
| GDP | 2,149.6 | 5,804.9 | 25,090.7 | 69,076.0 |
| GDP per capita | 1,482.0 | 2,798.0 | 10,394.0 | 25,677.0 |
| Export Earnings | 3,477.1 | 4,755.8 | 41,452.3 | 95,206.0 |
| Agri & Fishing | 3.8 | 2.2 | 1.1 | 0.3 |
| Quarrying | 0.2 | 0.2 | 0.2 | 0.2 |
| Manufacturing | 16.6 | 24.8 | 29.5 | 28.6 |
| Utilities | 1.7 | 1.9 | 2.0 | 2.1 |
| Construction | 5.3 | 9.5 | 7.1 | 6.1 |
| Commerce | 24.6 | 22.0 | 18.9 | 17.5 |
| Transp't & Communic'n | 8.8 | 7.3 | 12.0 | 14.3 |
| Fin'l & Business Services | 14.0 | 16.9 | 20.9 | 27.4 |
| Others | 19.6 | 14.9 | 11.6 | 10.1 |

Source: Ministry of Trade and Industry, *Economic Survey of Singapore, 1991* .

The major shift in the economy when industrialization began to take off in the seventies was, of course, in the direction of the secondary sector, notably manufacturing and construction. The very rapid pickup in economic transformation, due in part to a reasonably developed infrastructure, is evident in the following figures. By 1980 GDP had grown to S$25,090 million and per capita GDP had leapt to S$10,394. The contribution of manufacturing and commerce had grown in significance while the financial and business services sector contributed 20.9% to GDP.

As Singapore begins the 1990s the transformation of the economy has been significant. The primary sector is contributing only .5% to GDP while the share of manufacturing and construction seems to have plateaued. Transport and communications, and financial and business services, however, continue to grow.

*Expansion and Investment in Education*

Table 2 indicates the broad picture of expansion in education in Singapore. Though there is a dip in enrollment between 1980 and 1985, the general trend is a steady, voluntary incorporation of the school-age population into the education system. The enrollment increase between 1965 and 1990 is 65%; enrollment at the primary level declined by 8.6% from a high point in 1975 due to a decline in the birth rate; even without compulsory schooling Ministry of Education (MOE) statistics show a 95% participation rate of children aged 6 in grade 1. The figures for secondary education are interesting, not only because they also show increases but also for the diversification of secondary education away from the academic. With industrialization growing apace in the seventies, it was both possible and necessary to invest in technical skills and this is reflected in the increase of 16,142 students (280%) between 1970 and 1980; an increase of 26,063 (956.7%) students between 1970 and 1990 in technical and vocational institutes parallels those in technical/vocational programs in schools. The general upgrading of secondary education in the seventies made possible the expansion of post-secondary education in the eighties, an increase of 32,929 (245.5%) between 1980 and 1990.

TABLE 2. Enrollment Changes in Educational Institutions (selected years), (in thousands)

| | *1959* | *1965* | *1970* | *1975* | *1980* | *1985* | *1990* |
|---|---|---|---|---|---|---|---|
| Primary | | 357,075 | 363,518 | 328,401 | 291,722 | 278,060 | 257,932 |
| Secondary & Junior Colleges | | 114,736 | 145,740 | 176,224 | 173,693 | 190,328 | 161,029 |
| Academic | 47 | 102,861 | 136,782 | 153,029 | 148,553 | 154,435 | 155,800 |
| Tech/Voc | | 11,875 | 8,958 | 23,195 | 25,140 | 35,893 | 35,659 |
| Tech & Voc Institutes | | 1,193 | 3,039 | 9,830 | 13,839 | 21,161 | 29,102 |
| Univ/Colleges | 7 | 13,807 | 13,683 | 18,501 | 22,633 | 39,913 | 55,562 |
| Total | 323,000 | 486,811 | 527,668 | 532,956 | 501,887 | 529,462 | 534,005 |

Sources: Chng Meng Kng et al., *Technology and Skills in Singapore*, Singapore, Institute of Southeast Asian Studies, 1985, Table 11, p. 47.
Singapore, Department of Statistics, *Yearbook of Statistics, 1985/86*, 1988.
Singapore Ministry of Education, *Education Statistics Digest*, 1990.

A more graphic way of demonstrating how the expansion and diversification changed levels of participation and qualifications at different levels of the education system is seen in Tables 2a and 2b. Tables 2a and 2b indicate that the number in the age group 25–29 years who had secondary qualifications more than doubled as did those with university qualifications. Since the success of the industrial policy depended in part upon the availability of technically/vocationally trained manpower, the dramatic increase in enrollment between 1981 and 1991—from 9% to 24% for polytechnics and from 6% to 21% for vocational institutes—demonstrates the government's success in re-orienting the pattern of educational involvement in the last decade.

TABLE 2A. Educational Qualifications of Singaporeans Aged 25–29 Years

| | *1980* | *1990* |
|---|---|---|
| Primary or lower | 69% | 38% |
| Secondary | 19% | 41% |
| U. Secondary | 8% | 13% |
| (of which Polytechnic) | na | 7% |
| University | 4% | 8% |
| TOTAL | 100% | (107%) |

Source: *Straits Times*, 16 January 1991.

TABLE 2B. Intakes into Non-School Institutions by Age Group

| | *1981* | *1991* |
|---|---|---|
| University | | |
| Number | 3,500 | 6,900 |
| % of Age Group | 6% | 14% |
| Polytechnic | | |
| Number | 4,800 | 10,200 |
| % of Age Group | 9% | 24% |
| VITB | | |
| Number | 3,500 | 9,000 |
| % of Age Group | 6% | 21% |

Source: *Straits Times*, 16 January 1992.

In many countries educational expansion has often been accompanied by a lowering, both of standards and of satisfactory levels of resource allocation as ministries often expanded education under political pressure but without the necessary resources. In Singapore's case there has been great care and attention paid to ensuring that standards were maintained in the face of expansion; indeed, many have complained that an overly academic view of student progress and achievement has denied many more students an opportunity to proceed beyond secondary education. As Table 3 indicates, in the three major examinations, the Primary School Leaving Examination, the Singapore-GCE "O" Level Examinations and the Singapore-GCE "A" Level Examinations there was improved student performance between 1975 and 1989.

Table 4 shows the pattern of government expenditure on education. According to the Ministry of Education its budget for the financial year 1992 is 15% of total government expenditure or 3.6% of the Gross Domestic Product. Total expenditure on education increased from approximately 217.5 million in 1969/70 to 1.7 thousand million in 1989/90. Impressive increases for secondary education, polytechnics as well as universities, indicate rising costs due to both expansion of students enrolled as well as infrastructural development.

*Orienting Education to Economic Development Purposes*

As noted previously there was early recognition that Singapore needed to transform its economy, both to create wealth for necessary infrastructural development and to meet the needs of a burgeoning population; in 1960, population growth was 4.6% per annum. The PAP's 1959 Election Manifesto, *Spring Source of Our Nation,* singled out industrialization as the basis of an economic strategy for modernization. Indeed, economics, in the possibility of a larger market with Malaysia, had as much to do as politics with the move to form the Malaysian federation in 1963. The Singapore Polytechnic had already been established in 1954 and when the Chan Chieu Kiat report on vocational and technical education (1960) recommended a tripartite system of academic, vocational and technical schools the government accepted them promptly. Thus at the beginning of the sixties the basic economic strategy and a rudimentary education and training system was in place.

The two decades 1960–80 saw considerable attention being paid to making schooling economically relevant, principally through diversifying the curriculum. Changes to schooling in the sixties followed conventional wisdom in the development of vocational schools in the belief that these would

Table 3. Summary Results of National Examination (Government & Government Aided School Candidates)

| *Year* | *Primary School Leaving Examination* | | | *GCE 'O' Level Examination* | | | *GCE 'A' Level Examination* | | |
|---|---|---|---|---|---|---|---|---|---|
| | No. Sat | No. passed | % | No. Sat | No. passed | % | No. Sat | No. passed | % |
| 1975 | 72,452 | 42,556 | 58.7 | 35,653 | 21,472 | 60.2 | 6,901 | 4,508 | 65.3 |
| 1980 | 49,237 | 41,118 | 83.5 | 32,668 | 22,360 | 68.4 | 5,736 | 3,836 | 66.8 |
| 1985 | 47,673 | 40,928 | 85.8 | 29,130 | 25,933 | 89.0 | 10,268 | 6,793 | 66.1 |
| 1989 | 39,598 | 35,021 | 88.4 | 38,405 | 33,835 | 88.0 | 15,089 | 10,345 | 68.5 |

Source: Ministry of Education: *Education Statistics Digest*, 1990.

Table 4. Government Expenditure on Education (selected years), (in thousands)

| *Fin'l Yr* | *Prim'y* | *Sec & Pre-U* | *VITB* | *Poly-techs** | *NIE* | *Univ* | *Others* | *Total Recurrent Expend* | *Devt Expend* | *Total Expend* |
|---|---|---|---|---|---|---|---|---|---|---|
| 1969/70 | 92,962 | 47,812 | 17,609 | 5,350 | 3,469 | 18.719 | 12,141 | 199,062 | 18,557 | 217,619 |
| 1979/80 | 186,266 | 181,545 | 25,000 | 20,516 | 7,831 | 68,185 | 2,971 | 503,137 | 54,137 | 557,528 |
| 1989/90 | 497,598 | 533,292 | 77,070 | 124,711 | 24,578 | 273,908 | 7,266 | 1,599,872 | 145,490 | 1,745,362 |

* 1969 figures for Ngee Ann Polytechnic are included under "Others."
Source: Ministry of Education, *Education Statistics Digest* (various years).

provide students with usable skills. However, the vocational schools proved unpopular and ineffective. In 1968 a national-level council, the National Industrial Training Council, was formed to coordinate training initiatives and this led to the establishment of a Technical Education Department within the Ministry of Education. Two major initiatives toward the end of the sixties must be noted, the creation of a Faculty of Engineering at the University of Singapore in 1969, and the shift of vocational training outside the school system, led by the rapid creation of no less than nine vocational institutes. Within the school system the Ministry of Education boosted the number of students having exposure to technical studies by requiring all male lower secondary pupils and 50% of girls to compulsorily take technical subjects and workshop practice.

The seventies must be regarded as the breakthrough decade for the training thrust. In 1973 an Industrial Training Board with strong industry links was formed to coordinate training initiatives, but even so full-time enrollment in ITB institutes was still less than 10,000 in 1978. A further development in 1979, the Vocational and Industrial Board (VITB), formed by the merger of the ITB and the Adult Education Board, led eventually to the creation of a more comprehensive and structured program of non-school-based skills-orientated training. In 1980 the VITB had twelve vocational institutes and about 11,500 full- and part-time students, up from about 6,500 in 1973. Developments in non-school-based vocational training were paralleled by the changes introduced to the school system by the Report on the Ministry of Education (Goh Report). The Report recommended diversification of the upper primary curriculum into a number of streams. Growth in enrollment at the Singapore and Ngee Ann Polytechnics (known as the Technical College until 1963) has also been impressive. At the Singapore Polytechnic enrollment jumped from 2,642 in 1966 to 8,337 in 1980, comprising 5,015 full-time and 3,322 part-time students. The Singapore Polytechnic alone has graduated more than 20,000 students since 1954 and currently graduates about 2,000 students annually. In 1979 the government established the Council for Professional and Technical Education (CPTE) to provide projections for skilled, technical and professional manpower requirements and to facilitate developments in post-secondary requirements, and in post-secondary and tertiary institutions, to meet enrollment targets. With the acceptance of the Report on Professional and Technical Education (CPTE) by parliament in 1981 polytechnic-level education took off. Enrollment rose to 29,550 by 1990, compared to less than 10,000 in 1978. Within the school system the number of students in the technical stream has fluctuated but there have been steady increases in the commercial and science streams (see Table 5).[2] This diversification and expansion of education has had important consequences both for individual and social development. The more systematic and unified training, coupled with a more relevant curriculum (greater emphasis on language, science and mathematics), has meant much wider occupational opportunity with commensurate benefits in terms of income and status. It has meant for Singapore a wider and more skilled pool of labour to sustain economic growth.

TABLE 5. Enrollment in Upper Secondary Technical, Commercial, and Science and Arts Streams

| | *Technical* | *Commercial* | *Science* | *Arts* |
|---|---|---|---|---|
| 1977 | 19,100 | 6,031 | 6,250 | 59,287 |
| 1980 | 17,332 | 7,808 | 23,697 | 35,163 |
| 1985 | 19,782 | 15,454 | 33,219 | 40,221 |
| 1991 | 15,330 | 19,198 | 43,044 | 35,522 |

Source: Ministry of Education, Singapore, *Key Education Statistics* (Various years).

*Orienting Education to Foster Cohesion*

It was noted earlier that when the first steps to self-government were being taken in the late fifties the challenges of nation-building loomed large. Education and social policy under colonial rule had resulted in a fragmented society, which in some instances accentuated original cleavages, and in others added new ones. For example, limited access to English-language schooling created language-based differences in the Chinese community. These differences could fairly be said to have raised serious questions about the viability of the fledgling state. Mr. Lee Kuan Yew's assessment both of the situation and of the role of the school is apt:

> If in the four different languages of instruction, we teach our children four different standards of right and wrong, four different ideal patterns of behaviour, then we will produce four different groups of people and there will be no integrated coherent society. What is in the balance is the very foundation of our society. For if we are not to perish in chaos caused by antagonisms and prejudices between watertight cultural and linguistic compartments, then you have to educate the right responses amongst our young people in school. (Lee Kuan Yew, 1959)[3]

The steps taken to inculcate the "right responses" have been many and varied. Over the years government policies have led to standardization within the system, especially in terms of bilingualism, curricular requirements and examinations, a unified teaching force, the establishment in the sixties of integrated schools, greater emphasis on non-communal extracurricular activities, an emphasis on uniformed groups, seen as particularly useful for boys in preparing them for National Service, and a daily flag raising and lowering ceremony with the singing of the National Anthem and the recitation of a pledge (Gopinathan, 1988).

Not unexpectedly, attention has also been paid to devising syllabi that would explicitly teach the values deemed desirable. Even in the fifties some attention had been paid to civics but it was not until the sixties that a fully articulated attempt was made to teach essential values. The "Education for Living" syllabus drew upon a nascent attempt to define an Asian cultural identity seen as both a feature of Singapore society and appropriate for it. It was suffused with values like filial piety, social and individual discipline, concern for family, neighborhood and nation. It was the beginning of an attempt to link the mother tongue and ethnic cultural identity, and to make both desirable for all citizens. However, the Report on the Ministry of Education found both the syllabus and teaching methodologies flawed and the Report of the Committee on Moral Education proposed alternatives. Soon, "Education for Living" was replaced by "Good Citizen" and "Being and Becoming" courses at the primary and lower secondary levels and a range of Religious Knowledge options, including a much-promoted Confucian Ethics course at the upper secondary level (Tham Seong Chee, 1980; Gopinathan, 1988; Eng Soo Peck, 1992). With the launching of a Confucian Ethics course came the most explicit formulation of Confucianism as an essential value system for Chinese Singaporeans. However, at the end of the eighties the Religious Knowledge options were withdrawn on the grounds that a secular state should not be seen as promoting religion. In their place a new civics syllabus was introduced. At the national level the earlier emphasis on promoting Confucianism, still seen as important, seems to have given place first to a search for a national ideology and now to the articulation of a set of core values.

Though civics deals, of course, with social institutions and the rights and responsibilities of citizenship, and of patriotic duty, it does these in general, unproblematic ways. Singapore's political history has been unique, as seen in examples of the existence of prolonged one-party rule, recent amendments to the constitution to establish an elected presidency, the creation of nominated members of parliament, of group constituencies, among others.

However, civics curriculum and teaching seem not to have taken advantage of the above developments to promote dialogue and critical awareness of political assumptions and processes.

## Education and Development in Singapore: Toward an Assessment

It would be useful to start an assessment of the contribution of schooling to development by identifying education's functions. Though functionalists and Marxists would disagree about educational process and eventual outcomes they would agree that schooling, the state-sponsored mass education variety, has consequences for individual development, economic growth, identity formation and group cohesion and is essential to the formation of new elites. All four "functions" are significant and need to be seen as interrelated. Where an expansion of education occurs within the context of economic growth and the former is characterized by new knowledge and skills, human capital is enhanced. The enhanced contribution of labor to the economy leads to greater growth, leading to increases in socioeconomic mobility which in turn fuel new demands for educational expansion. Further, it makes feasible new directions in economic growth and legitimates new and powerful roles for the skilled and educated. Personal efficacy and more opportunities for personal development are said to be possible under conditions of strong state stability and economic growth since schooling for development is seen at the individual level as modernizing individuals, giving them more valuable skills and a future-oriented outlook (Fågerlind and Saha, 1989).

While the above is how the education-development nexus is supposed to work, the development experience of the last four decades suggests, for a large number of developing countries, otherwise. Walters (1981) among countless others, has critiqued the simplistic assumptions. Walters points out the difficulties of estimating the independent contribution of schooling to national and economic development, that cause-and-effect relationships at the individual level cannot be assumed to hold at the aggregate level, and the limitations of cross-sectional analysis. Collins (1979) has argued that schools are an inefficient means of providing for occupational skills in any direct sense since a large number of skills are better learned at the job site and that educational expansion is due more to credential inflation. Other critics have long argued that the schooling-labor market link is elusive and more complicated than commonly assumed. In particular, they have made a case against early and school-based vocational training and the introduction of technical streams, especially if these are justified on the basis of economic relevance (Psacharopoulos and Loxley, 1985).

There are a number of factors which need to be held in mind in explaining Singapore's economic development experiences. Singapore is small in size, had at the beginning of its industrial phase no large primary sector but a useful, if narrowly confined and rudimentary, industrial infrastructure, well-developed communications (relative to the region) and a pivotal role in the commerce and trade sectors in the regional economies. What were major constraints were rapid population growth, and a fragmented language-divided education system.

What is remarkable is the drive, vision and cohesion of the political and administrative machinery that was thrown up to meet the development challenge. If the people of Hong Kong prospered because they were allowed unhindered to get on with the job, the people of Singapore were hectored ceaselessly to get on with the job by the government which supported efforts with training and an infrastructure. One party, the People's Action Party, has been in power since 1959, and until 1990, Lee Kuan Yew had been its leader and prime minister. Coupled with this longevity and continuity the PAP has been imbued with a hard-nosed pragmatic vision that eschewed wealth distribution policies in preference to wealth-creating policies.

The PAP's economic strategy over three decades has been founded on an acceptance of Singapore's small size and on building upon existing advantages and creating new ones. Thus trading links with the ex-colonial power were maintained and strengthened while new ones were established. Nationalization of foreign economic assets was ruled out. Multinational corporations were intensely courted to establish themselves in Singapore. The continued teaching of the English language was vigorously promoted as being of crucial economic significance in the face of some considerable opposition in the sixties. The government also established new economic institutions and incentives. The Jurong Town Corporation was established to provide basic infrastructure to ease the cost and time involved in starting up industrial operations in Singapore; the Economic Development Board (EDB) (1961) to sell Singapore abroad and to source for new capital and industries; the Development Bank of Singapore to provide for development financing; INTRACO to open up government-to-government trade with the Eastern bloc countries; and a National Productivity Board, among others. These were among several key parastatal organizations that provided both innovative economic policies and the necessary infrastructure. Indeed, the EDB itself jointly ran a number of critical and specialist training centers to provide workers with skills needed in the economy but which were not available in mainstream training institutions. Centers were established with the help of Rollei, Tata, Philips and the Japanese and French governments. The government itself invested heavily in the economy, in such companies as the Keppel Shipyard, Neptune Orient Lines, Singapore Refining Company, Singapore Airlines and the National Iron and Steel Mills.

It must also be noted that the sixties and seventies, when Singapore embarked on a single-minded push for economic growth, were also decades of global economic growth. Singapore's low-wage economy, docile labor force and political stability all contributed to the growth of investments and exports of a range of low-technology industrial products. Much of the manufacturing products produced in the sixties were done in small-scale production units, and typically consisted of food products, textiles and garments, wood and metal products. The expansion of the Vietnam War and the oil exploration boom in the region contributed as well to economic growth. All of the above contributed to strong foreign direct investment. It was only in the latter half of the seventies that the government began to emphasize the creation of technology-intensive industries.

It is in this economic context that we have to assess the contribution of schooling. Singapore's development planning experience is best understood in the context of the "strong state" thesis advanced by Hage, Garnier and Fuller (1988). Four characteristics singled out by them are control of state bureaucrats over education, proportion of the economy directly controlled or owned by the state, existence of a basic educational infrastructure and curriculum standardization. The state's ability to achieve a tight coupling between education and the economy will minimize the slippages between them and thus produce conditions for more direct impact of schooling on economic activity. It may be useful to distinguish between two periods of economic growth, 1960–80 and 1980 onward. The economic growth data shows that 1980 GDP figures and share of manufacturing in the economy were already impressive. It can be argued that this is principally due to the government's successful interventionist stance and the resultant capital intensification that were the principal contributors to the economy, rather than schooling.

One of the clues to be used in estimating education's contribution to economic growth lies in looking at the educational profile of the workforce in the seventies. In the 1979 Report on the Ministry of Education, the major concern was not with extolling the virtues of the educational system but with the problem of considerable underachievement in the seventies resulting in wastage. It is significant that the review which culminated in the Report was undertaken at a time when consideration was also being given to re-structuring the economy. An examination of the data in Table 6 indicates that 72.4% of new entrants to the workforce as late as 1980 had only "primary and below educational qualifications and only 3.6% had tertiary qualifications." Table 2a indicates that of the age group, 25 to 29 years, those most likely to have been employed in the economy, 69% had primary or lower qualifications. Further, as Table 7 shows, engineering enrollment in 1979 stood at only 514 students. Contrary then to popular belief it could be argued that Singapore had underinvested in its human resource. It certainly makes plausible the argument that while the expansion of education may have had other benefits, its contribution to sizable growth in the economy must be small.

TABLE 6. Country Comparison of Educational Profile of Workforce

| | *Singapore* | | *Taiwan* | *Japan* | *US* |
|---|---|---|---|---|---|
| | *1980* | *1990* | *1984* | *1982* | *1983* |
| Tertiary | 3.6 | 6 | 6 | 19 | 19 |
| Post-Secondary | 24 | 40.7 | 23 | 46 | 16 |
| Secondary | | | 26 | 35 | 50 |
| Primary & below | 72.4 | 53.3 | 45 | — | 15 |
| TOTAL | 100 | 100 | 100 | 100 | 100 |

Source: Ministry of Trade and Industry, Singapore (1986).

It would be possible to argue that the relationship between educational expansion and diversification may have been different in the eighties. For one thing, both the industrial and nonindustrial infrastructure was already in place, and Singapore had earned a justifiable reputation as a stable, work-oriented and relatively corruption-free society; most significantly, for Singapore's economic strategy the major multinationals had found Singapore a good place to invest in. The education and training infrastructure had also been considerably enhanced. More crucially, Singapore's economic growth strategy had begun to move into a new phase to include precision engineering, computer peripherals, software manufacturing and financial services. The establishment of a National Computer Board signalled the government's intention to harness new technologies to carve out niches in the newly emergent global economy. It could have been argued that this type of an economy required special skills, a well-balanced general education and opportunities for continuous retraining. Significantly, the major educational innovation at the beginning of the eighties was the establishment of the Nanyang Technological Institute to produce practice-oriented engineers and at the end of the decade to start up two more polytechnics to sharply expand the number of diploma holders. In the early nineties the establishment of the comprehensive Nanyang Technological University, an Open University, the phasing out of vocational institutes, the push for a 10-year general education regime for all students indicate a closer awareness of the ways in which education can be relevant to the economy. As a result of the phasing out of the vocational institutes some 20,000 additional students will have to be catered for in the educational system. Table 7 indicates the very considerable growth in polytechnic education between 1982 and 1990 with the two new polytechnics having yet to come fully on stream. The EDB continues to provide focused skill training with close industrial links in such areas as precision engineering, electronics design, and development, automation and mechatronics.

TABLE 7. Student Enrollment at Technical and Vocational Training Institutions and Engineering Faculties

| *Year* | *Polytechnics* | *VITB* | *EDB Training Institutes* | *NUS/NTI Engineering Enrollment* |
|---|---|---|---|---|
| 1976 | 10,529 | - | 584 | 330 |
| 1979 | 9,906 | 14,516 | 933 | 514 |
| 1982 | 13,407 | 16,974 | 1371 | 837 |
| 1985 | 21,610 | 22,276 | 2267 | 1143 |
| 1990 | 29,550 | 26,468 | 2634 | |

Source: Dept. of Statistics (Singapore) (Various years).

Dr. Goh Keng Swee, regarded by many as the architect of Singapore's economic transformation and in the early eighties Singapore's Minister for Education, noted recently that it was a combination of knowledge generation policies validated by the discipline of a competitive export market that explains the economic success of Singapore and the other "dragons." The production of engineers in the seventies and eighties was linked to the shift to technology-based higher value-added industries. He noted that at present Singapore's production of engineers, in proportion to its population, is nearly double that of Britain.

In summary, then, educational growth between 1960 and 1980 is important not for the direct economic benefits but in incorporating more and more young citizens into a modernizing social institution, and in providing wider exposure and opportunities to learn English. Increased literacy and completion of primary education are beneficial to the economy via making possible the later acquisition of occupationally valuable skills. In the second phase, 1980 onward, the contribution of manpower with polytechnic-type qualifications, and in the university sector, the production of professionals, and individuals with the capacity to innovate, to research and develop, may be more significant.

## Education and Social Development

If measuring the contribution of education to economic development has bedevilled researchers and policy makers there is far less consensus in the literature about the contribution of explicit and informal values teaching in schools to values acquisition and to adult behavior; indeed much of the research effort, except perhaps for political socialization, has gone into problems of moral development and evaluation of school-based programs. A number of significant institutions, family, peer groups, religious organizations and significant others all influence behavior. It is also acknowledged that adult experiences in the workplace or major political events like a civil war or a political assassination can radically transform, erode or replace values promoted earlier in schooling. Additionally, the various controversies that have followed attempts to teach values via sex education and religious instruction, for instance, have often affected implementation processes at the school level adversely. Finally, in a period of rapid social change and contentious ideological rivalry about the nature of the state and its relation with key social institutions it is difficult for teachers in schools to know what form of the future society pupils are to be socialized into.

Notwithstanding the above, it is an article of faith among education planners that some form of values education must be attempted. However, in assessing the contribution of values education to national development we need to consider as well non-school institutions and initiatives. Singapore's efforts to build a cohesive and productive society via education can be examined at the level of political socialization, of the management of ethnicity and efforts to create the new Singaporean. First, the need to develop a political identity. It was noted earlier that there were serious doubts about Singapore's political viability, and that the first attempt to shape it within the Malaysian federation failed. The principal fear among Singapore's neighbours was that the island's overwhelming Chinese majority would create a "Third China" and Singapore's political leadership had to demonstrate otherwise. The choice of Malay as the national language and one of the official languages was intended as one demonstration. At the school level cognitive and attitudinal dispositions were engendered through the inclusion of content on Singapore history, socio-demographic and economic characteristics, role in the region and information on political institutions. The raising of the national flag at the beginning of the school day, the singing of the national anthem, the recitation of a pledge affirming commitment to the nation's ideals of equality and multiculturalism, the creation of uniformed groups such as cadet corps and portraits of the president and his wife in the school hall are examples of efforts at school-based socialization. But perhaps the major move was a non-school one, in the institution of compulsory national service in 1967 for all males.[4] More than any other policy it captured the adolescent imagination, and the actual rigors and assumptions of national service reinforced the notion of duty and loyalty to country, a rite of passage into civic adulthood.

In some ways the management of ethnicity was more problematic. Assimilation into the majority Chinese culture was obviously not a feasible option. A commitment to equal treatment of all groups, languages and cultures was the fundamental political commitment. Multiculturalism was the chosen ideology, a commitment to preserving and enhancing ethnic cultures and traditions while striving for a supra-ethnic Singaporean identity, principally through the bilingual policy of mother tongue teaching and English, respectively. A notable feature was the stress on meritocracy which, while it acknowledged that minority groups like the Malays lagged behind in socio-economic terms, implied that while they would be helped to compete equally this would not be via the provision of job or educational quotas. Among other steps taken at the national level to enhance inter-ethnic harmony and religious peace and to thwart communalism were parliamentary legislation like the Maintenance of Religious Harmony Bill, and constitutional amendments to ensure that minority members are represented in parliament. These national-level policies were significant in signalling the government's determination to be even-handed in ethnic issues and more positively, to promote multiculturalism.

At the school level two major policies can be singled out for mention. It was noted earlier that upon independence Singapore inherited a segregated school system based on medium of instruction. A major policy move was to integrate these different media schools, to mix pupils up within one school setting, to promote inter-school activities that would cut across ethnic and cultural lines, and within schools, to promote integrated cultural activities, both for instruction and entertainment via extracurricular activities (Gopinathan, 1985). In the last decade the movement toward English (as main medium of instruction) schooling has in fact resulted in ethnically mixed schools, except in the case of the Special Assistance Plan Schools which cater to an overwhelmingly Chinese student population.

It is perhaps the bilingual education policy that is emblematic of the commitment to multiculturalism. All four official languages, English, Chinese, Malay and Tamil, can be learned in schools and students are required to learn English and their "mother tongue," the latter determined on the basis of ethnicity, i.e. Mandarin, for Chinese pupils. The commitment to bilingualism has been steadfastly maintained, even though the Report on the Ministry of Education and the Improving Primary School Education Report indicate that it is the demands of bilingual competence that are difficult for most pupils and primarily responsible for wastage. On the positive side, though, the language profile of the recently schooled population is moving towards the desired configuration; bilingual literacy has arisen, more and more students are mastering English and more and more Chinese households are using Mandarin instead of dialects. To the extent that the increasing spread of English-language competence among all ethnic groups promoted ethnic integration we can claim that the schools played a decisive role, for it was through the schools that competence in English was ensured. Singapore's management of multilingualism, in which the schools played a large and significant part, has been relatively successful; it has, in its turn, been helped by growth in the economy and the sacrifices that learning English entailed have been compensated for by increased occupational and social mobility (Kuo, 1980; Gopinathan, 1988).

Seen-Kong Chiew (1985, 1990) has examined the degree and processes of societal integration in Singapore. He reported in 1983 that on a number of indicators of structural integration, e.g., labor force distribution by economic sectors, neighborhood integration, inter-ethnic friendship, biliteracy in the recently schooled population, and on a number of indicators of national identity there was evidence that Singapore was becoming more integrated. Ethnic tolerance and overall national identity were high. His 1989 survey data showed that inter-ethnic friendships between the Chinese and Malays and Chinese and Indians have increased and are at high levels.

We now turn to examining the link between language and values. The early decision in Singapore to teach mother tongues was premised on the assumption that language was the primary carrier of values; not to know the mother tongue was to become, in Mr. Lee's words, "deculturalised." The concern for a cohesive set of social and personal values goes back to the mid-sixties when the emergence of interest in alternative lifestyles typified by "Hippie Culture" was seen as evidence of a hedonistic, self-serving, undisciplined morality which could not be allowed to infect Singaporean youth. A vaguely defined "Asian cultural heritage" to be accessed through mother tongue teaching was to be the antidote. In the seventies there was increasing elaboration of the characteristics of the Asian heritage, drawing principally from the Confucian ethical tradition and stressing filial piety, a commitment to consensus, respect for duty and obligations and a need for order, among others. The culmination of this trend is to be seen in the introduction of Confucian ethics in the early eighties as an examination subject, one of several options in a new subject, religious knowledge for upper secondary students.

As Singapore enters the mid-nineties societal challenges are beginning to multiply. On the economic front the decades of double digit GNP growth fuelled by low wage costs are over, and Singapore needs to find economic niches and to compete now with developed countries; it is estimated that economic growth for the rest of the decade will be between 4 and 6% though in 1994 it exceeded 10%. A growing middle class is now more vocal in demanding greater personal liberties and demands increasing participation in decision making. Singapore was not unaffected by the winds of religious evangelism sweeping Asia in the eighties, and the heightened religious activity and polarization in Singapore led to the government withdrawing the religious knowledge subject from the school curriculum; a newly revised civics and moral education course is now being implemented in the schools. Criticism of the effort to promote Confucianism, both from the minority groups and from English-educated Chinese, has led to its being quietly backgrounded and in its place a set of core values has been promoted.

Tensions and publicly voiced differences between English- and Chinese-educated Chinese (or more accurately, English and Chinese-competent Chinese) have been a feature of life since the mid-eighties. The old social contract in which the government imposed firm labor and social discipline in return for material rewards, jobs, good schooling, subsidized housing and effective transportation is weakening with the emergence of the middle class and the now vocal non-English-educated underclass. The latter group has made its displeasure known in recent elections which saw losses for the ruling party, and, allied with some Chinese-educated intellectuals, forced a government change in policy which resulted in greater opportunities for pupils weak in English. There has also been some questioning of the old assumptions that the mother tongue would be primarily used in the social, cultural and familial domains. The rising economic importance of China is given as one reason why Mandarin, in particular, should have an increased role in Singapore.[5] Finally, the government has been more open about acknowledging, first, the existence of educational underachievement among the minorities, and second, the needs of a Chinese-dominant underclass (Gopinathan, 1994).

The evidence from the schools is, not unexpectedly, mixed. There has been little empirical evidence of the effect of curriculum initiatives on the moulding of values. The Report on the Ministry of Education criticized the Education for Living syllabus in use in the seventies but did not undertake any studies of its own. The (Ong) Report on Moral Education was also long on recommendations but short on closely argued analysis of the case for values education and for its detailed recommendations. Eng Soo Peck et al. conducted a series of studies on the effectiveness of the moral education curriculum but the full data and analysis have not been released. Eng (1992) reported that "the class environment does not provide an optimal setting for values learning." Pupil–pupil relationships denoting caring and sharing are perceived as being weak and he speculates that "strong and unmitigated competitiveness . . . may have weakened the value of caring and sharing" (p. 20). Joy Chew, in her ethnographic study of school level implementation of moral education, concluded that the "national education system conveyed its own morality and set of values and was often in tension with the sociocentric focus of official moral education . . . [and that] pupils were confronted with . . . a social morality of co-operation and mutual supportiveness and an economic morality that encouraged individualism, competition, inequality and self-interest" (1988). Two earlier commentators, Leong and Pang and Lim, were also critical. Leong, studying national servicemen, concluded that ". . . theirs is a practical hardcrusted morality . . . there is more refraining than doing . . . largely negative moral behaviour and [goading this is] the fear of punishment" (Leong, 1978, p. 12). Pang and Lim state that "docility, obedience to authority and acceptance of hierarchy are encouraged by teachers' unquestionable authority in the classroom . . ." (Pang and Lim, 1976). This ties in neatly with Chan's 1976 observation of a political culture that discourages conflict, confrontation and bargaining. Chiew found in his 1989 survey that a significant number of Singaporeans, while being aware of national issues, had little or no interest in them. The "new Singaporean" is perhaps being rather well socialized for the reality of adult socio-political life in Singapore. However, these values fall short of the ideal of responsibility, principled morality and collaborative social life as set out in the core values formulation mentioned earlier.

The structure of the school system also has implications for socialization. One pattern that has been evident is the pattern of increasing differentiation in the school system. It will be remembered that Singapore inherited a divided education system and the major task of the 1956 All Party Report was to unify the system on the basis of equal treatment; the rationale then was clear cut, that a unified society could not be built out of disparate ethnic groups if the schools remained divided. School system unification was successfully done, even though the unique identity of the church and clan-aided schools remained distinct from the more numerous government schools. Then, as a follow-up to efforts to improve bilingual attainment and to preserve the unique and cultural identity of leading Chinese schools, the government introduced the concept of the Special Assistance Plan (SAP) schools, which, because they are all Chinese schools, are attended exclusively by high-performing ethnic Chinese pupils who are offered both English and Chinese at first-language level. In the latter half of the eighties and early nineties, in an effort to provide more school level administrative autonomy, the government allowed eight leading English medium schools to go "independent." The high fees that these schools charged led to public disquiet and the government has responded with a proposal to establish "government autonomous schools." For good measure the government has also given approval to the *Straits Times,* the leading English-language newspaper, to produce a list of secondary schools and junior colleges ranked according to academic performance. Since the leading edge of these innovations is to sharpen competition among schools so as to benefit from the discipline of the market, they are likely to weaken the system's commitment and contribution to collaboration and societal cohesion.

While both the independent schools and the SAP schools cater to the academic elite it is the SAP schools and to a lesser extent, the "Speak Mandarin" campaigns that have borne the brunt of criticism, especially from minority group leaders. Pupils in the SAP schools represent the cream of the primary cohort and thus can reasonably be expected to be part of the future elite. That they should be schooled in an exclusively single ethnic environment seems to many commentators untenable in a society committed to multiculturalism, and counter to other efforts to ensure a leadership that is both multi-ethnic and knowledgeable and committed to multiculturalism (Association of Muslim Professionals, 1990; Quah, 1990).

## Concluding Observations

While it is necessary to be skeptical of some of the more extravagant claims made on behalf of the schooling system in the context of its contribution to development, it is necessary also to acknowledge the system's capacity to change in desired directions. Since the mid-eighties, there have been in Singaporean education a number of innovations that, it could be argued, would promote processes leading to greater decentralization, professionalism and curriculum flexibility. A major change in Singapore's socio-political context has been the stepping down of Mr. Lee Kuan Yew as Prime Minister and the elevation of Mr. Goh Chok Tong to the post. Mr. Goh has promoted a more open, participative and consensual style of government, and the sphere for criticism and comment, not least in the media, has been considerably enlarged. As noted earlier an increasingly better-educated middle class is both demanding and making possible such a shift. One very good example in the educational domain is the open acknowledgement of minority educational underachievement, a willingness to reveal and to discuss data and issues.

The period of intense centralization in the fifties and sixties, largely as a response to the tensions and contradictions within the colonial-sponsored segmented system, has in the late eighties begun to give way to more decentralization, both in terms of control over some of the leading schools and in giving principals more latitude. Mr. John Yip, then Director of Schools, noted as early as 1982 that the Ministry's policy was "to decentralize the management of education . . ." and "to hand over more authority to principals as a critical factor for encouraging school-based initiatives in education" (Yip, 1982). While the clearest manifestation of this policy has been in the establishment of independent schools and the impending establishment of "government autonomous schools," it is important to note as well the greater professionalism of senior school executives made possible by specially tailored programs for school principals and heads of departments which have considerably enhanced leadership capacity in the schools. The greater use of school management committees and a commitment that parents will be given more choice in how they want their children educated and in what enrichment activities their children should participate strengthens this reform initiative.

While constant changes to curriculum are rightly criticized as unhelpful and probably not very effective, fundamental structural innovations like streaming do have the benefit of breaking up a lock-step curriculum and introducing greater curriculum variety and student options. The school curriculum has been progressively democratized and planned curriculum innovations like the Reading and English Acquisition Program (LEAP) and Active Communicative Teaching (ACT) program have improved competencies significantly, and curriculum innovation implementation at school level is more and more school-led with greater levels of teacher involvement. There has also been an acknowledgment of the need to pay more serious attention to aesthetic education, and a number of art and music elective programs have been implemented. Two major institutions for education in the fine arts, the Nanyang Academy of Fine Arts and the La Salle, a college of the arts, are thriving. While Victoria Junior College offers Drama Studies as an "A" level subject, other junior colleges offer Japanese, French and German. Schools and individual pupils have been provided additional funds and a cash sum respectively to use on enrichment activities.[6] More fundamentally, and perhaps under economic pressure, the government has committed itself to 10 years' general education and turned the pass-fail Primary School Leaving Examination into a placement examination. This hopefully should help free instructional practices. At the post-secondary level too, increased training opportunities are now available with the creation of two new polytechnics in the last three years. Polytechnic education itself has broadened its scope and now includes courses in design, information technology, occupational therapy, nursing and mass communications.

The role of education in societies like Singapore has been shown in this analysis to be complex and often contradictory. The overly optimistic formulations of the sixties have in some instances become now more darkly pessimistic, a view warranted only in some of the more extreme situations in which some developing countries find themselves. Education continues to have the potential to contribute to enhanced human agency, greater civic tolerance and pluralism, and indeed in meeting the legitimate claims of the state for national cohesion and economic viability.[7] The issues are less with goals and more with means. A possibilistic view of the relationship between education and development must inform both practice and theory.

## Notes

1. *Asiaweek*, October 9, 1982, p. 68.

2. A full account of the vocationalizing trends in Singapore education has yet to be written. Of interest are contributions by R.L. Skolnik, *The National Wide Learning System in Singapore* (1976), Linda Low et al., *Economics of Education and Manpower Development in Singapore* (1991), Soon Teck Wong, *Development of Human Resources and Technological Capability in Singapore* (1982) and Bikas C. Sanyal's "Economic Growth and the Training System in the Asian Countries." In general these works adopt an uncritical human capital stance to the contribution of vocational and technical training to economic growth.

3. Speech reported in the *Straits Times*, December 9, 1959.

4. Goh Keng Swee, then Minister for Defence, stated in Parliament, "Nothing creates loyalty and national consciousness more speedily and more thoroughly than participation in defence and membership of the armed forces. . . ."

5. The appeal of Confucianism as an organizing ideology continues to be strong, at a time when the West is seen as promoting an individual-based, human rights-biased democratic ideology. It has obvious appeals to the government of a Chinese-majority state which believes in social discipline. What began as a vaguely defined call to hold on to Asian values has now taken on new significance as Western commentators have sought to explain economic growth in the "four dragons" as being due to

Confucianist values of solidarity, thrift and effort. "Communitarianism" and "Soft authoritarianism" are currently fashionable.

6. The Education Endowment Scheme Act under which $40 million will be given out as grants to secondary schools and pupils next year is an interesting example of the high levels of funding the educational system enjoys and a further example of promoting curricular enrichment via choice.

7. It should be noted that while there has been some effort to think about what the re-structuring of the economy toward more knowledge-based industries must mean for learning processes and outcomes, no attention has yet been paid to how classroom instructional variables, including classroom climate, might affect knowledge and attitudes toward political participation. Harwood (1992) concluded that there were "consistent relationships between classroom climate and political interest, efficacy and confidence," and most of these relationships have been found to be positive. If we are to be more assured of more positive outcomes from civics education causes then a pedagogy characterized by knowledge, interaction, discussion of issues and community-oriented civic action will be necessary.

# 5 Taiwan

*Yi Rong Young*

## Introduction

Taiwan, known to the contemporary world as one of the "Four Little Tigers" in East Asia, is an island off the southeastern coast of the Chinese mainland. It has an area of 35,873 square kilometers, roughly the same as the Netherlands. The island of Taiwan together with the 64 small Pescadores islands and the 21 other scattered islands constitute the Taiwan Area, the seat of the Republic of China (ROC) since 1949. There are now twenty million residents of Taiwan, making its population density 565.5 per square kilometer, one of the highest on earth. The overwhelming majority of its population are ethnic Chinese, with about three hundred thousand aborigines who are descendants of early migrants from Southeast Asia.

What epitomizes Taiwan's development in recent decades is its economic success. In 1992, Taiwan was the thirteenth leading trading nation of the world; its foreign exchange reserves totalled over eighty billion US dollars, the highest in the world; per capita GNP was $10,215 by the end of 1992 (CEPD, 1993, p. 90). The "Taiwan experience" is now praised as "a model that inspires other developing nations" (Myers, 1990, p. 17). As more and more attention has focused on the miraculous economic achievements of Taiwan specifically and other newly industrializing Asian countries in general, a theory or model of "East Asian development" has emerged from political and economic studies of this region (Deyo, 1987; Bates, 1988; Berger and Hsiao, 1988; Winckler, 1988; Lau, 1990; Robinson, 1991).

This chapter will examine Taiwan's development focusing on the contributions of education. The relationship between education and development has long been a focus of study for both developmentalists and educationalists. Modernization theory and human capital theory generally regard education as an agent of social change, contributing to modernization and economic growth. Such approaches have been adopted, and sometimes challenged, when examining the case of Taiwan (Galenson, 1979; Li, 1988; Young, 1990; Smith, 1991; Woo, 1991); the questions of how and how much education is linked with economic growth have remained under debate.

## Political and Economic Development

### *Historical Background*

Taiwan is described as "having its own creation myth" (Long, 1991, p. 1) even for Chinese historians. Several waves of immigration from the mainland into Taiwan during recent centuries reinforced its cultural and political ties with China. In 1895 Taiwan was ceded to Japan by the Chinese government after the first Sino-Japanese war. The Japanese colonization lasted until 1945 when Japan's surrender ended World War II; Taiwan was then returned to China. Four years later the Chinese civil war broke out. The result was a divided China: the People's Republic of China (PRC) was established by the Communist government; and the ROC, led by the Nationalist President Chiang Kai-shek, secured its new capital in Taipei, a northern city of Taiwan, in December 1949.

In the early 1950s, when Taiwan was trying to recover from the ravages caused by war, over half of its then eight-million population were illiterate; 56% of its employed labor force were in primary industries; per capita GNP in 1951 was $145. It is from this base of an agricultural economy with low income and high illiteracy that Taiwan has gradually developed its modern, highly industrialized economy. Economists usually divide the contemporary history of Taiwan into the following four stages (Ranis, 1979, pp. 208–255): (1) 1895–1945 was the period of Japanese colonialism. (2) 1953–1962 was a decade of general rapid growth for Taiwan's industrial sector. (3) 1963–1972 was a decade characterized by a very rapid overall growth of the economy. It is during this period that Taiwan entered the stage of economic take-off. (4) The 1970s witnessed drastic shocks to the world economy, but "Taiwan demonstrated notable resilience in meeting these shocks. In fact, its ability to respond as it did represents a prime indicator of the increasing maturity of the economic system" (Ranis, 1979, p. 255).

### *Recent Economic Development*

A classification system established in the 1980s by the Organization for Economic Cooperation and Development (OECD) has identified Taiwan and ten other developing countries including Argentina, Brazil, Greece, Hong Kong, South Korea, Mexico, Portugal, Singapore, Spain and Yugoslavia, as Newly Industrializing Countries (NICs) (Todaro, 1989, pp. 14–15). The label "NIC" itself delineates to some extent the state of development of Taiwan. The structural changes occurring in the past four decades are very significant. The percentage of agricultural production in total GDP has dropped from 32.2 in 1952 to only 3.7 in 1991, while that of industrial production has risen from 19.7 to 42.3, services from 48.1 to 54.0 during the same period of time (see Table 1). Forty-seven percent of the labor force are now in tertiary industries (communication, transportation and other services), 40.1% in secondary industries, while only 12.9% remain in primary industries (CEPD, 1992, p. 18). Table 1 also shows other major indicators of the Taiwan economy: annual economic growth rate in the 1970s reached double-digits, and has remained high except during the world-wide economic crisis in the early 1980s; GNP per capita has doubled in each five-year period. Such economic achievements are praised as being "one of the highest growth rates of real output achieved by any country over a sustained period" (Lau, 1990, p. 187).

TABLE 1. Indicators of Taiwan Economy

| *Period* | *Economic Growth Rate (%)* | *Per Capita GNP (US$)* | *GDP by Activity (%)* | | | |
|---|---|---|---|---|---|---|
| | | | *Agriculture* | *Industries* | *Services* | *Total* |
| 1952 | 12.0 | 196 | 32.2 | 19.7 | 48.1 | 100.0 |
| 1962 | 7.9 | 162 | 25.0 | 28.2 | 46.8 | 100.0 |
| 1967 | 10.6 | 267 | 20.6 | 33.0 | 46.4 | 100.0 |
| 1972 | 13.4 | 522 | 12.2 | 41.6 | 46.1 | 100.0 |
| 1977 | 10.3 | 1,301 | 10.6 | 44.0 | 45.4 | 100.0 |
| 1982 | 4.1 | 2,653 | 7.7 | 44.4 | 47.9 | 100.0 |
| 1987 | 11.9 | 5,275 | 5.3 | 47.4 | 47.3 | 100.0 |
| 1991 | 7.3 | 8,815 | 3.7 | 42.3 | 54.0 | 100.0 |

Source: CEPD, 1992, pp. 1, 42.

Taiwan's economic achievements rest not only on rapid industrialization, but also on constant growth with a relatively even distribution of wealth. While many developing countries have suffered the problem of rapid growth distorting wealth distribution, Taiwan has not been greatly troubled by this dilemma. It is classified as a country with "low inequality" when the criteria of Gini coefficient smaller than 0.4 is applied (Todaro, 1989, p. 156). The disposable income of the highest 20% income group has been only four to five times that of the lowest 20% income group since the 1980s. In comparison with other developing and developed countries, Taiwan has therefore enjoyed a relatively equal distribution of income and has thus avoided the problems which accompany large income disparities.

Taiwan's development has been described as "a rags-to-riches story" (Li, 1988, p. xi), "an economic miracle by any definition" (Clark, 1989, p. 4) and "one of the few success stories of modern development" (Bates, 1988, p. 133). Political and economic studies on Taiwan have focused on answering the following question: "Taiwan constitutes a puzzle because its developmental history challenges the fundamental assumptions of both the developmentalist and dependency approaches" (Clark, 1989, p. 4), but little consensus has been reached regarding the major contributors to Taiwan's economic success. A general explanation includes such factors as land reform (Galenson, 1979; Kuo et al., 1981; Amsden, 1988), the crucial role of the government (Li, 1988; Lau, 1990), and education and human resources (Kuo et al., 1981; Sun, 1987; Li, 1988).

### *Political Development*

Although Taiwan is known to the world for its economic success, its international, legal and political status is less clear. The long-term separation of Taiwan from China has created a rather difficult political environment for the island. In the international community, the ROC is not recognized by most of the nations of the world, and is no longer represented in the United Nations and its affiliated agencies (Chiu, 1992). As far as Taiwan's domestic affairs are concerned, this political factor has affected Taiwan's overall development to the extent that the government had maintained an authoritarian rule by enforcing martial law for four decades. It was not until the mid-1980s that a series of critical events gave rise to the dawn of a new political era.

In 1986, the Democratic Progressive party, the first political opposition party in Taiwan's history, was established. On July 15, 1987, the government lifted the emergency decree that had kept martial law in force in Taiwan for nearly 40 years. This major political reform was followed by a series of other liberalization measures, including the abolition of most foreign exchange controls and newspaper restrictions, permission for Taiwanese residents to visit mainland China and official tolerance for public demonstrations. This move toward democratization has greatly changed Taiwan's internal political ecology, and has even overshadowed its economic success.

As Taiwan enters into the late 1990s, it has undergone another series of social and political reform movements. The government has responded to pressure to amend the ROC Constitution, to institutionalize two-party competition in elections, and to promote and ameliorate Taiwan's relation with mainland China as well as the international community. As a political observer points out, "the transition from an authoritarian dictatorship to a pluralistic representative system has now been completed" (Domes, 1993, p. 60).

One of the significant effects of this political reform on Taiwan's overall development is the gradual formation of an autonomous civil society. As a result of the loosening of the government's central control, different pressure groups have emerged which have played a more active role in the discussions and formulation of public policies. Once an area where the government had exclusive control, education, among other public services, has now become an area of public concern as well.

## Educational Development

### *The Educational System: Its Legal and Constitutional Basis*

Embedded in Chinese culture is the tradition of holding education in high regard. Policy makers have deemed education as a vehicle to preserve cultural heritage as well as to promote individual mobility. Therefore, it is constitutionally guaranteed and required that all citizens have an equal opportunity to enjoy a minimum level of education. In the Constitution of the Republic of China, several articles specifically aim at developing education and protecting the citizens' rights in this regard:

> Article 158: Education and culture shall aim at instilling in citizens a national spirit of self-government, national morality, healthy physique, scientific knowledge, and the ability to earn a living.
>
> Article 159: All citizens shall have an equal opportunity to receive education.
>
> Article 160: All children of school age from six to twelve years shall receive free elementary education. Those from poor families shall be supplied with books by the Government. All citizens above school age who have not received elementary education shall receive elementary education free of charge and shall also be supplied with books by the Government.

Articles 161 to 167 are also related to the government's responsibility of providing education at various levels. It is clearly stated in the Constitution that both public and private educational institutions shall be subject to state supervision, thus putting education under a central authority.

As far as funding is concerned, Article 164 of the Constitution stipulates that, "Funds earmarked for education, science, and culture shall be, in respect of the Central Government, not less than fifteen percent of the total national budget; in respect of the Provincial Government, not less than twenty-five percent of the total Municipal or County Budget." It is on this constitutional basis that Taiwan's educational development has been supported by government funding.

As mentioned earlier, Taiwan was under Japanese rule from 1895 to 1945, during which time the educational infrastructure including a massive "common school" system open to children aged seven to sixteen was established (Tsurumi, 1977, pp. 18–19). In 1949, when the Nationalist government relocated itself in Taiwan, the blueprint of a modern school system was introduced into the island. Through a number of modifications it gradually evolved into the current 6–3–3 school system. Article 160 of the Constitution requires that all 6- to 12-year-old children receive elementary education on a tuition-free basis. In 1968 compulsory and tuition-free education was extended from a length of six to nine years to cover both primary and junior secondary education. Beyond the compulsory education level, students may select—or, to be more accurate, be selected through the joint entrance examinations—to take vocational or academically oriented education in senior high schools. Higher education is provided by two- or three-year junior colleges, regular colleges and universities and graduate schools.

### *Administration*

The administration of education is subject to government control, and is divided into three levels in accordance with the hierarchy of the government system: the central Ministry of Education is in charge of legislation and administration of education in general; the provincial departments of education are in charge of provincial/municipal formal and non-formal education; and county bureaus of education are in charge of education in each of the counties. The nine years of compulsory and tuition-free education are effectively supervised by the Bureau of Education in each county, although by and large, the fundamental policies such as those on curriculum and personnel are decided by the central Ministry of Education.

It is obvious that the administration of educational affairs in Taiwan is highly centralized. To take elementary education as an example: all teachers and principals of public elementary schools have to go through the government "distribution" system to be appointed to their positions in schools. All textbooks used in elementary schools and junior high schools are published by the National Institute for Compilation and Translation since both of these levels of education fall within the nine-year compulsory system. The Ministry of Education also regulates such substantial matters as finance, personnel, curriculum, tuition, entrance examinations and student quotas for public schools at various levels. Moreover, it regulates the establishment and practice of private schools.

In 1972 the executive body of the government decided to freeze the establishment of private primary and secondary schools. Since then, no new private schools have been set up. Such a centralized administrative system has been criticized by Taiwanese scholars as being "unique" in the worldwide trend towards greater democratization (e.g., Huang, 1990, p. 565). It has also become a central target of reform in the recent wave of political and educational changes.

### *Educational Investment*

Education has been a major area of government investment in terms of public expenditure. As described above, the ROC Constitution makes it clear that at least 15% of the central government budget must be set aside for funding education, science and culture. However, this constitutional requirement was in practice, never fully met until 1990 in which year 15.19% of the central government expenditure was allocated to meet education/science/culture expenses (Ministry of Education, 1991, p. 50). With respect to the proportion of educational expenditure against the total expenditure for all levels of government, official statistics show that for two decades from the mid-1960s to the 80s, the ratio was around 15%, and reached 17.77% in 1991. The ratio of government educational expenditure to GNP was 5.45% in 1991; and 6.63% if both public and private educational expenditures are included. These figures indicate a constant increase in educational investment vis-à-vis the gross national product. (See Table 3.) Another official source shows that within the structure of government expenditures, the ratio of general administration and defence budget has decreased from 66% in 1951 and 68% in 1961 to 52% in 1981, and further decreased to 39% in 1991. By contrast, the budget for education and social security and welfare has constantly increased over the four decades (DGBAS, 1992, pp. 92–95). As in other East Asian societies education has not been solely provided by the state. In the case of Taiwan the government's policy since 1972 to freeze the establishment of private schools at the compulsory education level has meant that only 0.86% of expenditure on the nine years of compulsory education was privately financed in 1992. In contrast, however, 30.4% of expenditure at the upper secondary level and 29.9% at the tertiary level was privately financed in 1992. There are other indications to illustrate the government's increasing commitment to educational investment. Figure 1 shows the growth rate of GNP and that of the educational expenses in the past four decades. Given 1952 as the base year for calculating the indices of GNP and education expenditure (Index = 100 in 1952), the index of GNP in 1991 was 27,999.6 while the index for educational expenditure in that year was 100,102.5, thereby showing a much higher increase in the growth of education expenditure than that of GNP. In other words, the high growth of the educational expenditure not only is a consequence of a growing GNP, but also reflects the government's extraordinary investment in education. Figure 1 illustrates the disproportionately high growth of the education expenditure vis-à-vis the growth of GNP over the past decades.

FIGURE 1. Expansion of GNP and Educational Expenditure

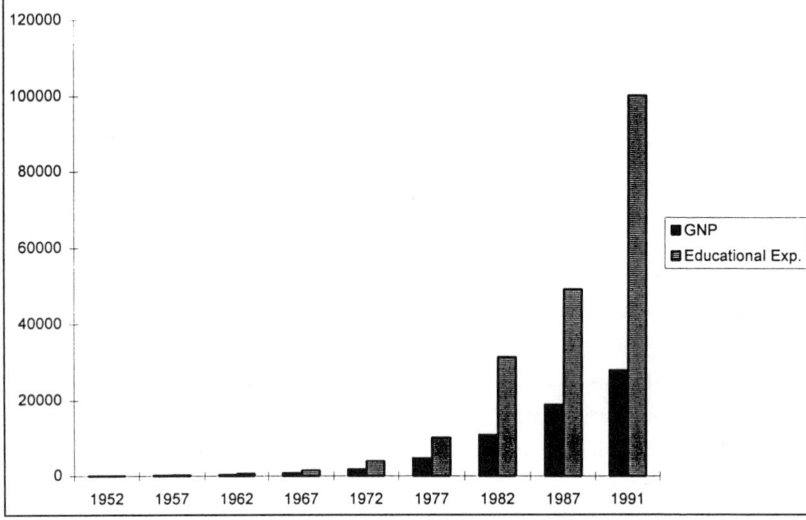


*The Expansion of Education and Current Figures*

The government's most significant achievement in education has been the phenomenal quantitative expansion of the school system as a result of central planning and government funding. According to 1992 official statistics, the number of schools at all levels in Taiwan has increased more than four times in the past four decades, from 1,501 in 1950–51 to 6,787 in 1991–92, and the number of students from one million to over five million over the same time span. The gross student enrollment rate in 1990–91 was 100.41% at the primary level, 98.43% at the junior secondary level, 91.01% at the senior secondary level, and 31.15% at the tertiary level (age 18–21) (Ministry of Education, Taiwan 1992, pp. 32–33). Table 2 compares the enrollment rates of different school levels in different countries in 1965 and 1986, respectively.

It is clear that in the two decades from 1965 to 1986, Taiwan and the Four Little Tigers considerably expanded secondary education, and began to catch up with the high-income economies by expanding higher education.

When making educational investments, the government has chosen to favour higher education. Public universities (and private universities as well, although to a lesser extent) have been heavily subsidized by the government; university students generally benefit from a low-tuition-fee policy. Table 3 contrasts the student ratio with the ratio of government's educational expenditure at various school levels. The small number of students receiving higher education (only 5.3% of the total student population) have enjoyed 14.6% of the education expenditure of the government, while those in pre-schools, primary schools and special schools are relatively disadvantaged in terms of allocation of government funding.

TABLE 2. Enrollment Rate

| | *Percentage of Age Group Enrolled in Education* | | | | | |
|---|---|---|---|---|---|---|
| | *Primary* | | *Secondary* | | *Tertiary* | |
| | *1965* | *1986* | *1965* | *1986* | *1965* | *1986* |
| Low-income economies | 73 | 103 | 20 | 35 | 2 | 3 |
| Middle-income economies | 93 | 104 | 26 | 54 | 6 | 18 |
| High-income economies | 105 | 102 | 62 | 92 | 21 | 39 |
| Taiwan | 97.15 | 99.57 | ... | 92.19 | ... | 25.18 |
| Korea, Rep. | 101 | 94 | 35 | 95 | 6 | 33 |
| Singapore | 105 | 115 | 45 | 71 | 10 | ... |
| Hong Kong | 103 | 105 | 29 | 69 | 5 | 13 |

Sources: 1. World Bank, 1989, pp. 220–221.
2. Taiwan data are from Ministry of Education, 1992, pp. 28, 32–33.

### *Educational Problems and Reforms*

While the above-mentioned data clearly demonstrate the very impressive quantitative growth of Taiwan's education on the one hand, they are, on the other hand, less convincing in demonstrating qualitative improvement. For example, the problem of overcrowded classrooms has existed for a long time. Government statistics show that in 1990 the average number of students in each class reached 41.94 in primary schools, 44.12 in junior high schools, and over 45 in senior high schools and vocational schools. The student/teacher ratio was 28.51 in primary schools and 21.55 in senior high schools

(Ministry of Education, 1991, pp. 34, 39). This phenomenon has aroused complaints by parents and criticism by scholars (Chiu, 1989). Another problem is the increasingly unequal distribution of educational resources. Namely, students in urban areas have generally enjoyed better teaching facilities and greater chances for advanced schooling than their peers in rural areas (Lee and Yang, 1987). In recent years, the problem of "educational unemployment," the highly educated being unemployed, has emerged and caused public concern. In 1992 those with college/university degrees had an unemployment rate of 2.28%, which is higher than the national average unemployment rate of 1.51%, and much higher than the unemployment rate of 0.53% for those with only primary education (DGBAS, 1993, pp. 70–71).

TABLE 3. Student Ratio and Government Expenditure Ratio (1990–91)

| | *Student Ratio (%)* | | *Government Expenditure (%)* | |
|---|---|---|---|---|
| Pre-school | 4.4 | | 0.3 | |
| 9-yr compulsory | 65.2 | | 47.0 | |
| (primary) | | (43.1) | | (29.8) |
| (junior secondary) | | (22.1) | | (17.2) |
| Senior secondary | 13.0 | | 14.6 | |
| (academic) | | (4.1) | | (6.4) |
| (vocational) | | (8.9) | | (8.2) |
| Junior college | 6.2 | | 2.7 | |
| Higher education | 5.3 | | 14.6 | |
| Special education | 0.1 | | 0.7 | |
| Adult education | 5.8 | | 6.3 | |
| Administration | — | | 11.8 | |
| Others | — | | 1.9 | |
| Total | 100.0 | | 99.9 | |

Source: Ministry of Education, Taiwan, 1992, pp. 18–19, 40.

Another major source of complaint is the centralized administration and "ideological control" exercised over education by the government. The government has put under its authority such fundamental elements of education as the compilation of textbooks, the training and provision of school teachers and the regulation of access to schooling at all levels. To challenge the government's tight control over education, a movement to reform the education system emerged and developed parallel to the more general political democratization movement that originated in the mid-1980s. The major platforms of this reform movement are to decentralize the administration of education and to grant schools and higher education institutions more autonomy. In 1987 alone, two nationwide teachers' organizations, the National Education Association and the Teachers' Rights Association, were established. In the following years, a Declaration of Students' Rights was signed by student groups and presented to the public; an Association for Higher Education Reform composed of academics from different universities was also organized. These pressure groups, each with its specific platforms, all aim to push the Ministry of Education to loosen its control over the school system.

In response to growing demands from within society, the government began to undertake reform measures. Currently the Teachers Law, the Universities Law and the Normal Education Law are being amended by the legislature, and this has resulted in great disputes among different interest groups. Other reforms have included the effort to extend compulsory education through an experimental plan started in 1990, to widen access to higher education by raising the student quota for higher education, to modify the current standardized and politically oriented school curriculum and to reform the uniform entrance screening system for senior secondary and higher education. The result is yet to be evaluated since many of the reform plans either have just begun, or have been pending for years. However, it is clear that the overall aim of these reforms is to grant more autonomy to the bodies concerned in the administration of education matters.

## Education to Accelerate Economic Growth

Ever since Schultz (1961) viewed education as a productive investment rather than simply a form of consumption, investment in education has been recognized by policy makers as a cause of both economic growth at the macro level and individual advancement at the micro level. The worldwide phenomenon of massive expansion in education after World War II was obviously influenced by this perception of the function of schooling (Hallak, 1990, pp. 7–23). However, the findings of empirical case studies in various societies have suggested that "it clearly cannot be assumed that the link between education and economic growth is a direct and linear one, or that it operates in the same manner for every kind of society" (Fågerlind and Saha, 1989, p. 80). In spite of the enormous efforts in the study of the role of education in economic development, it remains debatable whether education is a cause or effect of economic growth (Psacharopoulos, 1988, pp. 1–2).

In the case of Taiwan, along with the impressive economic growth of the past decades there was an even faster rate of growth of the government's investment in education (see Table 4 and Figure 2). However, no strong and direct evidence has been located to prove that education is a major contributor to the country's extraordinary economic success. Chiu's study (1989) shows that, in terms of international comparisons, Taiwan's educational investment is about average for that of developing countries in terms of the ratio of education expenditure to GNP, while its economic growth has remained much above average, thus suggesting that educational investment is neither an effective indicator of nor a sufficient explanation for economic growth (Chiu, 1989, p. 188–192). Woo's (1991) review of relevant studies of education's contribution to economic growth in Taiwan also fails to demonstrate a strong linkage. She contends that "it was probably not just investment in education alone, but the interaction between education, wage moderation, and the Taiwanese industrial investment strategy that led to such spectacular (economic) growth" (Woo, 1991, p. 1041).

It seems necessary that we look into other more indirect evidence to examine the relation between education and economy. Psacharopoulos's study suggests that education may well be an effect, instead of a cause, of economic growth (1988, pp. 1–2). The Taiwan Government's policy in 1968 to extend compulsory education from six to nine years, which led to the major expansion of the school system, may be an example to support Psacharopoulos's argument. Official statistics indicate that Taiwan experienced the first peak of economic growth in the decade between 1964 and 1973; the annual growth rate of the gross national product reached double digits in that decade. Chiang Kai-shek, then President of the ROC and the decision-maker who forcefully advocated the policy of extending compulsory education, contended in 1967 that "we need to solve the (financial) problem of nine-year compulsory education by our achievements in social-economic development at the current stage" (Research Committee on National Development, 1973, p. 8). Obviously it is the rapidly growing economy that made possible the most important educational expansion in Taiwan's history.

The sound financial condition of Taiwan supported the other major leaps in Taiwan's educational development, such as the 1987 move to upgrade all of the nine public teacher-training institutions from junior colleges to four-year regular colleges of tertiary level, and the 25% increase in educational expenditure in the one year from 1989 to 1990 in order to meet the constitutional requirement that education/culture-related expenditure should be at least 15% of the central government budget. In these cases, education is the effect rather than the cause of economic growth.

Scholars have adopted the human capital approach to evaluate the role of education in Taiwan's economic development, and have generally recognized its contribution (Ho, 1978; Kuo et al., 1981; Li, 1988). Government statistics (DGBAS, 1987) show that in 1966 20% of the total employed population were illiterate while only 3.9% of them received tertiary education. Thanks to educational expansion, the percentage of illiteracy in the labor force in 1986 dropped to 5.61, and roughly 13% of the employed population received tertiary education. This phenomenon suggests that the quality of the labor force has been improving due to the attaining of education.

One educational policy identified by policy makers as an important contributor to Taiwan's economic development is that of vocational education. As stated earlier, senior secondary education is divided into a vocational track and an academic track. Before 1970 there were more students in academic high schools than in vocational schools. However, as the government decided to expand vocational education in order to meet the needs of industry for qualified manpower, the student distribution in senior high schools has changed dramatically. By freezing the student quota for academic high schools, and expanding that for vocational high schools and five-year junior colleges—the latter being vocational in nature and enrolling graduates of junior high schools—the government has successfully allocated more students to vocational training programs. In just one decade the number of students in vocational schools doubled while that of academic high schools remained relatively stable. The ratio between the former and the latter was 5.0 : 5.0 in 1970–71, which means that roughly half of the 15- to 18-year-old students were in vocational schools while the other half were in academic schools. The first academic year that more students were enrolled in vocational schools than in academic schools was 1971–72; the ratio was 5.1 : 4.9. This ratio in the following two decades has continued to change as a result of the government's interventionist policies. It was 6.7 : 3.3 in 1981–82, and 6.9 : 3.1 in 1991–92, indicating that the number of students in vocational high schools is now over twice that of students in academic high schools (see Table 4).

TABLE 4. Academic High Schools and Vocational High Schools

| *School Year* | *Academic High School* | | *Vocational School* | | *Ratio(1)/(2)* |
|---|---|---|---|---|---|
| | *Schools* | *Students (1)* | *Schools* | *Students (2)* | |
| 1970–71 | 185 | 178,537 | 146 | 175,650 | 5.0–5.0 |
| 1971–72 | 199 | 190,798 | 168 | 198,969 | 4.9–5.1 |
| 1976–77 | 195 | 181,933 | 178 | 296,493 | 3.8–6.2 |
| 1981–82 | 180 | 182,391 | 196 | 374,206 | 3.3–6.7 |
| 1986–87 | 175 | 200,599 | 204 | 437,924 | 3.1–6.9 |
| 1991–92 | 177 | 218,061 | 212 | 475,852 | 3.1–6.9 |

Source: Ministry of Education, Taiwan, 1992, pp. 4–5, 20.

While this change of student ratio is often used to affirm the increasing need of the labor market for manpower trained for employment, it is worth noting that such a distribution is a result of the government's manpower planning based upon a "social demand approach." This attempts to provide educational opportunities beyond the level of compulsory education according to some definition of society's needs, while the "private demand approach" relies upon the demand for places in higher education institutions expressed by qualified individuals (Premfors, 1980). In his review of the policy behind Taiwan's development process, K.T. Li (1988), former Minister of both Finance and Economic Affairs of the ROC, has described in detail the evolution of manpower development planning in Taiwan. The official "Manpower Development Plan" was formulated in 1966 and heavily depended on advice from Western experts. It included projects to expand vocational education, to set up the "target ratio" between academic high school and vocational high school enrollments for different stages of economic development and to initiate the Science and Technology Development Program focusing on education and training at undergraduate and graduate levels (Li, 1988, pp. 83–91).

It is very clear that education is one element of the overall manpower policies in Taiwan and one of the instruments to push for economic growth. In another official document, the "Middle and Long Term Plan for Human Resource Development in Economic Construction in Taiwan: 1986–2000," the Council for Economic Planning and Development of the executive body makes specific suggestions, based upon economic considerations and human resource evaluations, that the Ministry of Education should regulate the access, content, and structure of education in accordance with the type and amount of manpower needed for economic development (CEPD, 1986). Such manpower policies and the centralized administrative system have enabled the Ministry of Education to regulate access to education, and to achieve official targets on the number of students enrolled at certain levels and in certain fields, for example.

So far there have been few studies on the physical contribution of the vocational-education-oriented strategy, among other centrally controlled educational policies, to Taiwan's overall economic development. Sun, former deputy director of the Council for Economic Planning and Development, and president of the leading National Taiwan University, specifically points out that the government's decision to put more emphasis on vocational education was made out of the considerations to (1) provide needed manpower to the labour market, and (2) moderate the keen competition for gaining admission to higher education (Sun, 1987, p. 4). However, the efficacy of

Taiwan's vocational education is yet to be evaluated. One study (Ma, 1988), adopting Harbison and Myers's (1964) model, proves that in Taiwan the correlation between GNP and the integrated education index is high (r = .67). However this finding fails to establish a cause-effect relation between education and economic development in the case of Taiwan. We could only confirm that a major function of Taiwan's education, from the viewpoint of the government's strategic planning, is to accommodate economic growth and to meet the needs of the labor market.

As the economy succeeds, Taiwan's educational policy is praised as "a case of successful planning." (Woo, 1991, p. 1029) However, scepticism also exists that "no firm conclusions can be reached about the economic efficiency of Taiwan's educational effort. Taiwan has invested fairly heavily in education, but whether the amount and the allocation of the investment provide an appropriate model for other developing countries is not clear" (Galenson, 1979, p. 399).

### Education to Maintain Political Stability and Cultural Identity

Confidence in the effect of education on economic growth is often accompanied by a similar confidence with regard to its effect on political development. Education is not only an agent of political development; in some cases, it is incorporated into the multi-dimensional political mechanism. "As is the state, so is the school," Coleman (1965, p. 6) so interprets this phenomenon, implying that schools are the forum for the political ideology of the state. Ironically, while education bears the power of shaping the political attitude of the public, education itself is usually shaped by its political context. Numerous studies have explored the relationship between education and politics. The earlier ones, following the approach of structural functionalism, usually confirm the contribution of schooling to democracy (Almond and Verba, 1965; Coleman, 1965). However, plenty of studies also question, if not refute, such optimism about the political function of education. Lipset (1981) contends that a high level of education is a necessary but not a sufficient condition of democracy. Kamens (1988) also notes that many of the taken-for-granted democratizing effects of education on individuals and society as a whole are not universal. It is, therefore, necessary to examine the particular role each educational system plays in its own social and political context before we can draw any general conclusion.

One consistent finding of various studies about the political function of education in Taiwan is that schools have been designated to fulfill the mission of maintaining political stability. Obviously this results from the fact that Taiwan has been separated from China for over forty years and that the state needs to maintain a stable political environment to secure its legitimacy. Education is one of the public domains that have been put under total governmental control. Wilson (1970), in his early study on political socialization of children in Taiwan, demonstrates how education has served as a stabilizing factor for political control. As he describes this phenomenon:

> In Taiwan considerable effort has successfully been expended through the educational system to reinforce a congruence between styles of authority in primary groups and those that exist between citizens and political leaders. Knowingly, or unknowingly, the patterns of authority that have been taught have been conducive to political stability. . . . Educational development has been characterized by a great mass of teachers cooperating effectively in inculcating in children support of the government. (1970, p. 146)

At all levels of education various measures have been adopted by the Ministry of Education to exercise political control over education. The centralized nature of educational administration as previously discussed is just one such example. Curriculum is another example. At the primary and secondary education level, curricular arrangements in all schools, public or private, have to observe the official "Curriculum Guidelines" (for primary schools, junior high schools, and senior high schools) which specifically mandate teaching hours, methods, goals, textbooks and objectives of each subject taught in schools. The textbooks, as stated earlier, are standardized and published by the National Institute for Compilation and Translation. The compilation of textbooks in each subject area have to follow and fulfill the specific "subject goals" set up in the general "Curriculum Guidelines." For instance, in the "Curriculum Guidelines for Primary Schools," the four general goals of the subject "Life and Ethics" (civics) are: (1) to foster a foundation of sound behavior; (2) to develop traditional mores and ethics; (3) to inspire patriotism and anti-communism; and (4) to cultivate students into good citizens (Ministry of Education, Taiwan, 1975, p. 15). For junior high schools, the "Curriculum Guidelines" sets the following as the primary goal for learning the subject of "Chinese": to guide students to continue their studies from primary schools, to enhance their life experiences, to inspire their thinking and reasoning abilities, to cultivate the concept of ethics, to inspire patriotism, and to promote Chinese traditional culture (Ministry of Education, Taiwan, 1985, p. 57). There is no doubt that cultivating patriotism and preserving traditional ethics among youngsters are two of the major functions of schooling.

From the foregoing description, it is clear that the government has deemed the fostering of a Chinese cultural identity among Taiwanese residents as a primary objective. The roots of the cultural identity lie in a Confucian heritage. In the face of the rapid industrial development and political separation from China, the government has been determined to restore a Chinese cultural heritage, both to demonstrate its culturally orthodox status and to work toward the long-term political goal of China's unification.

Martin, in her analysis of Taiwanese textbooks, concludes: "The Taiwanese Government is promoting a revitalization of the traditional Confucian system of social behavior and personal mores" (1982, p. 152). Her observations include: patterns of personal interaction in the Taiwanese textbooks appear to be hierarchical in nature, resting on traditional, ascriptive authority relations; the individual's focus is to the family unit; the role models appearing in textbooks are primarily traditional, historical persons. Another study which examines the curriculum guidelines shows that "most of the above mentioned subject goals aim at restoring traditional culture and imposing a sense of cultural linkage with and political loyalty to the fatherland. The affection for China as well as the knowledge about it (history, geography, language, etc.) are strongly emphasized while, on the other hand, little is mentioned about the land of Taiwan itself" (Young, 1992, p. 360). Altbach (1988) also notes that "(i)n Taiwan, issues relating to mainland China and to questions of independence for Taiwan are very sensitive. There seems to be relatively little research concerning Taiwan's history while most efforts are directed at Chinese topics. Research on specific Taiwan-related social issues must be handled carefully by scholars" (Altbach, 1988, p. 24).

Notwithstanding the fact that different studies have consistently pointed to the cultural and political functions of Taiwan's education system, one recent development worthy of attention is the effect of the strong public demand for reforms of educational policies. As described earlier, the overall political ecology of Taiwan has been greatly changed through reforms over the past decade. By and large the trend is toward democratization, liberalization, and the so-called localization: to put priority on securing the welfare of the twenty million residents of Taiwan over the once premier national goal of unification with China. One of the major consequences of this reform movement, as reflected in the education sector, is that authority is now committed toward developing a new set of curricula with greater emphasis on teaching local culture, dialect and history, which in the past were deliberately understated in the school curricula. This reform is obviously an epitome of the general political reform, demonstrating that, in Taiwan, education is shaped by its political context.

## Conclusions

In reviewing the evolution and development of Taiwan's education in its social/political context, one general conclusion we could draw here is that education in Taiwan has been a product of the government's central planning. Over the past decades those major educational policies that have dominated the content, process, ideology and institutions of education have been under total governmental control. From the government's point of view, education should serve the needs of the state, and be used to meet its social, economic and political goals. It is in this context that Taiwan has enjoyed such educational achievements as: a universal enrollment for the nine-year compulsory education, yearly increases in educational investment and rapid expansion of higher education. However, it is under the same policy that the operation of private schools, the professional autonomy of teachers and the participation of parents are constrained or even prevented. As a result, the pre-determined purpose that education should serve the state ensured that in the changing political and economic circumstances of Taiwan, questions about the relations between education and development could not always be comfortably or even consistently answered.

The discussions presented above suggest that we need to sort out the answer not by merely identifying a straightforward causal relationship, but by looking into the interwoven and interactive effect between education and development. The examination of educational policies against the background of Taiwan's economic development shows that the government has included education in its overall manpower development plan. The strategies used to execute the general principle of quantitative expansion were extending compulsory education and subsidizing higher education when the growth of the economy made this financially possible. In this regard, education can be viewed as an effect of economic growth in the early stage of development. The expansion of education in turn is expected to contribute to economic growth by providing well-trained manpower to serve the needs of industry. This is why the government started to enforce the vocational-education-oriented policy in the beginning of the 1970s, which is believed to have been one of the major contributors to the continuous growth in the following decade. However, the Chinese tradition that holds scholarly learning in high regard has made vocational education a second choice for the majority of the students. In other words, the dilemma here is not to decide on the cause-effect relationship between education and development, but to strike a balance between the demands of individuals and society as a whole.

The examination of the political function of education again addresses this problem. All of the evidence points to the conclusion that Taiwan's school system is subject to the state's control, and functions as a mechanism for political socialization. On the one hand, this device serves the state's interest to the extent that it has strengthened the regime's authoritarian rule through ideological control. On the other hand, the resultant long-term political stability, among other factors, has sustained economic growth. As Johnson (1987) convincingly argues, "(a)uthoritarianism can carry with it exceedingly damaging side effects, such as the suppression of human rights," but it is also one "that is only rarely accompanied by the trade-off of very high-speed, equitably distributed economic growth" (Johnson, 1987, p. 143). Huntington (1991) also notes that many authoritarian regimes have achieved "overall levels of economic development that provided an economic basis for democracy and that facilitated the transition to democracy" (Huntington, 1991, p. 59). In the case of Taiwan, the rapidly rising level of educational attainment of the public, which has been planned, supported and controlled by the government, has supported the emergence of a strong middle class that in turn has pushed for a more rapid process of democratization. It seems that education, initially a product of governmental planning, has gradually exerted a democratizing effect upon the society, and has become one contributor to the current political transition.

When Harbison (1967) asks the question "(s)hould education aim at satisfying the needs, desires and hopes of individuals, or should it be directed towards meeting the needs of the state," he himself points out that although the choice may be made in the light of a certain national philosophy, "the problem is not nearly so simple in the new, developing countries" (Harbison, 1967, p. 15). One problem revealed from Taiwan is that the goal of "development" may change as the social/political condition of a society changes. In the 1960s and 70s when most of "the new, developing countries" struggled to follow the developmental model of the then-developed Western countries (it was also the time when developmental theory prevailed in the international academic community), overall economic growth and industrial upgrading were the major goals which such countries sought. To a great extent, as Eisenstadt contends, "in many of the so-called new countries the goal of economic development is more of a political goal than a fact of economic life" (Eisenstadt, 1973, p. 73). Under that situation, education was not so much an end in itself as a means to reach the national goals of economic growth, and political stability conducive to such growth. However, as the concept of development has changed in more recent decades to a "human needs approach" which gives priority to individual welfare (Fågerlind and Saha, 1989, pp. 117–121), and coincidentally when the global democratic revolution has turned more than thirty countries all over the world, including quite a few East Asian societies, from authoritarian to democratic systems of government between the mid-1970s and 1990 (Huntington, 1991), the earlier view of development that gave legitimacy and praise to a strong state has been weakened. This is why the focal point of current public discussion of education in Taiwan is no longer about the efficiency of governmental planning, but more about the fundamental question of the legitimacy of governmental control. In other words, the changing notion of development has transformed people's evaluation of and expectations for education. It is only when education is examined against this changing social and political background that we can better understand and interpret its function, and its relationship with development.

# 6 South Korea

*Chon Sun Ihm*

## Introduction

This chapter presents an overview of how the formal school system has expanded in modern Korea, how it has been linked to industrial development and the problems and challenges it is facing. The discussion will deal with various policy changes that have affected schooling within the context of rapid industrialization and national development. A particular focus of the analysis is on how educational policy has been linked to human resources development. In this regard, the paper will deal with the problem of vocationalizing public education and examine the changes in the labor market status of recent graduates. The paper then examines recent policy reforms to restructure and diversify Korean secondary schools in an attempt to strengthen the link between schools and industrial needs. This is followed by a brief discussion of new issues and the prospects for Korea's future economic reforms.

## Economic Development and Industrialization in Korea

Economic conditions in Korea before the 1960s were extremely adverse. The colonization (1910–45) of Korea by Japan drained much of the nation's already meager resources, and the Korean War (1950–53) left much of the nation devastated. The division of the Korean peninsula into North and South divided raw materials, resources, production facilities and markets. Before the division, most natural resources and industrial facilities were located in the North. South Korea was left with only a few light industries and exports were insignificant.

Korea has been one of the fastest growing economies in the world during the past few decades. The average annual rate of real growth in GNP was 9.2% between 1962 and 1979. During the first (1962–66), second (1967–71), and third (1972–76) five-year economic development plan periods, the average annual growth rate of GNP was 7.8%, 9.7% and 10.1%, respectively. The real growth rate of GNP in 1987 was 12.2%, the highest in the world.

The effort to reconstruct the economy in the fifties from the ashes of the Korean War was carried out mainly with massive foreign economic aid. Entering the sixties, the government implemented an aggressive national development policy which was embodied in a series of five-year economic development plans. The export-oriented policy was officially implemented with the first economic development plan (1962–66). With the initial success of the plan, Korea was able to realize rapid growth of commodity exports. The volume of exports grew at an average annual rate of almost 40% during the period of the first five-year economic plan. The average rate of growth of exports between 1962 and the early 1980s was 35%.

Per capita GNP in real terms grew at an annual average rate of 1% prior to 1962. But real GNP per capita grew rapidly thereafter with the success of the export-oriented policy and decreases in the population growth rate from 2.7% to 1.6% (Kim and Park, 1985). The per capita GNP was $6,749 in 1992 (Table 1), compared with a mere $80 in 1962.

TABLE 1. Per Capita GNP

| | |
|---|---|
| 1962 | 80* |
| 1975 | 594 |
| 1980 | 1,592 |
| 1985 | 2,194 |
| 1990 | 5,659 |
| 1991 | 6,498 |
| 1992 | 6,749 |

*In current U.S. dollars.
Source: Bank of Korea.

The ratio of income from exports to GDP grew from 10.7% in 1970 to 18.8% in 1975, 22.7% in 1980 and 25% in 1982 (Lee et al., 1983). Most of the export increase came from the nation's rapidly expanding manufacturing sector. The share of total exports arising from manufactured goods rose from a mere 20% in 1962 to more than 90% in 1982. The growth of the manufacturing sector was particularly notable during the second (21.8%) and third (18.7%) plan periods. The share of GNP contributed by the manufacturing sector increased from 14.3 in 1962 to 30.9% in 1984.

The effect of this on employment was even more significant. The number of persons employed in export-oriented industries rose by four times (from 406,000 in 1970 to 2,112,000 in 1982), while that of total employment increased during the same period by about 80% (3,786,000 to 6,780,000). Initial efforts focused on simple household appliances and consumer products, which required a relatively simple level of skills and technology. Many products were sold with foreign product names.

In the mid-seventies, the government's development strategy focused on developing heavy and chemical industries. Table 2 below shows the changes in the composition of export commodities. As can be seen the reliance on light industries, such as textiles, was greatly reduced by 1983.

TABLE 2. Share of Commodities in Total Exports

| | *1970* | *1975* | *1980* | *1983* |
|---|---|---|---|---|
| Machinery | 7.4 | 13.8 | 19.7 | 32.2 |
| Electrical Machinery | 5.3 | 8.7 | 10.9 | 12.1 |
| Ship/Transport Equipment | 1.1 | 3.6 | 6.6 | 17.1 |
| Other Machinery | 1.0 | 1.5 | 2.2 | 3.0 |
| Iron and Steel | 1.6 | 4.6 | 9.4 | 7.5 |
| SUB-TOTAL | 9.0 | 18.4 | 29.1 | 39.7 |
| Textile/Clothing | 35.7 | 36.0 | 29.4 | 25.0 |
| Footware | 2.1 | 3.8 | 5.0 | 5.1 |
| Fishery Products | 4.9 | 7.1 | 3.9 | 3.0 |
| Others | 48.3 | 34.7 | 32.6 | 27.2 |
| TOTAL | 100.0 | 100.0 | 100.0 | 100.0 |

Source: Bank of Korea, *Economic Statistics Yearbook*.

As the table clarifies, the composition of heavy industries rose quite dramatically: machinery from 7.4% in 1970 to 32.2% in 1983; iron and steel from 1.6% to 7.5% in 1983. On the other hand, more traditional exports fell (e.g., fishery products from 4.9 to 3.0%) in the same period. Korea today is now known in the international community as a highly competitive producer and exporter of quality automobiles, semi-conductors, personal computers and other sophisticated electronic goods such as television sets, VCRs and so on. It is also known for having the world's most efficient steel plant and one of the largest shipbuilding industries. As such, the country was able to develop a broad and diversified manufacturing sector in the space of merely a few decades. The rate of economic growth was sustained during the first half of the seventies and surpassed an 11%

annual average rate. This was despite the worldwide recession after the oil crisis of 1973 and subsequent reductions in world trade resulting from the protectionist policies of the major industrialized nations. The economy was then subjected to the impact of the second oil crisis, leading to its first negative growth rate since 1962 and it experienced extremely high rates of inflation (at 30 to 40%) and a trade deficit of $5.3 billion. The worldwide recession continued into the early eighties, potentially threatening the export-oriented economy. Korea, however, was one of the few developing nations that was able to survive the adverse world market conditions in the eighties.

The achievements of the Korean economy have been attributed partially to the effective and flexible economic policies that the government formulated in a series of five-year economic development plans, which were launched from the early sixties. With few resources and technical know-how, the country invested in labor-intensive, low-technology, light industries in the initial stages. For example, in its aggressive effort to promote exports, the government provided various incentives for export industries, including a preferential tax system, credit subsidies, and exemptions from the tariff on imported raw materials used for producing export goods. There was also an abundant supply of educated and well-disciplined workers by the early sixties, and this inexpensive labor was easy to mobilize and train. The surplus labor kept wages low, enhancing the competitive advantages of Korean products in the world market.

The skeptics may point out that huge amounts of foreign aid had played a key role in stimulating growth. That is not a sufficient argument, however, because many other countries received large amounts of economic aid but did not effectively use it to stimulate the economy. Strong government control of the implementation of the development plans and perhaps large amounts of economic aid did contribute. But, in the opinion of many, it was investment in education that provided the springboard as well as the necessary support for the country's development.

## Education and Development in Korea

Modern schools were first introduced into Korea in the 1880s by Christian missionaries. A Royal Decree for Educational Reform in 1885 established modern state schools, including primary schools, and vocational schools in the capital (Seoul) and the provinces. Many private schools were also established around the country. However, during the Japanese colonial period from 1910 to 1945, Japanese education supplanted Korean schools and much of their identity was subsequently lost. The level of education access was minimal and only about 20% of the population were barely literate during this period.

The government adopted in 1949 a 6 (primary) –3 (middle ) –3 (high) –4 (college) ladder system based on the American model as the structure of the formal school system. The system went through numerous reorganizations to date (refer to Figure 1). Schooling in Korea now consists of four stages: primary (1–6), lower secondary (7–9), upper secondary (10–12) and higher education (13–16). High schools are divided into general (academic) and vocational high schools. Vocational education is provided mainly at vocational high schools and two-year technical colleges. However, prevocational courses are provided even at elementary schools as a part of general education. Practical arts education is required for all students at the elementary school for orientation toward the world of work, job and technology.

A distinct feature of contemporary Korean education has been the rapid quantitative expansion of provision in the post-war period. In 1945, when Korea was liberated from 36 years of Japanese colonial rule which followed more than a thousand years of dynastic rule, only 30 percent of children between the ages of 6 to 11 years were enrolled in schools and the use of Korean language had been banned during the 36 years of colonial rule (1910–45). Soon after, during the Korean War, virtually all of the few available school facilities were destroyed. The Japanese colonial policy of limiting educational access of Koreans kept the illiteracy rate to more than 90% of the relevant school-age children (Sohn, 1971). One of the ways in which this was done was by exercising strong control over the traditional village schools, called "Sudang." The restrictive policy of Japanese colonists effectively reduced the number of Sudang. There were 21,057 Sudang estimated to be in existence in 1923. These were reduced to fewer than 5,000 by 1940. Education in the post-liberation period (1945– ) was, therefore, inevitably geared to strengthening literacy education for adults as well as to expanding provision for school-age children. Many institutes were established and nearly 2.4 million people went through Korean language courses offered by these institutes. Civic schools were also established in 1946 to undertake similar tasks.

The massive national campaign for literacy was disrupted by the Korean War of 1950–53. However, classes were held in makeshift barracks and tents even during the war. The priority given to literacy education was also politically motivated as large numbers of voters could not read or write the names of candidates for public offices. This priority was well illustrated by a proposal for a literacy campaign submitted by the Ministry of Education prior to the election of members of the National Assembly. Illiter-

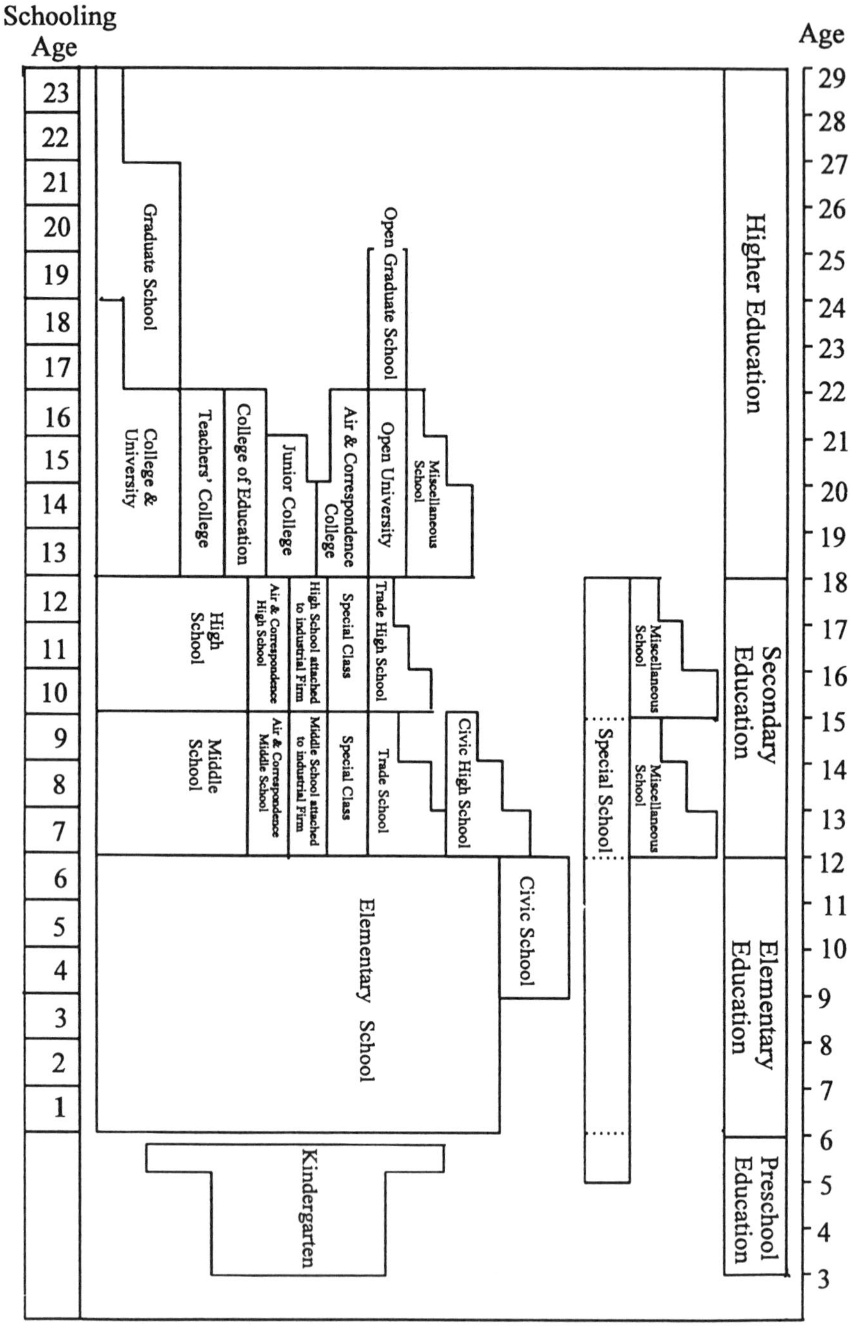


FIGURE 1. The School System in Korea (1992)

ate adults were required to attend literacy classes 70–90 days per year during off-farming seasons and to master rudimentary reading, writing and calculating skills. Through such efforts, the illiteracy rate of the population 12 years and over declined to 27.9% by 1960 from about 78% in 1945 (Choi and Baik, 1990). The efforts to achieve mass literacy were paralleled by a massive and rapid expansion of primary schooling. Universal enrollment in primary schools was achieved by 1960 and in secondary schools by 1980.

Today, the nation provides compulsory education up to primary school level and the most recent Seventh Five-Year Economic and Social Development Plan (1992–96) targets 1996 as the year to extend the compulsory years of schooling to the middle school level, equivalent to lower secondary school, at least for children in rural villages and counties. But, in reality, high school–level education is already universal, as about 90% of the relevant school-age population are graduating from high school, nationwide. As of 1993, the enrollment rate is over 100% for primary schools, 96.3% for middle schools, 90% for high schools, and 44.8% for tertiary education (Table 3).

TABLE 3. Enrollment Rate Changes by School Level (unit:%)

| *Year* | *Primary* | *Middle* | *High* | *Tertiary* |
|---|---|---|---|---|
| 1953 | 59.6 | 21.1 | 12.4 | 3.1 |
| 1955 | 77.4 | 30.9 | 17.8 | 5.0 |
| 1960 | 86.2 | 33.3 | 18.9 | 6.4 |
| 1965 | 91.6 | 39.4 | 27.0 | 6.9 |
| 1970 | 102.8 | 53.3 | 29.3 | 9.7 |
| 1975 | 106.1 | 72.6 | 41.8 | 10.3 |
| 1980 | 102.1 | 95.7 | 66.6 | 16.5 |
| 1985 | 101.0 | 101.0 | 79.0 | 35.1 |
| 1986 | 100.2 | 103.1 | 81.3 | 37.8 |
| 1990 | 101.4 | 97.8 | 87.6 | 38.1 |
| 1993 | 101.4 | 96.3 | 90.0 | 44.8 |

Note: Enrollment rate indicates percentage of students among the relevant school-age population.
Source: KEDI, *Educational Indicators in Korea*, 1993.

### *Education for National Development*

Korea has successfully implemented policies to link education as an integral part of the larger development strategies and especially to meet industrial manpower requirements. Below, the major educational policies which have attempted to link education to broader national development goals, and in particular to industrial manpower needs, are analyzed.

If the national policy on education was designed to induce development, an important part of the goals and content of the general education was designed deliberately to inculcate the values which were viewed as compatible with larger development objectives and with a deliberate effort to educate the individuals with an "industrial mentality." The development of the whole person, promotion of national identity, advancement of scientific mind and technological know-how, and moral maturity were the persistent themes throughout the various curriculum revisions.[1] The development of national identity has been regarded as very important in the light of the nation's unhappy historical past and political division. National identity education aimed at the development of students' understanding of the legitimacy of the nation and the inculcation of personal attitudes and a capacity to participate in improving national prosperity and development.

This was particularly evident during the period 1960–80 when the government attempted to justify its authoritative regime by emphasizing efficiency ("growth first" from early on, and "can do" slogans later). The development of positive, self-reliant and diligent persons was also emphasized in social campaigns, rural development education programs[2] and in the national curriculum of schools. The ruling elites and the development planners promoted a school curriculum which encompasses a combination of traditional values and industrial values (Kwak, 1990). In effect, the formal curriculum has fostered values and skills which are themselves conducive to developing an industrial mentality, productivity and growth—e.g., diligence, competition, and obedience. Consequently, a range of values such as entrepreneurship, achievement motivation and task-oriented personality has constituted the ideology of industrialization.

During the period of reconstruction in the later fifties, there was no apparent policy which was specifically geared toward national development, except for a massive expansion of formal schooling. Through massive literacy campaigns and with the implementation of compulsory primary education, a great reservoir of literate but unskilled workers became available to meet the demand of the manufacturing industries. As developmental planning became a key function of the government in the 1960s, human resources development became an integral part of overall developmental policies and planning. It was clear in the late sixties (during the second plan period) that the nation lacked a systematic means through which the skill requirements of the industry could be met. The significance of the policy switch in this period was that planners realized, for the first time, that formal education and vocational training should be provided on a more rational basis and based on the expected demand of manpower.

It was also realized that, as it takes a long time for education to have an effect, projections of manpower demand and related educational planning should be worked out on a long-term basis. Accordingly, the government produced the First and Second Manpower development plans as a part of the First and Second Five-Year Economic Development Plans. Then the government formulated and presented a twenty-year plan for long-term manpower supply and policy directions extending over the period 1967–86, which contained manpower supply-demand forecasts by industries, occupations and skills. This twenty-year plan is significant in that it presented a long-term blueprint and provided guiding principles for manpower development through education and occupational training.

In this regard, the deliberate effort to link national educational policy directly with industrial development has been an important and consistent feature of the developmental process. Through manpower forecasting, the government linked the training and supply of educated personnel to the specific needs of industry in each of the stages of Korean industrialisation. Under the strong control of the government, school enrollments were set, influenced by manpower planning goals, and explicitly stated in each of the five-year economic development plans from 1962. These were divided into sectoral plans, which included the education sector and manpower sector plans. As such, human resources development policies have been a vital element of the Five-Year Economic Development Plans and have provided the raison d'être for educational expansion and reform. As industry shifted from low-skilled labor-intensive industries toward export-oriented industries, human resources planning began to emphasize the training and supply of skilled manpower. Accordingly, the government increased investment in secondary school education with a strong vocational orientation.

### *The Vocationalization of Secondary Schools*

The seventies was the period when Korea launched its drive for the development of heavy and chemical industries. These industries began to require more skilled workers, and the government launched two very ambitious skills-training initiatives: the technical high schools and the public vocational training institutes. The training content of these two programs was almost exclusively to provide basic training to meet the emerging industrial needs.

Vocational high schools were given various kinds of institutional and financial support. The intensity of such support at national policy level was significant in changing the previously low public perception of agricultural, technical and commercial education.

There are five types of vocational high schools; agricultural, technical, commercial, fishery and marine, and home economics. With rapid industralization, the number of agricultural high school students has been gradually declining and this trend is expected to continue. On the other hand, technical high schools have been gradually expanded in order to meet technical manpower demands for industrialization. The number of commercial high school students accounts for more than 50% of the total number of vocational high school students and the number of female students has gradually increased at commercial high schools.

The shift toward capital-intensive industries in the seventies also brought new manpower needs and adjustments to manpower policy. This involved the need for qualitative improvements of technical education and an increase in the supply of middle-level technicians. Again, educational provision was adjusted following changes in central economic policy. Junior technical colleges, which offered two-year post–high school programs, were established. These focus on the training of middle-level technical and other para-professional workers. There were 128 such colleges, with a total of 174,964 students in 1993. They are grouped into technical, agricultural, fishery and marine, nursing, sanitation, commercial and business and so on. Most of the vocational colleges offer two-year programs, while others such as nursing colleges run for three years. In this way, the key changes to economic policy, such as the promotion of heavy and chemical industries in the seventies, were accompanied by adjustments to educational policy which emphasized training mid-level technicians by building two-year junior (vocational-technical) colleges in the seventies.

### *Other Policy Supports*

During the Third Plan period (1972–76), additional support measures were implemented by the government to improve the nation's human resources development system. These included the strengthening of vocational education in primary and secondary schools, as well as in vocational training centers. It was in this period that the National Technical Qualification Licence Law of 1973 was enacted. Under this new law, the national technical certification testing system was reorganized. The new legislation provided standard criteria for certification examinations. This was a first major step to incorporate the then loosely structured existing system into a single, formalized system. Furthermore, with the establishment of the Korea Skill Test Agency, various kinds of loosely organized examinations and certification systems for technicians and craftsmen were unified. It can be seen that the government took the initiative, during this period, devising drastic measures to support institutional, administrative and financial aspects of vocational education.

## The Expansion of Tertiary Education and the Paradox of Human Resources Development

The rapid expansion of enrollment in tertiary education institutions has been remarkable and consequently the opportunities for higher education have expanded massively in both absolute and relative terms. The tertiary education student population reached almost 1.7 million by 1993, as compared with 7,819 in 1945.[3]

As can be seen from Table 4, the number of students in tertiary education expanded dramatically in the 1950s, but slowed down in the 1960s and early 1970s. However, it jumped again in the late 1970s and in the early 1980s with the implementation of the (now defunct) graduation enrollment quota system. We shall return to this later.

Table 4. Quantitative Growth of Tertiary Education, 1945–93

| *Year* | *No. of Students* | *Ratio** |
|---|---|---|
| 1945 | 7,819 | 1.0 |
| 1950 | 11,358 | 1.5 |
| 1955 | 84,996 | 10.9 |
| 1960 | 101,041 | 12.9 |
| 1965 | 141,636 | 18.2 |
| 1970 | 201,436 | 22.7 |
| 1975 | 297,219 | 38.0 |
| 1980 | 615,452 | 78.7 |
| 1983 | 1,075,969 | 137.6 |
| 1985 | 1,277,828 | 163.9 |
| 1990 | 1,490,809 | 190.7 |
| 1993 | 1,687,222 | 215.8 |

Source: KEDI, *Educational Indicators in Korea, 1993.*
*Ratio of students with 1945 as base year.

The huge increase of tertiary education in the fifties was primarily due to the great enthusiasm for education that had been suppressed under the

Colonial regime (Kim, J., 1979). The policy of open entrance to higher education introduced in the fifties further accelerated the trend.[4] The drastic nature of the expansion can be seen more clearly if the changes in enrollment ratio of the college-age population (18–21-year-olds) are examined. College enrollment rates were 3.1% of the age group in 1953, 6.4% in 1960, 9.7% in 1970 and above 10% in 1975. However, the ratio increased rapidly in the late 1970s. The enrollment rate was 16.5% in 1980. But the big jump came in the mid-eighties to reach more than the 35% level. By 1993, 44.8% of the age group were enrolled in tertiary education.

The college enrollment quota system (maximum number of students by academic departments for each college and university in the nation) has been rigidly controlled by the government since the seventies. Under this system, student enrollments are set by the government with reference to the forecasted manpower demand of industries and the projected student demand for higher education (or social demand). The rigid application of this system in the seventies exaggerated the scarce value of college spaces and further fanned the competitive climate for college admission. The use of this approach, primarily based on manpower planning considerations, lost ground to the extremely competitive atmosphere of the college entrance examination race. This was reflected in the growth of examination repeater groups and an apparent shortage of college graduates, particularly in the sciences and engineering in the late seventies. The new military regime which came into power in 1981 moved to rapidly expand the enrollment quota, which resulted in a drastic increase in the number of students during the eighties. The measure was aimed at alleviating the accumulation of examination repeater groups and the extremely competitive atmosphere of the college entrance race (Kim, Y.C., et al., 1981). As the college enrollment ceiling was increased, an additional 30% and 15% of high school graduates were admitted to colleges and junior colleges, respectively. From 1980 to 1986, the enrollment rate doubled, with almost 38% of the school-age population attending colleges in 1986. By 1993, the proportion had further increased to 44.8%, with an expansion of enrollment quotas for engineering colleges and junior vocational colleges. The political and social pressures, as well as manpower considerations, resulted in a massive expansion of higher education. The motive behind the policy to continue to expand enrollment in tertiary education in this period was primarily a response to the ever-increasing social demand for college education, together with the recent enlargement of the quota for engineering students.

The sudden and drastic nature of the expansion had a significant effect on the labor market for educated workers. In this section, the discussion will focus on how the expansion of higher education has affected the status in the labor market of college graduates and also stimulated the competitiveness of the college entrance examination to a fever pitch.

The expansion of higher education created a surplus of graduates, resulting in a high rate of unemployment. As can be seen in Table 5, the output/supply of college graduates between 1965 and 69 decreased at an average yearly rate of 4% while employment increased at 0.7% during the same period. During 1970–79, the number of graduates increased at a rate of 7.3% per year, whereas employment in the economy generally grew at a rate of 9.9%. Clearly, employment opportunities were out-pacing the growth of supply. But since the 1980s, the number of college graduates has risen at an average rate of 17.4% compared to the increase of the average employment rate of 7.8% per annum. Supply has thus grown at a faster rate than the demand for educated manpower. In 1992 only 58% of college graduates were estimated to have found employment and the figure is even worse for female graduates.

Educational qualifications were, prior to the oversupply of graduates, the major criterion for selecting employees as employers "hoarded" workers with good college credentials, who were perceived to be in short supply. College graduates were perceived to possess certain professional characteristics such as clerical and/or managerial potential or ability. Credentials were commonly used as a minimum requirement in the first round of the selection process (Park, S., 1984; Kim, S., 1987). Selected individuals would then be subjected to further screening, such as tests or interviews, as well as considerations of their experience.

In the late 1970s, major firms competed to stock up on college graduates, and restrictions by the government on the enrollment quota served to fan social demand for higher education. In spite of rapidly growing industrial demand for college graduates, the Ministry of Education rigidly applied the enrollment quota system. The situation escalated because the wage gap between college and non-college graduates widened during the late seventies. The earnings ratio between all college males vs. all male workers during 1972–74 period was 1.85. This increased to 1.92 in the 1977–79 period. In contrast, high school graduates (males) vs. all workers (males) dropped from 1.05 in 1972–74 to 0.98 in the 1977–79 period (Park, S., 1984). This was due to the relative scarcity of college graduates. The widening gap in earnings was another signal which served to exaggerate the perceived value, and thus, the desire of high school students (and more important, their parents) to seek a college education.

TABLE 5. Changes in the Number of Tertiary Education Graduates and Employment

| *Year* | *Grads.* | *Increase(%)* | *Employed* | *Increase(%)* |
|---|---|---|---|---|
| 1965 | 36,180 | | 12,564 | |
| 1966 | 26,166 | -38.3 | 10,084 | -24.6 |
| 1967 | 22,338 | -17.1 | 10,123 | 0.4 |
| 1968 | 26,974 | 20.8 | 13,938 | 37.7 |
| 1969 | 22,648 | 18.9 | 12,659 | -10.1 |
| 1970 | 23,515 | 3.7 | 13,743 | 8.6 |
| 1971 | 27,168 | 15.5 | 14,448 | 5.1 |
| 1972 | 29,544 | 8.7 | 15,078 | 9.7 |
| 1973 | 28,776 | -2.7 | 16,139 | 7.0 |
| 1974 | 30,153 | 4.8 | 17,277 | 6.7 |
| 1975 | 33,610 | 11.5 | 19,635 | 14.0 |
| 1976 | 34,725 | 3.3 | 21,299 | 8.5 |
| 1977 | 37,374 | 7.6 | 22,087 | 3.7 |
| 1978 | 41,680 | 11.5 | 32,057 | 45.1 |
| 1979 | 45,424 | 9.0 | 29,378 | -9.1 |
| 1980 | 49,735 | 9.5 | 28,340 | -3.6 |
| 1981 | 55,846 | 12.3 | 28,524 | 0.6 |
| 1982 | 62,688 | 12.3 | 38,988 | 13.1 |
| 1983 | 77,272 | 23.3 | 38,489 | 13.2 |
| 1984 | 90,888 | 17.6 | 43,907 | 14.1 |
| 1985 | 118,584 | 30.5 | 48,552 | 10.6 |
| 1986 | 137,848 | 16.2 | 51,667 | 6.4 |
| 1965–69 | | -4.0 | | 0.7 |
| 1970–79 | | 7.3 | | 9.9 |
| 1980–86 | | 17.4 | | 7.8 |
| 1965–86 | | 7.9 | | 7.5 |

Source: MOE, Korea (1987), *Statistical Yearbook of Education*, 1965–86.

The outcome was an accumulation of a large pool of repeaters for the college entrance examination. As Table 6 below shows, there were 194,916 applicants for admission for an enrollment quota of only 56,580 college places in 1974. Among the applicants, 130,734 were 1974 high school graduates and 64,182 were repeaters, who had graduated from high schools in previous years. The number of exam repeaters increased to about 183,000 in 1980. Their predicament emerged as a major political and social issue.

TABLE 6. Number of College Applicants and Repeaters

| Year | 1974 Grads. | Exam Repeaters | Enrollment Quota |
|---|---|---|---|
| 1974 | 130,734 | 64,182 | 56,580 |
| 1976 | 177,466 | 76,211 | 60,555 |
| 1978 | 202,649 | 117,184 | 76,410 |
| 1980 | 317,606 | 183,909 | 205,835 |
| 1982 | 478,854 | 238,893 | 305,190 |
| 1984 | 431,875 | 249,914 | 323,678 |
| 1986 | 420,919 | 233,543 | 311,044 |
| 1988 | 598,781 | 340,757 | 296,820 |
| 1990 | 774,831 | 485,366 | 339,290 |
| 1991 | 801,873 | 548,460 | 347,100 |
| 1992 | 799,348 | 570,959 | 375,090 |

Source: MOE, Korea (1993).

The new military regime opted hastily in 1981 to increase the enrollment quota, to accommodate the explosive demand for college places and to deal with the problem of entrance examination repeaters. Part of the reason for the government's sudden decision to ease enrollment restriction was politically motivated as the repeaters seemed to be a major source of political opposition and social unrest. In effect, the pronounced scarcity (not in competitive terms, but in terms of demand from students, and from employers) of college graduates in the late seventies and continuing social, as well as political, pressures to deal with the problem of repeater groups have led to subsequent upward readjustments of the college enrollment quota in 1981.

The measure adopted in 1981 was too drastic and abrupt. The changes in the quota were made with little consideration of their potential impact upon the future labor market. Students entering college after the 1981 expansion of the college enrollment quota were due to graduate in 1985. Consequently, the unemployment rate among college graduates greatly increased. Table 7 shows the deteriorating employment conditions of college graduates. By 1985, the employment rate of college graduates had declined to 52% and the problem has continued to date. The reasons for this rise in unemployment among college graduates were the sudden increase in the supply of college graduates in 1981 and the cyclical downturn of the economy in the early eighties. The economy began recovering in the late eighties. Yet the high unemployment rate of college graduates has not receded and the problem persists.

TABLE 7. Employment Trends Affecting Four-Year Graduates

| *Classification* | *1975* | *1980* | *1985* | *1990* | *1992* |
|---|---|---|---|---|---|
| No. of graduates (A) | 33,610 | 49,735 | 118,584 | 165,916 | 178,631 |
| No. into grad schools (B) | 2,179 | 6,088 | 12,302 | 12,795 | 14,040 |
| Enlisted in military (C) | 4,076 | 4,796 | 13,163 | 7,831 | 6,897 |
| Employed (D) | 19,635 | 28,349 | 49,744 | 84,658 | 91,438 |
| Unspecified | 7,720 | 10,502 | 45,627 | 65,598 | 66,256 |
| No of grads entering market (E)=(A)–(B+C) | 27,335 | 38,851 | 95,371 | 150,256 | 157,694 |
| Employment Rate (D) / (E) % | 71.8 | 73.0 | 52.2 | 56.3 | 58.0 |

Source: MOE, Korea (1993).

*The Paradox of Human Resources Development*

The labor market for educated workers in Korea has recently been characterized as being in a paradoxical state: there is a shortage of lower-level skilled and temporary workers, and a surplus of white-collar workers. There is also a structural imbalance between the demand for graduates in the scientific and technical fields, on the one hand, and the excessive supply in the area of non-technical and liberal arts, on the other. This is despite the fact that the government intervenes in the admission process by setting quotas for different program fields, based on forecasts of demand and supply. The government revised its quota for different fields of higher education in the early seventies. Science and technology fields, such as engineering and basic sciences, were given an increased quota. This was in recognition of the expected shortages of science and technology manpower.

When the new enrollment quota policy was implemented, many private universities (two-thirds of all existing colleges and universities in Korea) preferred to enlarge enrollment in the humanities and social sciences over natural sciences and engineering colleges. This is because of the high cost of establishing or expanding facilities in the latter. From the point of view of a private university, it is much easier and less expensive, thus more profitable, to increase the enrollment in humanities and social sciences than it is in natural sciences and engineering fields of government specification. As a result, the share of engineering college students remained constant at 21.3% between 1975 and 1987, while the numbers studying literature and social sciences have increased quite substantially over the same period: 14.9% and

17.9%, respectively, in 1975 and 20.7% and 28.5%, respectively, in 1987 (Kim, S. 1987). Consequently while the overall rate of unemployment of college graduates has risen, the shortage of engineering and technical graduates has been aggravated. Students leaving high schools still choose to study social sciences in college despite the fact that there is a high level of unemployment of social science graduates and a shortage of engineering graduates. In the meantime, the gross contraction of employment opportunities for highly educated workers and the critical shortage of technical and skilled manpower continues.

The basic cause of this paradox is the exaggerated expectations from and demands for college education. Formal secondary education has been reduced to a vehicle to prepare pupils for the college entrance examination. Parents demand that schools focus on teaching only the subject matter that is relevant for the college entrance examination, at the expense of education for other important purposes, including that necessary for future employment. Presumably this is a rational decision on the part of parents and pupils in terms of job prospects and future earnings. Indeed, the impact of the college entrance examination system is one of the most crucial problems facing Korean education, threatening the once productive role of school education, particularly secondary school education.

In future, an industrial society will require individuals who can reason quickly and critically, be creative, communicate effectively, lead and serve society and socialize. But what is happening in the classroom remains oblivious to such needs. Educators fear that education has been reduced mainly to memorizing simple factual information. It is important that students at an earlier age be given some basic knowledge and practical skills to enhance their employability upon graduation. Students at early ages should be exposed to some type of vocational and technical training and an appropriate time to do this is in their middle or high school years. However, motivating the students to do so is not easy. Given the pervasive desire to go to college, there indeed is a great waste of human resources currently in Korean schools.

Only about two-fifths (actually 44.8%, as in Table 4) of all high school graduates go to colleges and universities. The remaining three-fifths either enter the labor market or reapply the following year. Meanwhile, those who fail to enter college suffer from having to redirect their focus on resitting the college entrance examinations or taking their chances for employment. The majority of non-college-bound high school graduates are not prepared for employment and would have benefited more if middle and high school curricula included some occupational preparation. Despite the important role the vocational education institutions have played in the earlier periods of economic growth in the sixties and seventies, these institutions in more recent years have failed to attract enough students. Students evade vocational high schools, an issue that we discuss further below.

*Problems of Vocational Educational Institutions*

Vocational high schools are institutions built with a specific mission: to prepare students for employment. However, despite many policies designed to improve the curriculum over the past decades they have experienced serious problems, especially with respect to the relevance and quality of the curriculum.[5]

A wide disparity exists between the technical or vocational competence demanded by industry and the training students receive from vocational educational programs. Individual employers complain that technical high schools do not train competent technicians who can work in factories as soon as they graduate. The utilization of the graduates of vocational programs presents a general problem. There are also specific criticisms that the knowledge and skills they learn in vocational high schools are outdated and do not keep up to date with the changes occurring in the workplace.

In the earlier periods, the low rates of employment of vocational high school graduates were a problem. In 1966, only 37.5% of vocational high school graduates were employed. After some fluctuation in the seventies and the early eighties, the rate rose to 63.3% in 1987. This was an increase of 7.6% from 1986 and 25.8% from 1966. The rate of employment in recent years has improved, at least at the initial entry point immediately upon graduation. This is especially true for the technical high school graduates. But recent studies (e.g., Ihm et al., 1992, 1993) indicate that many graduates do not stay long in their first job. This seems to be a result of poor working conditions, lack of promotion opportunities and a distaste for menial and repetitive tasks, which do not necessarily require three years of technical education at high schools. Ideally, technical high schools should be provided with a broad theoretical knowledge so that they can adapt themselves to situational variations of skill requirements. But this has not been the case.

Some employers also prefer and are more willing to hire those who complete courses at vocational training centers[6] rather than technical high school graduates, because the duration of the training in high school programs is three years and yet there is perceived to be little difference in the level of skill of the graduates of the two institutions (Kim, S., 1987). More recent surveys (Ihm et al., 1992, 1993) show mixed preference by employers for the vocational high school graduates and training center completers.

In practice, technical high schools offer a mixture of both general education to prepare pupils for college entrance and vocational training for employment. In trying to accomplish both, they cannot fully achieve either of their objectives. Furthermore, there is not really a clear role distinction between the training function of technical high schools and that of vocational technical colleges, which were built to meet the demands for mid-level technicians from heavy and chemical industries in the 1970s. Another problem is that there is still a widespread reluctance among middle school graduates to enter vocational high schools. The number of students enrolled in vocational high schools has been declining in recent years.[7] In 1987, for example, overall vocational high school enrollment was barely met with 98.2% of the target enrolled. For agricultural high schools, the ratio was as low as 86.3%.

There are many reasons for such a decline in student enrollment. The limited opportunities for vocational high school graduates to advance to tertiary education, particularly into four-year universities, and the large wage differentials between college graduates and high school graduates in the labor market (see Table 8) have certainly affected the desire of students to seek enrollment in these schools. There is also the persistent perception that a humanities (general) education is superior to a vocational one because of the greater prospects of advancement to higher-level education.

TABLE 8. Wage Levels by Educational Attainment Level

| *Year* | *Middle Sch. Graduate* | *High Sch. Grad.* | *Jr. Coll. Grad.* | *4-year Coll. Grad.* |
|---|---|---|---|---|
| 1976 | 59.1 | 100.0 | 145.3 | 229.7 |
| 1979 | 65.9 | 100.0 | 147.6 | 230.7 |
| 1982 | 69.9 | 100.0 | 130.7 | 221.6 |
| 1985 | 74.7 | 100.0 | 129.8 | 226.5 |
| 1988 | 82.1 | 100.0 | 121.1 | 202.7 |
| 1991 | 84.6 | 100.0 | 117.4 | 179.2 |

Note: Wage level of high school graduate = 100.
Source: Ministry of Labor, South Korea, *Report on Occupational Wage Survey.*

Despite improvements in the vocational colleges, they face similar problems. These are typically associated with higher education institutions, which mainly provide short-term vocational courses. Vocational colleges were originally intended to train highly competent middle-level technical manpower. However, this has not been the result. The low social status, low employment rate of graduates, and lack of recognition by parents—who would much prefer that their children enter four-year colleges—meant that people rated the alternatives to junior vocational colleges more highly. Few students who apply to vocational colleges have a strong commitment to the program, most students entering because they could not get access to a four-year university course. Also, most professors teaching in vocational colleges are themselves graduates of four-year universities. They tend to teach students (with regard to both subject area and method) in the style they became familiar with at university. Further, most professors in the vocational colleges have no experience in their fields, do not know how technicians in the field perform a task, and do not know what knowledge and skills are needed to perform the job. These problems and limitations are usually reflected in the quality of the curriculum and teaching methods used in these colleges.

### *Recent Policy Reforms: The Restructuring and Diversification of Secondary Schools*

In recognition of the problems and constraints outlined above, the government recently introduced various measures to strengthen the vocational education and training system. The most distinctive of these has been the restructuring of the whole secondary school system to achieve a greater vocationalization. In 1991, the government called for a major revision of the secondary education system to strengthen vocational and technical education. The policy goal was double-edged. First, it attempts to reduce the abnormally competitive climate of the college entrance examination by directing more students on to the vocational track and away from the humanities. Second, the vocationalization of secondary schools was a new response to the call from industrialists for an increase in the number of skilled workers produced by schools during a period of persistent shortage of production workers. This was in fact a new effort to link the needs of industries to secondary school education.

Apart from increasing the proportion of students following the vocational track, special vocational classes have been introduced into general high schools for humanities track students who want a vocational education. Boards of education are encouraging general high schools to establish more vocational classes and have financed them generously since 1988. The major objective is to provide students on the humanities track with the opportunity to explore a wide range of careers and to provide vocational skills for employment before graduation. An effort is also being undertaken to improve and modernize the system of commercial high schools. The government is also encouraging private firms to establish in-plant training programs. This is to reduce the government's role in training the technical manpower and providing for an increased role by the private sector.

Many of these measures are direct responses by the government to the call from industry for a greater vocationalization of schools. Yet the road to vocationalization is riddled with obstacles and controversies. There is, of course, the difficulty of providing massive funds for costly facilities and equipment for existing and new vocational schools. There is also the basic controversy surrounding the justification and validity of "hoarding" children on to the vocational track against the widespread sentiment of the parents and students who favor the humanities track leading, they believe, to university education. Most fundamental is the inherent contradiction of the situation that in expanding vocational/technical education, the government is investing in that sector of education which seems to have the lowest rate of economic return, if salaries can be taken as an accurate reflection of productivity.

### Prospects and Challenges

Despite these reservations and the paradoxical situation of human resources development, there is no doubt that the nation's rapid economic development has been supported by the educational system which has provided the human resources which have contributed to the export-oriented industrialization in the past few decades. What distinguishes Korea from many other developing countries is the way in which investment in general educational provision was made early on, after liberation, and well before the development of the economy. This was later augmented by the more deliberate attempt to make specific investments in technical education, as the primary vehicle for fostering development after the sixties. The post–Korean War campaign to eradicate illiteracy at all levels seems to have laid the foundations for economic development. This educational base supported economic development, particularly in the early phases of industrial growth.

The literacy base of the workforce was further augmented with more deliberate investment by the government to provide technical/vocational training in the period of rapid industrialization in the seventies and beyond. In this process, the provision of education programs, as well as the development of the economy, was pursued primarily through highly interventionist central control of educational policy.[8] This included the adoption of a manpower planning approach to educational provision, particularly since the early sixties, with the launching of the five-year economic development plans. Consequently, the policy of linking education to industrial requirements was instrumental in training and supplying employers with, at first, a large number of semi-skilled workers, and subsequently middle-level technicians. This was of course facilitated by the tight control of the government over the nature of the major shifts which occurred in the economy.

However, these attempts to link educational provision to the perceived needs of the economy have resulted in some severe mismatches in more recent years. The manpower planning approach (fit people to specific jobs) was perhaps in the case of Korea an effective instrument of human resource development in the earlier stages of industrialization and growth (i.e., in the sixties and perhaps in the seventies). However, subsequently, the rigid manpower planning approach has probably outlived its usefulness. There are strong signs of the limitations of rigid manpower planning, particularly at the higher education level. The return to investment in higher education, especially technically oriented courses, may have become negative, as evidenced by the serious levels of unemployment of college graduates. It has also contributed to the provision of highly specialized and rigid school tracks.

More recently, the mismatch in the employment prospects of manpower and the severe competition for college entrance have raised the need for a serious reappraisal of the role of the existing system of education as a vehicle for human resource development. The training of manpower has been the responsibility of the formal educational system, which has played a valuable and responsive role when the industrial and occupational structure of the nation depended primarily on a labor force with relatively simple skills and a basic level of education. Clearly the export-led growth strategy was effective and successful in the early stages of growth. The labor-intensive industries which formed the backbone of the industrial structure in the initial phases of economic takeoff were transformed into more technologically based industries. Looking ahead, one can expect that the nation's export sector will continue to play the leading role, whereas its domestic market must accept more foreign competition under increased pressures to liberalize imports.

Furthermore, with an increasing sophistication of industrial processes and deepening skill requirements in the future, the demand for production workers, with low levels of skills which the nation's secondary vocational schools have provided in the past, will decline. In contrast the demand for high-level technological manpower will increase. These prospects suggest that the importance of high and middle-level technical workers (engineers and technicians) will expand significantly. In particular, the demand for high-level science and technology-related manpower will greatly increase. In the meantime, the current problem of a shortage of semi-skilled and unskilled workers on industry's production lines remains.

What emerges therefore is the continuing challenge of enlarging the base of skilled and middle-level technical workers, while at the same time producing a large number of high-level technical or professional workers. This challenge will further increase the pressure for expanding opportunities for higher education. This calls for an assessment of the existing student quota policy and a commitment to allow greater autonomy to individual institutions of higher education. This is a delicate matter, however, since the expansion of the quota for higher education is the major cause of the problem of unemployment among highly educated workers.

The restructuring process also requires an updating of the skill requirements of workers in both the initial and retraining stages. But this poses the question as to whether schools—rather than the industries themselves—should be training workers. In many countries, this is the job of employers. There is a limit to what formal schools can do to continue to update the ever rapidly changing skill and work requirements of the industries. Such a task is difficult for the public sector to perform for a number of reasons.

A critical reappraisal and assessment is now necessary as to how the human resources role of the formal school system should be altered and modified to meet changing demands. In this regard, the role of public agencies in the development of human resources should be reestablished and their roles should be redefined. High technology industries require a continuous updating of skill and knowledge for which formal schools, even vocational ones, are inadequately prepared. It is the private sector's role to update and deepen skill levels and training requirements of entering workers, with only initial or preliminary training completed in the formal schools.

## Notes

1. The common curriculum was offered to all children for a given period of compulsory education in the formal education system. The first official national curriculum was enacted in 1954. Since 1954, there have been five completed revisions. The most recent (sixth) revision cycle began in 1992.

2. Another noteworthy feature was the national rural education campaign of the Saemaul Undong (New Community Movement) launched in the 1970s by the government. The movement began with the goal of modernizing rural villages with a focus on the improvement of the rural areas. It was essentially a cultural reform movement to awaken the sense of industriousness, self-reliance and cooperation among rural Koreans. The movement was later expanded to include even urban areas. It had a significant impact on changing the attitudes of people in the cities. In Kwak's (1990) terms, the movement seems to be a revitalized collectivism of traditional values within the context of rapid industrialization.

3. Here, tertiary education population includes those attending two-year junior colleges and graduate schools, but those attending four-year colleges alone recorded more than one million.

4. The privilege of special exemption from military service to those enrolling in four-year colleges has further fanned the enthusiasm for college enrollment.

5. The curriculum of vocational high schools offers various types of general and vocational subjects. The principal in each of the different types of vocational high

schools determines the ratio for the two subject areas in a range between 20% : 80% and 40% : 60%. In general the former is devoted to learning general subjects and the latter gives equal weight to theory and practice. Before graduation, all students are required to complete an in-plant apprenticeship ranging from one to three months. Quite recently there has been a national plan to expand the in-plant apprenticeship to one year out of the three years of high school.

6. The passage of the Vocational Training Act in 1967 launched full-fledged vocational training programs. The training centers were established to respond to the demand for skilled workers augmenting the function of vocational high schools. The legislation permitted establishment of two types of training programs: public vocational training offered by the central and local government and in-plant vocational training provided by private firms.

7. In the case of commercial high schools, the number of students has not changed as much as in other schools. This is because the budget requirements for facilities needed in laboratory work and practice are relatively small in commercial high schools, compared with other types of schools.

8. The policy of central planning evident in the economic sector was also evident in the planning and provision of education. Manpower planning was used to identify the needs of industry and education was expanded to fulfill those needs. The rapid industrialization and the subsequent shift to high-technology manufacturing seem to have been supported by the quantity and type of educational provision. However, more recent decisions to expand tertiary education have also been at least in part a response to political pressures.

# 7 MALAYSIA

*Hena Mukherjee and Jasbir Sarjit Singh*

## INTRODUCTION

The relationship between education and development in Malaysia cannot be examined solely in terms of linear economic growth. Rather, as two key policy statements below demonstrate, development is viewed multidimensionally with the role and contribution of education varying accordingly.

The theme of building a unified nation is a primary focus of all development plans:

> . . . education and training will continue to be geared towards fostering national unity and increasing participation of all Malaysians in national development. (5MP[1], 1986).

Emphases on other aspects of Malaysia's developmental task find expression in terms of human resource development goals to meet economic growth requirements, as well as the growth of a society attitudinally oriented to the goals of modernization.

> . . . . the role of education and training in Malaysia is to produce knowledgeable, trained, and skilled individuals to meet the manpower requirements as well as the growing social needs . . . [we] require manpower to be innovative and equipped with knowledge and training in science and technology, management, and related skills. Equally important is the need for the national education system to mould disciplined, diligent and motivated individuals. (6MP, 1991)

At each stage of development the authorities in Malaysia have resorted to education as the vehicle to either reinforce the status quo or to spearhead social change. In common with other developing countries in the post-war years Malaysia has selected education as one of the principal instruments for change and development. Taking lessons from Japan and other newly industrializing countries Malaysia set itself targets to achieve a modern and technologically developed society. Educational reform has been given high priority and since independence changes have been witnessed on many fronts: goals, structure, medium of instruction, curriculum, pedagogy and evaluation.

The Malaysian economy, based on primary products, chiefly rubber, tin, timber, and more recently oil and manufactured goods, has encouraged Malaysia to design an educational system that meets the needs of the economy. From the early development plans the concentration on producing the right manpower is evident, with attempts to gear the educational system towards producing manpower for modernization and economic growth.

At the same time, Malaysia's complex socio-political and demographic milieu has forced the debate on other national priorities to the forefront. Thus, while economic growth is a target, and an expanding economic pie has always been seen as the means to facilitate the achievement of its social restructuring objectives, the overarching objectives of development arise from its local context—the need to weld together a multi-ethnic and a multi-lingual population into a cohesive social entity. The government's strategy for achieving national unity is based on a multicultural model, the principal components of which have been declared to be the creation of a core of commonly ascribed values, the preservation of some degree of cultural diversity, and the attainment and maintenance of socioeconomic parity.

The development process in Malaysia and its outcomes can perhaps be best understood by non-Malaysians in terms of the social and cultural framework within which political decisions are made and which affects implementation in all sectors. The highly centralized, top-down, interventionist style of the government in post-independent Malaysia is effectively the outcome of a system of one-party rule. Although opposition political parties demonstrate an adversarial political style in the tradition of Westminster, the overt operational mode has been generally a consensual one, governed by pragmatic considerations in the interests of inter-ethnic harmony and political stability.

The thrust of development policies viewed from the citizen's experience of implementation demonstrates a concentration on achieving faster rates of economic growth, greater diversification of agriculture and industry, the creation of increased employment opportunities and the raising of the living standards of the rural population. Cutting across these development objectives is the high priority given, after the 1969 racial riots, to improving the disadvantaged lot of the indigenous people or the Bumiputeras. In operational terms this meant assisting them to become more competitive and to achieve a social and economic position comparable or superior to that enjoyed by other ethnic groups in the country. Education is seen as one of the pivotal instruments for achieving these goals.

Outcomes have not always matched goals and, to some extent, strategies and implementation processes have given rise to results that are sometimes at variance with the aims of national unity and equity. By way of illustration, the issue of sponsored higher education for the indigenous population has bred inter-ethnic resentment as well as intra-ethnic disparities which are issues discussed later in this chapter.

The implementation process is characterised by crucial interventions on behalf of the indigenous population by the ruling government, such as: quotas for university places and jobs, scholarships and awards for local and overseas education and training, favourable treatment under licensing and franchising regulations, state subsidies, concessional loans and grants to enter industry and trade as well as privileged access to capital markets. Government interventionist policies in education and training were planned as support measures for the major economic developmental goal—that of eradicating rural poverty by enhancing agricultural output and of enlarging the industrial base in urban areas. By limiting access and resources in educational and economic terms primarily to the indigenous population, which excludes close to 45% of Malaysia's citizenry, from this particular equation, the long-term negative impact of such a large-scale wastage of human resources is evident to planners and members of all ethnic groups. Equally evident is the fact that opposition to such strategies has not been sufficient to block policies from being implemented. The public face of the development process therefore shows a high level of consensus and support for the government's interventionist measures.

A culture of acceptance of far-reaching policies made by a small group of decision-makers has marked the response of the populace to the implementation of change. To date, in terms of economic growth, this seeming passivity appears to have worked, although its success, in terms of the equitable distribution of economic goods, is questionable. To political leaders elsewhere whose development plans are disrupted by internal unrest, this is an enviable position to be in. Generally, the acceptance of planned disadvantages by the large majority can be explained in two extremely simplified ways. Malaysians of Chinese and Indian origin but who are third or fourth generation Malaysians regard Malaysia as their home, and unless strong ties exist, are conscious that the Chinese mainland and the Indian sub-continent are not viable locations for their permanent domicile. Their acceptance of what may elsewhere be termed as discriminatory policies are taken as a recognition of political realities. Second, the extent to which the non-indigenous communities acquiesce in interventionist policies has also depended on the state of the economy. With favorable economic growth patterns where there is sufficient pie for all, going along with government policies does not seem to be a painful proposition. The acid test of a long-term recessionary economy might change the situation. One also should not underestimate the value of being able to practise one's religion and to keep to communal cultural mores, both allowing for an important and functional framework of personal and community freedoms.

This chapter discusses, within the constraints of space, what are perceived as the major efforts made by those responsible for national development policies and plans. Account is not taken of alternatives put forward by individuals and non-mainstream groups primarily because they are not seen by the writers as having any appreciable impact on the forces of change that the ubiquitous and powerful government machinery has pursued. The focus for the chapter therefore is the extent to which education and training have contributed to Malaysia's developmental process and the nature of that contribution.

Our investigation leads us to the conclusion that Malaysia's membership in the group of rapidly growing East Asian economies is not an instance of serendipity nor due only to extraordinarily successful leadership, planning and implementation. Rather it has resulted from a combination of private economic enterprise, which flourished in an infrastructure inherited from the colonial period, and government intervention. This chapter maintains that the latter is largely responsible for the pattern and shape of Malaysia's current socioeconomic landscape and provides an important source of explanations for the nature of policies, their implementation and outcomes. The supportive role of education and training in the developmental process is emphasized by the focus given in the country's strategies of implementation to three major policy instruments: institution building, fiscal policy management featuring large-scale subsidy programs, and a major program of land development and settlement (Mehmet, 1988). To reduce rural poverty, for instance, several land development schemes were established along with attendant institutions. These include the Federal Land Development Authority (FELDA), Federal Land Consolidation and Rehabilitation Authority (FELCRA) and the Rubber Industry Small Holders Development Authority (RISDA). State enterprises and public corporations were set up to deal with every sector of development including banks and financial institutions as well as the needs of the rapidly expanding manufacturing sector.

In this chapter, the complexity of the relationship between education and development in Malaysia is reflected in selected illustrative examples which mirror cases where education provides the foundation for growth;

where it is the principal means of changing social structure; where it is one of several supportive components of development mechanisms; or where it provides a common framework for diverse elements of growth.

## The Country's Background

Malaysia comprises Peninsular Malaysia with 40% of the total land area and the states of Sabah and Sarawak on the island of Borneo, which account for the remaining 60%. In 1990 the population was 17.1 million, of which 14.6 million or 82% lived in Peninsular Malaysia and 2.5 million or 18% lived in Sabah and Sarawak. In the Peninsula Malays and other indigenous groups known as ***Bumiputeras***, "sons of the soil," comprise 58.2% of the total population, 31.3% Chinese, 9.8% Indians and about 0.7% termed others. In the States of Sabah and Sarawak, Bumiputeras constitute 85% and 71%, respectively, of the population, the rest being predominantly Chinese. About 45% of the population in Peninsular Malaysia, 21% in Sabah and 26% in Sarawak live in urban areas.

### *Colonial Legacies*

Malaysia's current national development objectives have been influenced by legacies from its British colonial experience (1786–1957):

- The most important colonial legacy is the plural society of modern Malaysia. During the first four decades of the twentieth century, British immigration policy transformed a homogeneous Malay society into a heterogeneous society. By 1957, Malays comprised 49.8% of the population, Chinese 37.2% and Indians 11.3%. The population today retains its multi-ethnic character and the integration of its diverse population groups has assumed primary importance in the building of the post-independent Malaysian nation.
- Early efforts at urbanization and industrialization reinforced the existing ethnic divisions. The indigenous and rural-based Malays continued to work predominantly in the low-wage agricultural sectors while the immigrant Chinese and Indians were perceived as enjoying the fruits of modernization, thus creating both vertical and horizontal social divisions.
- In the economic arena the country inherited a classic export economy concentrating on the production and export of a few primary commodities: primarily rubber and tin. The heavy dependence on the export earnings of these commodities and the vagaries of the international commodity markets made it imperative for Malaysia at independence to seek new avenues for economic growth, and to plan for a supply of labor possessing appropriate skills.
- The new nation also inherited a communication infrastructure of

roads, railways and telecommunications, a civil service and other essential services that were required for the smooth functioning of Malaysia's export trade. This has been maintained and augmented.

## Development Trends

Malaysia's growth has been quite impressive in the thirty years since independence. In the first decade, covering the period of the Second Malaya Plan and the First Malaysia Plan (1961–70) an average annual growth rate in real GDP of 6.4% was recorded. In the second decade covering the Second Malaya Plan and the Third Malaysia Plan (1971–80) an annual growth rate in GDP of 7.0% was experienced. During the 1980s, the period of the Fourth Plan (1981–85) the growth rate fell but held at around 5.8% annually. For most of the Fifth Plan period (1986–90) growth was sluggish at around 4% annually. However before the end of the decade there were signs of an upturn in the economy and since 1988 the economy has steadily improved: in 1988 growth in real terms was 8.9% and for 1989 and 1990 growth was 8.8% and 9.4%, respectively (Mahathir Mohamad, 1991, p. 10).

The modern sectors of the economy—manufacturing, wholesale and retail trade—spearheaded development. The share of the agricultural, forestry, livestock and fishing sectors' contribution to GDP gradually shrank, while the shares of mining and manufacturing have increased significantly. The primary sector's contribution to GDP reduced from 30.8% in 1970 to 20.3% in 1985 while that of manufacturing increased from 13.9% in 1970 to 19.1% in 1985 and 27.0% in 1990 (Table 1).

Table 1. Malaysia's Source of Growth

| | *Average Annual Growth* (%)* | | *Share of GDP (%)* | | | |
|---|---|---|---|---|---|---|
| | *Achieved 1971-90* | *Target 1991-2000* | *1970* | *1980* | *1990* | *2000+* |
| Agriculture & Forestry | 1.0 | 0.5 | 29.0 | 22.9 | 18.7 | 13.4 |
| Mining & Quarrying | 0.6 | 0.1 | 13.7 | 10.1 | 9.7 | 5.7 |
| Manufacturing | 2.1 | 3.3 | 13.9 | 19.6 | 27.0 | 37.2 |
| Construction | 0.2 | 0.2 | 3.8 | 4.6 | 3.5 | 3.5 |
| Services | 3.0 | 3.4 | 36.2 | 40.1 | 42.3 | 45.4 |
| Import duties# | 0.2 | 0.5 | 3.4 | 2.7 | – 1.2 | – 5.2 |
| GDP | 6.7 | 7.0 | 100.0 | 100.0 | 100.0 | 100.0 |

* 1978 prices.
+ Projected.
# Less imputed bank charges.
Source: *Far Eastern Economic Review*, June 27, 1991, p. 16.

Since 1970 significant shifts have occurred in the size of employment opportunities in the different sectors of the economy. Between 1970 and 1985 the agriculture, forestry and fishing sector's share of employment dwindled from 53.5% to 35.9% while that of the manufacturing and related wholesale and retail sectors expanded from 20.1% in 1970 to 31.7% in 1985 (3MP, 1976; 4MP, 1981). Manufacturing was clearly the principal growth sector increasing its share to job creation from 18.4% in 1970 to 34.7% in 1985 and 31.0% in 1990.

*Development Targets*

National objectives have been very much influenced by the desire to achieve national integration within the context of economic growth. It is best epitomised in the Second Malaysia Plan (2MP) 1971–75, which introduced the New Economic Policy, which strongly reinforced the existing national development goals, with a more explicit pro-Bumiputera stance in terms of implementation procedures. Subsequent development Plans (3MP and 4MP) reinforced the same strategy with increasing emphasis upon restructuring as the primary goal of development, arguing that ethnic differences are always much sharper than economic differences: "hence . . . an important part of this task (of economic development) is to remove the glaring socio-economic differences among the major ethnic groups" (5MP, 1986). This was visibly demonstrated by the increased allocation of public sector development expenditure to poverty eradication and societal restructuring from 17.3% in the Second Malaysia Plan to 27.2% under the Third Malaysia Plan and then to 37.2% under the Fourth Malaysia Plan.

During the 1970s the predominant focus had been placed on aspects of restructuring, but as the 1980s progressed, a slower growth rate, falling prices of primary commodities, and a relatively weaker position among its newly industrializing neighbors caused the Malaysian authorities to review their development strategies including related manpower and education policies. From the second half of the 1980s Malaysia aimed for increased agricultural productivity, intensified resource-based industrial development and an expanded manufacturing base to include heavy and high-technology industries. With the current goal of producing "value-added" products with implications for a supply of workers possessing higher level technical and technological know-how, the quality and productivity of human resources has assumed central importance. Through the Industrial Master Plan (1986–95) and the Fifth Malaysia Plan, a science and technology policy underpinned the strategies for manpower development and industrial growth which stressed the need for a degree of self-sufficiency in industrial technology

(Malaysia, 1986a).

With the end of the NEP period (1990) and following its review, Malaysia has prepared a broad Second Outline Perspective Plan (OPP2), 1991–2000, which embodies the National Development Policy (NDP), which sets out "to guide the development of the nation in the nineties" (6MP, p. 3). Its first phase, as reflected in the Sixth Malaysia Plan (1991–95), concentrates on strategies to sustain the development momentum achieved during the past twenty years. Development will be spearheaded by expanding productivity in agriculture, expanding industrialisation and strengthening of structures for productivity, especially through accelerated scientific and technological development. The need for human resource development that will enhance the quality of labor to support these enterprises will continue to be crucial. While not losing sight of the distributional aspects of development and working for growth with equity, a shift is evident toward ensuring qualitative improvements of the labor force to enable those from the low-income groups to move into the modern economy and earn higher incomes while maintaining and developing a "more permanent participation of the Bumiputeras in the industrial and commercial sectors of the economy" (6MP). Its critical aspects comprise primarily "striking a balance between the goals of economic growth and equity" through policies that will "diversify the industrial base, enhance human resource development, provide technological upgrading and reduce structural imbalances among sectors and regions of the country" (6MP). In terms of human resource development, "greater attention will be given towards nurturing a higher quality of leadership, professional, technical, managerial and entrepreneurial skills to enable Bumiputera to manage their wealth effectively in order to lay the foundation for further creation of wealth on a sustainable basis" (6MP).

The Malaysian Prime Minister, Mahathir Mohamad, has set the year 2020 as the target for Malaysia to be included among the developed nations of the world. He has frequently elaborated upon the need to promote development in Malaysia "in our own mould." He explains that Malaysia should not only dwell upon economic development but also become developed along all dimensions: economic, social, political, spiritual, psychological and cultural. "We must be fully developed in terms of national unity and social cohesion, in terms of our economy, in terms of social justice, political stability, system of government, quality of life, social and spiritual values, national pride and confidence" (Mahathir Mohamad, 1991).

In terms of priorities of national development, the creation of a united and cohesive Malaysian nation remained as the most fundamental. But as the seeds of disunity often rest upon economic disparities, the focus of developmental planning quite evidently turns to economic development from two perspectives: the raising of the general level of national productivity with a view to raising the living standards of the most economically disadvantaged; and in tandem with economic growth, the enhancement of economic social justice which is primarily directed at reducing ethnic differences in access to education, jobs and high incomes. While maintaining concern about merit and quality the policy of social restructuring hopes to achieve a viable and robust Bumiputera commercial and industrial Bumiputera community.

## The Context of Educational Development

Malaysia has experienced three distinct periods of development: the colonial period from the founding of Penang in 1786 until independence in 1957; the post-independence period of reconstruction and Malaysianization between 1957 and 1970; and the period which began with the commencement of the New Economic Policy in 1970 and which set out to restore the primacy of the Bumiputeras. In each of these periods education played a distinctive role, leading to the shaping of the National Development Policy, which was formulated as a result of reviewing past efforts and achievements.

### *The Colonial Period*

Parallel systems of education emerged during the colonial period, which was characterized by the transformation of the homogeneous Malay society into a multi-ethnic society. The vernacular system with Malay, Chinese and Tamil schools enabled children from these language groups to receive the rudiments of schooling in their mother tongue and created a small literate group that served the respective communities. The Malay system was highly subsidized by the British government and was intended to promote among the indigenous Malays basic literacy, the foundations of agriculture, and the capacity to become more astute farmers and fishermen who could guard against being swindled by other communities. The Chinese system reinforced links with China and created a workforce for Chinese enterprises. The Tamil medium schools, centered in the rubber estates, provided elementary reading and writing skills in Tamil. At the same time a small urban-based English school system was attended largely by the immigrant Chinese and Indian middle classes. It provided limited opportunities for higher education in Singapore and abroad as well as access to the administrative and clerical services of the colonial government and the small modern economic sector.

The colonial government did not develop considered policies for education, national development or national integration. In fact, the disparity in access and the different opportunities for economic advancement inherent in the colonial system emerged as the principal issue of contention among the ethnic groups. Similarly, the indigenous systems that followed curricula imported from overseas appeared to be divisive rather than unifying.

### *Post-Independence Period*

In the post-independence period the instrumentalist function of education surfaced strongly; education was seen as the principal tool for both national integration and for the development of human resources that was expected to be the engine for economic growth. Two reports—the Report of the Education Committee (Razak Report) and the Report of the Education Review Committee (Rahman Talib Report)—laid the foundation of the post-independence education system in Malaysia. The new system aimed to set up a national education system with a view to making *Bahasa Malaysia* the national language while preserving the language and culture of the other races. The key components of the system were to be a common language of instruction, a common curriculum and common examinations. The system also ensured nine years of schooling to all children allowing them to move up the school ladder automatically.

Despite rapid growth of enrollments at all levels averaging close to 6% annually at the primary level, 39% at the lower-secondary level, 29% at the upper-secondary level, 78% at the post-secondary level and 8% at the tertiary level (Aziz et al., 1987), the system contributed significantly to enhanced ethnic cleavages. Most evidently the distribution of opportunities for schooling were grossly uneven, favoring the immigrant communities who were better placed in the urban areas to seize the new opportunities for education. By 1970, the Malay representation at most levels of education remained below their proportion in the population. In the occupational structure Malays were unable to compete with the Chinese in the high-productivity commerce and manufacturing sectors. In attempting to analyse the root causes of communal violence in May 1969 the authorities were compelled to examine the bases for economic and social development and the crucial role that education had played in it. In this context the New Economic Policy was born.

### *The New Economic Policy*

To achieve the socioeconomic restructuring proposed by the New Economic

Policy (NEP) education was assigned a key role. Education would promote national unity and integration through: the staged implementation of Bahasa Malaysia as the medium of instruction in the common curriculum; reducing the gap in educational opportunities between social and ethnic groups and geographical regions; and expanding and reorienting education to meet national manpower needs, especially in science and technology.

Since 1970 all development plans viewed education as a "tool for nation building and an agency for human resource building" to spearhead development (Rudner, 1975). The NEP was based on the belief that education, properly managed, could act as an agent of social change and transformation. The twin objectives of alleviating poverty and social restructuring would be achieved through increased educational opportunities for all Malaysians irrespective of race and special sponsorship for the Bumiputeras. The enhanced educational and occupational attainment of the indigenous Bumiputeras to the level of those of Chinese and Indian origin was expected to remove ethnic inequities as well as remove invidious comparisons which were at the root of national discontent.

Investment in education has been constantly rising but is lower than neighboring new little dragons such as Thailand and Indonesia (Schlossstein, 1991). The expenditure on education increased from MR179 million in 1960 to MR522 million in 1970, to MR2,786 million in 1980 and jumped to MR6,032 million in 1990. This expenditure represented a range of about 13% to 21% of government spending. However, as a percentage of gross national product education expenditure increased from 3.1% in 1960 to 6.7% in 1972 and in subsequent years fluctuated between 5.5% to 6.5%.

During the two decades of the NEP (1970–90) significant shifts took place in educational opportunities for all, especially the Bumiputeras. Participation rates in education improved quite dramatically in the primary, lower secondary and upper secondary levels. By 1980, nearly 96.8% of the 6- to 11-year-olds, 81.7% of all 12- to 14-year-olds, 36.1% of 15- to 16-year-olds, and 4.3% of the 17- to 18-year-olds were in school. By 1990 primary enrollments had reached 99.8%, lower secondary 83.0%, upper secondary 49.1%, and post-secondary enrollments (17- to 18- age group) improved to nearly 19%. The Bumiputera share of enrollments increased conspicuously, for instance, at the upper secondary level from 48.8% in 1970 to 68.1% in 1985, and at the post-secondary level from 43.3% to 56.9% during the same period. By 1990 the Bumiputera share of total educational opportunities in all local educational institutions constituted 60%, considerably in excess of their proportion in the population (Table 2).

TABLE 2. Percentage Distribution of Enrollment by Educational Level and Ethnic Group, 1970–1988

| | *Percentage Distribution of Enrollment by Ethnic Group and Year* | | | | | | | | | | | | | | |
|---|---|---|---|---|---|---|---|---|---|---|---|---|---|---|---|
| *Educational* | *Bumi-putera* | *Chinese* | *Indian* | *Others* | *Total* | *Bumi-putera* | *Chinese* | *Indian* | *Others* | *Total* | *Bumi-putera* | *Chinese* | *Indian* | *Others* | *Total* |
| | | | 1970 | | | | | 1980 | | | | | 1988 | | |
| Primary | 53.4 | 36.0 | 10.0 | 0.6 | 100.0 | 58.4 | 32.2 | 7.7 | 1.7 | 100.0 | 62.2 | 28.1 | 7.7 | 2.0 | 100.0 |
| Lower Secondary | 51.0 | 38.8 | 9.6 | 0.6 | 100.0 | 60.3 | 30.0 | 8.5 | 1.2 | 100.0 | 55.9 | 34.9 | 8.1 | 1.1 | 100.0 |
| Upper Secondary | 48.8 | 43.4 | 7.0 | 0.8 | 100.0 | 66.3 | 27.0 | 6.0 | 0.7 | 100.0 | 66.1 | 26.8 | 6.1 | 1.0 | 100.0 |
| Post-Secondary | 43.4 | 49.6 | 6.0 | 1.0 | 100.0 | 61.4 | 32.9 | 4.7 | 1.0 | 100.0 | 54.3 | 39.5 | 5.4 | 0.8 | 100.0 |
| Tertiary | 53.7 | 38.3 | 5.3 | 2.7 | 100.0 | 60.4 | 32.7 | 6.1 | 0.8 | 100.0 | 74.9 | 20.9 | 3.6 | 0.5 | 100.0 |
| Percentage Distribution of Population | 53.0 | 35.6 | 10.6 | 0.8 | 100.0 | 58.1 | 32.3 | 9.1 | 0.5 | 100.0 | 60.1 | 30.9 | 8.4 | 0.6 | 100.0 |

Sources: Malaysia, *Third Malaysia Plan, 1976–80*, p. 400; *Fifth Malaysia Plan, 1986–90;* Ministry of Finance, *Economic Report 1988/89*, p. 7.

### *The New Development Policy*

Toward the achievement of the NDP, announced in 1991, education and training will be geared to improve the knowledge and skills base as well as to inculcate norms and values appropriate for development in the Malaysian context. In particular the programs will attempt to develop a technically competent labor force that will make the Malaysian economy more competitive. Education is expected to continue assisting the process of poverty eradication and restructuring by a better delivery system that will serve the low-income and the undeveloped regions to obtain better access to education and training (6MP).

### *Global and Regional Orientations*

Until two decades ago, the direction of educational reform in Malaysia tended to reflect her British colonial past. School leaving examinations that were set and marked by the Cambridge Overseas Examination Syndicate are an illustration of the links that were more than ones of structural similarity. Educational interactions tended to be limited to Britain and other developed Commonwealth countries such as Canada and New Zealand, exceptions being Egypt and Saudi Arabia chiefly in relation to Islamic religious education.

The pattern evolving since the sixties reveals that while relations with traditional Commonwealth partners have continued, emerging significantly are bi-lateral educational interactions with non-traditional partners, particularly the United States and Japan, and a range of Islamic nations. Particularly significant is the well-established participation in international and regional educational development organizations such as the activities of UNESCO's Principal Regional Office in Bangkok and the substantial work organised by the South East Asian Ministers of Education Organisation (SEAMEO) (SEAMEO 1971; Hayashi 1984). Regional and international dialogues provide Malaysia's educational personnel with windows on global trends. While direct impact is hard to discern, the general impression is that the sharing of experiences with other countries has given Malaysia more insight into the real problems commonly faced by Asian countries and also the opportunity to consider suitable alternatives for their solution.

## Human Resource Development (HRD)

> Human resource development will be a major thrust in the Sixth Malaysia Plan as the achievement of socio-economic objectives depends on the availability of educated, skilled and trainable labour force. Towards this end, education and training programmes will be further

> expanded and improved, not only to equip individuals with the appropriate knowledge and skills but also to produce responsible citizens with strong moral and ethical values. In addition, such programmes will help to develop a technically competent labour force that will enhance the competitiveness of the Malaysian economy. (6MP)

In the sixties, a major systemic reform was put in place when the Secondary School Entrance Examination was abolished in 1964, resulting in a situation where pupils enjoyed automatic promotion throughout the six years of primary and the three years of lower secondary education (Ministry of Education, Malaya, 1964). At the end of the three years, pupils would sit for the Lower Certificate of Education Examination which was conceived as an aptitude test. On the basis of their performance in the examination, pupils could move on to upper secondary level which had differentiated curricular foci—academic, technical, agricultural, commercial or home sciences. The plan was that the selection process would be assisted by professional educational counselors. "At the end of the two-year programme, pupils would be equipped with the knowledge and skill to follow a vocation, . . . and be employed" (ibid.). The reform was designed to raise the educational levels in the whole country, an aim which it clearly achieved as evidenced in the rapidly increasing enrollment rates in this period; to provide a system which took individual differences and preferences into account; and to provide, through the technical and vocational tracks, skilled workers for the economy which was beginning to move toward modernization and industrial diversification.

A senior official suggested three major aims for the system:

> . . . to foster greater interest towards technical, scientific and vocational education; to improve the quality of instruction offered in our schools; to expand our post-secondary education in order to develop high-level manpower especially in the field of technical and technological know-how so as to further our industrial and economic progress. (Report of the Seminar on Contemporary Educational Practices in Relation to Goals, University of Malaysia, 1968)

*Technical and Vocational Education: Secondary Schools*

Although overall secondary enrollment rates grew steadily from 25% of the total school population in 1970 to 31.7% in 1990, the entrance examination became a different animal. Since there was not a cadre of trained counselors, selection into the various tracks could no longer be based on aptitude but on examination scores, resulting in stratification with high scorers moving into the academic stream and the low scorers being deposited in the vocational. This perpetuated the traditional view of the latter track being the receptacle for low achievers. The pattern and ethos of secondary schooling resembled the elitist mode of the English school system with greatest value placed on academic training. Since these graduates also won the best jobs as clerks and low-level administrators in the growing economy managed by the colonial government, parents and pupils preferred the academic track. Until the middle eighties, the fact that the technical and especially the vocational tracks were terminal courses with no access to further or higher education within the national system served to cast further ignominy on them. The conditions prevailing in technical and vocational schools did little to improve the scene: classrooms were ill-equipped and teachers were not adequately trained. Technical/vocational curricula were not marked by sensitivity to local and changing requirements with the result that they received lukewarm support from parents and pupils.

Prior to 1987, the two-year vocational education program was narrowly vocational, perceived by all as a terminal program and deservedly unpopular. The expectation was that, on completion, students would be employed as semi-skilled workers in the industrial, agricultural or commercial sectors. Currently, the program is characterized by a larger general education component which, according to its statement of objectives, aims to provide a flexible and broad based curriculum to meet not only immediate needs but also future needs and changes in technology and to provide the foundation for skills and knowledge on which to build subsequent education and training. The strong pre-vocational element is far removed from the initial "trade school" approach to the vocational program as conceived in the 1964 Committee Report.

Students in the vocational stream now follow academic and vocational courses in the first year of their two-year upper secondary program. At the end of the first year, based on their performance, students are channeled either into the "academic" or vocational stream leading to the Malaysian Certificate of Education (Vocational) or MCE(V), or to the skill training track where students are prepared for the examination conducted by the National Industrial Training and Trade Certification Board. The significant difference between the two is that successful completion of the former enables students to compete for entry into tertiary education with important spin-offs for the quality of the program and motivation of students.

As the economy expanded in the middle seventies, continuing its growth well into the eighties, conscious efforts were made by the government to revamp this sector of the educational system. Primary impetus for this came from the needs of industry for trained manpower at all levels. Greater attention to the curricula of the technical and vocational components of schooling and to prospects for moving into other levels of education and training have been responsible for bringing about a steady increase in enrollments over the last ten years or so. From a low of 3.33% in 1970 (2MP, 1970) of all secondary school pupils, enrollments rose to 6.10% in 1985 and 8.42% in 1990 with a projected increase to 8.85% in 1995 (6MP, 1991). During the 6MP period, a further six vocational schools are to be built in anticipation of projected demand.

Programs designed for the upper secondary academic and technical streams are fairly similar, providing general education with some elements of specialization in the arts, science or technical subjects (largely basic engineering courses) leading at the end of the two-year program to the Malaysian Certificate of Education (MCE) examination or the MCE(V) (for the vocational stream). Successful completion of the MCE enables students to move to the sixth form or pre-university programs which prepare them for entry into tertiary institutions.

Technical stream students have the option of enrolling in (a) the sixth form, or (b) matriculation classes in one of the local universities, or (c) gain direct entry to the Universiti Teknologi Malaysia (Technology University) or the Universiti Pertanian Malaysia (Agriculture University). This two-year program, which has a strong general education component as well as a technical emphasis (e.g., Engineering Workshop Practice, Surveying and Building Construction, Agricultural Engineering and Farm Management), aims "to provide scientific and technical education to students who have the aptitude for such subjects and to foster and maintain that interest" and generally "to raise the level of skilled manpower to meet the industrial needs of the country."

Of note in the technical and vocational programs is the ever-increasing emphasis on general education, evidence of the growing conviction that within the context of modernization, industrialization and rapid changes in technology, the school should focus on basic skills especially in language (literacy) and mathematics (numeracy), and more generalized skills such as problem-solving and knowledge of social issues. They reflect the conviction that it is the school's role to prepare the ground for training that takes place on the job rather than to provide occupation-specific skills, a task it is not equipped to do.

One of the underlying principles of the New Primary and Secondary

School Curricula, introduced in 1983 and 1989, respectively, was to improve the quality of basic and more generalised skills. Such a move reflects current thinking (e.g., Commonwealth Secretariat, 1988; Lauglo and Lillis, 1988; World Bank, 1991a) that school-level work orientation programs need to focus on producing "trainable" rather than trained graduates who are ready to receive on-the-job training in a range of specific occupational skills. More recently the pragmatic decision was taken to give renewed importance to the teaching of the English language, which is now recognized as an international commercial language. This is a status which it lost when Malay became the main medium of instruction in 1970, reflecting arguments based on nationalist fervor.

*The Polytechnic Sector*

The seven polytechnics in Malaysia (there was only one between 1969 and 1976) provide diploma-level opportunities to pupils who choose to continue their technical education on successful completion of their MCE or MCE(V). Polytechnic graduates may go on to degree programs in the local universities, thereby providing another route or second chance to those who had not gained direct access to pre-university programs.

During the eighties, educational institutions were able to keep pace with the skills required by the world of work when Malaysia's agricultural economy was dependent on the export of primary products. A slight shift in skill requirements occurred with early efforts at diversifying the economy through industrialization with a focus on the import substitution of consumer goods. However, over the last one-and-a-half decades or so, Malaysia moved into a more aggressive phase of developing its export-oriented manufacturing industry (currently responsible for approximately 30% of GDP) which is beginning to make inroads into heavy and high-level technology. An appreciation of the value of industry or job-based, post-school training appears to be gaining hold among planners simultaneously with renewed measures (demonstrated in the recent introduction of "Living Skills," which incorporates aspects of entrepreneurship, commerce and technology into the Integrated Secondary School program) to bring about and maintain understanding, support and interest of pupils in the world of work.

The planning and implementation of the polytechnic and school level technical/vocational sector in education requires some mention. By reviewing and monitoring the system, learning lessons from its unpopularity and unattractiveness due to low-status and terminal characteristics; by providing more than one route into tertiary education; by reviewing and renewing curricula; and by providing more resources to improve physical facilities and training of instructors, the sector is increasingly marked by greater flexibility and less wastage through attrition. That the originally low-status polytechnic and vocational segments of the system have to a large extent come into their own is demonstrated by both public recognition of the role technical personnel play in national development, and more importantly, by the employability of its graduates in the job market.

TABLE 3. Distribution of PTV Graduates by Level of Income (in percentages)

| *Level of Income* | *Vocational* | *Technical* | *Polytechnic* |
|---|---|---|---|
| $500 & below | 43.3 | 20.5 | 24.7 |
| $501-750 | 35.0 | 21.5 | 49.5 |
| $751-1000 | 15.5 | 23.5 | 12.9 |
| $1001-1250 | 3.2 | 17.5 | 5.1 |
| $1251-1500 | 1.6 | 7.0 | 2.9 |
| $1501-1750 | 0.4 | 4.5 | 2.7 |
| $1751-2000 | 0.3 | 2.0 | 1.0 |
| $2001 & above | 0.7 | 3.5 | 1.2 |
| TOTAL | 100.0 | 100.0 | 100.0 |

Source: Universiti Teknologi Malaysia, *Tracer Study on Graduates of Polytechnics, Technical and Vocational Schools*, 1989.

In a study conducted at the tail end of a recessionary period (1987–88), researchers found that job prospects for graduates of polytechnics, technical and vocational schools were good. As Table 4 shows, polytechnic graduates were the most easily absorbed into jobs followed by technical and then by vocational school graduates. Earnings of technical school graduates were generally higher, however, which the report ascribes to better planned courses which were more effectively geared to market demands. But the findings reported in Table 3 need to be taken with some caution since many of the technical school graduates had followed higher-level courses not indicated by the categories selected. A fair comparison is also difficult as data were not controlled for years of service. For all three categories of graduates incomes were higher among those employed in technically related jobs (ibid.) as Table 5 shows.

TABLE 4. Post-graduate Wait Periods prior to Employment

| *Category* | *1 year after* | *2 years after* |
|---|---|---|
| Polytechnic | 80.7% | 95.6% |
| Technical school | 70.4% | 86.2% |
| Vocational school | 57.0% | 81.0% |

Source: Universiti Teknologi Malaysia, *Tracer Study on Graduates of Polytechnics, Technical and Vocational Schools,* 1989.

TABLE 5. Comparison by Means of Salaries Earned by Occupation: Relatedness of Training of Polytechnic, Technical and Vocational Graduates (Salaries in M$)

| *Occupation Relatedness to Training* | *Polytechnic* | *Technical* | *Vocational* |
|---|---|---|---|
| Technically Related | 615 | 833 | 518 |
| Technically Non-Related | 523 | 650 | 220 |
| Non-Technical | 280 | 595 | 200 |
| Group's Mean Salary | 578 | 778 | 455 |

Source: Universiti Teknologi Malaysia, *Tracer Study on Graduates of Polytechnics, Technical and Vocational Schools,* 1989.

The report highlights the fact that during the course of their investigations "industry leaders do not seem to be unduly worried about the present unemployment situation. They are more concerned with our ability and commitment to train a more sophisticated work force for the next phase of industrialisation."

During the 1980s, when Malaysia's abundant natural resources provided a comparative advantage and contributed to the development of a resource-based manufacturing sector, such complacency of industry leaders could perhaps be accepted. But maintaining the momentum of economic growth (averaging approximately 8% in 1991 and 1992) in an increasingly competitive arena requires leaders in the public and private sectors to reconsider policies relating to raising levels of public education, to increasing investment in research and development and to strategies for capturing the country's best talents.

Especially relevant to the continued ability of the technical/vocational school and polytechnic sector to contribute to growth is the move toward value-added manufacturing products (6MP). The immediate implication of such a policy is an increased need for higher level training in terms of technological know-how including information technology, which is essential if a competitive edge is to be maintained. The extent to which public expenditure and policies reflect these requirements will indicate Malaysia's ability to keep up the momentum of growth.

In an analysis of the three Southeast Asian "new little dragons"—Indonesia, Thailand and Malaysia (Schlossstein, 1991) it is posited that among other factors such as an authoritarian political system, an outward economic orientation and increased private savings, an "unswerving commitment to public education" characterizes the successful newly industrialized countries such as Taiwan, South Korea, and Singapore. Malaysia's allocation of 5.3% to education in her national budget compared unfavorably with the 13% (a median figure) allocated by Hong Kong, Taiwan and Singapore (Schlossstein, 1991). More significantly, comparison with neighboring "little dragons" also put Malaysia at the bottom of the pile with Indonesia allocating 6.7% and Thailand a high of 16% (ibid.). Furthermore, unlike Malaysia, their educational systems are typically highly competitive and merit-based, allowing for the nurturing of the countries' best talents.

### *The Role of Universities*

During the NEP period tertiary education served both the need for high-level manpower to boost economic development as well as the restructuring objectives of the government. A considerable degree of control is maintained over the higher education sector. This is exercised through the large state subsidy which comprises nearly 95% of the recurrent and developmental costs of universities and colleges, as well as legislative enactments such as the Colleges and Universities Act (1971), that empower the government to intervene and moderate all aspects of their programs. The Ministry of Education exercises control over the establishment of institutions, student enrollments, staff appointments, curricula and financing. The five-year plans have regularly reviewed their contribution toward national targets.

Recognizing the higher education system as the valued producer of high-level manpower, and the principal vehicle for enabling Bumiputeras to move into the upper echelons of the occupational structure, the government has been willing to invest in it. Expenditure on higher education has grown during the five-year plans relative to other sectors of education. In 1985 Malaysia was spending 6.9% of its GNP on education, with 15.6% of it spent on higher education (Singh, 1991a, p. 38).

With the growth of the manufacturing base of Malaysia's economy, the higher education system has been ascribed the role of the major supplier of high-level scientific, technological and managerial manpower as well as the creator of a research and development environment that would sustain indigenous industrial development. More specifically, Bumiputeras are provided with opportunities to take up high-level scientific, technical and research positions.

The high investment in tertiary education is paralleled by increased enrollments, averaging 20% in the decade from 1971 to 1980 and around 13% in the period 1981 to 1990. To the one university in 1969 were added four more by 1972 and a sixth in 1984. These universities, together with seven polytechnics, the MARA Institute of Technology, Tengku Abdul Rahman College and various private institutions, supply high-level manpower. A large number are trained overseas and more recently twinning programs between private institutions and overseas universities and colleges have mushroomed.

Malaysia inherited an unbalanced higher education system which overproduced arts and social science graduates and under-produced scientific, professional and vocational graduates. An imbalance also existed in that there was a larger output from the universities than from the colleges which offer diploma and certificate courses. Since the 1980s, efforts have been directed toward enlarging the pool of scientific and technological manpower and research personnel. By deliberately adjusting the admission quotas and promoting specialised science and technology institutions, a ratio of three science to two arts and humanities graduates in secondary schools has been achieved. Instead of one comprehensive university—the University of Malaysia—specialized universities in science, agriculture and technology were established which began to develop postgraduate courses in science, medicine and engineering. A reduction in the share of arts students from 56.8% in 1970 to 45.8% in 1980 was evident accompanied by an increase in the share of science students from 43.2 to 54.2% over the same period. Since then expansion in business, commerce and accountancy studies has taken place.

While science-based studies have expanded, enrollment has still tended to be in the basic science courses of biology, chemistry, physics and mathematics with nearly 45% of all science students in the 1980s graduating in these fields. Graduates in the technological-based engineering faculties remained low at about 24% of science graduates and with the majority graduating in civil engineering. Enrollments in applied scientific fields were around 3% and in postgraduate studies were only about 4% of total enrollments.

Universities have been given a central role in development plans but they remain peripheral to scientific research relevant to national development. Most of the early significant research on national products such as rubber and oil palm was undertaken by specialized research institutes with the universities playing the role of trainers and teachers of scientific manpower. With the introduction of the Industrial Master Plan (1986–91) and the identification of research priorities, the universities are being brought into the broad framework of research to support industry.

Universities themselves are keen to improve their research profile and have since 1985 made strenuous efforts to reorient their research agendas to national priorities. New multi-disciplinary research institutions and consultancy-type agencies have been established within universities to provide new frameworks from which to contribute to the research output. Nevertheless, their function of teaching and training the scientific and research manpower remains prominent, with universities expected to carry out about 22% of planned research and development.

Bumiputeras obtained increased opportunities to acquire higher education both at the diploma and college levels. Between 1970 and 1980, diploma and college level enrollments locally increased from 41.0% to 65.8% and in the degree level courses from 40.2% to 63.0% while the Chinese share of enrollments declined from 56.6% to 30.5% in certificate courses and from 48.9% to 29.7% at the degree level. In the last decade of the NEP (1980–90), Bumiputera numbers further increased in all local public institutions and the non-Bumiputera proportion continued to decline. By 1988, Bumiputeras occupied 74.9% of the total places in higher education institutions.

Bumiputeras also began to increase their share of the medical, scientific and engineering places in higher education in readiness to move into the equivalent posts which in the past had tended to be dominated by the non-Bumiputeras. Detailed analyses of enrollments by ethnicity and discipline are not available but by 1985 at the University of Malaysia 25.7% of the undergraduates in engineering, 56.8% in medicine and 48.4% in science were Bumiputeras. The university system has gradually restructured the output of manpower to create a large stock of Bumiputera scientific manpower (Singh, 1989).

The non-Bumiputeras responded to the situation by striving, often at great personal expense, for openings in the private sector locally and in overseas institutions. It has been calculated that at any one time there are as many students overseas as in the local institutions (60,000 were enrolled overseas in 1985 [6MP]). Since the 1980s a plethora of local private institutions have tried to tap the overseas market by establishing split-site courses, providing cheaper studies than abroad but relative to local public universities quite considerably more expensive.

There was one abortive attempt in 1981 spearheaded by the Chinese community to establish a privately funded university teaching in Mandarin. It was declared unconstitutional by the government. As far as the government was concerned the numbers of Chinese overseas balanced the number of Bumiputeras locally and an overall balance in educational opportunities was claimed in the development plans that regularly reviewed progress under the NEP. While quiet resentment smouldered and was expressed by members of the opposition and activist groups such as Aliran and Insaf, many Malaysians forked out the enormous sums for private education, calculated in 1984 to be RM 1.3 billion spent on private sector education (Kua Kia Soong, n.d.). During the mid-1980s resentment grew further as employment opportunities became scarce with the spectre of recession, and many non-Bumiputeras felt that despite adopting the Malay language and having acquired higher education without state sponsorship, the reward of employment was still eluding them. The ranks of the unemployed swelled and larger than ever numbers showed an intent to migrate to Australia and Canada in search of jobs. However, with the improved state of the economy since 1988, the trend seems to have been reversed and young Malaysians are increasingly seeking employment locally.

## Poverty Reduction and Social Restructuring

Social restructuring is the centrepiece of the NEP. Education and training were identified as the principal instruments which would equip Bumiputeras with the proper skills to relocate into the new occupational structures. In the Malaysian context, education was readily accepted as the legitimate route to social and occupational mobility and restructuring. Since the colonial period its value has been recognized as the arbiter of prestigious occupations and it carries with it notions of fairness and open competition. Only a few voices were raised against the continued advantages that would be bestowed upon the traditional elite to be able to secure the best positions for themselves, providing a continuity between the old aristocracy and the modern Malay elite (Mokhzani, 1965). Although a strong relationship has been shown to exist between social background and school achievement (Murad, 1973; Hussain, 1979) as access to schooling was extended, the traditional barriers to entrance into the education system have been removed (Hoerr, 1973; Hirschman, 1979).

The impact of the NEP on social restructuring has been depicted through the changes in the ethnic distribution in the different educational and occupational levels. Significant changes in the educational structure were paralleled by changes in the occupational structure, moving Bumiputeras into the tertiary sector, from 21.7% in 1970 to 40.5% in 1990 (*Far Eastern Economic Review*, 1991). The Bumiputera share of professional and technical occupations increased from 47% to 60% and among service workers their share rose from 44% to 61% during the NEP phase of development (Table 6).

TABLE 6. Peninsular Malaysia: Employment Structure by Ethnic Group and Occupation, 1970-1990

| | *1970* | | | | |
|---|---|---|---|---|---|
| *OCCUPATION* | *Bumiputera* % | *Chinese* % | *Indian* % | *Others* % | *Total* *(000)* |
| Professional & technical | 47.0 | 39.5 | 10.8 | 2.7 | 136.7 |
| Administrative & managerial | 24.1 | 62.9 | 7.8 | 5.2 | 30.7 |
| Clerical & related workers | 35.4 | 45.0 | 17.2 | 1.5 | 142.5 |
| Sales & related workers | 26.7 | 61.7 | 11.1 | 0.4 | 258.5 |
| Service workers | 44.3 | 39.6 | 14.6 | 1.5 | 225.8 |
| Agricultural workers | 72.0 | 17.3 | 9.7 | 1.0 | 1,278.7 |
| Production, transport & others | 34.2 | 55.9 | 9.6 | 0.3 | 777.4 |
| TOTAL | 1,477.6 | 1,043.6 | 301.4 | 27.7 | 2,850.3 |
| | (51.8) | (36.6) | (10.6) | (1.0) | |

| | *1980* | | | | |
|---|---|---|---|---|---|
| *OCCUPATION* | *Bumiputera* % | *Chinese* % | *Indian* % | *Others* % | *Total* *(000)* |
| Professional & technical | 50.0 | 36.9 | 11.4 | 1.7 | 236.2 |
| Administrative & managerial | 31.6 | 57.0 | 6.1 | 5.3 | 51.2 |
| Clerical & related workers | 55.3 | 36.2 | 6.9 | 1.7 | 306.5 |
| Sales & related workers | 23.1 | 69.2 | 7.6 | 0.2 | 432.3 |
| Service workers | 47.9 | 39.9 | 11.6 | 0.5 | 351.3 |
| Agricultural workers | 67.7 | 19.7 | 11.9 | 0.9 | 1,474.8 |
| Production, transport & others | 45.4 | 42.6 | 11.4 | 0.5 | 1,412.1 |
| TOTAL | 2,211.5 | 1,558.0 | 460.7 | 34.2 | 4,264.4 |
| | (51.9) | (36.5) | (10.8) | (0.8) | |

| | *1990* | | | | |
|---|---|---|---|---|---|
| *OCCUPATION* | *Bumiputera* % | *Chinese* % | *Indian* % | *Others* % | *Total* *(000)* |
| Professional & technical | 60.3 | 30.8 | 7.7 | 1.2 | 580.8 |
| Administrative & managerial | 33.3 | 58.7 | 5.3 | 2.7 | 162.4 |
| Clerical & related workers | 54.9 | 36.9 | 7.8 | 0.4 | 645.9 |
| Sales & related workers | 36.0 | 56.5 | 6.5 | 1.0 | 761.3 |
| Service workers | 61.5 | 27.0 | 10.6 | 0.9 | 770.3 |
| Agricultural workers | 76.4 | 15.8 | 7.0 | 0.8 | 1,872.5 |
| Production, transport & others | 48.5 | 40.4 | 10.7 | 0.4 | 1,827.8 |
| TOTAL | 3,825.4 | 2,182.2 | 562.7 | 50.7 | 6,621.0 |
| | (57.8) | (32.9) | (8.5) | (0.8) | |

The link between education and the movement into occupations is supported by some of the empirical research into occupational mobility carried out in Malaysia. A close relationship between education, income and employment has been demonstrated (Singh, 1973). In Petaling Jaya, Malaysia, it was shown that educational attainment exercised a considerable influence over job entry and career advancement. Education was the key variable in the placement of individuals in the social structure. However, the effects of social origins were also strongly felt, largely indirectly through education. The trend was toward increased dependence on education for status achievement, while the effects of social origins correspondingly declined. Lee Kiong Hock (1980) found significant inter-racial differences in the impact of education on occupational status, occupational mobility and the openness of their educational structures, which in general tended to favour the Chinese. Rabieyah Mat (1986) found enhanced educational opportunity in Peninsular Malaysia between 1972 and 1982 and, furthermore, confirmed that those who experienced greater educational equality also experienced greater opportunity for upward social mobility. She found educational achievement more important than socioeconomic background in determining survival for all groups—Malays, Chinese, rural, urban, male and female, except among the Indians, for whom socioeconomic background is more important. The effects of socioeconomic background for all groups remained significant. She concluded that "today Peninsular Malaysia more closely approximates a meritocratic society than some more industrialised societies" (Rabieyah Mat, 1986).

For the poorer groups in society, education has been identified as the key determinant of upward social mobility. The higher the educational attainment the greater the prospects of those from poorer backgrounds to occupy at least middle-level occupations. The benefits from education accrued with each increment of education. In relative terms the most disadvantaged social groups—the Malays, those from the rural areas and females—benefited the most from increased educational opportunities. This does not, however, obviate the fact that there remained a considerable proportion (about 33% compared with 25% in the non-poverty group) who continued in low status occupations despite obtaining secondary education. Undoubtedly the attainment of education has helped the poor to climb out of their poverty, but the group that has had access to this avenue remains considerably smaller relative to the middle and upper social groups within the country (ibid.).

A more recent survey of the labor force to assess the relationship between socioeconomic environment, academic achievement and occupational opportunities in Malaysia highlighted the continued dependence of the Bumiputeras and Indians on education for their occupational status. The data confirmed that middle- and low-status Malaysians relied heavily on education to move into high-status occupations. The analysis further illustrated the relative weakness of social origins acting alone and the dominance of education as a determinant of status; "the higher the educational level of the respondents, the greater the capacity to obtain the best available positions in the group" (Singh, 1989).

The studies consistently portray the very positive role that education has played in enabling all Malaysians, especially the Bumiputeras, to move out of poverty into middle- and high-level occupations. However, all the studies have not discounted the effects of social origins; they are agreed that education has played a moderating role by transmitting the advantages and disadvantages of social origins.

Empirical research has also pointed to the relationship between economic growth and the upward trend in social mobility resulting from education. Much of the enabling power of education appears closely related to the creation of new jobs and opportunities in the expanding public sector and state-promoted industries. Two pieces of evidence support this. Time series analyses reveal a declining dependence on education for mobility. There are signals that the younger Bumiputeras are less likely to reap the benefits from education that have been enjoyed by their parents. The capacity of ethnic groups whose options for employment in the public sector have been visibly reduced through restrictions imposed by the NEP, as in the case of the Chinese, have over time shown a reduced dependence on educational achievement as the prime determinant of occupational status. In such circumstances, it is argued that entrance into the labour market, which is the greatest predictor of future career mobility, becomes subject to a greater extent to influences from family and other "pulls."

Note should be taken of the special educational support structures and mechanisms which enabled the Bumiputeras to seize the opportunities in education created by the NEP, that is, enabled education to perform its instrumental role in development. These included the conversion of the medium of instruction in all secondary schools from English to Bahasa Malaysia, placing Malay children in a favorable position to benefit from schooling; the provision of special residential schools and preferential entry to institutions of higher education; fixing quotas and providing generous scholarships; special provision and entry into science and technological fields at all levels of the education system; the establishment of professional studies and special sponsorship for studies abroad primarily through a special agency—the *Majlis Amanah Rakyat* (MARA) or the

Peoples Trust; reorganization of higher education to meet the aspirations and demands of the Malay medium system with the establishment of the National University (Universiti Kebangsaan) at its apex; and making adjustments in the hierarchies of education and the civil service which placed Malays in the upper echelons.

Broadly speaking the government, represented by the alliance party with the United Malays National Organisation (UMNO) as the dominant component, was able to put in place legislation designed to safeguard the goals of the NEP and to accord the Malays a favored position. Furthermore, through a gradual process of promoting Malays into senior positions within the different services, Malays occupied key positions in the power hierarchies to promote the interests of the Bumiputeras in all matters pertaining to recruitment and promotion. Thus, educational expansion went hand in hand with strong interventionist measures by the government to achieve the affirmative action targets for this ethnic group.

In the Malaysian context it has been constantly pointed out that as the competition for education and jobs has increased among members of each ethnic group, and especially among the Bumiputeras, the intra-ethnic gaps have widened. As a direct result of the capabilities of those from high social status to capitalize on the opportunities made available to the group through the NEP, the traditional Malay elite dominate the social, political and economic arenas. Since the primary focus is on ethnic restructuring, this is tolerated by the Malaysian authorities who prefer to see more Malay than non-Malay rich providing the role models for the rest of the community.

Social restructuring has proved to be a two-edged sword. While appeasing the Bumiputera demands for greater participation and benefits from the economy new inequities have become evident. These are sharp in the context of a shrinking economic pie. A high degree of alienation and a feeling of despair is evident among the non-Malays in the face of privileges accruing to the Bumiputeras in excess of their proportion in the population. At the same time among the Bumiputeras are large numbers of lower and middle class who feel that the NEP has enabled a few privileged Malay businessmen to seize for themselves the best opportunities in education, employment and business and to become extraordinarily wealthy. The NEP has been especially instrumental in exacerbating Malay divisions by creating and empowering a Malay elite in federal administrative positions. Having taken control of key development mechanisms "to manage Malaysia's ethno-centric capitalist state," the new Malay elite have behaved like a "cartel" that, while espousing the cause of Bumiputera development and poverty eradication, have enriched themselves. As a result the ever-widening intra-ethnic gaps are today much more evident than the historical inter-ethnic disparities (Schlossstein, 1991).

The problem may be viewed in terms of the different organizing norms of the major groups. The Indians and Chinese subscribe to meritocratic or contest norms and firmly believe that they have the right to work hard and enjoy the fruits of their labor. The Malay elite, in possession of the instruments to promote their own mobility, are able to place a limit on the "contest" on an inter-communal basis. The difficulty arises from placing two conflicting norms "under the same institutional roof" (Bock, 1978). Malay sponsorship has erected institutional barriers to the operation of "contest mobility" as it is normally understood (Tham Seong Chee, 1977).

Contradictions have also arisen from the "dualistic interpretation" of national integration and unity. At one level national unity is the product of a common experience in school and working together to increase productivity to benefit all groups. On another level, social restructuring and the advancement of the Bumiputeras is crucial to promote national unity. Political and economic resources have been mobilised along ethnic lines to achieve the latter, exacerbating ethnic cleavages (Reid, 1988).

### *Scholarships for HRD/Malay Sponsorship*

The award of scholarships for higher education provides a lucid example of how government policies favored the Bumiputeras as a group and created divisions among them by favoring the better-off Bumiputeras over those from the really low-income group. Mehmet (1988) illustrates how the "trusteeship" role of the government worked in this sphere. The government created the demand for Malay manpower and through its expanded education facilities and special sponsorship of the Bumiputeras signaled to them "that the path out of poverty and under-development was through the acquisition of human capital. The trustees, of course, retained the power of sponsoring this acquisition" (through scholarship) and certifying its quality (by recognizing the degrees and diplomas earned).

The study of Malaysian graduates of 1982–83 revealed that the high-level manpower served primarily the requirements of the Malaysian government (67% worked for the government and another 14.5% for statutory bodies with only 16.2% for the private sector). Most of the scholarships were awarded in generalist disciplines (76.6%) rather than in the professional fields. In terms of social rates of return, there was evidently over-investment in the educational sector, providing a rate of return for scholarship holders of less than 5%. However private rates of return have been extremely profitable (15–20%) (Mehmet, 1988).

Most important, the scholarships have not promoted the poor as much as those from well-off families. The poor households (income less than RM$300 per month) who comprised 49.4% of the population received 12.3% of the scholarships while the richest 10% of the population enjoyed 25% of the awards. The regressive nature of the scholarships appeared to be acutest among the Malays. For every chance a poor Malay household had of receiving a government scholarship, the rich Malay group had 21 chances. The relative figures for the rich Chinese and Indians were 13 and 10 respectively. Mehmet concludes "the scholarships policy has become a public policy tool generating inequality in income distribution and promoting an elitist concentration of human capital" (ibid.).

## Values and Educational Development

### *The School Moral Education Programme*

In 1983, after several years of public debate and unprecedented consultation with various sectors of the population, the Malaysian government introduced the "moral education" (ME) curriculum into schools. The preamble to the syllabus states that its function was to provide:

> a means of maintaining and improving the moral consciousness of society. Such a strengthening of the moral fibre of the nation can form the basis for political, economic and social stability as well as for unity within the context of a plural . . . democratic society. (Curriculum Development Centre, 1982)
>
> The moral education programme is thus conceived as "a planned sequence of experiences and activities, both formal and informal . . . (in order) to assist pupils to identify, clarify and internalise values based on the religions, traditions and values of multiracial Malaysian society as well as universal moral values that are in accordance with the principles of the Rukunegara." (ibid.)

The long-term objective of the eleven-year curriculum is the development of a morally autonomous person who would be able to make moral decisions reached through rational, problem-solving processes, and act upon them. Sixteen "core" values provide the focus for teaching and learning and these include: cooperation, moderation, diligence, honesty, respect (for king and country, for all religions, for the environment, for parents and elders etc.) and public spiritedness.

The nature of the moral education curriculum and the course it has travelled since its inception give rise to issues linked with the process of educational development through centralized curriculum planning and implementation as well as the role of education in nation building, particularly in the case of a plural society.

*Genesis*

The Curriculum Development Centre identified several sources as triggering off proposals for an ME program in schools. Schooling as a process that shapes future citizens received particular attention after 1969—a year generally recognized as a watershed in educational decision-making as Malaysia sought to pull itself together after the worst-ever racial riots in the country. Parliamentary discussions on education during the early and middle seventies refer to growing street violence, drug abuse, indiscipline in schools and the need to identify school-level strategies which could help repair the delicate ethnic fabric which the race riots had torn apart (Mukherjee, 1983).

Parliament referred the matter to the Cabinet Committee on Education, which proposed the eleven-year curriculum. The initial understanding generally was that this would be intended for pupils of all races. Contrary to this belief, in 1979 the Cabinet Committee Report (Malaysia, 1979, par. 127.1) categorically stated that the new curriculum was to be planned for non-Muslim children, to be taught while their Muslim school-mates studied Agama (Islamic Religious Studies), the reason being that the Agama course included Akhlak (Islamic Ethics). The upshot of this decision was that Malaysian children would not be sharing common experiences in an area which was claimed as crucial to the country's future.

As in curriculum development exercises elsewhere, the events leading to the formulation and implementation of ME in Malaysian schools had a larger than local framework. Moral education (or Values Education as some label it) was receiving attention in industrializing as well as industrialized countries. In Japan, the National Institute for Educational Research working with UNESCO was involved in a state-of-the-art study of thirteen Asian countries, including Malaysia (UNESCO-NIER, 1981); the contributions of people such as R.S. Peters (1981) in the United Kingdom; and in the United States Lawrence Kohlberg's six-stage moral theory (1976), which claimed cross-cultural validity—all provided a fertile context for the school ME program.

*Implementation*

In 1983 ME was launched as part of the new primary school curriculum, being taught for three periods a week to non-Muslims while their friends studied Akhlak. Non-Islamic religious leaders and parents were uneasy: in their opinion the sub-text was the Islamization of their children. The fact that the first set of prototype materials was only available in the Malay language and not in Chinese and Tamil seemed to confirm their fears. The furore this set in train came to a head in a protest led by Chinese and Tamil school teachers who declared that the teaching materials, primarily reflecting Malay culture, were an attempt to indoctrinate non-Muslim/non-Malay children. Ineptitude and lack of sensitivity were closer to the truth than Machiavellian machination. The Ministry of Education had studied the ME program of Japan and South Korea prior to introducing their program in Malaysia. These countries had a long history of ME programs in the school curriculum. However, both countries had very homogeneous populations, unlike Malaysia. Lessons drawn from their experiences were thus of limited use to Malaysia's multi-religious and multilingual population. More appropriate would have been Singaporean strategies, directed to its plural population.

Implementation was dogged by a set of contradictions. A humanistic approach to values education directed to the development of a moral agent where the final court of appeal is the agent's own autonomously held universal principles sits uneasily in an authoritarian and hierarchical societal framework. Equally at dissonance with mainstream beliefs marked by faith in a supernatural being is the notion of the moral authority of the individual. Perhaps the most significant of dissonances exists between the values that are promoted, such as cooperation, public-spiritedness, value of the individual as an end (which are all in tune with universally held virtues in democratic states) and the impact on non-Malay pupils of the structural and policy framework in education.

The constitutionally backed privileges of the Bumiputeras within the publicly funded educational system that parcels out rewards in terms of educational and occupational opportunities provides the root cause of the deep-seated anguish of the other ethnic groups. When life chances are perceived to be restricted by design, a values-oriented curriculum can very quickly become an object of cynicism for those teaching as well as the taught. The special policies and implementation strategies (refer to previous section) designed to improve the occupational and social mobility of Bumiputeras permeate the school, creating a climate of resentment and distress which formal classroom work can do little to dispel. Competition rather than cooperation, loyalty to one's own community as a source of strength rather than king and country take precedence in the growing child. Character traits like honesty, integrity, diligence, respect for private property have little chance to take root in a context that is perceived as fundamentally unjust.

The Malaysian ME curriculum assumes much about what schools can achieve in terms of values inculcation. In a more homogeneous society such as Japan, what is taught in schools is continuous with the values held or at least overtly supported at home. In the Malaysian situation, the school is seen as a channel for decreasing the cultural heterogeneity in relation to value orientations by providing formal classes three times a week to some segments of the main players. From the official perspective the positive view is one that talks about "building consensus." The literature on values formation/ inculcation points to the overwhelming odds such a strategy is attempting to take on. Recent thinking in Malaysia indicates growing awareness of the situation and plans are afoot to provide reinforcement in the form of a "values across the curriculum" approach.

*Dissonances*

That social restructuring policies, acting through the instrumentality of education, and their impact on individuals have had a negative impact on national integration objectives is borne out not only through anecdotal reporting but also by a number of research studies. Among the more positive findings have been the effects of learning of Bahasa Malaysia (the national language) on Chinese students' national identity and integration (Lee, 1987) but evidence in general portrays the dysfunctional outcomes of the schooling process.

At all levels of education the realities of the opportunity structure outside institutional walls have had a more permanent and fundamental effect on the formation of attitudes and values than experience at school. Schools themselves primarily orient their learning strategies toward helping students obtain good qualifications (Leong, 1981) and even in the middle eighties teachers, expressing their firm conviction that their task was to enable pupils to pass examinations, were unable and in some cases unwilling to make any connection between national integration goals and classroom practice (Mukherjee, Ahmad, et al., 1984).

Chillingly, findings from the eighties seem to confirm investigations of the previous decade where ethnic relations in educational institutions were found to be based on distrust and fear (Singh, 1991b). In 1973 Takei, Bock and Saunders pointed out that the government's efforts at educational sponsorship of the Malays and their restructuring efforts had heightened ethnic sensitivities since each ethnic group viewed the system as benefiting the others. Students in the ethnically heterogeneous national schools were more alienated from the other ethnic groups due to the conflict between the contest and sponsored norms that characterize Malaysian society (Bock, 1978). This was found to be true in the tertiary educational sector as well. The ethnic factor was dominant in all spheres of interaction—at lectures, tutorials, the library, the canteen, the hostel and in the sports field (Mudzaffar, 1984).

A twist to the tale emerges in a study of three categories of Chinese students (Yew, 1982): those in national type schools (the most heterogeneous being previously English medium schools), in homogeneous Chinese medium schools within the national system and in independent Chinese schools outside the national educational system. The investigation affirms that the less students felt threatened by the political system, the more they identified themselves with the political system irrespective of their different backgrounds (ibid.). Despite better facilities and better job opportunities, students in the ethnically heterogeneous and competitive environment of the national schools felt more threatened and revealed more anxiety regarding socioeconomic mobility, employment and educational opportunities than those in the homogeneous national schools while this second category had a lower level of security than those in the independent schools.

The political and economic underpinnings of educational reform are dramatically demonstrated in the national language policy that served to change the entire face of the system as well as its nuts and bolts. According to one analyst, "the issues of national language and education featured prominently in the bargaining between Malays and non-Malays prior to 1957" during the period of pre-independence negotiations (Mah Hui Lim, 1985).

In his work on *Inequality and Economic Development in Malaysia*, Snodgrass highlights the following analysis by Silcock:

> The English educated Malays could capture power only by coming to terms with the Chinese. Having a majority of the electorate, as well as a greater participation in the British system of government, they had superior bargaining power, and they realized that emphasis on English education would favour the urban non-Malays. They could not, however, press for a complete Malay system of education without alienating the essential minimum of Chinese support. As a result, a mixed system with gradual pressure toward Malay as a national language was introduced. (cited in Snodgrass, 1980)

When Bahasa Malaysia began to replace English as the medium of instruction in 1970, English as the colonial language was dropped from the core of the common content curriculum. Recently it has made a re-appearance within the context of its contribution to national development. Being the major international language of commerce and international trade, science and technology and diplomacy, substituting it hastily with Bahasa Malaysia with its modern, technological vocabulary still in a state of evolution is now recognized unofficially as a retrogressive step. An unexpected outcome of this policy was the facility developed by urban Chinese and Indian national school pupils in the national language: this, coupled with their mastery of English, tended to give them a head start in overseas training institutions as well as in the private sector as employment opportunities for non-Bumiputeras in the government sector proceeded to contract in line with speedily implemented affirmative action policies.

A key strategy in the implementation of the national language policy was the development of textbooks in the national language that in the post-1969 period were expected to serve the government's social and political goals. The British-oriented content of texts still in use more than a decade after independence was to be replaced by an ethos identifiably Malaysian. Investigations demonstrate that the plethora of texts that invaded educational institutions in the early seventies interpreted "Malaysian" as "Malay" and this was true for texts in English as well as Malay (Mukherjee and Ahmad, 1988). Of the 476 comprehension passages analyzed in the English language texts, about 63% focused on Malays, 21% on Chinese, 10% on Indians and 6% on the indigenous from the East Malaysian states of Sabah and Sarawak. Significantly, less than 14% of the passages referred to the various races interacting with each other. Development-oriented messages such as starting up a small business always used Malay role models with the other groups in a subordinate power/authority relationship. Similar verbal and visual messages recurred across the board in terms of regional sensitivities, the rural-urban dimension, social class and cross-cultural awareness. In sifting through implementational tools such as textbooks through which the largest number of Malaysians are subject to a nationally designed curriculum over a sustained period of time, it is difficult to conclude whether the substance selected is the outcome of conspiracy, insensitivity or ignorance.

## Conclusion

In the introduction to this chapter it was held that the relationship between education and development in Malaysia is a complex and multi-dimensional one. Additionally, educational policies and the effects of implementation point to the fact that education's role is a dynamic one, with characteristics, aims and the manner of implementation altering as situational specifics change.

From a historical perspective education's contribution may seem almost chameleon-like. For a decade or so after independence in 1957, the educational system continued in the four media of instruction as in pre-independence days but sharing a common curriculum. High-status jobs continued to be the preserve of the English educated. In the last two decades, aggressive pro-Bumiputera affirmative action policies, especially at the tertiary level, have altered radically the profile of the high-status job-holders, most visibly in the government and parastatal sectors.

Broadly speaking the government, represented by the Alliance party with the United Malays National Organisation (UMNO) as the dominant component, was able to put in place legislation designed to safeguard the goals of the NEP to accord the Malays a favored position. Furthermore, through a gradual process of promoting Malays into senior positions within the different services, Malays occupied key positions in the power hierarchies to promote the interests of the Bumiputeras in all matters pertaining to recruitment and promotion. Thus, educational expansion went hand in hand with strong government interventionist measures to achieve the targets.

Where economic growth is concerned, the role of education may be said to be largely supportive as seen in policies consciously directed to human resource development objectives at various levels in response to the needs of the industrializing economy. Schools, training institutes, polytechnics and universities have played important parts in producing skilled and trainable school leavers, middle-level technicians and high-level scientific, technological and managerial personnel. Education and training provided by overseas educational institutions have augmented numbers trained for the Malaysian labor market. Also perceived as supportive of growth has been the emphasis on ethical and religious education which is expected to help develop a stable, unified and development-oriented society. Education's instrumental role is probably best demonstrated in the educational support structures that were established to enable Bumiputeras to access opportunities made available through the New Economic Policy.

Another way of understanding the consequences of educational reforms in Malaysia may be to view them from the following vantage points:

a. at a global level in order to promote economic growth per se, education took on a strong human resource orientation in order to be internationally competitive during the process of industrialization;

b. at the national macro-level, education brought about social restructuring through strategies providing indigenous groups special access to education and occupation opportunities; and

c. at the micro-level, curricular reform was set in train within educational systems in order to support and to help operationalize global and macro level objectives.

Educational planners have generally adopted a structuralist-functionalist approach to change aimed at achieving equilibrium between its disparate groups to meet the needs of a modern industrial society. Nevertheless, internal group conflicts have persisted and it has not altogether been possible to eradicate the inequities. Rather, new disparities have emerged with some of the existing contradictions being further exacerbated. Perhaps Indonesia's success in reducing the incidence of poverty (from 58% in 1970 to 17% in 1987 compared with Malaysia's own impressive fall from 37% in 1973 to 15% in 1957 according to World Bank's figures) without resorting to race-directed redressal policies should give Malaysia's planners pause for thought. In the words of *The Economist* (May 4, 1991a), it "suggests that Malaysia might have done better without the waste of economic apartheid." On the other hand nations chart their courses in ways that are a result of their unique histories.

Malaysia has been perhaps more proactive and interventionist in its educational policies than many other developing countries. In this it has been assisted primarily by the prevalent authoritarian ethos which provides an environment whereby the major ethnic groups tend to accept the pronouncements of the government. For more than thirty years Malaysia has had a strong and confident Alliance government with UMNO at the helm which is able to legislate and oversee implementation of policies. The hand of government intervention is evident at all levels of the education process—entry to school, selection and access to higher education, quotas in employment and education. All three ethnic groups historically are not alien to authoritarian rule and find the "guided democracy" a model they can live and work with. Besides, some degree of consultation is seen to take place and through the presence of each of the ethnic groups in the coalition government, a semblance of consensus is preserved. Furthermore both the immigrant groups, finding themselves in a weakened political position, have adopted a pragmatism that prevents open opposition which could only serve to damage everyone's prospects. As far as possible they tread carefully in order not to upset the delicate balance that has been established, displaying what has been termed as "the egg-shell syndrome."

## Note

1. There have been six national development plans since 1965. These range from the First Malayan Plan (1MP: Malaysia, 1966 [1966–70]) to the Sixth Malaysian Plan (6MP: Malaysia, 1991 [1991–95].

# 8 Macau

*Mark Bray*

The links between education and development in Macau have received little attention by researchers. One reason is that Macau has seemed small and idiosyncratic, very different from other parts of Asia and apparently with few instructive messages for neighbouring and other countries.

However, during the last two decades the neglect has been at least partly rectified. With its marked economic growth and expanded population, Macau can no longer be described as a sleepy backwater. Also, the operation of the university which was founded in 1981 has helped create a local research community. This is in itself an aspect of the linkage between education and development with which this chapter is concerned.

Because research traditions in Macau have not been strong, much of the data necessary for full understanding of the links between education and development in the territory is lacking. Nevertheless, sufficient evidence is available to indicate that the relationship is far from straightforward. Like other parts of the book, this chapter is particularly concerned with links between education and economic development. Macau has achieved a great deal in economic development in recent decades, but it is far from certain that the economic growth is a direct result from investment in education.

## Background

### *History and Politics*

Macau takes 1557 as the year of its foundation. At this time, after several unsuccessful attempts dating back to 1513, Portuguese traders finally secured from the Chinese authorities rights of settlement in the territory. Some constitutional specialists argue that the arrangement was a lease rather than a cession (Afonso and Pereira, 1986, pp. 28–33). However, the Europeans were allowed considerable autonomy, and an 1887 treaty brought explicit recognition of Portuguese sovereignty.

Macau had confirmed itself as the keystone of the Portuguese trade-empire soon after its establishment. Portuguese trade in spices, silk, porcelain and silver was virtually unrivalled during the period 1570 to 1640. Almost all China's foreign trade passed through Portuguese hands, and Macau was among the world's foremost entrepôts.

Macau also played a major religious and cultural role. In 1576 the territory was made the center of a diocese which included all of China and Japan. The church established many schools, one of which became a university in 1594. It operated until 1762, and taught theology, humanities, Greek, Latin, rhetoric and philosophy (Pires, 1991, p. 16). Teixeira's (1982) historical account shows that Macau well deserved its appellation "The City of Schools."

After the mid-seventeenth century, Macau's fortunes declined. Portugal proved unable to hold her empire together, and competition for East Asian trade intensified. The foundation of Hong Kong in 1842 was a particularly serious blow, in particular because its far superior port led Hong Kong to take over the strategic significance that Macau had previously enjoyed.

After the end of World War II, the Nationalist government in China wished to repossess the territory. However, the Chinese authorities were unable to force the issue, especially after civil war broke out, and even after the Communist victory in 1949 the issue was not pressed. During the Korean War Macau was used for smuggling raw materials and munitions into China. The People's Republic of China therefore came to consider Macau more valuable as a Portuguese colony than as an integral part of China (Edmonds, 1989, p. xxiii).

The Indian takeover of Portuguese Goa in 1961 led many people to wonder how long Portugal would hold on to Macau, especially since China expressly supported the Indian stance. During the 1960s, tension with the Chinese government mounted. The outbreak of China's Cultural Revolution in 1966 led to violent riots in the territory and to vigorous anti-Portuguese propaganda both locally and in China itself. Unexpectedly, however, as soon as the Portuguese announced that they intended to leave, the Communists immediately altered their stance (Edmonds, 1989, p. xxv). It may be assumed that the Chinese authorities were conscious of Macau's valuable role as an outlet for international trade, and again found it more useful to retain Macau as a foreign port than to repossess it.

Eight years later, Portugal itself experienced a revolution. The new government had a very different view of world affairs, and immediately set about decolonising its African territories. In Asia, East Timor was unilaterally seized by Indonesia, and matters would perhaps have been more simple for Portugal if China had similarly seized Macau. However, the Chinese continued to view the Portuguese administration of Macau as an asset for foreign trade, and did not attempt to reassert sovereignty.

Finally, in 1987 the Portuguese and Chinese governments agreed that Macau would revert to China in 1999. This will be two years after a similar resumption of sovereignty in Hong Kong. Like Hong Kong, Macau is expected to remain a Special Administrative Region for at least 50 years after the transition. Meanwhile, Macau is officially regarded as a "Chinese territory under Portuguese administration."

### *Geography and Population*

The territory of Macau consists of a small peninsula plus two adjacent islands. The total land area is just 18 square kilometers, and the surrounding territory belonging to the People's Republic of China (PRC) is easily visible from many points.

The 1991 census indicated a population of 401,900, of which 47,000 were non-residents (Macau, 1991a, p. 10). This implies a density of 22,300 persons per square kilometer, which makes Macau the most densely populated territory in the world. Hong Kong, by contrast, had just 5,600 persons per square kilometer in 1991. Macau's population has grown rapidly over the last few decades. It was estimated at 268,000 in 1980, and 169,000 in 1960 (Chan and Tan, 1991, p. 219). Much of the population increase has been the result of immigration, particularly from the PRC, rather than of natural increase.

Over 90% of Macau's population is Chinese by ethnicity. Two significant minority groups are a small cadre of Portuguese and a mixed-race group known as the Macanese (Zepp, 1991, p. 153). Many of the Portuguese are descendants from long-established families, though others have been recruited on short-term contracts to assist with administration, education and other social services.

A considerable proportion of Macau's food and other daily necessities is imported each day across the Chinese border. Macau also has excellent communications with Hong Kong, which is only 38 nautical miles to the east and is easily reached by jetfoil, hydrofoil and ship. The significance of the links with Hong Kong is demonstrated by the extent of the traffic. During 1992, for example, visitor-arrivals from Hong Kong totaled 6.2 million, of which 4.9 million were Hong Kong residents (Macau, 1993, p. 20).

### *Economy*

Macau's economy compares well with others in the region. In East Asia, it ranks fifth in per capita Gross Domestic Product (GDP), after Brunei Darussalam, Japan, Singapore and Hong Kong (Cremer, 1989, p. 221). The territory ranks sixth in hospital beds, second in medical doctors, sixth in infant mortality rate, second in life expectancy at birth and fifth in private cars per 100 persons. Imprecise as these comparisons are—for instance because of different statistical measurement concepts—they nonetheless show that Macau has a notable economy and standard of living.

Official figures placed the 1990 GDP per head at $8,100 (Macau, 1991b, p. 3). Manufacturing comprises 40% of GDP. According to *The Economist* recent years have also brought major growth of the tourist sector, much of which is linked to gambling in the casinos. Cremer (1989, p. 227) reports that of the 4.5 million tourists coming to Macau in 1985, 85% were gamblers. The direct and indirect contribution of gambling to Macau's GDP was estimated at 15–20%, and taxation on gambling provided nearly half of the government's total revenue. Being a highly urbanised society in which land commands substantial prices, Macau has a negligible agricultural sector.

Sit et al. (1991, pp. 12–18) divide analysis of the process of industrialisation in Macau into four phases: early industrialization, Portugal-led transformation, take-off led by textiles and garments, and industrial diversification. Subsequent sections of this chapter will comment on the role that education did or did not play in these phases, but meanwhile it is useful to outline the key features of each period.

The early period covers the years up to the 1930s. The principal manufactured products were matches, fire-crackers and incense. In 1930 their combined share in total exports was 37.8%, and in 1958 they still generated 28.5%. Fishing was at that time the dominant employer, but handicraft industries, especially production of matches, fire-crackers and incense, were the second largest.

The decline of Macau's traditional industries was mainly due to the loss of the American market following a removal of tariff preferences. Fortunately, new opportunities arose from free movement of goods into Portugal and its African colonies, and the period 1930 to 1958 brought structural change from traditional handicrafts to textiles, wigs and other light manufactured consumer products. The phase was truncated in the 1960s when the "duty free" privileges of Macau products to enter Portugal and Portuguese colonies were withdrawn.

The industrial take-off phase resulted from Hong Kong's success as a base for light industry and trade. Under the pressure of increasing restrictions placed by foreign countries on textile and garment exports from Hong

Kong, some Hong Kong industrialists set up production facilities in Macau, which was not then subject to similar restrictions. Macau had the additional advantage of lower labour and rental costs. This period saw particular growth in the textile and garment industry, which formed 58.2% of total exports in 1970 and peaked at 90.0% in 1979.

The fourth phase, of industrial diversification, took place in the 1980s. Excessive concentration on textiles and garments proved dangerous, and Macau was soon put under restraint by the major overseas markets. Industrialists accordingly developed new products, including toys, artificial flowers, electronic goods and leather articles. Many of these products went to the United States rather than to Europe. During the period 1979–88, domestic exports grew by an annual rate of approximately 23%.

Turning to the service sector, the contribution of tourism has already been mentioned. The number of hotel rooms increased from 3,200 in 1980 to 5,000 in 1990. Many of the visitors came from Hong Kong for short periods primarily for gambling, but other tourists, about a quarter of the total in 1990, were from further afield. In addition, a significant proportion of hotel rooms were occupied by businessmen from the PRC and elsewhere. The tourist sector has been greatly stimulated by improved transportation between Macau and Hong Kong. The combination of new hotel facilities and good communications has encouraged some companies and organizations to choose Macau as a venue for conferences since the costs are much lower than in neighboring Hong Kong.

The 1970s and 1980s also witnessed emergence of the banking sector. Following passage of a banking ordinance in 1982, the number of banks increased from 15 to 23 with a total of 90 branches. By 1990 the number of banks had reduced to 21, but the number of branches had increased to 102 (Macau, 1991c, p. 328). During the 1980s total savings in all banks increased by an average of 20% per annum; and in the late 1980s the government also investigated the feasibility of a stock exchange (Hui and Noronha, 1991, p. 17; Feitor and Cremer, 1991, p. 186).

## The Nature of Schooling

In the late 1980s, the government embarked on a series of major education reforms (Rosa, 1990; Macau, 1990; Macau, 1991d; Cheong, 1993). The chief stimulus for this activity was awareness that in 1999 sovereignty over the territory would revert to China. It was clear that considerable preparation was needed to ensure that Macau could exercise autonomy as a Special Administrative Region within the PRC, and this preparation was needed in education as well as other sectors. The impetus for reform may also be traced to certain key individuals, and it was facilitated by the improved economic performance of the territory during the 1980s.

One factor behind the need for reform was that Macau had never had a single, distinctive education system. Instead it had an uncoordinated collection of systems based on models used in Portugal, the PRC, Taiwan and Hong Kong (Alves Pinto, 1987, pp. 20–21; Bray and Tang, 1993). The number of years in the primary, junior secondary and senior secondary cycles varied according to the model. The Portuguese model followed a 4+2+3+2+1 pattern, the PRC-oriented schools had a 6+5 structure, pro-Taiwan schools had a 6+3+3 system and most schools following Hong Kong curricula had a 6+5+1 structure.

However, even the categorization into four basic systems is to some extent a simplification. A 1987 survey showed a bewildering total collection of combinations (Table 1). The existence of these different systems reflected the haphazard way in which education in Macau had been allowed to develop (Rosa, 1992, pp. 63–64).

TABLE 1. Number of Schools, by Type and Level, 1987/88

| *Level/Combination* | *System of Curriculum* | | | | | | |
|---|---|---|---|---|---|---|---|
| | *Taiwan* | *PRC* | *Hong Kong* | *Portuguese* | *Luso-Chinese* | *Other* | *Total* |
| Pre-School | 4 | | 2 | 2 | | | 8 |
| Pre-School & Basic | 21 | 10 | 6 | 2 | 3 | 1 | 43 |
| Pre-School, Basic & Secondary | 8 | 2 | 1 | 1 | | | 12 |
| Basic | 2 | | | 2 | | | 4 |
| Basic & Secondary | 2 | 1 | 4 | 1 | 1 | | 9 |
| Basic & Secondary Tech-Professional | | 1 | 1 | | | | 2 |
| Secondary | 4 | 2 | | 1 | | | 7 |
| Secondary & Teacher Training | | | | | | 1 | 1 |
| Secondary & Higher | | | 1 | | | | 1 |
| Teacher Training | | | | 1 | | | 1 |
| Nursing School | | | | 1 | 1 | | 2 |
| Higher | | | 1 | | | 2 | 3 |
| TOTAL | 41 | 16 | 16 | 11 | 5 | 4 | 93 |

Note: The original table referred to the "Anglo-Saxon" rather than the Hong Kong model. "Hong Kong" seems a better descriptor, since the model was adopted from there rather than directly from the United Kingdom.
Source: Macau, 1989a, p. 40.

Another striking aspect of education in Macau is the distinction between official and private schools. The former comprise only 11% of primary schools and 6% of secondary ones. The vast majority of schools are private institutions run by religious bodies, social service organisations, commercial enterprises and individuals. A small number of private schools operate a curriculum which parallels that of the official Portuguese schools, but the curriculum of the majority is very different from that in official schools.

Table 2 provides data on the institutions existing in 1991–92, classified by the medium of instruction. The majority of institutions used Chinese as the medium of instruction (except when teaching other languages as classroom subjects). Most of these institutions were private. Sixteen institutions, which were all private, used English as the main medium of instruction.

TABLE 2: Schools and Pupils, by Medium of Instruction, Macau, 1991/92

| *Type of School/Language* | *Pre-Primary* | | *Primary* | | *Secondary* | |
|---|---|---|---|---|---|---|
| | *Schools* | *Pupils* | *Schools* | *Pupils* | *Schools* | *Pupils* |
| Official | | | | | | |
| Chinese | 7 | 1,126 | 6 | 1,458 | 1 | 402 |
| Portuguese | 1 | 225 | 2 | 646 | 1 | 1,318 |
| Private | | | | | | |
| Chinese | 56 | 19,562 | 57 | 32,342 | 24 | 13,997 |
| Portuguese | 2 | 198 | 4 | 564 | 2 | 346 |
| English | 3 | 364 | 6 | 3,530 | 7 | 3,277 |
| TOTAL | 69 | 21,475 | 75 | 38,540 | 35 | 19,340 |

Note: The totals in this table diverge from those in Table 1. This is partly because figures refer to a different year, but also because of a different definition of "school." For example it seems that an institution teaching at basic and secondary levels was considered one institution for Table 1 but two (or even three?) institutions here.
Source: Direcção dos Serviços de Educação, Macau.

The government's Portuguese medium schools exist mainly to serve the Portuguese expatriate population, local Portuguese families, and others who either have or desire close links with Portugal. Until recently, all government jobs required fluency in the Portuguese language, and many recruits for government posts were drawn from these schools. The government also operates Luso-Chinese schools, which use Chinese as the main medium but also teach Portuguese. For many years the Luso-Chinese schools operated only at the primary level, but a Luso-Chinese secondary school was opened in 1985 (Rosa, 1992, p. 64). By 1991–92 enrollments in Luso-Chinese official primary schools were over twice those in the Portuguese primary schools, but the picture was reversed at the secondary level. The Portuguese official schools are really European schools operating in Asia (Bray and Hui, 1991, p. 187). Their students use Portuguese textbooks, learn about Portuguese history, geography and botany, and follow the Portuguese assessment system.

## The Nature of University Education

Like the school sector, the tertiary education sector in Macau differs markedly from those in other East Asian countries. This is partly because of Macau's unusual history and circumstances, and partly because the territory has a small population (Bray and Hui, 1989). The recent history of the university sector again illustrates first the laissez-faire government, followed by a more interventionist policy.

The first section of this chapter noted that a university was founded in Macau in 1594. When that institution ceased to function in 1762, the territory was again left without local provision of higher education. Only since 1981, with the foundation of the University of East Asia (UEA), has Macau again had a tertiary institution of its own. In 1991 the UEA was renamed the University of Macau.

The university was established primarily as a commercial venture—a fact which again reflects the government's lack of interest in education at the time. The university's founders had identified considerable unsatisfied demand for education in Hong Kong, and were keen to tap that demand. Hong Kong law prohibited establishment of private universities in the territory, and there seemed little prospect that the law would be changed. Macau had no comparable prohibition, and its authorities were much less antagonistic to the concept of a private university. Macau therefore seemed a good site, within easy reach of Hong Kong and also with its own tertiary educational needs. The businessmen proposing the institution felt that additional demand might be found among Chinese communities in Malaysia and elsewhere. This desire to have international appeal in part explains why at that time the institution was called the University of East Asia rather than the University of Macau (Mellor, 1988, pp. 3–6).

The background to this university, established by Hong Kong businessmen unable to operate such an institution in Macau, has a parallel with the textile operations set up in Macau by Hong Kong businessmen, mentioned above. Since the university was a commercial venture, its principal objective was to secure financial profit; and since it existed primarily to tap demand from outside Macau its principal working language was English rather than Portuguese. The staff were mainly recruited from outside Macau, and the courses were primarily oriented to non-Macau students.

With the political changes associated with the timetable for resumption of Chinese sovereignty, by the late 1980s the government had become more sensitive about its lack of leadership in the educational sector. One major action in 1988 was governmental purchase of the main body of the university. Although the influence of the original philosophy and mode of operation remained strong, the change of ownership of course brought a change in outlook. In 1990, the university changed the basic length of its degree courses from three to four years. In part, this change resulted from the need to facilitate and attract direct entry from local secondary schools so that the UEA could become the normal first choice for Macau school leavers. The change also brought the university into line with the dominant models in Portugal, the PRC and North America, and it enabled the UEA to strengthen the quality of its programmes and thereby to facilitate recognition both locally and abroad.

The change of ownership also brought efforts to increase the proportion of local students. In 1986–87 only 10.5% of the students came from Macau (Mellor, 1988, p. 187). By far the largest number came from Hong Kong, though significant numbers were also recruited from China and Malaysia. Only in the Junior College did Macau students comprise the largest group, and even there they represented only 40.0% of the total.

However, the largest numbers of Hong Kong students were in the Graduate and Open colleges, which were not purchased with the main body of the institution. The separation of these two colleges markedly reduced the enrollment, but significantly tilted the balance in favor of Macau. Figures for 1989–90 showed an institution with just 1,648 students compared with 8,329 two years previously; but 73.9% of the students in 1989–90 were from Macau compared with about 10.0% two years previously (Rangel, 1991, p. 320).

### Technical Education and Training

Until the 1980s, Macau had little formal technical education and training. One factor behind the lack of demand for technical training in government institutions was the language of instruction. Macau's manufacturing and commercial sectors have always operated primarily in Chinese, and training through the medium of Portuguese attracted few applicants.

The lack of governmental provision was only partially alleviated by the private sector. One institution operated by the Roman Catholic church provided technical training at the secondary level, but it had an enrollment of only 500 male students (no females) in Grades 7–11. Almost no formal training was provided by enterprises themselves. The vast majority of firms were very small, with 30% of companies in the mid-1980s having fewer than five employees. Few companies were interested in provision of formal training, and in any case most were too small to be able to undertake it. Most firms preferred either to recruit technicians who had trained in Hong Kong or elsewhere, or to encourage their workers to learn informally on the job.

The establishment of the University of East Asia in 1981 brought important change. The university had a College of Continuing Education, which in 1986 was renamed the Polytechnic College (Mellor, 1988, p. 184). It had only 200 places, but was nevertheless of considerable significance. In 1990 the college was separated from its parent body and, together with the Junior College, became an independent polytechnic. It currently offers programs in computer studies, hotel management, tourism and social work, and also has a range of extra-mural and pre-university programs (Rangel, 1991, p. 319).

Another important innovation was the foundation of the Industrial Training and Development Centre (CADI) in 1985 under the umbrella of the government's Department of Industry. It had an annual budget of $250,000 for full- and part-time training, and by 1988 had enrolled over 2,000 students on various short courses at technician, craftsman and operative levels (Sit et al., 1991, p. 186). The long courses at the technician level include the Diploma in Fashion, which trains people who are not in the trade but who want to join it. Shorter craftsmen and operative courses serve sewing machine mechanics, cutting operators, pattern graders and similar personnel.

The Association of Industry also offers regular Industrial Training courses, with subsidies from the government; and the Macau Management Association runs a Vocational Training Centre which offers courses on languages, computers, banking and advertising. Also, since the early 1980s the government has operated a Nautical Training School, a Hotel and Tourism Training School, and various schemes within its specialist departments. Recent years have therefore brought major growth. The sector remains poorly coordinated, but is at least better developed than before.

## Links between Education and Social Development

Despite the government's neglect of education until the 1980s, Macau could still be described, as in the title of Cremer's book, as a city not only of commerce but also of culture (Cremer, 1987, 1991). Education has played a key role in developing that culture. However, the precise definition of culture may be elusive. Cremer did not indicate explicitly what he meant by the word, though the emphasis of his book seems to be on the "high" culture of religion, art and architecture. Of additional importance is what Wielemans and

Chan (1992) call the industrial mentality.

Beginning with a historical note, it is useful to recall that in the sixteenth to eighteenth centuries Macau was a major conduit through which Western education and science entered China, Japan and Korea. Although Macau's economic place was eclipsed by the foundation of Hong Kong in the nineteenth century, the territory remained a centre of learning of considerable note. Pires (1991, pp. 18–19) emphasizes the blend of Portuguese and Chinese cultures, and highlights Macau's reputation for publication and scholarship.

Among the most significant actors in Macau's social development has been the Roman Catholic church. Teixeira (1991, p. 43) describes Macau as "the Rome of the Far East," and documents significant aspects of church history and work. Even today, the church operates a large proportion of the territory's schools, and it is partly because of the influence of the church that despite the absence of compulsory education Macau has had a primary school enrollment rate exceeding 95%.

Turning to the notion of industrial mentality, Wielemans and Chan (1992, p. 1) defined the phrase to mean:

> the typical mentality of man living in an industrial world which dominates both his perception and interpretation of his relationships toward nature, with his fellowmen, toward his self and in his transcendental relationship.

Taking this definition, Wielemans and Chan organized a major comparative education research project focusing on China, Hong Kong, Japan, Korea, Malaysia, the Philippines, Singapore, Taiwan and Thailand. It is regrettable that Macau was omitted from their list, for in terms of the proportion of GDP contributed by industry it is more industrialized than any of these places. It would be an instructive future exercise to explore in detail the Wielemans and Chan hypotheses with reference to Macau, and to add the findings to the international picture.

Meanwhile, however, it is at least possible to make some comparisons with Hong Kong, which shares many characteristics with Macau. The Hong Kong chapter in the Wielemans and Chan book was written by Luk (1992). He observed (p. 117):

> Unlike most national governments with its own cultural agenda to follow and the interests of its domestic power-base to promote through its educational policies, the colonial government of Hong

> Kong has not tried to impose its own or any one group's core values on the populace; rather, it has allowed the various groups to "do their own things," and to thrive, wither, or change in the evolving socio-economic environment.

In so far as this was true of Hong Kong, it was even more true of Macau. It is perhaps an overstatement to describe the philosophy of the Portuguese and Macau governments as laissez faire, for it has really been one of neglect. Indeed, in 1984 the Governor of Macau himself admitted that the territory's social system had "undoubtedly been characterised by enormous inertia" (de Almeida e Costa, 1984, p. 4). With specific reference to education, whereas the Hong Kong government passed an ordinance in 1913 to give it powers to control aspects of education in non-government schools (Sweeting, 1990a, pp. 283–9), only in 1991 was a similar step taken in Macau. Rosa (1992, p. 65) highlights a 1939 official document in which the Portuguese authorities described Macau's private schools as "foreign schools for foreign peoples." It was through this philosophy that the government was able to justify to itself neglect of the institutions.

A second point made by Luk concerns the origins of the Hong Kong population. Hong Kong is a society of migrants and their children. The latter may have been born locally, but most of the migrants came from China during the last four decades either in flight from political turmoil or in search of economic gain. Again, the parallels with Macau are very clear. Many of the migrants in both places came from peasant backgrounds, and have had to undergo profound changes in attitudes and habits to fit into the industrialised society. Luk's (1992, p. 12) comments on Hong Kong could as easily refer to Macau:

> The vast majority of . . . people live in high-rise residential buildings with several apartments to each floor. The scale of housing, and the degree of mobility, are such that no one is likely to be acquainted with all the neighbours even on one's own floor. . . . One's work and rest is regulated by the Gregorian calendar, while the traditional farming calendar is also observed for certain old festivals which have lost much of their agricultural connotations. The human life cycle is punctuated not only by the natural stages of generation, but also by the steps of schooling and career in an industrial society. Gender role restrictions have blurred, but have not entirely disappeared; and in education, in employment and in social life, there is much more equality and openness between the sexes.

The last two sentences of the above quotation make a link between social change and education. Luk proceeds with observations about the nature of schooling (pp. 138–9), including the ways that the Hong Kong educational system inculcates awareness of cultural heritage, respect for authority and valuation of time. Again, such observations are also applicable to Macau.

Among ways in which Macau differs from Hong Kong, however, is in the fragmentation of educational provision. Macau has many different models of schooling, all of which have largely external orientations. Following its non-interventionist policy, until the late 1980s the government did nothing to change this situation. The government has not produced any textbooks for Macau schools; and because of the small size of the market the commercial sector has not bridged the gap. As a result, almost all textbooks used in Macau have been written for other societies. In official schools most books come from Portugal, and in private schools they come from Hong Kong and, to a lesser extent, the People's Republic of China and elsewhere (Bray and Hui, 1991; Tang, 1991). Macau even lacks a set of basic history textbooks oriented to the local society (Tan, 1993). The result is that pupils using Hong Kong textbooks learn about the Hong Kong currency, the Hong Kong transportation systems, and the Hong Kong system of government. Pupils using PRC books learn about the virtues of socialism and the People's Liberation Army; and pupils using Portuguese books read about Portuguese social values and aspirations. In such a setting, it is hardly surprising that Macau seems to have an even greater identity crisis than Hong Kong. Macau's schools have not been used very effectively as a vehicle for resolving that crisis.

## Links between Education and Economic Development

The introductory sections to this chapter highlighted Macau's impressive recent economic growth. This has generated funds for the expansion of education. Government investments increased markedly in the 1980s and early 1990s, with the purchase of the main campus of the university, creation of a separate polytechnic, provision of grants to private schools and expansion of general support services.

As well as having a larger total budget, the government devoted a greater proportion of the budget to education. In 1975, the government spent only 2.2% on education. By world standards that figure was very low. World Bank statistics (1980, p. 67) show that at that period the average for industrialised countries was 15.6%, and that for developing countries was 15.1%. However in the 1980s the picture began to change, and by 1989 the allocation had risen to 7.6% (Bray, 1991, p. 15).

While economic growth certainly permitted expansion of education, it is more difficult to say that economic growth depended on education. Education may be necessary to underpin future growth; but it was not a major ingredient in the 1970s and 1980s. As noted by Feitor and Cremer (1991, p. 189), the five main factors contributing to economic growth were:

- favorable geographic location, especially the proximity to Hong Kong (from which there was a spill-over of development) and to mainland China (which provided cheap food, raw materials and other necessities);
- a liberal economic system, with limited government intervention;
- comparatively favorable access to foreign markets;
- a nucleus of dynamic entrepreneurs with positive attitudes toward risk-assumption; and
- high elasticity of labor supply, especially of unskilled labor, and correspondingly low wages.

Notably absent from this list is any reference to education.

Concerning the industrial sector, much valuable information for deeper analysis is provided by Sit et al. (1991), who in 1987 investigated small and medium-sized establishments in Macau. Their survey included interviews in 100 establishments, which represented 24.9% of the total. They showed (p. 57) that the majority of entrepreneurs were first-generation migrants. Studies elsewhere (e.g., Wong, 1988) have indicated a strong connection between immigrant status and the drive toward economic development and risk-taking. Sit et al. found that 38.8% of entrepreneurs had arrived since 1971, and that 57.2% had arrived since 1964. This contrasted with a survey in Hong Kong, which found respective figures of 9.7 and 19.4%. The statistics reflect Macau's more recent development. Because in the 1940s and 1950s Macau was an economic backwater, most migrants were drawn to Hong Kong rather than Macau. It was only when Hong Kong had become established as a manufacturing center that there was a diversification into Macau. Indeed, 21% of the entrepreneurs who had migrated to Macau since 1949 were of Hong Kong origin.

Sit et al. also provide information on the educational levels of the entrepreneurs. Table 3 compares the researchers' survey results with 1981 census data on the educational levels of the total working population. As might be expected, the entrepreneurs had higher levels of education than the working population as a whole. However, particularly striking, in a community which had no university until 1981, is that 7.2% had tertiary education. The majority were schooled in the Chinese mode, and may have turned to entrepreneurship because they lacked the type of qualifications required for stable, salaried work with the government and similar employers.

TABLE 3. Educational Attainment of the Working Population (1981) and of Entrepreneurs (1987), Macau (%)

| *Education Level* | *Working Population* | *Entrepreneurs* |
|---|---|---|
| No Schooling | 9.9 | 6.0 |
| Primary | 53.7* | 25.0 |
| Secondary | 34.4** | 61.9 |
| Tertiary | 2.0 | 7.2 |
| TOTAL | 100.0 | 100.0 |

* Including 27.2% graduating from "preparatory" classes for secondary school.
** Including 2.3% at matriculation level.
Source: Sit et al., 1991, p. 70.

The entrepreneurs were relatively well educated, but only 1.9% had received technical or pre-vocational education at the secondary level. In reply to a separate question, 63.3% indicated that they had received no technical or managerial training at any level (Table 4). When asked to specify the source of their knowledge, over a quarter said that they did not know and could not give an answer. Of those who could give a specific reply, many learned though direct experience on the jobs they held before becoming owners. Some 72.6% and 66.2% respectively derived their technical and managerial knowledge in this way (Table 5).

TABLE 4. Technical and Managerial Training of Macau Entrepreneurs

| *Training* | % |
|---|---|
| None | 63.3 |
| Apprenticeship | 21.1 |
| Industrial Process | 6.7 |
| Business Administration | 4.4 |
| Accounting | 3.3 |
| Designing | 1.1 |
| TOTAL | 100.0 |

Source: Sit et al., 1991, p. 72.

TABLE 5. Source of Technical and Managerial Knowledge of Macau Entrepreneurs

| *Source* | *Technical Knowledge (%)* | *Managerial Knowledge (%)* |
|---|---|---|
| Former job | 72.6 | 66.2 |
| Self-study | 13.7 | 13.8 |
| Schooling | 8.2 | 10.8 |
| Apprenticeship | 2.7 | 9.2 |
| Relatives and Friends | 2.7 | — |
| TOTAL | 100.0 | 100.0 |

Source: Sit et al., 1991, p. 73.

Feitor and Cremer (1991, p. 196) make some further observations which can provide a useful summary. They point out that the government's priority in the 1980s was improvement in the skills of common industrial workers and in the preparation of low-to-intermediate personnel. These are the kind of personnel that factories need in large numbers, absence of which would represent a bottleneck to development. However, Feitor and Cremer stress that more attention is needed to higher-level training in order to reduce the territory's dependence on outside sources of supply and to enhance local entrepreneurial and technological capacity. Similar comments could be made about the service sector, which has moved toward more sophisticated types of activity such as banking. The government has recognized this need, which is one factor behind its more active involvement in secondary and tertiary education.

## CONCLUSIONS

Macau has a long history of education. The territory was formally established in 1557, and was for centuries a major regional center of culture and learning. However, Macau cannot be described as a cohesive society. The schools have done little to promote a sense of territorial identity, and there has always existed a sharp divide between the official and the private schools. Much of the official system operates in Portuguese, and is oriented toward Portugal itself and the territory's civil service. The majority of private schools operate in Cantonese, though also with some English and Portuguese, and there is little coordination between them.

Although in the sixteenth to eighteenth centuries Macau was a major economic pivot within the region, its fortunes declined in the nineteenth century. However, the economic growth of the last two decades has been dramatic, and the territory might lay justifiable claim to be considered alongside East Asia's other "little dragons." Macau's current per capita GDP ranks far ahead of most other parts of the region. As noted at the beginning of this chapter, in East Asia the territory ranks high on several indices including the numbers of doctors and hospital beds per head of population, infant mortality and life expectancy rates, and the number of private cars per 100 persons.

Education certainly does not head the list of factors explaining Macau's recent economic success. More obvious factors have been the territory's operation as a trading post for China, the fact that it provided a new base for Hong Kong entrepreneurs when they began to face protectionist restrictions, the arrival of large numbers of talented and hard-working migrants, a liberal economic system, high elasticity of labor supply and access to foreign markets.

This is not to say that education has been unimportant. A survey in 1987 of the background of entrepreneurs indicated that 7.1% had tertiary education and that an additional 61.9% had secondary education. Most of these entrepreneurs were migrants, and their general level of education was far above that of the population as a whole. It seems that the education of these entrepreneurs was an important enabling instrument. Interestingly, very few of the entrepreneurs had any technical training; but this does not seem to have blocked their advance.

However, these entrepreneurs received the bulk of their education outside the territory. The government has recognized a need to strengthen local provision, without which it is to be doubted whether future economic growth will be achieved. Although in the past Macau has benefited from regional and historical circumstances, its economy has been imitative rather than aggressively innovative. If Macau is to be able to grow further in competition with its neighbors, or even to maintain its present position, then upgrading of education and training will be essential.

The government's educational expansion and reform initiatives will also have an impact on social development. The government aims at universal and compulsory education of six years' duration in the first instance and later nine years' duration. Efforts to coordinate the schools will provide the basis for a more integrated educational system, and it seems likely that textbooks will be written specifically for Macau schools and will help promote a sense of identity. The challenge for the future will be to dovetail a specific identification with Macau and a broader identification with the People's Republic of China.

# 9 The People's Republic of China

*Yat Ming Leung*

## Contextual Background

The People's Republic of China (hereafter referred to as China) was founded in 1949 by the Chinese Communist Party. The term "New China" was often used as holy writ to signify a new path of national development. Yet it is more appropriate to see China as a civilization of 5,000 years striving for industrialization and modernization. China acquired its present territorial dimension in the fifteenth century, but regrettably its self-contained agrarian economy and highly centralized feudal bureaucracy inhibited the technological and organizational breakthrough comparable with the Industrial Revolution in Europe. The quest for Westernization started after the humiliating defeat in the Opium War of 1840 but thereafter the Qing dynasty declined into "semi-colonial" status under foreign aggression. China became a republican state in 1911 but the country was further torn by warlord infighting, civil wars and Japanese invasion. In 1949 China was an underdeveloped and devastated country properly described by Mao Zedong as "poor and blank."

China is situated in the northeastern part of the Asian continent. It is the world's third largest country, possessing 9.6 million square meters of land of which only 12% is cultivable (Jowett, 1990). Its physical and climatic environments display great diversity, ranging from temperate prairies in the northeast to tropical forests in the southwest, and continental deserts in the northwest. Two-thirds of the country consists of high plateaus and mountains, whereas alluvial lowlands are found mainly along the coastal regions.

China is the world's most populous country, with a population of 1,143 million people (1990 census). This accounts for about one-fifth of the world's population but the country only possesses 7% of the world's arable lands. The population, which has increased by over 600 million since 1949, is considered by the Chinese government as too large and growing too rapidly. The optimum population that can be supported is estimated to be 1,500 million, beyond which there will be disasters (Chinese Academy of Science, 1991). The government therefore adopted strict population control policies to curb the population explosion.

The 1990 census shows that about 26.4% of the population are urbanized. The dominant Han-Chinese account for 93% of the population and there are 55 officially recognized national minorities amounting to about 70 million people. The age composition of the Chinese population has moved from a "youth type" to an "adult type," with 28.8% of the population under-15s and 65.7% between 15 and 64 years old. The dependency ratio of under-15s is 39% and compares favorably with many developing countries, for example India (62%) and Thailand (51%). Nevertheless, the huge population has exerted great pressure on employment and schooling. It is estimated that each year there are 20 million children waiting to enter primary schools and another 20 million secondary school graduates entering the job market (Hu, 1993).

It is unrealistic to view China as a single entity in the light of its vast territory and geographical contrasts. Rural-urban and regional socioeconomic disparities are great. These disparities intensified after 1978 because the leadership favored a "get rich first" development strategy which allows the coastal regions and newly established "special economic zones" to enjoy special tax exemptions and preferential investment terms designed to attract foreign investment. Figure 1 depicts the sharp regional economic and geographical differences of the thirty administrative regions in China. Chinese planners have divided China into five income categories: the municipalities of Beijing, Tianjin and Shanghai, high income, upper-middle income, lower-middle-income and low-income regions. In 1991, GDP per capita for the richest region (Shanghai) was 5,699 yuan but it was only 790 yuan in the poorest region in Guizhou (SIHRD, 1992). The wealth gap between the coastal regions and the poor inland regions is widening.

## Development Challenges and Strategies

An understanding of the role of education in China's development requires an awareness of the major political shifts which the country has experienced and to which education was harnessed. When the People's Republic of China was proclaimed in 1949 two major development challenges were faced by the Chinese leaders. The first was to rebuild a bankrupt economy devastated by the Japanese War (1937–45) and the Civil War (1945–49). The second was to consolidate the newly established communist regime. These tasks of economic reconstruction and nation building had to be accomplished in an insecure and hostile Cold War atmosphere for most of the period between

1950 and 1978. The Korean War (1950–53) solidified the hostility between China and the West. Soviet assistance was terminated after China's ideological quarrel with the USSR in 1958. Mao Zedong's vision of a world revolution and the zeal of Chinese nationalism frightened the Southeast Asian countries. China was therefore subjected to an international market blockade and military encirclement. Unlike Japan and the "four little Asian dragons," which benefited from their good relationship with the West and enabled them to enjoy export-oriented economic growth, China was excluded from the world trade market. Its share of world trade dropped from 1.4% in the mid-1950s to 0.4% in the mid-1970s (Teng, 1992) and its annual volume of foreign trade averaged no more than 4% of the GDP in the same period (Philips and Yeh, 1990).

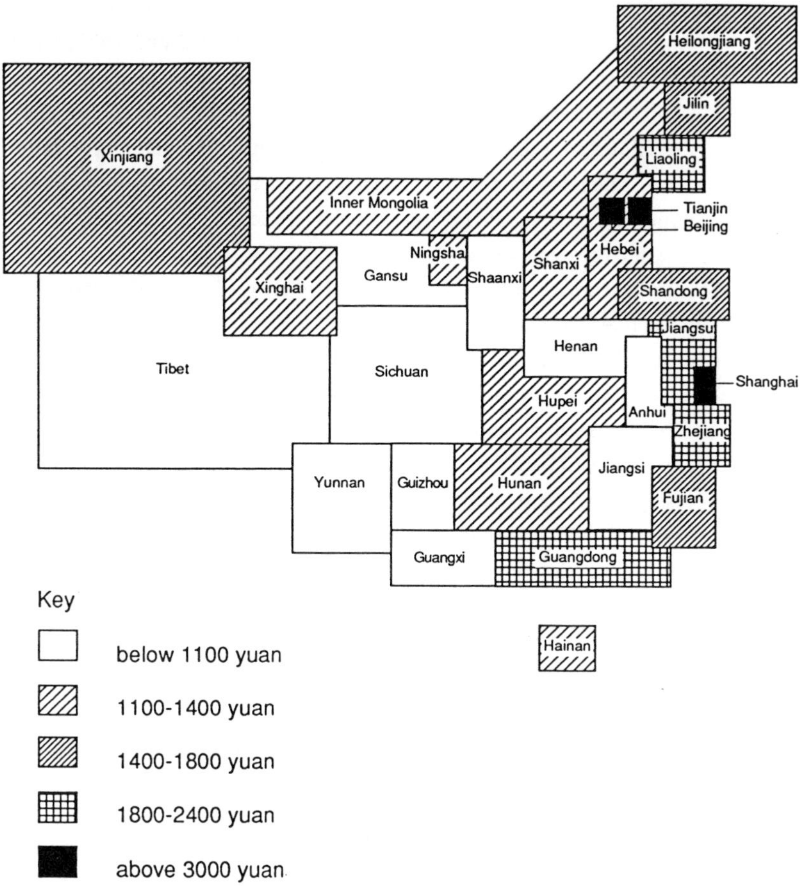


FIGURE 1. Economic Disparities between Provinces (as measured by per capita income, 1991).

The development strategies pursued in China were determined by the ideological outlook of the Chinese leadership and this was heavily influenced by their interpretation of the external world conditions. Under the unfavourable conditions of the Cold War in the 1950s and 1960s, the Chinese Communist Party gave top priority to policies which maximised political control and indigenous economic development. China opted for a strategy that involved a highly centralised planned economy and a priority for the development of agriculture and heavy industry to sustain capital formation. Consequently, until the Open Door Policy was adopted in 1978, the Chinese economy was almost a closed system based on self-reliance and seclusion to avoid "contamination" by the capitalist world. At the risk of oversimplification, one might identify two distinct models of economic development in the course of China's economic development: the Stalinist model of a planned economy, which was adopted between 1952 and 1978, and the post-1978 model of "Open and Reform" with its acceptance of transition towards "market socialism."

China adopted a Stalinist model of economic development in 1952 because it blended well with China's traditional centralist political culture and the "barrack socialism" experienced by the Chinese Communist Party in its armed struggle for power. Moreover, it was the only real option available in the climate of the Cold War confrontation. The model, though designated the "Chinese road to socialism" and strongly marked by Mao's own socialist ideals, exhibited distinct Stalinist features: monolithic administrative planning; a high degree of central control over the accumulation and reinvestment of capital; top-down directives implemented by a centralized bureaucracy commandism; elimination of competition, entrepreneurship and the pursuit of profit; five-year plans; collective farms (People's Commune) and state-owned enterprises; the absence of markets for capital or labor; relative isolation from the international economy; mass restriction of individual liberties in the name of "proletariat dictatorship." This highly centralized one-party system allowed the "Great Leader and Teacher," Mao Zedong, to dictate his own ideological-political perspectives in China's socialist transformation. Mao believed that it was possible to change social consciousness away from individualism towards collectivism and patriotism through mass construction campaigns (for example, huge irrigation projects and the "Great Leap Forward") and ideological indoctrination. These measures were designed to liberate people's creative energies, which would, in turn, induce the rapid socioeconomic transformation of a "New" China (Howell, 1978; Maxwell, 1979). Mao's notion of education was broader than formal schooling and involved indoctrination and remolding the political culture through highly politicized activities.

The death of Mao in 1976 and the downfall of the "Gang of Four" marked a turning point in the contemporary history of China. Between 1976 and 1978 there was intense political infighting between the neo-Maoists led by Hua Guofeng, and the pragmatic moderates led by Deng Xiaoping. Eventually in December 1978 Deng won the upper hand and initiated a new direction for economic development. The Third Plenary of the Eleventh Central Committee called for a shift in emphasis away from Mao's notion of "Take Class Struggle as the Key" to the development of the forces of production for accomplishing the Four Modernizations (of industry, agriculture, science-technology and defence). The Stalinist model of economic development was abandoned because of its two major shortcomings: (a) a high rate of accumulation at the cost of improvement in the standard of living of the people; (b) an irrational economic structure biased toward heavy industry at the expense of light industry and agriculture. The "Great Proletariat Cultural Revolution" was denounced by the new leadership as a "national catastrophe" which had brought China's economy to the edge of collapse (Foreign Language Press, 1984). Eventually a new developmental strategy was adopted for the Seventh Five-Year Plan from 1986 to 1990. The new strategy formally discredited the Stalinist model in stating that:

> Our strategy for economic and social development has changed from a lopsided pursuit of increased output and output value of industry, especially heavy industry, to place emphasis on the need for the balanced development of agriculture, light industry and heavy industry, and for all-round economic, scientific, technological, educational, cultural and social development, with focus on the achievement of better economic results. (Foreign Language Press, 1986)

In 1987 the Chinese Communist Party reshaped its conception of socialism and its basic ideology. The term "primary stage of socialism" was coined to describe the backward stage of socialist development in China, which was, according to Deng Xiaoping, falling at least twenty years behind the advanced capitalist countries of the world. A GDP-growth target was set forth which aimed at doubling China's GDP of 1980 by the year 2000 to achieve a GNP per capita of US $800, bringing China to a "relatively well-off stage." The post-1978 leadership gradually formulated a new model of development described as "Open and Reform" (kaifang kaige), which exhibited the following features: dissolution of the People's Commune and the introduction of the production responsibility system, specialisation in the rural economy, relaxation of controls on the movement of surplus rural manpower, reduction of the rigid central control over the national economy, devolution of state-owned industry to the provinces, the pursuit of intensive growth rather than extensive growth strategy via productivity improvement, greater emphasis on consumption welfare, more reliance on market mechanisms, encouragement of non-state-owned enterprises, and an "open door" to foreign investment and trade in the Special Economic Zones (Nolan and Dong, 1990; Hsueh and Woo, 1991).

## Economic Transformation and Achievements, 1949–1990

Despite extreme policy contradictions, sharp economic fluctuations, low efficiency and serious micro-level imbalances, China's economic development since 1949 has impressed the world with its high growth rate, especially since 1978. Simultaneously China has undergone a socioeconomic transformation in five aspects, as described by the Chinese Academy of Social Sciences: namely, "transformation from a society of product economy for self-sufficiency to a society of planned commodity economy; from a closed and semi-closed society to an industrial society, from a rural society to a heterogeneous and diversified society, and from a society based on moral principles to a society based on legal principles" (Lu and Lin, 1991). The leadership has also taken a broader view of national development to include social aspects. In 1986, for example, the seventh five-year plan was announced as "The Five-Year Plan of Economic and Social Development."

China's industrial take-off is said to have begun in 1965 after a period of extensive state-controlled capital accumulation (Lofstedt, 1990). Ironically this occurred just before the devastating "Cultural Revolution" that was inaugurated in 1966. The period between 1949 and 1965 is referred to by Chinese scholars as "the preparatory stage for modern economic development" (Chinese Academy of Science, 1991). In the early fifties, China exported raw materials and farm products to the Soviet Union in order to acquire a variety of industrial turnkey projects that formed the core of the Chinese heavy industry. Myers noted that by 1956 the ratio of capital formation to GDP in China was 14%, a very high rate for a country with a per capita income of less than one hundred U.S. dollars in the 1950s. After the deterioration of the relationship with the USSR, China adopted a policy of "self-reliance and arduous struggle" which further raised the capital formation to GDP ratio to between 23 and 30% in the early sixties (Myers, 1980). Such a high ratio was maintained at the sacrifice of a general improvement in the living standards of the population.

Table 1 (a). Major Indicators of Economic Growth in China, 1952–1990

| *Indicator* | *1952* | *1965* | *1978* | *1985* | *1990* |
|---|---|---|---|---|---|
| Population (billion) | 5.74 | 6.46 | 7.25 | 10.6 | 11.4 |
| Net Material Product (billion yuan RMB) | 1015 | 2695 | 6846 | 16582 | 37,969 |
| GDP/per capita (yuan RMB) | 104 | 129 | 315 | 668 | 1267 |
| Gross Value of Agricultural Output (billion yuan RMB) | 461 | 833 | 1397 | 3619 | 7662 |
| Gross Value of Industrial Output (billion yuan RMB) | 349 | 1402 | 4237 | 9716 | 23851 |
| Annual Output of Iron and Steel (million tons) | 1.4 | 12.2 | 32.2 | 41.7 | 60.1 |
| Annual Output of Crude Oil (million tons) | 0.04 | 11.3 | 104.0 | 124.9 | 180 |
| Percentage of Urbanized Population | 12.5 | 18 | 18 | 23.7 | 26.4 |

Sources: State Statistics Bureau, *Statistical Yearbook of China,* 1992a; State Statistics Bureau, *State Development Report,* 1992b.

Table 1(a) and (b) summarize the key economic indicators of China's economic development between 1952 and 1990. It can be seen that both the volume and rate of growth are impressive. Gross material product (GMP),

Table 1 (b). Average Annual Growth Rate of the Chinese Economy, 1949–1990

| | *Average Annual Growth Rate (%)** | |
|---|---|---|
| | *1953–78* | *1979–90* |
| Population | 2.2 | 1.4 |
| New Material Product | 7.9 | 10.3 |
| Gross Value of Agricultural Output | 2.7 | 6.1 |
| Gross Value of Industrial Output | 11.4 | 12.0 |
| Heavy Industry | 13.0 | 10.0 |
| Light Industry | 8.7 | 14.1 |
| Export Trade | 10.0 | 16.7 |
| Import Trade | 9.1 | 14.2 |

Source: You and Wu, *Socialism in China,* 1991.
*One U.S. dollar is equivalent to 5.7 yuan at 1993 exchange rate.

a term used by the Chinese as equivalent to GDP, grew at an annual average rate of 7.9% between 1953 and 1978 and over 10% since 1979. This is a strong performance compared with China's past and with most developing countries (Nolan, 1990). China's tempo of industrial growth in the 1980s, which averaged 10.6% per annum, was faster than that of the developed countries (2.7%) and the developing world (3.1%) (State Statistics Bureau, 1992b). The country is now viewed as one of the countries constituting the third phase of rapid growth in East Asia (World Bank, 1993).

Significant structural changes and shifts in intersectoral growth have taken place in China's GDP composition by sectors of industry and labor distribution. From Table 2 it can be seen that, in terms of GDP shares, the economic structure shifted rapidly away from the primary toward the secondary sector while the tertiary sector began to expand in the late 1980s. The primary sector generated about 58% of GDP in 1952 but declined sharply to 28.4% in 1990. Nevertheless, it was still very labor intensive and had low productivity. Its share of labor force only dropped from 83.5% to 60% between 1952 and 1990. The manufacturing sector grew from a share of 23.1% of GDP and 7.4% of labor force in 1952 to 44.3% and 21.4% in 1990 respectively. The tertiary sector, which provided 27% of GDP and 18.6% of labor force in 1990, was relatively small even if compared with the average of 46% and 29% in lower-middle countries (World Bank, 1991a).

TABLE 2. Change of China's Economic Structure, 1952–90

| *Year* | *Percentage of GDP* | | | *Percentage of Labor Force* | | |
|---|---|---|---|---|---|---|
| | *P* | *M* | *S* | *P* | *M* | *S* |
| 1952 | 57.7 | 23.1 | 19.2 | 83.5 | 7.4 | 9.1 |
| 1955 | 52.9 | 26.5 | 20.6 | 83.3 | 8.6 | 8.1 |
| 1960 | 52.8 | 27.2 | 20.0 | 65.8 | 15.9 | 18.4 |
| 1965 | 46.2 | 40.2 | 13.6 | 81.6 | 8.4 | 10.0 |
| 1970 | 40.4 | 45.1 | 14.5 | 80.8 | 10.2 | 9.0 |
| 1975 | 37.8 | 50.5 | 11.7 | 77.2 | 13.5 | 9.3 |
| 1980 | 36.0 | 53.9 | 10.1 | 68.9 | 18.3 | 12.8 |
| 1985 | 35.4 | 50.8 | 13.8 | 62.5 | 20.9 | 16.6 |
| 1990 | 28.4 | 44.3 | 27.2 | 60.0 | 21.4 | 18.6 |

P: primary sector; M: manufacturing sector; S: services sector.
Source: *Chinese Statistical Yearbook* (Zhongguo Tongji Chubanshe), 1991.

About 80% of China's foreign currency earnings are generated by merchandise exports. These rose from $5.5 billion in 1950 to $273.5 billion in 1985 and $1,357 billion in 1991, ranking China as twelfth in the world's export trade (State Statistics Bureau, 1992b). The export growth rate was as high as 14.2% per annum between 1979 and 1990, despite the fact that this was a period of decline in world trade (World Bank, 1991a). Nevertheless, China's share of world trade is still very small. It rose from 0.8% in 1978 to 1.9% in 1991, and the ratio of its exports to GDP rose from just 5% to 13% in the same period (State Statistics Bureau, 1992b).

China is a giant in terms of GDP but a dwarf in terms of GDP per capita. In 1990, GDP amounted to 3,565 billion U.S. dollars, ranking China in absolute terms the ninth in the world. But due to huge population, China's GDP per capita was only about $370, ranking 99th in the world. The World Bank puts China among the 37 "Low Income Economies" (World Bank, 1991). Chinese economists reckon that per capita measures have been underestimated, and claim that in real purchasing value China should have a GDP of $5,868 billion and a GDP per capita of $535 (You and Wu, 1991).

China's achievements in poverty relief have been praised by the World Bank, which stated that "the speed and scale of the improvement is probably unprecedented in human history" (World Bank, 1986). China also has one of the world's lowest levels of income inequality. This was mainly due to an "egalitarian" wage structure and, in particular, to heavy governmental subsidies to stabilize the price of the major consumer commodities. In 1978, China's Gini coefficient was 0.20 at the national level, 0.18 in urban areas and 0.21 in rural areas. When China gradually moved toward a market economy in the 1980s, the income gap widened and the Gini coefficient increased to 0.27, 0.22 and 0.3, respectively, in 1989 (You and Wu, 1991). Yet the figure is still lower than many developing countries. In 1993, China's level of social development, which is an aggregated comparative evaluation of the country's different aspects of quality of life, was self-estimated to rank 68th among 119 countries (Chinese Academy of Social Sciences, 1993). The World Bank rates China as one of the HPAEs which enjoys much higher per capita income growth with highly equal income distribution and drastic improvement of human welfare, such as life expectancy and infant mortality rate (World Bank, 1993).

From this brief review it is evident that China has successfully laid down a substantial foundation of modern industry and agriculture by "self-reliance and frugal struggle." Economically, China is today one of the world's production giants. In sheer volume of production, China ranks the first in world production of grains, cotton, clothes, coal and cement; second in television sets; third in chemical fertilizers; fourth in steel, crude oil, synthetic fibers and electricity; fifth in crude oil and sugar (State Statistics Bureau, 1992a). It also has a $122 billion current account surplus, one of the world's largest, and $430 billion of foreign reserves, an amount exceeded in Asia only by Taiwan and Japan (*Asia Week*, 1992). China is ready for a "blast-off" in the nineties, particularly in Southern China which has recorded exceedingly high annual growth rates of about 25% (World Bank, 1993). Politically, China has resumed independent sovereignty and plays a significant role in world affairs.

The Chinese government has set an ambitious medium- and long-term development target for the country. In a strategic projection prepared by the Chinese Academy of Science under the sponsorship of the State Council in 1988, it was projected that China's GDP will rank the fifth in the world by the year 2000, the fourth by 2020 and the third by 2050 (Chinese Academy of Science, 1991).

## Educational Development in China

It is now generally acknowledged that the relationship between education and different aspects of national development is better seen as a non-linear and interactive process rather than as a direct cause-and-effect relationship (Ahmed, 1991). There are four basic functions that education is expected to contribute towards national development, namely, (a) the provision of basic education as an essential prerequisite for a pool of vocationally skilled and adaptable labour force, (b) the provision of different categories of skilled manpower to match specific economic needs, (c) as a political tool to foster national identity and citizenship and (d) as a social tool to promote human development which embraces both personal efficacy and social equity (Fågerlind and Saha, 1983; Kostecki, 1985; UNDP, 1991; Ahmed et al., 1991; Murray, 1992).

In the following sections, an attempt is made to review the key aspects of educational expansion and development in China since 1949, with special emphasis on the impact of policy shifts on educational development in the pre-1965 period, the Cultural Revolution and the post-1978 periods. This review will provide essential background data for understanding the relationship between education and development. The key aspects of Chinese education examined are (a) national goals of education, (b) the educational infrastructure, (c) national investment in education, (d) expansion in school enrollments, (e) vocational and technical education, (f) ideopolitical education and (g) school curriculum.

### *National Goals of Education*

Parallel with the shifts in national developmental goals, China's educational goals have undergone a process of transformation since 1949. After the People's Republic was founded in 1949 the hegemonic Chinese Communist

Party inherited the tradition of using education as an instrument for sociopolitical and economic transformation, but on a scale and in a manner that surpassed that used by previous governments. Under the Marxist-Leninist doctrine, education was basically seen as an ideopolitical instrument of the state apparatus, with the function of eliminating class distinction, consolidating the proletarian dictatorship, building socialism and combating subversion. In the course of socialist development, education was expected to play a dual task of supplying both the "political capital" and "technological manpower" for China's national development. This was manifested in the overarching educational goal set by Mao Zedong in 1957:

> Education must serve the politics of the proletariat and must combine with productive labour so that those being educated develop morally, intellectually and physically, and become workers with socialist consciousness and culture. (Mao, 1965)

As a policy statement, this goal resonated well with the country's dual development tasks of economic reconstruction and nation building. Mao Zedong also coined the phrase "being both red and expert" to imply an idealised harmonious relationship between the political and economic orientation of education. However, the problem was that the two tasks became mutually exclusive at the implementation level because the relative emphasis on each task resulted in the so-called two lines of struggle between "politics in command" upheld by Mao and his radical supporters, and "economics in command" favoured by the more pragmatic Liu Shaoqi, Zhou Enlai and Deng Xiaoping. The outcome of this leadership contradiction was a zero-sum pattern of educational development which was manifested in a perpetual swing between the "revolutionary" and "academic" model of education (Fraser and Hawkins, 1973; Chen Hsien, 1974).

The "Great Proletariat Cultural Revolution" of 1966–76 marked the extreme of this zero-sum game arising from the continuing struggle between two opposing strategies for the transformation of China. Politically it was a shrewd attempt of the radical Maoists to eradicate the remnants of capitalist tendencies in Chinese society (Kwong, 1979). Unfortunately, education was a major battlefield in this struggle and it resulted in "extreme hyperpoliticisation and radicalism" (Sautman, 1991) in which education was exclusively used to consolidate the dictatorship of the proletariat, to prevent capitalist restoration and to build socialism (*China Reconstructs,* 1973). Paradoxically, the Cultural Revolution turned out to be a "decade of internal turmoil" and was officially condemned for its "criminal acts" against education, namely (a) the degeneration of academic education into the crudest form of anti-intellectualism, (b) the opposition to the study of basic theory, science and technology, (c) the instigating of pupils to anarchism and outright hooliganism and (d) the discrediting and purging of intellectuals (Hongqi, 1977; CCP, 1981).

After the death of Mao Zedong and the downfall of the "Gang of Four" in 1976, the leadership gradually redefined national educational goals in a way that mirrored the tenets of human capital theory. Deng Xiaoping's educational goal was to speed up China's economic, scientific, technological and general social progress by the expansion of educational provision, meritocratic competition in examinations, curriculum modernization and high-level academic interchange with the outside world. In May 1985, the Chinese Communist Party explicitly oriented education to economic development and announced, in the "Decision of the Central Committee On the Reform of the Educational Structure," that

> Education must serve socialist construction, which in turn must rely on education. Our massive socialist modernisation programme requires us not only to give full rein to the skilled people now available and to further enhance their capabilities, but also to train, on a large scale, people with new types of skills who are dedicated to the socialist cause and to the nation's economic and social progress into the 1990s and the early days of the next century. (CCP, 1985)

After the proclamation of the Law of Compulsory Education in 1986, China further redefined educational goals in order to incorporate a human development perspective in national development. The latest version of the goal for education proclaimed by the State Education Commission reflects this new philosophy:

> The goal of basic education is to foster among children and adolescents all-round education so that they can develop morally, intellectually and physically in an active way and with initiative, so as to raise the quality of the whole nation, and to prepare well educated builders of socialist construction who have lofty ideals, moral integrity and self-discipline. (Zhongguo Jiaoyubao, 1991)

It has taken China forty years to move away from a strong politically oriented and narrow manpower matching conception of education to a human resource development perspective that puts emphasis on developing the qualities and competencies of the Chinese citizens, not only for economic development, but also for the full realization of their individual potential. Yet it is too early to say whether this represents an acceptance of another new dogma by the leadership which has historically sought for a single correct orthodoxy, or a genuine policy shift to a broader and more comprehensive development strategy that better coordinates various formal and informal educational activities, and a more cost-effective mobilisation of resources. In a diversified country like China, the implementation of a centrally decreed policy is often confronted by the problem of "intention-becoming-facade" (Lewin, 1981; Guthrie, 1986).

### *The Educational Infrastructure*

The structure of formal primary and secondary schooling is 6+3+3, which was adopted in 1922 when Chinese educators abandoned a hybrid German-Japanese model in favor of a more ostensibly American school system based on John Dewey's progressive education ideas. After 1949, several attempts were made to shorten it to a 5+3+2 system during the "education revolution" of the Great Leap Forward (1958–60) and the Cultural Revolution (1966–76). After the introduction of nine years of compulsory education in 1986 some provinces experimented with a 5+4+3 system of primary and junior secondary education but the main form is still the 6+3+3 model. Higher education consists of short-term non-degree specialized courses (2 years) and undergraduate courses (4–5 years).

Progression through the formal schooling system is highly pyramidal and based on keen competition. The flow of students through the different levels decreases sharply toward higher education. In 1987, the enrollment rate of the school-age cohorts was 23% at the preschool level, 97% at the primary level, 56.2% at the junior secondary level, 16.2% at the senior secondary level and 2.3% at the higher education level (Zhou Beilung, 1990b).

There is a large non-formal adult education system that is parallel to the formal system. This originated from the Mass Education movement, which was launched by intellectuals after the May Fourth movement in 1919 to educate the illiterate majority. Non-formal education covers the provision of literacy programs, general basic education, general vocational upgrading of grassroots level workers, specialized upgrading of mid-level and high-level technicians, and spare time tertiary distance education (e.g., TV university and correspondence university). The total enrollment in the non-formal sector amounted to 121.8 million in 1990, of which 85 million were at the elementary level, 34 million at secondary level and 2.5 million at the tertiary level (*Chinese Population Yearbook*, 1990).

The Communist Party established a highly centralised and monolithic system of educational administration after 1949 and until 1985, the Ministry of Education (MOE), which is one of the State Council's 74 ministries, was the highest authority that governed all educational matters. With 20 departments, the MOE faithfully executed the educational policies formulated by the Communist Party and initiated laws and directives governing educational work in the whole country. This hierarchical system of administration was used to ensure that key decisions of the Communist Party and the central government were uniformly implemented nationwide. This administrative machinery was condemned in the Cultural Revolution as the "black headquarters of the capitalist-roaders" and crushed. After 1976 the Ministry of Education was re-established and in 1985 it was replaced by the State Education Commission (SEdC), which enjoys a higher status than a ministry. The SEdC coordinates the educational work of various ministries and departments, and provides overall plans and guidance on educational developments. Overall, there is a trend toward the devolution of educational responsibilities to the grassroots levels. Educational provision at the provincial and local levels is undertaken by provincial education commissions and education bureaus which are directly responsible to their respective level of the People's Congress.

Another key feature of the Chinese educational system is that the state monopolizes the provision of education. As a result, private investment on education is extremely small. In 1993, there were 13,000 private kindergartens, 900 private primary schools, 700 private secondary schools and 10 private tertiary institutions recognised by the SEdC (China News Agency, November 7, 1993). There are largely unexploited opportunities for a more balanced partnership between the public and private providers of educational resources. However, the government has been ambivalent in its policy on private education. On one hand, it supports private initiatives in education to alleviate the problem of insufficient educational resources. On the other hand, it is concerned with the quality and status of private educational institutions.

### *National Investment in Education*

In parallel with the major ideological shifts there was, until 1978, a general reluctance to invest in education at all levels. The underlying reason was that education was generally seen as a form of social consumption and its economic benefits were not easily recognized. Paradoxically, while the study of the economics of education began to blossom in the West during the 1960s, the discussion of a possible causal relation between education and economic growth was discouraged and eventually banned in China.

Budgeted Educational Expenditure (BEE) is the Chinese term that is the equivalent of public educational expenditure (PEE) used in UNESCO statistics. Two calculations are adopted in China. The "standard calculation" only includes four main items: (a) general expenditure, (b) capital expenditure, (c) expenditure earmarked for technical and craft schools and (d) administrative expenditure in education departments. Other planners use an "elaborated estimate" which puts together all kinds of special subsidies, unbudgeted funds and World Bank loans (Li Shouxin, 1988a). The two calculations yield different sets of figures. For example, according to the standard calculation, public educational expenditure was 2.5% of the GDP in 1987 but this rises to 3.2% if based on the elaborated calculation (Cheng, 1989).

Whatever calculation is adopted, China's investment in education remains low by world standards. Table 3 shows China's public education expenditure as a percentage of GDP and government expenditure between 1952 and 1992. Zhou Beilung (1990a) calculated that China's public education expenditure as a percentage of GDP ranged from 2.2 to 3.7 and averaged 3.05% between 1952 and 1992. The lowest percentage was 1.5% in 1970, which was significantly below the world average of 5.5% and the 2.9% average for developing countries in the same year (UNESCO, 1990). The post-1978 leadership supports greater educational expenditure but according to the standard calculation the PEE as percentage of GDP climbed only from 2.2% to 3.7% between 1978 and 1992, with the highest ratio of

TABLE 3. PUBLIC EXPENDITURE ON EDUCATION IN CHINA, 1952–1992

| | *1952* | *1965* | *1975** | *1980* | *1985* | *1990* | *1992*** |
|---|---|---|---|---|---|---|---|
| Total Government budgeted expenditure (billion yuan) | 183 | 437 | n.a. | 1085 | 1866.4 | 3244.8 | 4189 |
| Public Expenditure on Education (billion yuan) | 11.6 | 35.9 | n.a. | 113.2 | 224.4 | 433.9 | 551.4 |
| Public Education Expenditure as % of government expenditure | 6.6 | 8.2 | 5.9* | 10.4 | 12 | 13.4 | 13.2 |
| Public Ed. Expenditure as % of GDP | 2.2 | 3.1 | 1.2* | 2.6 | 2.7 | 3.1 | 3.7 |

Sources: Zhou Beilung (ed.) *Chinese Education Towards the 21st Century,* 1990a.
* Data taken from Wang Shangmai, "A historical analysis of the percentage of educational investment in the national economy," *The Future and Development of Higher Education,* 1986.
** Data taken from Hu Ruiwen, *Chinese Education: Development and Perspectives,* Shanghai Institute of Human Resource Development, 1993.

3.8% in 1988 (Zhou Beilung, 1990a; Hu, 1993). However, educational expenditure as a percentage of the annual government budget had increased sharply in the 1980s. It is estimated that 1% of GDP growth was matched by a 1.5% increase in government expenditure on education between 1953 and 1988 (SIHRD, 1991b).

Since 1980 Chinese economists and educators have begun to lobby for a guaranteed increase in educational expenditure in a way which reflects a strong faith in the tenets of human capital theory. Two policy guidelines have been suggested. The first proposes that the annual growth rate of government expenditure on education should be parallel in China's annual economic growth rate (Li Yining, 1981). The second proposes that the growth rate in educational investment should be ahead of the economic growth rate to ensure that education serves as the "engine-for-growth" (Chin and Zhou, 1984). In a research project sponsored by the SEdC on "the appropriate ratio of education investment in relation to the national income," it was suggested that the ratio of educational expenditure as a percentage of investment in GDP should not be less than 4.06% (Chen Lianghun et al., 1986). Yet this ratio has never been achieved. According to the basic calculation, China's PEE as a percentage of GDP averaged 3.5% between 1978 and 1990 (Zhou, 1990a). This percentage fell behind the world average of 5.5% and 4.2% in developing countries in the same period (UNESCO, 1990). It has been argued that if the PEE does not rise to 6 or 7% of GDP, education will not be able to fulfill its strategic objectives of promoting economic development by the end of the current century (Zhou Beilung, 1990a).

After 1985, the SEdC advocated a "multi-channel" strategy for raising educational funds from all possible sources. Local education authorities were encouraged to raise funds through an educational surtax, profits from school-run enterprises, school fees and different kinds of donations. It is estimated that non-budgeted funds averaged up to 30% of education revenue in all provinces in 1991 (SIHRD, 1991b).

In terms of educational expenditure per capita China's record is low by world standards. The figure was about $39 in 1989, which ranks China eleventh among twenty-six low-income countries (Hao Keming et al., 1991). Consequently, schools in China generally suffer from poor physical conditions and inadequate supporting facilities. Thus a survey conducted in 1985 revealed that 20% of primary and secondary schools in China lacked desks and chairs (Jing, 1987). The percentage of dilapidated school buildings was as high as 17% in Hainan Province in 1990 (SIHRD, 1991b). Moreover, the actual increase in educational spending was eroded by inflation, wastage and educational funding being diverted illegally for other purposes by local authorities. It was admitted by the director of the SEdC that despite the growth in educational expenditure in the last decade the acute shortage of educational funding had remained unresolved. In September 1993, a total of 6 billion yuan of teacher wages could not be paid by local education bureaus (Zhongguo Jiaoyu Bao, October 29, 1993).

There is also a marked over-investment in higher education at the expense of basic education. As Table 4 shows, the average public educational expenditure per student in 1991 was 114.8 yuan for primary students, 254.6 yuan for secondary school students and 3269.1 yuan for university students, a ratio of 1 : 2.2 : 28.6 (Hu, 1993). This kind of lopsided distribution of educational investment has prevailed since 1952 and it contrasts sharply with the major public policy in East Asia, where the share of PEE allocated to basic

TABLE 4 (A). Average Public Expenditure per Student in China (in yuan RMB), 1952–1991

| | *1952* | *1965* | *1980* | *1985* | *1991* |
|---|---|---|---|---|---|
| Higher Education | 830 | 917.7 | 1752.4 | 2477.3 | 3269.1 |
| Secondary Education | 111.5 | 88.9 | 60.1 | 128.5 | 254.6 |
| Primary Education | 7.4 | 20 | 23.2 | 47.3 | 114.8 |

Source: Hu Ruiren, *Chinese Education: Development and Perspectives,* Shanghai Institute of Human Resource Development, 1993.

TABLE 4 (B). Proportions of Public Educational Expenditure by Levels of Education, 1991

| *Level* | *% of Pupil Population* | *% of Total Expenditure* |
|---|---|---|
| Higher Education | 8.3 | 21.54 |
| Secondary Education | 20.1 | 35.78 |
| Primary Education | 44.6 | 35.02 |
| Preschool Education | 8.9 | 1.34 |
| Others | 18.1 | 6.32 |

Source: Hu Ruiren, 1993; *Chinese Statistical Yearbook,* 1992.

education is consistently higher (World Bank, 1993). It is unfavorable for both the development of higher education and basic education. In 1991, university students, who comprised only 8.3% of the total student population, consumed 21.5% of total education expenditures. Higher education has become very expensive and its expansion cannot be accelerated despite the presumed overall shortage of university graduates. At the same time, the quality of basic education has been undermined by the disproportionately small share of educational investment. The secondary and primary school pupil population, providing 20% and 45% of the total student population, only shared 35.8% and 35% of the budget. As outspoken Chinese economist Qian Jiaju remarks: "Our education policy has always emphasized higher education at the expense of basic education. We are the only country in the world that has free university education but requires payment for attending primary schools" (Qian, 1986).

### *Expansion of School Enrollment*

Despite the low level of investment in education, the quantitative expansion of formal schooling since 1949 has been remarkable. Tables 5a and 5b show the expansion of formal education in terms of student numbers and enrollment ratios. There has been a general expansion in gross enrollments, with the exception of primary and junior secondary enrollment as a result of the decline in the birth rate since the late 1970s. But there is an imbalanced development of enrollment ratios for different levels of schooling. Preschooling is the most underdeveloped sector because the majority of rural children stay at home until they reach the age for primary enrollment. Despite the huge quantitative expansion in enrollments, only 20% of the age cohort was actually enrolled (Zhou, 1990a). This implies that China has not fully recognised the growing international evidence that effectiveness of human capital depends on a better quality of early stimulation. At the primary level the high cohort enrollment rate must be carefully weighed against a high dropout rate and a low completion rate. It was estimated that the completion rate in six-year primary education was only 55% in the mid-1980s before the introduction of nine years of compulsory education in 1986 (World Bank, 1985). In 1989, about 80% of rural children received six years of primary education and this was projected to reach 93% by the year 2000 (Hao Keming et al., 1991).

TABLE 5 (A). Expansion of Formal Schooling in China, 1949–90

| | *1949* | *1952* | *1958* | *1965* | *1979* | *1985* | *1990* |
|---|---|---|---|---|---|---|---|
| *Primary* | | | | | | | |
| Schools (thousands) | 347 | 527 | 777 | 682 | 924 | 832 | 766 |
| Enrollment (millions) | 24.4 | 51.1 | 86.4 | 116.2 | 146.6 | 133.7 | 122.4 |
| *Secondary* | | | | | | | |
| Schools (thousands) | 3.2 | 4.2 | 28.9 | 18.1 | 144.2 | 93.2 | 87.6 |
| Enrollment (millions) | 1.4 | 2.4 | 8.5 | 14.4 | 60.3 | 47.0 | 45.8 |
| *Higher Education* | | | | | | | |
| Universities/Colleges | 201 | 205 | 791 | 434 | 633 | 1016 | 1075 |
| Enrollment (millions) | 0.15 | 0.19 | 0.66 | 0.67 | 1.02 | 1.7 | 2.1 |

Source: *Chinese Statistical Yearbook*, 1990.

The figures for secondary education are interesting. The enrollment ratios for junior and senior secondary schooling reached their historical peak by 1965 but it was openly acknowledged by Chinese educators that these high ratios were only a facade because it was "a rash advance promoted by the erroneous thoughts of 'left' deviation, marked by excessive targeting, boastfulness and without quality assurance" (Zhou Yuliang, 1990). The post-1978 leadership has adopted a more realistic approach to secondary education expansion which, coupled with a declining birth rate, has precipitated a drop in both in gross enrollments and cohort enrollment ratio.

TABLE 5 (B). Enrollment Ratio* and Promotion Ratio** (in percentage) at Different Levels of Schooling, 1949–1990

| | *1952* | *1958* | *1965* | *1975* | *1978* | *1985* | *1990* |
|---|---|---|---|---|---|---|---|
| Primary* | 49.2 | 67.0 | 80.0 | 96.8 | 95.5 | 96.0 | 97.8 |
| Junior secondary** | 17.0 | 44.2 | 82.5 | 90.6 | 87.7 | 68.4 | 74.6 |
| Senior secondary** | 20 | 38.0 | 70.0 | 60 | 40.9 | 41.7 | 40.6 |
| Higher education* | n.a. | 1.6 | n.a. | n.a. | 1.4 | 1.6 | 4.0 |

Source: *Chinese Statistical Yearbook*, 1990.

The expansion of higher education has been carefully monitored by the Chinese government to maximise the output of high-level specialized professionals. The Russian model of higher education was transplanted into the Chinese system in 1950 because its high degree of specialization and central control was seen to be relevant to Chinese needs. State planners decided the volume and capacity of higher education in accordance with the "needs" of the national economy as projected in the five-year plans. University students were viewed as state assets, and this is still reflected in the practice that the government pays all their educational expenses and allocates them to jobs after graduation.

With the exception of the period during the Cultural Revolution between 1966 and 1976, an elitist selection system based on a highly competitive university entrance examination has prevailed in an attempt to ensure that the candidates selected (about 1.4% of the age cohort ) are of top quality. The Cultural Revolution destroyed the higher education system completely and enrollment dropped to the lowest record of 48,000 in 1970. It was estimated that the higher education system failed to produce 1.5 million graduates between 1965 and 1979 (Zhou Beilung, 1990a). To compensate for the acute shortage of urgently needed high-level manpower, the post-1978 leadership boosted tertiary education at such a drastic speed that full-time university enrollments jumped from 1.3 million to 2.1 million between 1979 and 1990, at an annual growth rate of 8.3%.

There are two major deficiencies in China's higher education. First, the expansion of higher education is severely constrained by insufficient resources caused by high unit costs, internal inefficiencies, overstaffing, small scale operations and repetition of courses so that the perceived demand for qualified manpower for the country cannot be met. Second, as Table 6 shows, the higher education structure exhibits a lopsided distribution of graduates among the different disciplines. Just as there is an overconcentration of heavy industries in the economy, the higher education system has traditionally focused on engineering and science whilst agriculture, humanities and social sciences are poorly provided for. The oversupply of engineers and scientists contrasts sharply with an acute shortage of agriculturalists, lawyers and various types of manpower for the rapidly expanding tertiary industries. This trend has only been slightly adjusted in recent years and it poses a serious mismatch with China's rapidly shifting economic structure.

TABLE 6. Distribution of University Graduates (as percentage) in Higher Education by Disciplines

| | *1955* | *1962* | *1965* | *1978* | *1981* | *1986* | *1992* |
|---|---|---|---|---|---|---|---|
| Engineering | 38.1 | 41.6 | 43.8 | 33.6 | 36.0 | 34.5 | 40 |
| Science | 6.9 | 10.7 | 9.2 | 7.5 | 7.8 | 5.4 | 5.2 |
| Agriculture & Forestry | 7.4 | 9.7 | 9.4 | 7.2 | 6.8 | 7.2 | 5.0 |
| Medicine | 12.7 | 13.1 | 12.3 | 13.2 | 12.4 | 9.1 | 10.4 |
| Education | 21.1 | 16.6 | 14.0 | 29.2 | 25.1 | 25.6 | 21.4 |
| Arts & Humanities | 6.6 | 4.8 | 6.8 | 5.4 | 5.4 | 6.8 | 4.8 |
| Finance & Economics | 3.9 | 1.5 | 2.7 | 2.1 | 3.7 | 9.0 | 9.4 |
| Law | 1.7 | 0.5 | 0.6 | 0.2 | 0.8 | 2.3 | 2.1 |
| Sports | 0.8 | 0.7 | 0.6 | 1.0 | 0.9 | 0.8 | 0.7 |
| Fine Arts | 0.8 | 0.8 | 0.6 | 0.6 | 0.6 | 0.7 | 0.7 |

Sources: State Education Planning Office, *Achievement of Education in China, 1949–1983*, People's Education Press, 1984; idem, *Summary of Educational Statistics*, 1992.

### *Vocational and Technical Education*

The government has devoted special efforts to fostering a pool of mid-level craftsmen and technicians for different industries and trades. Vocational and technical education was given emphasis in 1958 when the concept of "dual-tracking" was introduced to diversify senior secondary education. Between 1958 and 1965 there was a proliferation of different kinds of agricultural secondary schools, technical secondary schools, vocational secondary schools and craft schools, covering 385 specialities. As shown in Table 7, the number of students in the vocational and technical streams of senior secondary schools had exceeded that in the general stream in 1965. This was a surprising achievement because there was a strong Confucian tradition of disdaining skill-oriented studies. During the Cultural Revolution the dual-tracking system was terminated for its discrimination against the children of workers and peasants. In 1981, Premier Zhao Zhiyang called for the full-scale revival of the dual-tracking senior secondary educational system. In the 1985 restructuring of the educational system, a target ratio of 5 : 5 between academic and vocational secondary education at the senior secondary level was set for the year 2000. Since then the percentage of senior secondary students attending technical and vocational schools has risen and reached about 50% in 1990. Implementation of vocational and technical education has been hindered by the lack of qualified teachers and funding. As a result, most of the so-called vocational and technical schools are in fact grammar schools merely offering one or two vocational courses to pupils in the specialized stream. For example, it was reported that none of the vocational and technical schools in the Pearl River Delta region had met the official requirements of facilities and teacher qualification (Xu, 1992). Vocational and technical education has greater popularity in the more developed regions where jobs can be guaranteed by linkage with the flourishing local enterprises and service industries. In the rural areas, vocational and technical education is perceived as a second-class education which goes against the expectations of pupils and parents of finding a permanent job in cities through an academic qualification (Hou, 1988).

TABLE 7. Composition of Students at Senior Secondary Level (in percentage), 1952–1990

| | *1958* | *1965* | *1980* | *1985* | *1990* | *1992* |
|---|---|---|---|---|---|---|
| General | 58 | 48.2 | 81.1 | 64.1 | 54.3 | 50.7 |
| Vocational & Technical | 42 | 51.8 | 18.9 | 35.9 | 46.7 | 49.3 |

Source: State Education Planning Office, *Summary of Educational Statistics,* 1992.

Besides formal vocational and technical education, the "Education-with-Production Movement" was initiated in 1954 with the goal that labor skills would be introduced into all primary and secondary schools as a way of promoting respect for labor. Students had to spend four to ten hours a week on manual labor depending on their level of education. In 1957, a formal system of "Hard Work and Thrifty Study" (Qingong Jianxue) was introduced in the school system for pedagogical (integration of theory and practice), ideological (respect for labor) and economic (income-earning) reasons. As much as 20 to 40% of the school year could be devoted to production work in different kinds of workshops, school-run factories, orchards and farms. The post-1978 leadership criticized the excesses of labor education and greatly reduced the time allocated to manual labor. The 1991 Curriculum Outline for nine-year compulsory education stipulates that 2.2% and 6.8% of the timetable should be devoted to labor at the primary and secondary level. In 1988, about 72% of schools claimed to have hard-work and thrifty-study programs and the total value of production of goods reached one billion yuan RMB (Zhongguo Jiaoyubao, November 17, 1988). In reality most school-run factories employ full-time workers for production. Students and teachers take a very limited, if any, part in productive work. Most schools use the labor time for campus cleaning or vocational lessons, such as typing and domestic science.

In 1990, the Chinese government began to experiment with what was termed the "Integration of Three Educations" project in selected rural regions. This tries to better integrate formal education, adult education and vocational-technical education in such a way that rural school children and adult farmers can acquire fundamental knowledge as well as useful agricultural skills. The ultimate purpose is to help peasants earn more money by improving their farming skills, and to make schooling more relevant to local needs (Gu Jianjun, 1992). It is too early to evaluate the effects of this experiment.

*Ideopolitical Education*

The Chinese Communist Party deliberately uses education as an important instrument for fostering political integration and national cohesion. After 1949, a rigid system of ideological and political education was established at all levels of schooling through the formal and informal curriculum. Political indoctrination was seen as "the command and the soul" by the Communist Party, but the degree to which education is politicized has fluctuated according to the macro political goals of the state in different time periods. A pattern of rational politicization (1949–65), hyperpoliticization (1966–76), depoliticization (1976–89) and repoliticization (1989 onward) has been observed (Sautman, 1991). Broadly speaking, ideopolitical education in the 1950s and 1960s was primarily a process of canonization and deification in which the students were to be converted to become Mao Zedong's ideal-type revolutionary successors—ascetic, fearless, disciplined, selfless and fighter-ideologues. At the zenith of the Cultural Revolution, the extreme form of ideopolitical education led to violent activities by the Red Guards. After 1978, the pragmatic leadership replaced "putting polities in command" by "putting moral education in the first place," and diluted political education toward the inculcation of patriotism and civic morality. Lin (1992) notes that in the post-Mao era political education no longer portrayed Mao as the supreme leader and savior of the Chinese people, and no longer put class struggle as the core of all textbooks.

In the formal school curriculum ideopolitical education is implemented through the teaching of "Politics," which is an umbrella term covering moral and civic education, legal education and basic courses on Marxism at different levels of schooling. "Politics" occupied 2.9% to 12% of the primary and secondary school timetable between 1954 and 1990 (Leung, 1991). But political education permeates all school subjects and curriculum content is regularly revised by official curriculum planners to respond to political tensions or special missions dictated by the political leaders. For example, Chinese history texts in Hong Kong and Taiwan describe the periods of Mongol (A.D. 1271–1370) and Manchu (A.D. 1644–1911) rule as the "invasion of barbarians" but in the PRC these periods are described as "periods of harmonious integration of the Han-Chinese with other ethnic groups" in order to promote a sense of brotherhood among the fifty-six ethnic groups. After the Tiananmen incident in 1989 the Party Secretary Jiang Zhemin instructed history teachers to strengthen the teaching of contemporary Chinese history, with a special emphasis on foreign invasions and subversion. Supplementary texts along these lines were written and delivered to schools for use.

The teaching of Chinese language in schools serves a dual task of indoctrination and promoting national cohesion. Chinese language texts and reading materials are carefully selected and revised by official curriculum planners to inculcate moral and political values that are seen as congruent with the prevailing political climate. A curriculum material analysis project revealed that 41% of the lessons in the 1988 version of primary Chinese contained political elements (Wang Zhenjie, 1992). Moreover, Chinese language is taught in "Putonghua," which is the national spoken language, and school children learn the pinyin (alphabetic) system of Chinese writing. Other subjects are also expected to be taught in Putonghua but in most cases teachers use the local dialect.

The popularization of Putonghua in the last forty years has helped to promote a common spoken language in a country where there are thousands of dialects. The most obvious success is the example of the newly established Shenzhen Special Economic Zone. Putonghua makes possible the working together of the two million population who come from different parts of the country. Other national minority groups can learn in their own mother tongue but usually those who can speak Putonghua and read Han Chinese can pursue higher education and become government officials. Thus young Tibetan children are selected and educated in boarding schools specially set up in adjacent provinces to facilitate better interaction of the Tibetan and Han Chinese culture.

Political education is also reinforced through informal channels such as the Young Communist Pioneers for primary students and the Communist Youth League for senior secondary and university students. The political background (class origin and family background) and political behavior of each student is carefully documented in a personal file which has a profound influence on the student's career development. Every candidate must get a pass in the subject of "politics" at the university entrance examination in order to be enrolled. Important government posts are usually reserved for those who are members of the Communist Party or active members of the Communist Youth League.

Ideopolitical education in the 1990s has been re-orientated to stress patriotism and civic morality in the "Four Haves" (ideals, morality, culture and discipline). The major values and attitudes promoted include the "Five Loves" (love the motherland, public property, manual labor, science and the Chinese Communist Party), the "Four Beauties" (of the mind, language, behavior and environment), a sense of responsibility to the nation, determination to sacrifice oneself to the interests of the state, adoption of a dialectical materialistic viewpoint, self-respect, frugality, interpersonal relations, diligent study, filial respect and internationalism. Pupils are expected to observe "rules of conduct" which range from proper hairstyle and dressing to decorum before state symbols. Pupils are also guided to follow models of moral rectitude, such as Chinese patriots in history, contemporary Chinese revolutionary leaders, martyrs, successful scientists and champion sportsmen. Citizenship education for primary and secondary schools stresses collective interest above individual interests.

Through its stringent political education network, the Party had been successful in maintaining its political control over the younger generation in the 1950s and 1960s. But the post-1978 decades of open door policy and depoliticisation have greatly diluted the ideological orientation of the youth towards communism. The Pro-Democracy movement in 1989 astounded the Marxist fundamentalists, who became concerned at the weakening of ideopolitical education in schools. There were attempts to reinforce political education but the results have not been very effective. According to a national survey of senior secondary school students conducted by the Central Institute of Educational Research, 32% of the students responded that they were not interested in politics, but had to study "politics" as a school subject because it is still the stepping stone to further studies and career development (Pan, 1992).

### *Curriculum Modernisation and Relevance*

The Chinese government exercises tight control over curriculum development both for ideopolitical and pedagogical purposes. After 1952, a uniform national curriculum for primary and secondary education, known as the General Teaching Outline, was devised by the central government through the People's Education Press. Standardized textbooks were written by full-time professionals to ensure uniformity and maintain academic standards. As Table 8 shows, the overall curriculum organization for primary and secondary schools remained quite consistent although there were adjustments in time allocation. Repeated attempts were made to make the school curriculum more pragmatic and relevant to the majority of school children. Yet the formal school curriculum is academic and the teaching approach didactic. As succinctly summarized by a Chinese educator, "the curriculum stresses too much on theories, established laws, formula and facts while too little attention is paid to experiments and inquiry. Every pupil is expected to be capable in all disciplines. This leaves little room for the individual development of pupils. Their talents and creativity are suppressed" (Qin Xin, 1987).

The Cultural Revolution had swung the pendulum to one extreme by making the school curriculum a nursery ground for the promotion of Mao Zedong's thought with the inclusion of some down-to-earth production skills, such as pig rearing and the maintenance of water pumps and tractors. By contrast the post-1978 leadership was so obsessed with curriculum modernisation initiatives in order to try to catch up with the world's advanced countries that curriculum developers directly transplanted knowledge, especially in science and mathematics, from advanced countries such as Japan, United States and West Germany. As a result of this kind of curriculum borrowing, which had also happened in the 1950s when Russian textbooks were transplanted, the revised 1981 national curriculum became highly academic and examination oriented. Curriculum content became divorced from the realities of the majority of schools and was irrelevant to rural needs (Hu, 1980; Jiang, 1988). Eventually, the Chinese government had to declare that the 1981 curriculum was the result of "'haste-makes-waste': neither can teachers teach well nor pupils follow" (Yang Zehong, 1986).

TABLE 8. The National Curriculum of Primary and Secondary Schools in China, with the Percentage of the Total Teaching Time by Different School Subjects

(A) Percentage of the total teaching time by different school subjects in the secondary school curriculum 1954–81

| | *1954* | *1958* | *1963* | *1978* | *1981** |
|---|---|---|---|---|---|
| Politics | 4.4 | 7.1 | 6.2 | 7.2 | 12 |
| Chinese language | 23.0 | 20.0 | 21.8 | 18.3 | 17–22 |
| Foreign language | 6.7 | 7.7 | 18.7 | 15.1 | 16–17 |
| Mathematics | 19.6 | 20.7 | 18.1 | 20.7 | 16–19 |
| Physics | 7.5 | 8.3 | 9.4 | 11.4 | 5–10 |
| Chemistry | 5.9 | 6.0 | 6.2 | 7.2 | 5–8 |
| Biology | 5.0 | 6.5 | 3.6 | 2.2 | 3.5 |
| Hygiene | 1.0 | — | — | 1.1 | 1.2 |
| History | 10.0 | 17.7 | 4.7 | 4.6 | 4.5–6.5 |
| Geography | 6.7 | 5.3 | 3.1 | 3.6 | 4–6 |
| Physical Education | 6.7 | 7.1 | 6.2 | 7.2 | 6.9 |
| Music | 2.4 | 1.8 | 1 | 0.7 | 1.7 |
| Arts | 2.4 | 1.8 | 1 | 0.7 | 1.7 |

Source: *Chinese Education Yearbook 1949–1981*, PEP.
*The 1981 timetable allows flexibility between the arts and science classes.

(B) Percentage of the total teaching time by different school subjects in the primary school curriculum 1955–81

| *Year* | *1955* | *1963* | *1978* | *1981* |
|---|---|---|---|---|
| *Subject* | | | | |
| Politics | — | 4.2 | 2.9 | 3.7 |
| Chinese language | 44.6 | 48.0 | 41.2 | 38.5 |
| Foreign language | — | — | 9 | 4.4 |
| Mathematics | 24.4 | 25.0 | 24.8 | 43.7 |
| General Science | 3.4 | 2.2 | 2.8 | 4.4 |
| History | 2.7 | 2.2 | — | 1.5 |
| Geography | 2.7 | 1.1 | — | 1.5 |
| Physical Education | 8.1 | 6.7 | 7.7 | 7.4 |
| Arts | 4.0 | 3.3 | 5.4 | 6 |
| Music | 6.1 | 5.6 | 6.2 | 7.4 |
| Craft and Labor | 4.0 | 1.7 | — | 1.5 |

Source: *Chinese Education Yearbook 1949–1981*, PEP.

After the proclamation of nine-year compulsory education in 1986, the State Education Commission took measures to make the school curriculum more relevant to the school children. First, it was decreed that the curriculum for basic education, which was to be implemented in 1991, had to be designed for the 80% of pupils who live in the countryside. This resulted in an overall reduction of curriculum content, emphasis on fundamental skills and concepts, applications in daily life situations and curriculum diversification to allow more optional subjects, extracurricular activities and vocational courses. Second, a modified system of curriculum development was introduced which removed the monopoly of the People's Education Press in the production of nationally standardized textbooks. Following the national curriculum guides, six designated regional publishing centers produced different versions of textbooks to address regional realities. For example, Guangdong produced the "coastal version" of textbooks while the People's Education Press caters for the needs of the majority of school children.

In 1988, Shanghai and Zhejiang province were given the right to design their own curriculum for the nine years of basic education. Eventually, Shanghai produced a curriculum which intentionally represents the socioeconomic features of "a centre city with a developed economy, advanced technology, rational industrial structure and a higher degree of socialist civilisation, special role of leadership, pioneer and a show case of opening to the outside world" (Wang, 1990). The Shanghai curriculum reflects a number of unique features that differ from the national curriculum, including (a) teaching foreign languages (English, French and Japanese) at primary three, instead of junior secondary, (b) reduction of the weighting for compulsory subjects to give place to more optional subjects, (c) promotion of subject integration by introducing general science and social science as alternatives to the traditional subjects, (d) increasing pupils' knowledge of the outside world to match with Shanghai's export-oriented economic strategy, (e) reduction in the depth and difficulty of mathematics, (f) introduction of computer literacy and (g) introduction of basic life skills and career education (Leung, 1992a).

Zhejiang province developed a curriculum for basic education that is oriented to "the new socialist countryside that is developing rapidly" (Zhejiang Education Commission, 1991). The new curriculum attaches greater importance to physical and health education, which occupies 11% of the total curriculum time and ranks third in the overall timetable after Chinese language and mathematics. Integrated science and social studies are introduced in all junior secondary schools. The weighting for optional vocational courses accounts for 390 teaching hours of the total curriculum (164 hours in the national curriculum) and seventy-nine possible optional subjects are suggested, covering basic vocational skills such as woodcarving, bicycle repairs and vegetable farming (Leung, 1992a).

There is a huge gap between curriculum intentions and implementation, especially in the countryside where a shortage of qualified teachers directly causes the nonimplementation of school subjects. For example, in Dapu county which is a poor rural district in northwestern Guangdong, 80% of the primary schools cannot offer fine arts and music simply because teachers are not available (Leung, 1992b). Officials in Zhejiang province worry about the implementation of the junior secondary English curriculum, which is written by British language experts sponsored by a large publisher in England and follows the communicative approach. Local teachers lack the required skills to implement the approach and in-service teacher training lags behind (Shen, 1993).

## Educational Achievements in China: A Preliminary Assessment

Although there has been significant quantitative growth and expansion of China's education, the impact of education on human resource development is problematic. China's educational development since 1949 has reduced the illiteracy level of the population from around 80% in 1949 to 15.8% in 1990. The mean years of schooling of the adult population increased from 2.3 to 5.5 years in the same period. This is above the mean of 3.5 years for developing countries but compares less favorably with other Asian territories like Japan (10 years), South Korea (6.6 years), Philippines (6.4 years) and Hong Kong (6.2 years) (UNDP, 1991). Moreover, the quality of human capital in terms of the level of educational attainment of the population is low. The 1990 census revealed that 37% of the population over 15 years old had primary schooling, 23.3% had junior secondary schooling, 8% had senior secondary education and only 1.4% had received university education. As Tables 9a and 9b portray, only 0.07% of the workforce and 1.2% of the pupil population have acquired university education. This compares very unfavourably with many countries. It is estimated that China ranks 101st among 120 countries in the number of university students per 10,000 inhabitants (Zhou Nanjiao, 1992).

The figures in Table 9b also reveal that the educational attainment level of the entire working force is very low—37.7% of the Chinese workforce were primary school graduates and 17.3% were semi-illiterate or illiterate in 1990. This meant that 55% of the workforce received no more than primary education. The agricultural labor force exhibited a noticeably low level of educational attainment—22.6% of the farmers were illiterate or semi-illiterate and 45.3% had only received primary education.

Perkins (1988) comments that the quality of China's labour force was comparable to that of South Korea and Taiwan in 1965. It is evident that China's economic performance, which impresses the world, is backed by a workforce most of which had access only to primary education.

TABLE 9 (A). Number of Pupils (per thousand inhabitants) at Different Levels of Education & as Percentage of Pupil Population, 1949–1990

| *Year* | *Student Population As % of Population* | *Primary* | *Secondary* | *University* |
|---|---|---|---|---|
| 1949 | 4.7 | 450 (94.6%) | 23 (4.9%) | 2.2 (0.5%) |
| 1957 | 11.1 | 994 (89.5%) | 110 (9.9%) | 6.8 (0.6%) |
| 1965 | 18.9 | 1,602 (88.6%) | 197 (10.9%) | 9.3 (0.5%) |
| 1978 | 22.2 | 1,519 (68.5%) | 690 (31.1%) | 8.9 (0.4%) |
| 1985 | 17.6 | 1,263 (71.8%) | 481 (27.3%) | 16.1 (0.9%) |
| 1990 | 15.4 | 1,071 (69.7%) | 447 (29.1%) | 18.0 (1.2%) |

Source: *Chinese Population Yearbook* (Zhongguo Tongji Chubanshe), 1990.

TABLE 9 (B). Level of Education of the Workforce (as percentage) in 1990

| | *Occupational Sector* | | | | | |
|---|---|---|---|---|---|---|
| | *Government administration* | *Industrial sector* | *Agricultural sector* | *Commercial sector* | *Service sector* | *All Workforce* |
| Illiterate & Semi-illiterate | 0.06 | 3.5 | 22.6 | 5.0 | 4.7 | 17.3 |
| Primary | 12.5 | 24.8 | 45.3 | 23.2 | 14.1 | 37.7 |
| Junior Secondary | 33.3 | 50.9 | 27.4 | 49.8 | 17.2 | 33.1 |
| Senior Secondary | 33.7 | 19.9 | 4.8 | 4.9 | 64.0 | 11.3 |
| Specialized Sub-degree Courses | 13 | 0.05 | 0.01 | 1.0 | 0.01 | 1.2 |
| Tertiary | 6 | 0.01 | 0.00 | 0.3 | 0.00 | 0.07 |

Source: *Chinese Population Yearbook*, 1990.

Inequalities in educational opportunities are evident among females and national minority groups in China. Such inequalities have undermined the contribution of education to promoting social equity and national cohesion. The problem of gender inequalities in education is a complex one which is related to a deeply rooted gender stratification system in Chinese society. In spite of the efforts made by the government to promote the liberation of women, the problem of gender inequalities in education is serious. Of the 180 million illiterates in 1990, 66% were females (1990 census). In the underdeveloped regions, as many as 80% of the female cohort group were deprived of any educational opportunities (Li Habwing, 1991). As Table 10 shows, the proportion of females in the student population has always been lower than the percentage of females in the population, and the continuation rate of female students decreases toward higher education. This contrasts quite markedly with the reality that the participation rate of Chinese women in the paid labor force is outstandingly high among developing countries (Landes, 1989) and in East Asia (World Bank, 1993). In particular, the near universal employment of urban women, with nine of ten urban women working, is among the highest in the world (Bauer et al., 1992). Raising the educational level of the female population in China is not only important for promoting social equity but is also crucial for the success of China's population policy. The 1990 census shows that illiterate mothers averaged 4.7 births, those with primary education 3.8, senior secondary education had 2.4 births and those with tertiary education had only 1.9 births. A calculation of the elasticity coefficiency indicates that one additional year of schooling for fertile Chinese women would result in a fertility reduction of 3.8% (Ahmed, 1991).

TABLE 10. Proportion of Girls in Schools, 1952–1992

| | *1952* | *1965* | *1980* | *1985* | *1992* |
|---|---|---|---|---|---|
| Postgraduate Research | n.a. | 11.4 | 11.8 | 18.6 | 24.8 |
| Tertiary | 23.4 | 26.9 | 23.4 | 30.0 | 33.7 |
| Secondary | 23.5 | 32.2 | 44.6 | 44.8 | 46.0 |
| Primary | 32.9 | 35 | 44.6 | 44.8 | 46.0 |
| % of Females in Population | 48.1 | 48.8 | 48.5 | 48.3 | 48.5 |

Source: *Chinese Population Statistics*, 1992.

Another educationally disadvantaged group are the national minorities. Significant gaps exist between the educational accomplishments of the national minorities, which constitute 8% of the Chinese population, and that of the Han majority group. In the southwestern and northwestern parts of China where most of the national minorities reside, the illiteracy rate of the adult population ranged between 48% in Yunnan to 70.5% in Tibet (Wang and Bai, 1986). By 1987, the number of national minority children who had attained junior and senior secondary education was only 68% of the figure achieved by the country as a whole (Kwong and Rong, 1989). National minorities are also very underrepresented in university level education. The Chinese government is very anxious to reduce educational inequalities among the national minorities because the issue is a sensitive one in the light of a growing "national" consciousness among the minorities. Yet there is a dilemma that increasing the university student population of the national minorities may also increase the likelihood of student political activism which was demonstrated in the Pro-Democracy movement of 1989 (Postiglione, 1992).

## Education and Development in the PRC: A Critical Examination

The international literature on education and national development abounds with correlations between education and indicators of economic development, in particular with reference to productivity and GNP-oriented growth. The simplistic assumption that education plays an engine-for-growth function and that greater investment in human capital formation automatically leads to higher economic growth (Schultz, 1961; Anderson and Bowman, 1963; Harbison and Myers, 1964; Denison, 1967) has been followed religiously by many developing countries and yet the results have often been frustrating. The World Bank concludes that investment in education buys no guarantee of economic prosperity (World Bank, 1991a). As Foster (1975) remarks, "The specific problem of measuring the effects of enhanced educational inputs upon economic outputs must be seen within a broader historical and sociological perspective which attempts to examine the problematic relationship in the widest sense." Moreover, discussions on the relationship between education and development are often confined to how education contributes to national development unilaterally, rather than how developmental policies and political development affect the progress, or even retrogression, of education.

In the case of the People's Republic of China, special caution is needed when applying Western theories in explaining the relationship between education and national development. This is not to support the idea of "Chinese exceptionalism" (Harding, 1984), which argues that the country is so unique that its experiences cannot be explained by Western theories. But one must carefully take into account the ideological and historical context, otherwise the discussion will commit the mistake of "pseudo-sophistication" which implies a misuse of Western social sciences models and propositions in explaining Chinese developments.

For example, a "diachronic" approach was used by Lofstedt (1980) to correlate China's educational effort and performance with the economic level of development. The method was to match a number of basic development indicators, such as per capita production of items (e.g., steel, crude oil) vital for industrialisation, and educational indicators, such as enrollment in per cent of total population, and then arrange them chronologically over a thirty-year period between 1949 and 1978. The conclusions were (1) quantitative expansion of higher education coincided closely with the pattern of industrialization; (2) there was a fairly high degree of correspondence between increase in per capita steel production and secondary school enrollment as a percentage of the population. This diachronic approach suggests a causal relationship between education and economic development, but it has problems of oversimplification and data matching.

There are also methodological problems which undermine any simplistic explanatory relationship between education and economic development in China. First, it should be noted that prior to 1978, the Chinese government had never adhered to the Western concept of human capital, and did not use education as an engine-for-growth. In fact, correlating education investment with any increase in productivity was a taboo, and even a curse because the term "productivity" was considered synonymous with revisionism and capitalism. Even in 1984, a course book for students at the Beijing Normal University labelled Schultz as "a bourgeois economist upholding the human capital banner to defend the interest of the capitalists," and human capital theory was perceived as "hypocritical and its fundamental viewpoints are wrong" (Beijing Normal University, 1984). Second, the relationship between human capital and the labor market in China is complicated by the allocation system which, until the 1980s, committed people to lifelong confinement within a specific work unit. As a result, the mobility rate of professional manpower in China is about 2% compared to 29% in the United States (Liu, 1988). Also the wage structure is inversely related to the educational attainment level. In the wage system manual laborers can earn more than highly educated professionals and experts. There are Chinese sayings such as "being poor as a professor" and "the surgeon's scalpel is less profitable than the barber's knife." Calculation of private rates of return to education is not meaningful in China. Third, there is a problem of the underutilization of trained professionals and the mismatch between qualifications and labor deployment. For example, it was estimated in the 1980s that about 25% of engineers and scientists were employed in jobs they had not trained for, and 60% of agronomists were employed in other fields (Zhou Beilung, 1990a). Fourth, even the Chinese officials doubt the credibility of the qualitative aspects of economic and educational development. As Li Yuanhun (1990) remarks, economic growth in

China in the fifties and sixties was marked by "high investment but low effectiveness; high capital and low consumption; great wastage and little practical returns." Educational expansion in the fifties and sixties was often inflated while the quality of education was overlooked. Statistical data for the period between 1966–78 were considered incomplete and seldom quoted in the Chinese literature.

In fact, Chinese leaders and educators still hold negative views about the contribution that education made to the country's development before 1978. The common view is that (1) the role of education in China's socioeconomic development has never been fully recognized, as indicated by the low level of educational investment, (2) the course of educational development has been sluggish and lacks a consistent direction because it has been seriously affected by political blunders, (3) the educational system has failed to satisfy the country's manpower needs, (4) the school curriculum indoctrinates pupils with biased viewpoints and wrong concepts which are harmful to the pupils and the country and (5) the educational system is of low efficiency and poor quality (Wan, 1985; Chen, 1986; Wang, 1986; Li Shaoyuan, 1989; Wu, 1991; Xu, 1992).

Indeed, educational development in the People's Republic of China has always been the appendage of political goals set by the state's leadership. Up to 1965, the overarching development goal was dominated by "politics in command." Education served as a useful tool for achieving the economic and social transformation of China. The prime motive for expanding basic education and removing illiteracy was to build broad-based political support through a highly politicized curriculum. Educational provision was also seen as conducive to removing gender and ethnic inequalities. Initial industrialization was achieved by the high rate of physical capital accumulation through the elaborate articulation of successive five-year plans while political consolidation was accomplished by a radical sociopolitical transformation of the Chinese society through waves of political campaigns launched in the name of the "proletarian dictatorship" and "permanent revolution."

Although investment in education was low, great strides were made in the provision of education for the masses. Literacy programs were successful and the popularization of elementary education had led to 80% of enrollment of the primary age cohort by 1965, one of the highest rates among developing countries. The formal school system exhibited pyramidization, academization and bifurcation. After 1960, the manpower-matching function of education was stressed. The dual track senior secondary school system greatly promoted vocational and technical education for the production of mid-level technicians. The transplanted Russian system of highly specialized university education enabled China to acquire high-level experts for the key areas of scientific and technological development. Physical and human resources were mobilised with special emphasis on setting up China's paramilitary industrial industries. There were impressive developments in nonformal educational opportunities, and attempts to bridge the gap between school and the world of work were notably implemented through "hard work/frugal study" programs. Ideopolitical education was directed to inculcate patriotism among the fifty-six Chinese nationalities and foster morality.

By 1965, the People's Republic of China had not only survived military containment and international economic sanctions; it had built a self-sustained economic system and become a nuclear power. It could therefore be argued that educational development synchronised with China's development strategy in the period of preparatory stage for modern economic development. Nevertheless, the PRC did not reach five-year universal primary schooling before the foundation of comprehensive industrialisation was laid in 1965. The literacy rate of the population over twelve years old was only 62% (1964 census). The public educational expenditure was very low, ranging between 2.2 and 3.1% of GDP. Per capita educational expenditure on primary education was low. These aspects of educational performance were contrary to the proposition that industrialisation and economic expansion cannot occur if not backed by high educational investment and until 80% of the population is literate (Bowman and Anderson, 1973a, b).

It was only after 1978 that the leadership expected education to play a more significant role in China's modernization programs in response to the policy shift from "politics in command" to "economics-in-command." Deng Xiaoping's conception of education and national development is that education must be coordinated with the vitalization of China's economic, scientific, technological and general social progress. The specific mission of education is to speed up modernization so as to allow the country to catch up with the advanced countries. This newly endorsed education policy sparked a debate on the nature of education in March 1978. An outspoken economist, Yu Guanyuan, openly refuted the Marxist dogma that education is merely the superstructure of the state apparatus. The debate gave birth to the "genesis of the economics of education" (Han Zongli, 1987) and was directed to "propagandise the viewpoint of equating investment in education with investment in production, to oppose those viewpoints of polarising educational investment with production investment" (Qian Jiaju, 1983).

Ironically, Chinese educators uncritically accepted the tenets of human capital theory in the 1980s when the theory was receiving severe criticism in the international literature. Since 1978 numerous articles have appeared in China affirming the newfound belief that (a) education is the foundation of the modern economy, (b) education is the major means of raising labor productivity, (c) education is the prerequisite for vigorous economic development, (d) investment in education can be transformed into material productive forces, (e) education is a kind of investment in intelligence and (f) there is a strong correlation between levels of educational development and regional economic development (Li Yunkun, 1983; Qian Jiaju, 1983; Sun Jinlan, 1988; Li Shaoyuan, 1989). Scholars also tried to prove the reciprocal correlation between education and economic development by asserting the association between a quantum of education and certain developmental benefits in a causation-by-correlation fashion. In particular, Japan and West Germany were identified as two model countries which created economic miracles after the Second World War by investing heavily in human capital (Zhou Beilung, 1990a).

For example, Wang Shouan et al. (1981) conducted several investigations in Changchun city, an industrial center in the northeast, to prove the correlation between levels of educational attainment of workers and different aspects of production. One of their findings was that 91% of the industrial accidents in the Changchun Number One Automobile Factory in 1980 were caused by workers with primary and junior secondary education, whereas 9% were caused by workers of senior secondary schooling and none by university graduates. This crude analysis is obviously unconvincing because it ignores the basic fact that engineers are not involved in shop floor tasks at all and thus bear no direct responsibility of industrial accidents, which are often caused by factors such as machine breakdown and poor safety rules rather than the fault of workers.

Studies conducted by scholars in the late 1980s focus on correlating educational levels with income levels in China. For example, it is argued that levels of educational attainment of the rural population positively correlate with their earnings and productivity in Liaoning Province. The annual income of peasants with senior secondary level of education is 993 yuan. The figure declines to 816 yuan for junior secondary level, 774 for primary education and 312 yuan for illiterates (Li Shouxin, 1988b). Another study claims that Liaoning's high per capita income of 1,155 yuan is correlated with a 78.2% primary enrollment rate, whereas in Guizhou province,which is the poorest province in China, the low per capita income of 670 yuan is due to a low primary enrollment rate of 43% (Lo Bunong, 1985). One national study concludes that those provinces with literacy rates above 60% have proportionally more than twice as many employees in township enterprises than is the case in provinces with a lower level of literacy. The fact is that the higher literacy level has facilitated the peasants moving from farm to factories (SIHRD, 1991a).

The above cited evidence put forth by scholars in China has tried to demonstrate a causal connection between educational level and earnings. However, they suggest only a simplistic and temporal coincidence without examining the more complicated socioeconomic contexts. There is very strong evidence to argue that education has been the cart rather than the horse in China's economic development even in the post-1978 period of high growth.

First, as previously noted, China's rapid economic growth has not been backed by a pool of well-educated labor. One might therefore argue that rapid growth is possible so far as the growth involves a reliance on labor-intensive primary and secondary industries of a low and mid-level of technological sophistication. Second, the level of economic development of a province in China is determined by its geography and historical record of industrialization. In 1990, the coastal regions generated 49.3% of China's total export earnings and attracted 61% of the country's foreign investment (Maruya, 1992). In the affluent coastal regions, the illiteracy rate is below the national average of 22.3% and the enrollment rate for nine-year compulsory education is about 80%. It can be seen from Table 11, and also Figure 1, that the five richest regions in China are located on the coastal plain with a medium-sized population of 10–20 million and they have experienced industrialization since the last century. The five poorest provinces are all located inland with unfavorable geographical conditions and poor access. The affluent areas are therefore able to spend more on education and provide school leavers with more opportunities, or attract skilled manpower to settle there.

The data in Table 11 do not demonstrate a direct relationship between affluence and good educational performance. Some provinces, like Guangdong, Jiangsu and Zhejiang rank very high in GNP per capita but their level of educational development, as indicated by educational spending per capita, illiteracy rate, and the number of university students in population, is far from outstanding. On the contrary, some poor provinces like Honan and Shanxi have an educational performance similar to that of the rich regions.

Several recent studies have argued that level of economic development has a negative significance on educational provision. It is reported that rural counties in China need to acquire an annual per capita income of above 300 yuan in order to provide six years of primary education and 600 yuan to provide junior secondary education. This implies that 68% of the counties, comprising 60% of the rural population in the 300–600 yuan bracket, cannot implement nine years of basic education in the near future, especially under the existing policy of financial devolution which requires local regions to provide their own educational expenditures (Hao Keming et al., 1991).

TABLE 11. Economic and Education Performance of China's Richest (top ten) and Poorest Provinces (bottom ten), 1990

| *Province/ Region* | *GDP/Capita (yuan)* | *Ed. Expenditure per Capita (yuan & Ranking**)* | *Illiteracy Rate (%)* | *No. of University Students per 10,000 population* |
|---|---|---|---|---|
| Shanghai | 5,699 | 118 (2nd) | 11.4 | 6,534 |
| Beijing | 4,717 | 126 (1st) | 15.8 | 9,301 |
| Tianjian | 3,451 | 100 (3rd) | 8.9 | 4,668 |
| Liaoning | 2,460 | 71.4 (7th) | 8.8 | 2,596 |
| Guangdong | 2,379 | 69.3 (9th) | 10.5 | 1,338 |
| Jiangsu | 2,003 | 48.2 (16th) | 17.3 | 1,474 |
| Zhejiang | 1,998 | 49.8 (15th) | 17.4 | 1,170 |
| Heilungjiang | 1,799 | 53.9 (14th) | 11.0 | 1,139 |
| Xinjiang | 1,612 | 75.3 (4th) | 12.7 | 1,854 |
| Jilin | 1,612 | 48.0 (17th) | 10.8 | 2,154 |
| Hunan | 1,157 | 42.9 (22nd) | 12.0 | 1,138 |
| Shanxi | 1,152 | 46.7 (18th) | 17.6 | 1,672 |
| Jiangxi | 1,111 | 37.0 (26th) | 16.2 | 991 |
| Anhui | 1,088 | 30.4 (28th) | 24.4 | 883 |
| Yunnan | 1,073 | 45.0 (20th) | 25.4 | 807 |
| Sichuan | 1,066 | 31.9 (27th) | 16.2 | 961 |
| Honan | 1,061 | 46.0 (19th) | 16.3 | 848 |
| Gangsu | 1,018 | 42.7 (24th) | 28.0 | 1,104 |
| Guangxi | 933 | 40.6 (25th) | 20.6 | 791 |
| Guizhou | 790 | 29.9 (29th) | 24.5 | 777 |

Source: *Chinese Population Yearbook*, 1990.
***Report on Local Educational Expenditure*, 1990.

Unless special measures are taken, it will be very difficult to universalize basic education in the poverty-stricken regions (SIHRD, 1991). It is obvious that poor economic performance generates low revenue for educational expenditure, which in turn undermines the contribution of education to development. The vicious cycle will prevail in China for a long time.

Second, rapid economic growth in China has been primarily the result of factors other than educational investment. A typical example is the annual output of grain. It staggered from 164 to only 194 million tons between 1952 and 1965 because the commune system of "eating from the same big pot" discouraged peasant enthusiasm for agricultural production. When the leadership changed the land ownership and production system in 1978 there was an incentive for farmers. Annual grain output leaped to 305 million tons in 1978 and reached a historical peak of 407 million tons in 1985 (Teng, 1982). The explosion of grain productivity after 1978 was mainly the result of market policy changes rather than raising the educational level of the peasantry.

The get-rich-overnight success of the Shenzhen Special Economic Zone, which is adjacent to Hong Kong, is another example of how "miraculous" economic growth was caused by market-oriented policy changes rather than the engine-for-growth function of educational investment. Shenzhen was originally a small agricultural county with a population of about 310,000. It was chosen by Deng Xiaoping in 1979 as the first "special economic zone" to experiment with his open door and get-rich-first economic development strategy. The introduction of various special economic privileges, such as exemption from tax and cheap industrial land, was granted by the central government and backed by heavy government investment in the infrastructure. Shenzhen subsequently became China's most modernized metropolitan city in ten years, with an immigrant population of 2.4 million and a GNP/ per capita of 6,963 RMB (the highest in China) in 1990. The expansion of schooling and, in particular, the proliferation of vocational education in Shenzhen is impressive but that was only a response to social and economic demand arising as a result of development. The director of the Shenzhen Education Bureau acknowledged that the economic boom had brought the flourishing of educational institutions in Shenzhen. Economic growth generates more government revenue which, together with the 3% education tax on foreign enterprises, enabled Shenzhen to enjoy a higher educational expenditure per capita (Shenzhen Educational Science Research Institute, 1991). Between 1980 and 1990, the Shenzhen government on average spent 18.1% of its government budget and 2.3% of its GNP on education (Shenzhen Education Bureau, 1991). If compared with the national average of 16.1% and 3.4% in the same period, Shenzhen's level of educational expenditure was not very impressive despite its relative affluence. Similarly, Guangdong province was criticized for its reluctance to spend more on education although it experienced an average annual growth rate of 20% in the late 1980s (Xu Mingdi, 1992).

It should also be noted that Shenzhen offers attractive incentives (e.g., permanent right of abode, better housing, higher wages and living allowances) to recruit 70% of its high-level and middle-level manpower from all over China, especially from the inland regions which have a large pool of skilled manpower. This pool of openly recruited skilled manpower forms the backbone of Shenzhen's economy at the expense of a brain drain experienced by other regions. Another important factor that accounts for Shenzhen's prosperous economy is its ability to provide cheap labor at a daily wage of 30 yuan per day (about five U.S. dollars), to attract manufacturers from Hong Kong, Taiwan and multinational enterprises to shift their labor-intensive production base to Shenzhen. Maruya (1992) remarks that there is high labor mobility from the low productivity agricultural sector to the high productivity manufacturing sector in Shenzhen and the Pearl River delta in Guangdong province. Surplus agricultural labourers from the poor regions of Guangdong and other provinces flood into Shenzhen to fill up various factory and construction vacancies. In 1990, these internal immigrants, locally called "temporary residents," accounted for 66% of Shenzhen's total population and 36% percent of them were females. Female workers usually worked in the labor-intensive manufacturing industry, such as electronics, garment and textiles and toys, which provided 65.6% of Shenzhen's GDP in 1990 (Shenzhen Statistics Bureau, 1991). Male laborers worked in construction industry. The level of education of the workforce was relatively low. According to a sample survey conducted in Guangdong province, 37% of the migrant peasant workers had received six years of primary education and 44% had not completed primary education (Wu, 1991). This can be taken as a close description of the educational background of the migrant labor force in Shenzhen.

Third, China's education system has been unable to satisfy the country's assumed short-term and long-term manpower needs despite the rapid expansion of specialized secondary schools and tertiary institutions. In 1984 a comprehensive national manpower projection was made. It was estimated that a total of 49 million skilled professionals were required by the year 2000. This represented a 350% increase of skilled professionals over the figure for 1983, and implies that China's tertiary institutions and secondary specialized schools would have had to graduate 34 million people in the ensuing 18 years. Of this pool of professionals, 7.8 million have been degree holders, 7.8 million graduates of specialized colleges and 17 million graduates of secondary specialized schools (Zhou Beilung, 1990a). However, from the graduation pattern already shown and even taking the output of adult education into consideration, it has proved difficult for the education sector to approach the projected manpower needs. The shortfall was about 60% (Lo, 1991). It is paradoxical for China to adopt a dogmatic manpower planning approach at a time when its economy is becoming more dynamic and when a freer labor market has been formed. Moreover, the lopsided manpower distribution pattern, as shown in Table 6, is still unfavorable for China's economic shift toward the tertiary sector. The educational system itself still contains many qualitative and structural deficiencies which reduce its capacity to yield the desired educational outcomes.

## Concluding Remarks

In this summary of China's economic and educational performance since 1949, only key aspects of development are reviewed and discussed. Surely education contributed toward China's national development in the political and economic consolidation of the newborn regime amid a hostile international climate. But the evidence suggests that the intended contribution had been greatly undermined by policy contradictions of the leadership and resulting political turmoil. The evidence argues against any simplistic and unilateral explanation of the correlation between education and development in China which focuses on the "engine-for-growth" function of education advocated by human capital theorists in the West and which is currently accepted as a new dogma by some Chinese planners.

Education in China has for most of the time served as an appendage to political goals, and remained the wagon rather than the locomotive in China's socioeconomic transformation. Looking ahead, while the Chinese leadership has set an ambitious national development goal of making China the world's third greatest economic giant after the United States and Japan by 2050, the accommodative capacity of education to sustain the realisation of such a goal should not be overestimated. This is because China's educational system at present contains many qualitative and structural deficiencies that cannot be easily removed. As the director of the State Education Commission admits, the pace of educational reform and development still lags behind socioeconomic needs (Zhongguo Jiaoyubao, October 29, 1993). Moreover, the widening gap between the rich coastal regions and the poor inland regions may lead to a polarized pattern of socioeconomic development, which implies that the majority of the Chinese people in the disadvantaged areas will continue to suffer from ignorance and poverty. What is even more worrying to see is that the country's rapid economic expansion and gigantic development projects have created huge demand on capital and it is educational expenditure that is likely to be squeezed. A more deepseated constraint on educational development is that the Communist Party, like many other ruling regimes in developing countries, only expects education to yield to the officially described aspects of socialist modernization, but not at the cost of social disorder or provoking the existing structures of authority and control. Education will remain as a state-controlled and mimetic enterprise, rather than a transformative and liberating endeavor.

# 10 Education and Development in East Asia

## An Overview

*Paul Morris and Anthony Sweeting*

Our goal in this chapter is to identify and compare the role education has played in the development of the eight East Asian societies. We will try to highlight both the common aspects and differences across the societies. Our analysis begins by tracing the relationship between education and development with reference to the three basic levels of educational provision: namely, primary, secondary and tertiary. Subsequently, we analyze the roles of technical and vocational education and of the nature of the curriculum.

Preceding chapters have separately analyzed the role of education in the development of eight societies in East Asia. Each of these societies has achieved high levels of economic growth and a general improvement in its peoples' living conditions. This commonality, along with their location in East Asia, masks a number of important differences, apart from their obvious differences in size, political system, and culture.

One significant difference relates to the distinction made in the Introduction to this book between *growth* and *development*. As we emphasize above, all of the eight East Asian societies which we examined experienced considerable *growth* in the latter half of the twentieth century. In the sense of significant changes to societal structures, values and attitudes, however, not all of them have *developed* to anything like the same extent. Malaysia and Macau, for instance, reached take-off toward development much more recently than Japan, Hong Kong, Singapore, Taiwan and South Korea. China is only now arriving at its developmental launch-pad. Variations in the extent and the rate of development are open to numerous explanations.

Such variety is reflected in the different emphases which our authors have adopted in analyzing the relationship between education and development. Concerning the People's Republic of China, Leung has illustrated how the Chinese leadership has used education as an accommodative vehicle for achieving their hegemonic political goals in different historical periods. With regard to South Korea, Chon Sun Ihm emphasizes the highly interventionist role of the government in linking educational provision, through manpower planning, to the perceived needs of the economy. In Taiwan, Yi Rong Young also focuses on the critical role of the government, but stresses the way that schooling generally and the curriculum specifically have been used to promote a strong sense of cultural and national identity. Similarly in the multi-ethnic societies of Malaysia and Singapore, Mukherjee and Singh in the former case and Gopinathan in the latter highlight the part played by education in forging social cohesion and a strong national consciousness which have provided a stable context for growth, while encouraging pride in economic progress and national development. Wing On Lee stresses the key role education has been accorded in Japan in both maintaining national pride and promoting values consistent with a competitive economy. Bray in the case of Macau and Sweeting for Hong Kong, however, both underline the minimalist role played in these societies by the governments and, in the case of Hong Kong, the extent to which education has expanded in response to economic shifts.

A more general feature which emerges from the analyses of the earlier chapters concerns the impact of the basic urge toward political survival upon economic health. We are struck by the extent to which the development of each of the societies investigated has been influenced by an *antagonistic* or, at least, strained and insecure relationship with a neighboring power. The potential threat to national security has served to stimulate efforts to promote economic growth. Thus Taiwan's development, especially during the early stages, was strongly affected by its antagonism toward the People's Republic of China. Similarly, the relationship between South and North Korea and, in the 1960s, between Malaysia and Singapore as well as between Malaysia and Indonesia, contributed important influences to development. These situations were effectively exploited by politicians to maintain a climate of opinion in which social cohesion and economic growth appeared to be two sides of the same vital coin. Education was certainly used to reinforce the significance of national unity and, at least in prospect, to prepare for economic well-being. The tenuous position of the two colonies as enclaves on the coast of China has, as Sweeting shows in the case of Hong Kong, been a major factor influencing both the direction of the economy and the nature of the school curriculum. In the post–Second World War period and especially since the establishment of the People's Republic, China's xenophobia has coupled with a persistent Cold War mentality to affect both economic planning and the nature of schooling. In this case, it is not one neighbor but the "West," including, for much of the time, Russia and Japan, which played the part of adversary and stimulant. Japan might appear to be the exception, but in this case, its defeat and humiliation at the end of the Second World War contributed toward a determination to substitute economic for military glory and also toward the fashioning of its post-war educational system.

This does not mean, however, that development in each of these societies was introverted or that relationships with neighboring states were inevitably hostile and asymmetrical. As Leung demonstrates, Hong Kong industrialists have been a major force in the rapid industrialization of southern China generally and Shenzen particularly. Japanese capital and enterprise have certainly contributed to the development of such societies as Hong Kong, Malaysia and Singapore. Singaporean capital has, in turn, played an important part in the Malaysian economy. In general, it seems important to recognize the influence within societies both of external factors and of a degree of insecurity or even feelings of antagonism on public policy in all fields. Essentially, in the societies which we have examined in East Asia, the survival of the state became associated with economic well-being. In each of the societies under investigation, this goal was pursued single-mindedly and successfully.

## Primary Schooling

We focus first on the early period of growth. In all of the societies investigated, the early growth period was the outcome of a process of industrialization which involved the low-cost, labor-intensive mass production of goods for export. This period occurred in the 1950s–60s in Japan, mainly from the mid-1960s in Hong Kong, Singapore, Taiwan and South Korea, from the 1970s in Malaysia and Macau and from the early 1980s in the case of the People's Republic of China. These periods in each of the respective countries were associated with a common set of educational conditions. The most notable was the high level of access to "basic" or primary education prior to industrial "take-off." By 1900, Japan had achieved universal primary education. By 1965, the enrollment rates for primary education in South Korea, Singapore and Hong Kong were all over 100% of the official estimated age-cohort[1] and in Taiwan the figure was 97.15%. In the low-income economies of the world, on the other hand, average enrollment in that year was 73%. In the PRC, expansion of primary education was accorded first priority and the primary school enrollment rate had reached 80% as early as 1965.

The high levels of access to basic education were also reflected in the relatively high levels of literacy which were achieved. Furthermore, the expansion of basic education was not gender-specific. Both boys and girls benefited. This had the effect of rapidly reducing the discrepancy which had existed between male and female access and also in respective literacy rates. Existing differences in literacy rates between males and females in the societies we examined arise largely from adult literacy estimates and are a legacy of the period before universal provision of primary education. The general effect of this situation was the relatively new and easy availability of literate and numerate women as well as men for the workforce at the time of rapid industrialization. The only obvious source of variation in connection with primary school provision was that Japan achieved universal access to primary schooling and a high level of access to secondary schooling long before the other societies and, thus, there was a far longer time lag between universal provision and fully fledged industrialization.

The overall pattern which emerges from the analyses in our country chapters highlights the sequential nature of educational provision. In the early stage of growth and industrialization, the expansion of primary education took priority. At this stage, overall, much less proportionately was spent on secondary and tertiary education. Subsequently, however, motivated both by changes in the economy and by the rising expectations of parents whose children were completing their primary schooling, first secondary and then tertiary education became the focuses for expansion. Table 1, below, provides a summary of data which illustrate this pattern as it manifested itself in the 1980s.

TABLE 1. Percentage Distribution of Current Expenditure by Level of Schooling

| *Country or Territory* | *1980* | | | *1990* | | |
|---|---|---|---|---|---|---|
| | *Pre-Primary & 1st Level* | *2nd Level* | *3rd Level* | *Pre-Primary & 1st Level* | *2nd Level* | *3rd Level* |
| China | 27.6 | 34.3 | 20.0 | 32.7 | 34.4 | 18.6 |
| Hong Kong | 33.7 | 35.7 | 24.6 | 29.8 | 40.7 | 28.8 |
| Japan | 39.5 | 34.6 | 11.1 | 29.3 | 32.2 | 22.5 |
| Malaysia | 35.0 | 34.0 | 12.4 | 37.9 | 37.7 | 14.9 |
| Singapore | 35.8 | 41.1 | 17.1 | 28.7 | 36.5 | 30.7 |

Source: UNESCO, *World Education Report*, 1993.

On the other hand, further investigation of educational expenditure indicates that the expansion of secondary and tertiary education was not accompanied by a reduction in the per capita expenditure on primary pupils, as Table 2 shows for the decade of the 1980s. This was partly the consequence of an increase in the gross level of expenditure and, most important, of a decrease in the size of the school age population. The latter was a direct result of the decline in fertility rates which was achieved by each of the countries in the 1970s. In each of the societies which we investigated, an increase in per capita expenditure on primary pupils became apparent after basic provision and universal access had been achieved. It coincided with the "post-early industrialization" period when the various economies were becoming technologically more sophisticated. In Table 2, it can be clearly seen that the expenditure per pupil improved during the 1980s in those countries of East Asia for which data are available, but that this improvement was not typical of developing countries in Africa.

TABLE 2. Current Expenditure per Pupil as a Multiple of GNP per Capita

| *Nation* | *1980* | | | *1990* | | |
|---|---|---|---|---|---|---|
| | *Pre-Primary & Primary* | *Secondary* | *Tertiary* | *Pre-Primary & Primary* | *Secondary* | *Tertiary* |
| China | 0.04 | 0.13 | 3.62 | 0.05 | 0.15 | 1.93 |
| Japan | 0.13 | 0.17 | 0.21 | 0.14 | 0.16 | 0.49 |
| S. Korea | 0.11 | 0.10 | 0.16 | 0.12 | 0.11 | 0.06 |
| Malaysia | 0.11 | 0.22 | 1.49 | 0.13 | 0.26 | 1.24 |
| Singapore | 0.07 | 0.13 | 0.43 | 0.09 | 0.14 | 0.55 |
| India | 0.09 | 0.14 | 0.72 | 0.11 | 0.15 | 0.83 |
| Kenya | 0.15 | 0.34 | 9.82 | 0.13 | 0.47 | 6.80 |
| Malawi | 0.08 | 1.33 | 13.71 | 0.07 | 0.94 | 10.32 |
| Brazil | 0.08 | 0.11 | 0.59 | 0.11 | 0.13 | 1.10 |

Source: UNESCO, *World Education Report*, 1993.

Table 2 shows the expenditure per pupil as a multiple of GNP per capita for each level of education in the years 1980 and 1990 in several of the countries which we have studied and in a selection of other countries. As far as the East Asian NICs are concerned, the data demonstrate that, with the exception of South Korea where primary education is more expensive than secondary, each successive level of education is more expensive in per capita terms. It also illustrates that the proportional reduction in overall expenditure on primary schooling was actually accompanied by an increase in expenditure per primary pupil in the decade of the 1980s. In addition, it contains interesting information about expenditure per secondary and tertiary student over the same period, which we will consider further in our sections on secondary and tertiary education.

In terms of the sources of funding for primary education, the pattern is not a consistent one. In China, Japan, South Korea, Taiwan and Malaysia, the state provided basic education, while in Hong Kong and Macau, the early demand was satisfied mainly by private schools. Thus, in the majority of the societies which we examined, the state played the critical role. It decided who should be educated and provided either the schools themselves or the financing for the schools. In Hong Kong and Macau, however, the governments allowed the public demand for primary and subsequently secondary education to be satisfied initially by private suppliers. These included missionary bodies, benevolent organizations, often of local origin, and profit-making businesses. Subsequently, the state increasingly took over the provision of primary education in an attempt to remedy the inequalities which became prevalent and to improve the base-line of physical conditions. This intervention essentially involved the phasing out of private profit-making schools and their replacement by "aided" schools (subsidies from public funds to non-profit-making provisioners). In Japan, the state was the main provider of formal primary and secondary education, but the private sector developed a parallel system of education designed to offer pupils extra tuition to prepare them for the highly competitive public examinations. In China, whilst the state was the sole provider of education, schools were encouraged to generate funds from other sources. With the advent of universal primary education, both social demands for education and state reforms of education shifted to the secondary sector.

As far as the nature of the primary school curriculum is concerned, the goal has been to provide pupils with high levels of achievement of basic literacy and numeracy, to promote in them social cohesion and the sense of national identity and to maximize their chances of access to a prestigious secondary school. The nature of the language in those societies which use an ideographic system encourages a style of teaching and learning which stresses the importance of memorization and diligence, while requiring an application of discipline and perseverance from early years. These characteristics may have been transferable to adult life. If so, they became highly prized components of the profiles of East Asian workforces.

## Secondary Schooling

The key features which emerge from the country chapters relate to the timing of the expansion of secondary education, the sources of its provision and the balance between general/academic and technical/vocational education.

In connection with the timing of secondary school expansion, the key periods are those which preceded each significant shift in the economic structure. The periods prior to industrialization saw systems of secondary education which, in general, were selective, elitist and academic with regard to curricular orientation and highly competitive with regard to admissions. They were in effect the centrepiece of a pyramid, one of their key goals being to prepare a minority of pupils for entry to the final stage of formal education. Thus in 1965, the enrollment rates in secondary schools in South Korea, Singapore and Hong Kong were 35%, 45% and 29%, respectively. As their economies grew, so people's living standards and aspirations increased. This coincided with increases in the governments' revenues. In the more interventionist societies of South Korea and Taiwan, the state responded to public demand and/or to its own desire to invest in human and political capital by rapidly expanding secondary education. Consequently, by 1986, the enrollment rates for secondary schools in Taiwan had risen to 92%, in South Korea to 95% and in Hong Kong to 69%. However, this expansion was not always publicly funded.

In Hong Kong and Macau, the response was, until recently, more one of pragmatic scepticism with regard to public provision. The state responded slowly to public demand, often as a type of indirect reaction to a political crisis which threatened the government's legitimacy. Such a tendency may be attributed to a mixture of motives. These included inertia, the concern of a colonial government about the consequences of having to deal with a more highly educated population and the desire to pursue a policy of "positive non-interventionism" especially when private provision was available. The absence of government provision on a large scale resulted in the rapid expansion of private secondary schooling which paralleled the earlier situation concerning primary education. In Taiwan, whilst virtually all primary and junior secondary schooling was publicly funded, over 30% of senior secondary or high school places were in the private sector. In most of the other societies which we investigated, the early phase of secondary school expansion coincided with rapid economic growth and depended heavily on private funding. In Japan, on the other hand, the expansion of secondary schooling occurred prior to the period of rapid economic growth and industrialization. This was accompanied by the emergence and expansion of a parallel system of private tuition, taking opportunity of the perceived need to make up for the defects of the official system and to prepare candidates for public examinations.

The two tables on educational expenditure reveal that, for secondary education, the situation varied across the subjects of our study in the 1980s. In some cases—for example, most notably Hong Kong and Malaysia—there was a significant relative increase in expenditure as a whole on secondary education and this was accompanied by improvements in the per capita expenditure. In the case of China, there was a small increase in overall relative expenditure on secondary education, accompanied by improvement in per capita expenditure on the secondary pupil. With Singapore and Japan, however, there was a decrease in overall relative expenditure. In Singapore, this was offset by an improvement in per capita expenditure. In Japan, which was the most advanced of all the societies in technological terms, the decrease in overall relative expenditure on secondary education was also accompanied by a reduction in per capita expenditure when factored against per capita GNP. As might be expected, however, in Japan's case, the decade of the 1980s witnessed very significant increases both in overall relative expenditure and in per capita expenditure on tertiary education.

Despite the general quantitative expansion of secondary education, the curriculum, teaching and assessment methods tended to reflect the earlier systems of the pre-rapid economic growth periods. The focus was on achievement and selection to the next stage of education. Both preference and expected returns favored academic specialization. The systems were broadly meritocratic, rewarding conformity and diligence. Each level of educational attainment was known to ensure a higher rate of future earnings in all of the societies except the PRC, where the higher level of educational attainment was valued more because it brought with it a job in the cities or in the government. Also, with the exception of Hong Kong and Macau, educational policy and practice placed a premium on providing pupils with a strong sense of national identity. The policies and practices adopted distinctive focuses in the different social and political contexts, which we will examine further below.

## Vocational and Technical Education

This area of educational provision displays the greatest diversity. In each of the societies we examined, vocational and technical education was initially provided for only a very small proportion of pupils in periods prior to industrialization and rapid economic growth. The need of employers was primarily for diligent, literate and trainable employees. What technical skills were required were mainly learned on the job. Further, the status of technical education was low as it was not seen to provide the same opportunities as a more academically oriented curriculum and, in some societies, was associated with the rehabilitation of criminal and less able youth. Thus, it is difficult to ascribe an instrumental role to technical and vocational education in the early stages of development. Its role and size have, however, changed as the economies shifted from the labor-intensive mass production of cheap export goods to more capital-intensive, expensive and technologically sophisticated products and, subsequently, as in the cases of Singapore and Hong Kong, toward an increasing reliance on the provision of commercial and financial services.

In Japan, the technical and vocational sector did expand in the 1950s and 1960s, but it was mainly the employers who took on the task of providing their employees with the necessary job-specific skills. Firms recruited the best available school leavers, as identified through conventional academic tests, in anticipation of providing those skills. The pattern in Hong Kong was similar, with the major expansion of technical education occurring in the 1970s and 1980s when the economy was already moving toward a greater reliance on tertiary production. However, that expansion resulted only in the proportion of pupils in technical/vocational education increasing from 4% in 1969 to 6.23% in 1979 and 8.96% in 1989. In Hong Kong's case, it certainly appears as if the courses provided by training agencies on behalf of groups of employers (e.g., the building industry) constituted the form of technical education which was most appreciated both by aspiring employees and by employers precisely because it focused on basic applied skills which were immediately usable in practical employment situations. In Malaysia, technical schooling was a small, neglected and low-status sector within the education system. In 1970, it recruited only 3.3% of the age cohort. As the economy expanded, it grew slowly and the government responded to the demands of employers by a general upgrading of its status and curriculum. By 1990, 8.4% of the age cohort were in technical education. Singapore exhibits a similar pattern, with the low status of a small technical sector in the 1970s being enhanced partly through government exhortation and intervention and partly through changes in parents' and employers' attitudes influenced by the mass media as well as expectations of economic rewards. However, as with Malaysia and Hong Kong, technical education has remained a relatively small sector in the overall system of education. The vast majority of pupils follow a general/academic secondary school curriculum.

In contrast, in the PRC, South Korea and Taiwan, the provision of a large-scale program of technical and vocational education has been a central element in long-term planning, especially in the periods which immediately followed early industrialization. In Taiwan before 1970, there were more students on the academic track than on the vocational track. The government decided to reverse this trend in 1970 to meet the future needs of industry. By 1991/92, the ratio had shifted to 2 : 1 in favor of the vocational track. In South Korea, the government has also invested heavily in technical/vocational education in an attempt to provide for the future needs of the economy. The persistence of problems in this field, provoked mainly by the continuing prestige associated with academically oriented tertiary education, is indicated, however, by the alarming suicide rate connected with failure to obtain places in universities and relegation to the technical/vocational institutions. In the PRC, the situation was somewhat more convoluted. Initially, there were clear intentions to promote technical and vocational education even before major industrialization and a rapid growth rate occurred, but these were punctuated by political upheavals. Thus, as early as the 1950s, China began to introduce a dual-track secondary school system by giving emphasis to technical and vocational education in an attempt to foster a pool of mid-level craftsmen and technicians. By 1965, the number of students enrolled in the vocational and technical streams of senior secondary schools exceeded that of students in the general stream. However, the dual track system was completely destroyed in 1966 with the onset of the Cultural Revolution. It was, however, fully revived in 1981 and, by 1990, the percentage of students attending technical and vocational schools had risen to about 50% of the age cohorts.

Macau represents the other extreme in terms of the provision of technical education. Only recently has any technical education been provided by the state in Macau.

## Tertiary Education

The expansion of tertiary education broadly followed the achievement of high levels of access to secondary schooling. For most of the countries in the early periods of industrialization and growth, tertiary education was a small, elite sector of the educational system, providing a highly academic curriculum for students considered to be the cream of the secondary schools. Access to tertiary education ensured employment in the civil service, some socially prestigious and financially rewarding professional areas (such as medicine, law and engineering) and teaching. Thus, for example, in South Korea, Singapore and Hong Kong, the percentage of the age group who survived up to tertiary education in 1965 was 6%, 10% and 5%, respectively. In the 1970s, these societies achieved high levels of access to secondary education and public demand for enhanced opportunities at the tertiary level grew. Responses were varied. The more interventionist governments of South Korea and Taiwan moved quickly to expand tertiary provision. By 1986, the enrollment rates in tertiary education had grown to 25% and 33%, respectively. In contrast, in Hong Kong it grew only to 13% by 1986. Japan had achieved an enrollment rate of 38% by 1985. But here, as in the case of countries like the Philippines, which have not yet experienced rapid industrialization and impressive economic growth but which can boast of very high enrollment rates in tertiary education, one might question the quality of at least some of the tertiary education on offer, as well as its likely contribution to national development. Both South Korea and Hong Kong have fairly recently embarked on massive expansion programmes for tertiary education. In South Korea, this resulted in 44% of the age group enrolled in institutes of tertiary education; in Hong Kong the target is 25% by 1995. Both these expansions were justified officially via reference to manpower needs, but our authors interpret them as being responses to political crises in the respective countries.

Two other variables were also evident: namely the differential sources of funding and the degree of governmental control. Concerning funding, we see a mixed pattern. The two extreme groups comprise Hong Kong, the PRC, Taiwan and Singapore on the one hand, and Japan, South Korea and, for much of the time, Macau, on the other. In the former group, tertiary education is predominantly funded publicly, either directly through the government or indirectly through an official agency which disperses public funds. The cost to the individual student is relatively low, but has, along with the expansion of tertiary education and consequent increases in public expenditure on this level of education, been rising. In the second group, a substantial proportion of tertiary education is provided by the private sector. This increases supply, but may depress academic standards. For this group in particular, and to some extent for the other societies we have examined, there is a general tendency, especially in the early phase of expansion, for tertiary education to involve a greater degree of private provision than the other levels of education. This is most marked in the cases of Japan, South Korea and Taiwan, where a very significant proportion of tertiary education is privately provided and funded. In contrast, in the PRC, Hong Kong, Singapore, Malaysia and, more recently, Macau, private funding is less significant, although there are some signs of expansion of the private sector with, for example, the establishment of the Open Learning Institute in Hong Kong and the opening up of joint venture degree programmes in Malaysia and Hong Kong.

Moreover, it must be recognized that the characterization and categorization we outline above apply only to provision within the eight different East Asian societies. Large numbers of students, especially those from Hong

Kong, Singapore and Malaysia, purchase education overseas. Many of them return to work in their countries of origin. In some cases, such as Taiwan and Malaysia, substantial numbers of students are sent to study abroad and supported via public funds. In Malaysia and Singapore, the governments have encouraged collaborative ventures (e.g., split-site courses) between local and overseas institutions which have relied, for the most part, on privately funded students. This has served as an alternative route for qualified ethnic Chinese and Indians whose access to tertiary education in the public sector in Malaysia has been limited by governmental regulations on admissions quotas based on ethnic origin. The predecessor of the University of Macau was established at least partly to cater for such students. In more general terms, the relatively high level of access of students to tertiary education opportunities in overseas countries has also served as an effective instrument of technology transfer, a channel through which scientific and technological advances could be rapidly and economically assimilated. The data provided in our Tables 1 and 2 do not reveal the substantial expenditure on overseas education by significant numbers of young people and their families from the East Asian societies we have investigated. As they stand, therefore, they seriously underestimate the importance of private funding at the tertiary level.

With regard to the extent of governmental control over tertiary education, we see high levels of control in those societies, like South Korea and Taiwan, with unfinished civil wars, and in the PRC where education is very closely linked to the promotion of the legitimacy of the role of the state generally and of the Chinese Communist Party in particular. This manifests itself in rigorous control of access and of the nature of the curriculum, although the extent of control was being reduced in the last decade, at least until the outbreak and suppression of the Pro-Democracy movement in 1989. The development and expansion of tertiary education in the PRC are dictated by the government's perceived manpower needs, which, together with political sensitivity toward the humanities and social sciences, has caused a lopsided distribution of graduates among the different disciplines. The outcome has been an oversupply of engineers and scientists, which contrasts sharply with the acute shortage of graduates for the currently expanding tertiary industries. In South Korea, the role of tertiary education has been closely linked, especially by governmental policy, to the perceived needs of the economy. Consequently, major shifts in economic policy, such as the government-initiated emphasis on heavy engineering and chemical industries, were reflected in an expansion of what were considered to be appropriate technical and vocational courses in the tertiary and secondary sectors of education.

However, problems of mismatch have arisen. On the supply side, the private institutions and students have responded to market forces which place a premium on general education. On the demand side, employers attest to the need for employees with appropriate technical skills, but in practice often prefer both to employ students with the "best" academic results and to pay them more. The result, most evident in South Korea, is that parents and pupils follow the signals of the labor market in which a general education produces the highest return. In contrast, governmental policy invests in and attempts to direct students into technical and vocational education. Similarly in Taiwan, the government has explicitly linked educational provision at all levels to the needs of the economy and seems to have been more successful at channeling students into technical and vocational streams. However, while 70% of all students aged 17 to 19 are in vocational schools, the status of these schools remains low because they enroll those students who have failed to obtain a place in more academic and general secondary schools. In both of these societies, as tertiary education expands, so the mismatches between education and employment become more pronounced and, along with an increasingly pluralistic political environment, this is resulting in a reconsideration of the role of manpower planning as a basis for determining educational access and the nature of specific courses.

In contrast, in Hong Kong, the degree of governmental control over access to, and the nature of, tertiary education has been less directive and not as immediately based on the perceived future needs of the economy. Tertiary education has grown, and often this is the result of governmental initiatives to introduce new programs which are thought to be desirable, perhaps even necessary. Thus, much of the expansion has been in technological and professional areas, such as engineering, computing, business studies, law and medicine, though, as Sweeting notes in the case of dentistry, failure to take into consideration such factors as the supply of qualified manpower from abroad has led to less than perfect matching between training and employment vacancies. On the whole, however, while there has been a tendency to respond to the manpower requirements of the economy as they seem to emerge, the link between employment and education is less planned than in South Korea and Taiwan.

It is also worth noting the possible political connotations of the conjunction of policies about the source of tertiary educational opportunities and the directiveness of government influence on students' career paths. Some of the societies examined here and others in East Asia rely heavily on the private sector for the provision of tertiary education. Examples of these include, as noted above, Japan, South Korea, Taiwan, the Philippines and Indonesia. In all of the societies we examined a large number of young people make use of overseas facilities for tertiary education: in some, like the PRC, Taiwan and South Korea, they are sponsored by and quite strictly controlled by their governments. Concerning both the young people studying locally and those enabled or permitted to study abroad, the countries we examined differed in terms of the extent of channeling into particular occupations on the basis of manpower needs' forecasts. As noted above, the PRC, South Korea, Taiwan and Japan exhibited the most rigorous attempts at planning, while Hong Kong and Macau exhibited the least. It may, therefore, be more than coincidental that the societies which have experienced the most serious political disturbances involving students at the tertiary education level are South Korea, Taiwan, the PRC and Japan where manpower planning has resulted in structural mismatches between the demand for and supply of labor.

The inter- and intra-country distributions of per capita expenditure on the different levels of education exhibited by Table 2 above indicate that:

- relative to other countries, Japan, Singapore and South Korea had the lowest degree of variation across the levels of education in 1980 and 1990 and that tertiary education has in per capita terms consumed a relatively lower level of expenditure;
- the expenditure on tertiary education per capita has declined in the PRC, South Korea and Malaysia from 1980 to 1990.

This clearly supports our earlier assertion that, while the expansion of education was sequential, it occurred along with a redistribution of expenditure that has resulted in relatively less being spent on each tertiary student and relatively more on each primary student. The situation appears to be especially true of the earlier phases of economic growth and development. If we extrapolate from the recent historical experiences of the most advanced of the societies included in our sample—Japan, Singapore and Hong Kong—then we might anticipate greater relative expenditure on tertiary education as a whole as well as improved per-student expenditure in the future, as the other societies develop further. However, such a prediction must, of course, be subject to the possible interference of overriding political and social factors.

## The Curriculum

With regard to the formal curriculum of schools we have seen a major difference between the societies in the relative emphasis on a general academic education and a technical/vocational education. In some societies, the latter has been a very small sector of the school system; in others, such as South Korea and Taiwan, it constitutes the main stream of secondary schooling. It was also evident that vocational/technical education continued to be plagued by its perennial problem of being seen to be a second-best alternative by pupils and parents. Consequently, the substance, as opposed to form, of such an education was sometimes very similar to that of academic institutions. In South Korea, teachers implement the curriculum in ways that reduce its vocational and technical orientation. Parents, pupils and teachers are unwilling to forsake the opportunity of competing in the arena which offers the greatest opportunities and rewards. In this sense, the system remains highly meritocratic. Further, the expansion of vocational and technical education at secondary and tertiary levels has had the effect of increasing the competition for the reduced number of places in general/academic courses.

As far as the nature of the curriculum is concerned, the pattern which emerged across the societies was more uniform. Teaching and learning were viewed instrumentally with regard to the goal of maximizing success in highly competitive selection examinations. In South Korea and Japan, the college entrance examination was described as the major determinant of what went on in schools and, often, outside schools—and this situation was in educational systems where over 40% of students proceeded to tertiary education and where graduate unemployment was a growing problem. Despite the problems and the periodic cases of oversupply, higher levels of education still provided the most readily available vehicle for upward socioeconomic mobility. Similar scenarios were evident in Hong Kong, Singapore and the PRC where examinations were described as the "conducting rod" of the educational system. However, in Macau and Malaysia, these aspects were not stressed to anything like the same extent. This is probably a reflection of the absence in Macau of any system of public assessment and in Malaysia of the fact that access to higher education is competitive up to a point but is also partly determined by consideration of ethnic origin.

The prevailing pattern is of an educational system which is meritocratic, competitive and highly instrumental. Higher levels of education are rewarded with higher lifetime earnings within a socioeconomic context where public provision for the disadvantaged (unemployed, old, physically or mentally different) is minimal as compared with the provision in the West. Access to each level of education is, within selective systems, a function of performance in public examinations. Where provision became universal, the examination performed the function of determining the stream of education (i.e., academic/general or technical/vocational) or the status of the institution (e.g., an elite metropolitan university or a regional college) a student entered. Thus, the selective function of education has prevailed even in the context of mass provision.

With regard to educational process, the patterns of teaching and learning have been shaped by and have also reinforced the competitive ethos. The knowledge and skills transmitted to pupils have focused on what was perceived to be necessary for the public examination. Pupils are encouraged to remember information and the key to success is diligence, which is premised on the belief that, with sufficient hard work, all pupils can succeed. Consequently, parents and pupils are often willing to persevere despite frequent disappointments. A thriving private school sector catering for repeaters in Hong Kong, Singapore and Japan and a large cohort of repeaters in the school system in South Korea attest to both the competitiveness of the systems and the perseverance of the consumers. As noted above, the practice of similar forms of diligence, perseverance and discipline when learning ideographic languages may provide at least some of the East Asian workforce with, if not a headstart, a predisposition toward and an amenability for the processes of modern industry.

The careers-motivated instrumentality and competitiveness within the educational system operate in parallel with a form of socio-political instrumentality. In the societies we have analyzed, again with the notable exceptions of Hong Kong and Macau, education generally and the curriculum specifically are overtly harnessed through centrally controlled curricula to the task of inculcating a strong sense of social cohesion through the promotion of national identity, consciousness and purpose. This takes a different form in the ethnically homogeneous societies, the multi-cultural societies and the colonies. In a post-revolutionary society like the PRC, a rigid system of ideopolitical education was established at all levels of schooling to ensure that the Maoist revolutionary ferment was maintained and that students were converted into ideal-type revolutionary successors. Later, in the post-Mao era, ideopolitical education was diluted into forms which focused more on the inculcation of patriotism, collectivism and civic morality. In those societies with homogeneous populations and unfinished civil wars, namely South Korea and Taiwan, where a central goal of schooling is to promote patriotism and encourage support for the goals of national advancement, the socializing role of education was most explicit and, in the early stages of statehood, took the form of a siege mentality. In contrast, in Hong Kong, this role of education was minimal as the state pursued a policy of apoliticization. The lack of an autochthonous curriculum in Macau both ensured and reflected a neglect of civic, social and political education, at least in institutions and through means sanctioned by the government. The multi-ethnic societies have had a more complex task in socializing populations that did not share a common set of religious and social values.

In Malaysia, the educational system has been harnessed to development through a manipulation of the access system to favor indigenous Malays, through the promotion of Bahasa Malaysia as the national language and through a curriculum which promotes a relatively tolerant, co-existing multi-ethnic society. Despite the inherent contradictions of these roles, the policy has served to minimize social and political protest. It has also allowed the society to benefit from the skills and business acumen of the predominantly Chinese urban population. Even in the realm of language-usage, it is interesting to note recent demands for the re-emergence of English as a medium of instruction in some subjects in universities and its re-emergence as the language of commerce in Malaysia. Now that a stable form of polity has been achieved, English will serve as the language of science, technology and commerce. To reduce the risks of serious disunity which religious fundamentalism could create among Malaysia's multi-credal populace, while Islamic values and the Koran are part of the curriculum for Muslim students, a secular curriculum based on universal values is included for non-Muslims. The goal is to achieve social consensus.

In Singapore, the educational system has similarly been harnessed to minimize ethnic conflict and promote political and social stability. But this has not involved the use of an ethnically preferential access system to higher education. Instead, it has focused on providing a competitive and meritocratic system which is streamed to provide for different ability ranges. Within this system, English has been used as the unifying national language and the curriculum has fostered a strong sense of national cohesion and identity. The increased materialism and individualism accompanying economic growth have resulted in attempts at remedy through the promotion in schools of core values and, especially for the Chinese, of Confucian values. This, however, has been problematic as it was inconsistent with the values of the minority groups (Indians and Malays) in the society. It thus mirrored the problems encountered in the promotion of Islamic values in Malaysia. This delicate relationship between social values and their promotion through schooling suggests that schools are effective for promoting the prevailing social values, but less effective for changing values or inculcating alternative sets.

In sharp contrast to the role of education as an explicit agent for political socialization and promoting a set of values which embody the national identity were the colonies of Hong Kong and Macau. Until recently, school curricula in Hong Kong were distinctly apolitical. Published curriculum statements deliberately avoided any attempt to focus on Hong Kong's political status, a Chinese cultural identity, or even the existence of the PRC. More important, the same attitudes affected curriculum implementation. In effect, curriculum content focused on classical Chinese studies of history and literature, non-controversial science and mathematics and, as an anodyne form of civic education, the description of governmental functions and services. No attempt was made to develop an explicitly Hong Kong identity and this was consistent with Hong Kong's status as a colony, allowed to thrive mainly through the acquiescence of the PRC. The situation changed rapidly in the early 1980s when it became clear that the territory would be taken over by the PRC in 1997. This led to an accelerated politicization of the curriculum to promote both an awareness of a Chinese cultural identity and an awareness of concepts consistent with democracy and a liberal political culture. In Macau, there was not only an absence of any attempt to promote through schooling a sense of national consciousness and identity; there was not even the vestige of a unified or national curriculum.

## SUMMARY

One lesson which emerged clearly from the country chapters concerns the need to distinguish between the rhetoric of political leaders and the reality of developmental processes and management. If we believed all the rhetoric, then most, if not all the countries in East Asia (and, probably, in the rest of the world) would be experiencing unproblematic development, based on the wise forethought of their leaders who had chosen to "invest in the future" and thus accumulate valuable human capital via expenditure on education. As was clearly illustrated in the cases of Hong Kong, South Korea and Macau, the expansion of educational provision was often motivated by a desire to legitimate the government during periods of political tension, rather than to invest in human capital.

Our analysis indicates a substantial degree of variation across the societies we have examined in terms of: the source of funding for educational purposes; the responsiveness of the state in providing education, especially tertiary education; the extent of state control; the extent of reliance on technical and vocational education; and in terms of the nature of the school curriculum.

Some broad patterns did emerge, however, across most of the societies which we have studied that have clear implications for policy. It is appropriate that a brief delineation of these distinctive patterns takes up the last words of our book. Paramount, in our opinion, was the role of primary schooling in providing a basic level of literacy, numeracy, and social cohesion in the period of early industrialization. In each of the societies we examined, high levels of basic education and literacy for males and females were available prior to economic take-off.

Second, as the respective economies grew, the move from low-technology, labour-intensive production to more technologically sophisticated and higher-value production was accompanied by the quantitative expansion of secondary education and qualitative improvements of both primary and secondary schooling. Subsequently, as some of the economies grew and developed further, this process was accompanied by an expansion of tertiary educational opportunities. This phenomenon suggests a general trend applicable to the East Asian societies which we examined, but not, for example, to the developing nations of Africa and Latin America. In the eight East Asian societies, educational expansion was largely sequential, with first priority being given to primary education, then later to secondary education, and most recently to tertiary education, generally in response to changes in the economy. Third, it is also evident that as the expansion process moved up the educational "ladder" toward tertiary education, the more the new opportunities were provided and funded privately. In a few of the cases, the expansion of secondary and tertiary education was related to the provision of specific job-related skills. But in most cases, the focus was on the provision, through formal schooling, of a general, academically oriented education.

Fourth, with the exception of the colonial societies where the governments had a more tenuous and temporary legitimacy, the educational systems have been explicitly associated with the goal of fostering social cohesion and political stability. While democratic political systems have clearly not been a necessary condition of development, the governments have achieved a high level of legitimacy through the single-minded pursuit of economic growth which has been reasonably equitably distributed. The schools have played a central role in maintaining the governments' legitimacy, encouraging competition and diligence and promoting a sense of national pride. By becoming the primary vehicle for upward socioeconomic mobility, schools provided a relatively open and fair access to improved socioeconomic status. This role has served to minimize the conflict which can arise when increased wealth is either not redistributed or is distributed according to manifestly unfair criteria.

The predominant role of education which thus emerges from these portrayals is not one which stresses the direct impact of investment in education on subsequent economic growth. Education has not played the part of the primary source or engine of growth. Rather it has performed a necessary but essentially supportive or facilitative range of roles in the processes of development. The precise nature of this range and these roles has varied according to the context in which it has operated, but in all of the societies, it has operated through a highly competitive and meritocratic educational system.

Finally and most important are the implications for economic rather than educational policies. In each of the societies we examined, export-orientation and a rapid decline in population growth-rates have been common. Both economic growth and development have become a matter of national priority. They have been pursued single-mindedly, albeit through different means. When growth has occurred, this has been ploughed back into improving the infrastructure, including transport facilities, housing, medical services and education. Further, the benefits of economic growth have been broadly distributed. Access to education has provided the principal means for personal socioeconomic advancement. Thus, access to the fruits of economic growth has been ostensibly open. The implications of this are that the first and foremost condition for economic development is the pursuit of effective economic policies.

We are aware that our analysis applies most sharply to the more or less "newly industrialized countries" (NICs or "little dragons") of East Asia: namely Hong Kong, Singapore, Taiwan, South Korea and Malaysia. The group of societies which we investigated, however, includes the two extremes of what might be termed post-rapid economic development and pre-rapid economic development. These happen to be politically the heavyweights of East Asia. On the one hand, Japan, having already passed through the white-hot development phase, is currently experiencing a slow growth rate. On the other hand, China, though clearly at or near a take-off point, has, so far demonstrated impressive economic *growth* but not, as yet, long-term development based on significant changes in structure.

We must conclude that neither economic growth nor economic development is a perpetual phenomenon and that no society, however cleverly its educational or its career incentives are organized, has a divine right to continuing prosperity. Nor can any society, in East Asia or elsewhere, anticipate, no matter how far-sighted its educational and manpower policies, continuing high rates of growth and persisting socially cohesive development.

Finally, it is to the pursuit of sensible economic policies and to hard work, perseverance, adaptability, a readiness to take risks and to plough the benefits of economic growth back into educational and social equities that we attribute the basic reasons for the successful development of the countries which we have studied. A measure of good fortune has contributed, too, as well as such variables as geographic location and either the existence or the dearth of natural resources. But the "East Asian Miracle" is not a story of several like-minded Jacks, each of whom serendipitously acquired some magic beans which would flourish equally well, producing the same results, if transplanted to some other soil or social system. Instead, the miracle is based on the sort of economic system and the sort of virtues which would have comforted Adam Smith and Samuel Smiles.

## Note

1. Enrollments may be over 100% of the age-group because of pupils repeating years of study plus other over-age pupils.

# Bibliography


Action Committee on Indian Education, Report of the (1991). *At the Crossroads*, Singapore.

Adams, D.K. (1977) "Development Education," *Comparative Education Review*, 21 (Nos. 2, 3), 296–310.

Afonso, R. and Pereira, F.G. (1986). "The Political Status and Government Institutions of Macao." *Hong Kong Law Journal*, 16, 1, 28–57.

Ahmad, B. and Blaug, L.M. (eds.) (1973). *The Practice of Manpower Forecasting*. San Francisco: Jossey-Bass.

Ahmed, M., with Cheng, K.M., Jalalludin, A.K. and Ramachandran, K. (1991). *Basic Education and National Development: Lessons from China and India*. New York: UNICEF.

Almond, G.A. and Verba, S. (1963). *The Civic Culture: Political Attitudes and Democracy in Five Nations*. Boston: Little, Brown & Company.

Altbach, P.G. (1988). "Academic Freedom in Asia: Learning the Limitations." *Far Eastern Economic Review*, June 16, 1988, 24–25.

Alves Pinto, M.C. (1987). *Ensino em Macau: Umas Abordagem Sistémica da Realidade Educativa*. Macau: Gabinete do Secretário-Adjunto Para a Educação e Cultura.

Amsden, A.H. (1988). "Taiwan's Economic History: A Case of Etatisme and a Challenge to Dependency Theory." In: Bates, R.H. (ed.) *Toward a Political Economy of Development*, 142–175. Berkeley: University of California Press.

Anderson, C.A. and Bowman, M.J. (1963). "Concerning the Role of Education in Development." In: Geertz, C. (ed.) *Old Societies and New States: The Quest of Modernity in Asia and Africa*. London: Collier Macmillan.

Anderson, R.S. (1975). *Education in Japan: A Century of Modern Development*. Washington, D.C.: US Department of Health, Education and Welfare, National Institute of Education.

Applebaum, R.P. and Henderson, J. (eds.) (1992). *States and Development in the Asia Pacific Rim*. Thousand Oaks, Ca.: Sage.

Aran, L., Eisenstadt, S. and Adler, C. (1972). "The Effectiveness of Educational Systems in the Process of Modernization." *Comparative Education Review*, 16, 1, 30–43.

Archer, M.S. (1979). *The Social Origins of Education Systems*. London: Sage.

*Asia Week* (1992). "Ready for Blast-off." July 10.

Aso, M. and Amano, I. (1983). *Education and Japan's Modernization*. Tokyo: The Japan Times Ltd.

Association of Muslim Professionals (1990). *Forging a Vision*. Singapore: AMP.

Aziz, U.A., Chew, S.B., Lee, K.H. and Sanyal, B.C. (eds.) (1987). *University Education and Employment in Malaysia*. Paris: International Institute for Educational Planning, IIEP Research Report No. 66.

Bates, R.H. (ed.) (1988). *Toward a Political Economy of Development.* Berkeley: University of California Press.

Bauer, J., Wang, F., Riley, N. and Zhao, X. (1992). "Gender Inequality in Urban China." *Modern China,* 18(3), 333–370.

Becker, G.S. (1964). *Human Capital: A Theoretical and Empirical Analysis, with Special Reference to Education.* New York: Columbia University Press.

Beijing Normal University Theory Group on Economics of Education (1984). *Economics of Education.* Beijing: Normal University Press (in Chinese).

Benedict, Ruth (1961). *Patterns of Culture.* London: Routledge & Kegan Paul.

Berg, I. (1971). *Education and Jobs: The Great Training Robbery.* Boston: Beacon Press.

Berger, Peter L. (1990). "An East Asian Development Model?" In: Berger, Peter L. and Hsiao, H.H. Michael (eds.) *In Search of an East Asian Development Model.* New Brunswick: Transaction Books, pp. 3–11.

Berger, Peter L. and Hsiao, H.M. (eds.) (1988). *In Search of an East Asian Development Model.* New Brunswick: Transaction Books.

Blaug, M. (1976). "The Empirical Status of Human Capital Theory: A Slightly Jaundiced View." *Journal of Economic Literature,* 14.

Bock, J.C. (1978). "Countervailing Outcomes of Malaysian Education: National Identity and Political Alienation." *Education and Urban Society,* 10, 2.

——— (1982). "Education and Development: A Conflict of Meaning." In: Altbach, P. (ed.) *Comparative Education.* New York: Macmillan.

Boltho, Andrea. (1975). *Japan: An Economic Survey.* London: Oxford University Press.

Bond, M.H. (1991). *Beyond the Chinese Face: Insights from Psychology.* Hong Kong: Oxford University Press.

Bowles, S. and Gintis, H. (1976). *Schooling in Capitalist America: Educational Reform and the Contradictions of Economic Life.* New York: Basic Books.

Bowman, M. and Anderson, Arnold C. (1973a). *Human Capital and Economic Modernization in Historical Perspective.* Paris: Mouton Press.

——— (1973b). "Human Capital and Economic Modernization in Historical Perspective." In: F.C. Lane (ed.) *Fourth International Conference of Economic History.* Paris: Mouton Press.

Bray, Mark (1991). "Strategies for Financing Higher Education: Perspectives from Hong Kong and Macau." *Higher Education,* 21, 11–25.

Bray, Mark and Hui, Philip (1989). "The Implications of Size for Educational Development in Small Territories: The Case of Macau." *International Review of Education,* 35, 129–43.

——— (1991). "Curriculum Development in Macau." In: Marsh, Colin and Morris, Paul (eds.) *Curriculum Development in East Asia.* London: Falmer Press.

Bray, Mark and Tang, K.C. (1993). "Three Plus Two Equals Six? Imported Curricula and the Search for a Macau Education System." Paper presented at the International Symposium on Curriculum Changes for Chinese Communities in Southeast Asia, The Chinese University of Hong Kong.

Bronfenbrenner, U. (1974). *Two Worlds of Childhood.* Harmondsworth: Penguin.

Burks, Ardath W. (1981). *Japan: Profile of Postindustrial Power.* Boulder, Colo.: Westview Press.

Cantor, Leonard (1985). "Vocational Education and Training: The Japanese Approach." *Comparative Education,* 21, 1, 67–76.

CCP (Chinese Communist Party) (1981). "Resolution on Several Historical Issues since Establishment of the People's Republic." In: *Chinese Education Yearbook 1949–1981* (in Chinese).

——— (1985). "Decision of the Central Committee of the Communist Party of China on the Reform of the Educational Structure, May 27." Beijing: Foreign Languages Press.

Central Council for Education, Japan (1971). *Basic Guidelines for the Reform of Education.* Tokyo: Ministry of Education.

Chan Chieu Kiat et al. (1960). *Report of the Commission of Inquiry into Vocational and Technical Education in Singapore.* Singapore: Government Printer.

Chan Heng Chee (1976). "The Political System and Political Change." In: Hassan, R. (ed.) *Singapore: Society in Transition.* Singapore: Oxford University Press.

——— (1989). "The PAP and the Structuring of the Political System." In: Sandhu, K.S. and Wheatley, P. (eds.) *Management of Success: The Moulding of Modern Singapore.* Singapore: Institute of South-East Asian Studies.

Chan, K.C.L. (1990). *China, Britain and Hong Kong, 1895–1945.* Hong Kong: The Chinese University Press.

Chan, S.K. and Tan, W.G. (1991). "Urban Development and Pollution in Macau." In: Yuan, D.Y., Wong H. K. and Martins, L. (eds.) *Population and City Growth in Macau.* Macau: Centre of Macau Studies, University of East Asia.

Chen, A.H.Y. (1989). "Law in a Foreign Language: the Case of Hong Kong." In: Cheek-Milbey, K. and Mushkat, M. (eds.) *Hong Kong: the Challenge of Transformation.* Hong Kong: Centre of Asian Studies, 212–238.

Chen, E.K.Y. (1979). *Hyper Growth in Asian Economies.* London: Macmillan.

Chen Hsien, T. (1974). *The Maoist Educational Revolution.* New York: Praeger.

Chen Lianghun et al. (1986). "An International Comparison of the Ratio of Educational Investment in GDP." *Journal of Higher Education,* 1, 28–34 (in Chinese).

Cheng, K.M. (1989). "Financing Education in Mainland China: What Are the Real Problems?" Paper presented at the Conference on Education in Mainland China, Taipei, July.

——— (1991). "Educational Policy Making in Hong Kong: The Changing Legitimacy." In: Postiglione, G.A. and Leung. Y.M. (eds.) *Education and Society in Hong Kong: Toward One Country and Two Systems.* New York: M.E. Sharpe, 97–116.

Cheong, C.M. (1993). "A Educação na Lei Básica da RAEM: Análise e Comentário." *Administração,* 19/20, 177–84.

Chew, Oon Ai, Joy (1988). "Moral Education in a Singapore Secondary School." Unpublished Ph.D. dissertation, Monash University.

Chia Siow Yue (1989). "The Character and Progress of Industrialization." In: Sandhu, K.S. and Wheatley, P. (eds.) *Management of Success: The Moulding of Modern Singapore.* Singapore: Institute of South-East Asian Studies.

Chien Liu and Armer, J. Michael (1993). "Education's Effect on Economic Growth in Taiwan," *Comparative Education Review,* 37, 3.

Chiew, S.K. (1985). "The Socio-Cultural Framework of Politics." In: Quak Jon, S.T., Chan, H.C. and Seak, C.M. (eds.) *Government and Politics of Singapore.* Singapore: Oxford University Press.

——— (1990). "National Identity, Ethnicity and National Issues." In: Quak Jon, S.T. (ed.) *Search of Singapore's National Values.* Singapore: Times Academic Press.

Chin Yang and Zhou Hua (1984). "Reform Educational Thought to Welcome Technological Revolution." *Educational Research (Jiaoyu Yanjiu),* 6 (in Chinese).

*China Daily.* November 15, 1986.

*China Reconstructs* (1973). "Documents of The Tenth National Congress of the Communist Party of China." November.

Chinese Academy of Science (1991). "Survival and Development: A Study of China's Long Term Development." Kehua Publishing Company (in Chinese).

Chinese Academy of Social Sciences (1993). "Report on the Social Development of China." Quoted in *Wen Wei Pao,* Hong Kong, December 15, 1993 (in Chinese).

*Chinese Education Yearbook* (1949–1981). Beijing: Encyclopaedic Press (in Chinese).

*Chinese Education Yearbook* (1985–86). Beijing: People's Education Press (in Chinese).

*Chinese Population Statistics* (1992). Beijing: Zhongguo Tongji Chubanshe (in Chinese).

*Chinese Population Yearbook* (1990). Beijing: Zhongguo Tongji Chubanshe (in Chinese).

*Chinese Statistical Summary* (1986). Beijing: Zhongguo Tongji Chubanshe (in Chinese).

*Chinese Statistical Yearbook* (1990). Beijing: Zhongguo Tongji Chubanshe (in Chinese).

*Chinese Statistical Yearbook* (1991),. Beijing: Zhongguo Tongji Chubanshe (in Chinese).

Chiu, H.Y. (1989). "Education and Social Change in Taiwan." In: Hsiao, H.M., Cheng, W.Y. and Chan, H.S. (eds.) *Taiwan: A Newly Industrialized State*. Taipei: National Taiwan University, 187–205.

——— (1992). *The International Legal Status of the Republic of China* (revised edition). Occasional Papers/Reprints Series in Contemporary Asian Studies, No. 5–1992 (112), School of Law, University of Maryland.

Chng Meng Kng (1985). *Efficient Mechanisms for the Enhancement of Technology and Skills in Singapore*. Singapore: Institute of Southeast Asian Studies.

Choi, P.K. (1990). "A Search for Cultural Identity: The Students' Movement of the Early Seventies." In: Sweeting, A. (ed.) *Differences and Identities: Educational Argument in Late Twentieth Century Hong Kong*. Hong Kong: Faculty of Education Paper 9, 81–107.

Choi, U. and Baik, E. (1990). *A Study of the Current Status of Literacy in Korea*. Seoul: Korean Educational Development Institute (KEDI).

Clark, C. (1989). *Taiwan's Development: Implications for Contending Political Economy Paradigms*. Westport: Greenwood Press.

Colclough, C. (1982). "The Impact of Primary Schooling on Economic Development: A Review of the Evidence." *World Development*, 10, 3, 167–186.

Coleman, J. S. (ed.) (1965). *Education and Political Development*. Princeton: Princeton University Press.

Collins, R. (1979). *The Credential Society*. New York: Academic Press.

Commonwealth Secretariat (1988). *Survey of Vocational Oriented Education in the Commonwealth*. London: Commonwealth Secretariat.

Council for Economic Planning and Development (CEPD) (1986). *The Middle and Long Term Plan for Human Resource Development in Economic Construction in Taiwan, the ROC, 1986–2000* (in Chinese). Taipei: CEPD.

——— (1992). *Taiwan Statistical Data Book*. Taipei: CEPD.

——— (1993). *Industry of Free China 80*. Taipei: CEPD.

Cowen, Robert and McLean, Martin (eds.) (1984). *International Handbook of Education Systems*. Chichester: John Wiley & Sons.

Cramer, J.F. (1959). "The Chinese Colleges in Hong Kong." *Comparative Education Review*, 3, 1, 26–29.

Cremer, R.D. (1989). "The Industrialization of Macau." In: Jao, Y.C., Mok, V. and Ho, L.S. (eds.) *Economic Development in Chinese Societies: Models and Experiences*. Hong Kong: Hong Kong University Press.

——— (ed.) (1987). *Macau: City of Commerce and Culture*. Hong Kong: UEA Press.

——— (ed.) (1991). *Macau: City of Commerce and Culture*, second edition. Hong Kong: API Press.

Cummings, William K. (1980). *Education and Equality in Japan*. Princeton, New Jersey: Princeton University Press.

——— (1982). "The Egalitarian Transformation of Postwar Japanese Education." *Comparative Education Review*, 26, 1, 16–35.

Curriculum Development Centre (1982). *Sukatan Pelajaran Pendidikan Moral* (Moral Education Syllabus). Kuala Lumpur: Government Printers.

Davies, S. and Roberts, E. (1990). *Political Dictionary for Hong Kong*. Hong Kong: Macmillan.

De Almeida e Costa, Vasco (1984). "New Year Message." Foreword to Government of Macau. *Sectorial Policies Investment Plan (Public Sector)*. Macau: Government Printing Press.

Denison, E.F. (1962). "Education, Economic Growth and Gaps in Information." *Journal of Political Economy*, 70.

——— (1967). *Why Growth Rates Differ? Post-War Experience in Nine Western Countries*. Washington: Brookings Institution.

Department of Statistics, Singapore (Various years). *Yearbook of Statistics*. Singapore: Department of Statistics.

Deyo, F. (ed.) (1987). *The Political Economy of the New Asian Industrialism*. Ithaca: Cornell University Press.

Directorate-General of Budget, Accounting and Statistics (DGBAS), (1987). *Yearbook of Labor Statistics*. DGBAS, Taipei.

——— (1992). *Yearbook of National Income*. DGBAS, Taipei.

——— (1993). *Annual Statistic Report of Human Resource Survey*. DGBAS, Taipei.

Doi, T. (1973). *The Anatomy of Dependence*. Tokyo: Kodansha America Inc.

Domes, J. (1993). "Taiwan in 1992: On the Verge of Democracy." *Asian Survey* 33, 54–60.

Dore, R.P. (1976). *The Diploma Disease*. London: Allen and Unwin.

——— (1987). *Taking Japan Seriously: A Confucian Perspective on Leading Economic Issues*. Stanford: Stanford University Press.

——— (1988). "Confucianism, Economic Growth, and Social Development." In: Berger, P.L. and Hsiao, H.H.M. (eds.) *In Search of an East Asian Development Model*. New Brunswick, N.J.: Transaction Books.

Duke, Benjamin (1975). "Statistical Trends in Postwar Education." *Comparative Education Review*, 6, 3, 213–218.

——— (1986). *The Japanese Schools: Lessons for Industrial America*. Hampshire: Macmillan.

Durkheim, E. (1977). *The Evolution of Educational Thought*. London: Routledge and Kegan Paul (first published in 1922).

Ebbeck, M. (1993). *Training Needs Analysis of Early Childhood Workforce in Hong Kong*. Hong Kong: Hong Kong Council for Early Childhood Education and Services.

Economic and Foreign Affairs Research Association (1982). *Statistical Survey of Japan's Economy, 1982*. (1982) Tokyo: Economic and Foreign Affairs Research Association.

Economic Planning Agency (1967). *Economic and Social Development Plan 1967–1971*. Tokyo: Ministry of Education.

——— (1970). *New Economic and Social Development Plan 1970–1975*. Tokyo: Ministry of Education.

*Economist, The* (1990). *The Economist Book of Vital World Statistics*. London: Hutchinson.

——— (1991a). "Building on Success." May 4.

——— (1991b). "Survey of East Asia." November 16.

——— (1993). "Where to Live: Nirvana by Numbers." December 25, pp. 73–76.

Edmonds, R.L. (1989). "Introduction." In: Edmonds, R.L. (ed.) *Macau*. World Bibliographical Series, vol. 105. Oxford: Clio Press.

Education Department (1979). *Director of Education, 1977–78 Annual Summary*. Hong Kong: Government Printer.

Eisenstadt, S.N. (1973). *Tradition, Change, and Modernity*. New York: Wiley.

Eng Soo Peck (1992). "The Environment for Values Learning." *Singapore Journal of Education* 12, 1.

*Facts and Figures of Japan* (1985). Tokyo: Foreign Press Center.

Fågerlind, I. and Saha, L.J. (1983). *Education and National Development*. Oxford: Pergamon Press.

——— (1989). *Education and National Development: A Comparative Perspective*. Oxford: Pergamon Press.

*Far Eastern Economic Review, The* (1991). June 27.

Feinberg, W. (1975). "Educational Equality Under Two Conflicting Models of Educational Development." *Theory and Society*, 2, 2, 183–210.

Feitor, R. and Cremer, R.D. (1991). "Macau's Modern Economy." In: Cremer, R.D. (ed.) *Macau: City of Commerce and Culture* (second edition). Hong Kong: API Press.

Foreign Language Press (1984). *China Handbook Series: Economy*. Beijing: Foreign Language Press.

Foreign Language Press (1986). *The Fourth Session of the Sixth National People's Congress*. Beijing: April 1986, 11.

Foreign Press Centre (1985). *Facts and Figures of Japan*. Tokyo: Foreign Press Centre.

Foster, P. (1975). "Dilemmas of Education Development: What We Might Learn from the Past?" *Comparative Education Review*, 19, 375–392.

——— (1982). "Economic Development and Education." In: *The International Encyclopaedia of Education*. London: Pergamon.

——— (1992). "Comparative Education." In: *The Encyclopaedia of Educational Research*. Washington: AERA, sixth edition.

Fraser, S.E. and Hawkins, J.N. (1973). "Educational Reform & Revolution in the People's Republic of China." *Phi Delta Kappan*.

Fukutake, Tadashi. (1981). *Japanese Society Today*, second edition. Tokyo: University of Tokyo Press.

Fuller, N. (1988). "Capital and Economic Growth: France 1925–1975." *American Sociological Review*, 53, December.

Galenson, W. (ed.) (1979). *Economic Growth and Structural Change in Taiwan: The Postwar Experience of the Republic of China*. Ithaca: Cornell University Press.

Gittings, J. (1989). *China Changes Face: Socialism and Reform 1949–1989*. Hong Kong and Oxford: Oxford University Press.

Goh Keng Swee (1992). "Ascent of the Dragons." *Asian Business*, July.

Gopinathan, S. (1974). *Towards a National System of Education in Singapore 1945–1973*. Singapore: Oxford University Press.

——— (1985). "Education." In: Quah, J.S.T., Chan Heng Chee and Seah Chee Meow (eds.) *Government and Politics of Singapore*. Singapore: Oxford University Press.

——— (1986). "Bilingualism and Bilingual Education in Singapore." In: Paulston, C.B. (ed.) *International Handbook of Bilingualism and Bilingual Education*. Westport, Conn.: Greenwood Press.

——— (1988). "'Being and Becoming': Education for Values in Singapore." In: Cummings, W., Gopinathan, S. and Tomoda, Y. (eds.) *The Revival of Values Education in Asia and the West*. Oxford: Pergamon Press.

——— (1992). "Education." In: *Singapore in The Year in Review, 1991*. Singapore: Times Academic Press.

——— (1994). "Language Policy Changes, 1979–1992: Politics and Pedagogy." In: Gopinathan, S., Pakir, A., Kam, Ho Wah and Saravanan, V. (eds.) *Language, Society and Education in Singapore: Issues and Trends*. Singapore: Times Academic Press (in press).

Government of Hong Kong (1978). White Paper on *The Development of Senior Secondary and Tertiary Education*. Hong Kong: Government Printer.

——— (1979). *Report of Committee on Diversification*. Hong Kong: Government Printer.

——— (1990). *A Statistical Projection of Manpower Requirements and Supply for Hong Kong*. Hong Kong: Education and Manpower Branch, Government Secretariat.

——— (1993a). Green Paper on *Equal Opportunities for Women and Men*. Hong Kong: Government Printer.

——— (1993b). *Hong Kong Census and Statistics Department: Estimates of Gross Domestic Product, 1966–92*. Hong Kong: Government Printer.

Green, A. (1990). *Education and State Formation: The Rise of Education Systems in England, France and the USA*. London: Macmillan.

Gregory, Gene (1985). "Science City: The Future Starts There." *Far Eastern Economic Review*, March, 28, 43–50.

Gu Jianjun (1992). "Rural Technical Education and Rural Technological Improvement." Paper presented in the Conference on Education, Social Change and Regional Development. University of Hong Kong, June 1992 (in Chinese).

Guthrie, G. (1986). "Current Research in Developing Countries: The Impact of Curriculum Reform on Teaching." *Teaching & Teacher Education*, 2, 1.

Haddad, W., Carnoy, M., Rinaldi, R. and Ormporn, R. (1990). *Education and Development: Evidence for New Priorities*. World Bank Discussion Paper, No. 95. Washington: The World Bank.

Hage, J., Garnier A.M. and Fuller, N. (1988). "The Active State, Investment in Human Capital and Economic Growth: France, 1925–1975." *American Sociological Review*, 53, December.

Hallak, J. (1990). *Investing in the Future*. Oxford: Pergamon Press.

Hamilton, C.J. (1957). "The Problem of People." In: *Hong Kong Annual Report, 1956*. Hong Kong: Government Printer, 1–31.

Hamilton, V.C., Blumerfeld, P.C., Hiroshi Akoh and Kanal Muira (1989). "Citizenship and Scholarship in Japanese and American Fifth Grades." *American Educational Research Journal*, 26, 1, 44–72.

Han Zongli (1987). "The Development of the Economics in Education in China." In: Hayhoe, R. (ed.) *Chinese Education*, 16, 1, 23–33 (in Chinese).

Hao Keming et al. (1991). "The Socioeconomic Environment for Making Compulsory Education Compulsory in China." *Chinese Social Sciences (Zhongkuo Shehui Kexue)*, 4, 145–158 (in Chinese).

Harbison, F. (1967). *Educational Planning and Human Resource Development*. International Institute for Educational Planning, UNESCO.

Harbison, F. and Myers, C.A. (1964). *Education, Manpower, and Economic Growth*. New York: McGraw-Hill.

Harding, H. (1984). "The Study of Chinese Politics: Towards a Third Generation of Scholarship," *World Politics*. 36, 2.

Harwood, A.M. (1992). "Classroom Climate and Civic Education in Secondary Social Studies Research: Antecedents and Findings." *Theory and Research in Social Education*, 20, 1.

Hayashi, Risuke (1984). "An Observation and Response to Malaysian Look East Policy." Paper presented at the Malaysian-Japan Colloquium. Malaysia: Institute of Strategic and International Studies.

Hirschman, C. (1979). "Political Independence and Educational Opportunity in Peninsular Malaysia." *Sociology of Education* 52, 67–83.

Ho, D.Y.F. (1986). "Chinese Patterns of Socialization." In: Bond, M.H. (ed.) *The Psychology of the Chinese People*. Hong Kong: Oxford University Press, 1–37.

Ho, H.C.Y. (1993). "The State of the Economy." In: Choi, P.K. and Ho, L.S. (eds.) *The Other Hong Kong Report, 1993*. Hong Kong: The Chinese University Press, 75–93.

Ho, S.P.S. (1978). *Economic Development of Taiwan, 1860–1970*. New Haven: Yale University Press.

Hoerr, O.D. (1973). "Education, Income and Equity in Malaysia." *Economic Development and Cultural Changes*, 21.

Hofheinz, R. and Calder, K.E. (1982). *The Eastasia Edge*. New York: Basic Books.

Holbrook, J. (1990). *Science Education in Hong Kong: Achievements and Determinants*. Hong Kong: Faculty of Education.

Holloway, S.D. (1988). "Concepts of Ability and Effort in Japan and the United States." *Review of Educational Research*, 58, 3.

Holsinger, D.B. (1974). "The Elementary School as Modernizer: A Brazilian Study."

*International Journal of Comparative Sociology*, 24, 24–26.

Hongqi (1977). "A Major Polemic on the Educational Front: Criticising the Two Evaluations Concerted by the Gang of Four." *Hongqi (Red Flag)*, 12, 3–13 (in Chinese).

Hou Yan (1988). "The Current Status, Problems and Solutions of Secondary Vocational and Technical Education." In: Li Shouxin (ed.) *Problems of Education Development in China*. Beijing: China Planning Press (in Chinese).

Howell, C. (1978). *China's Road to Development: A Basic Guide*. London: Paul Elek.

Hsueh, T.T. and Woo, T.O. (1991). *The Economics of Industrial Development in the People's Republic of China*. Hong Kong: Institute of Asia Pacific Studies, Chinese University of Hong Kong.

Hu Ruiren (1993). *Chinese Education: Development and Perspectives*. Shanghai: Shanghai Institute of Human Resource Development.

Hu Ruiren, Mao Hungchang and Jiang Minghe (1988). "Issues Concerning the Reform and Development of Education in China." In: *Special Issue on the Comparative Study of International Educational Development and Strategy*. Shanghai: Shanghai Institute of Human Resource Development (in Chinese).

Hu Yaobang (1980). "Opening Speech at the Second National Conference on Science and Technology." In: *Chinese Education 1949–1981*. Beijing: Ministry of Education (in Chinese).

Huang, B.H. (1990). "Prospect for the Higher Education Development in the 21st Century" (in Chinese). In: *Development and Trend of Higher Education in Taiwan in the 21st Century* (edited by the Education Research Center of the Tamkang University and the 21st Century Foundation), 513–580. Taipei: Shi-Da Publisher.

Hui, Baldwin Y.B. and Noronha, Carlos (1991). *Macau Tax and Economy*. Macau: Direccão dos Servicos de Financas/Macau Management Association.

Hung, C.T. (ed.) (1989). *Confucianism and Economic Development: An Oriental Alternative*. Washington, D.C.: Washington Institute Press.

Huntington, S.P. (1991). *The Third Wave: Democratization in the Late Twentieth Century*. Norman: University of Oklahoma.

Hussain Haji Ahmad (1979). "Achievement, Social Environment and Background Characteristics in Lower Secondary Schools in Peninsular Malaysia." Unpublished Ph.D. dissertation, Stanford University.

Ichigawa, S. (1979). "Finance of Higher Education." In: Cummings, W.K., Amano, I. and Kitamura, K. (eds.) *Changes in the Japanese University: A Comparative Perspective*. New York: Praeger.

Ihm, C.S. et al. (1992). *An Analysis of the Efficiency of High School Vocational Technical Education in Korea*. Seoul: Korean Educational Development Institute (KEDI).

——— (1993). *A Study of the Training and Utilization of Technical Manpower in Korea*. Seoul: Korean Educational Development Institute (KEDI).

IMF. (1991). *World Development Report*. Washington, D.C.: International Monetary Fund.

*Industrial Robot, The* (1984). "Steady Growth for Robots in 1984." No. 12, March 1.

Inkeles, A. and Smith, D. (1974). *Becoming Modern*. London: Heinemann.

James, Estelle and Benjamin, Gail (1987). "Educational Distribution and Income Redistribution through Education in Japan." *Journal of Human Resources*, 22, 4, 469–89.

Jamison, D. and Lau, L. (1982). *Farmer Education and Farm Efficiency*. Baltimore: Johns Hopkins University Press.

Japanese National Commission for UNESCO (1966). *The Role of Education in the Social and Economic Development of Japan*. Tokyo: Ministry of Education.

Jee Peng Tan and Mingat, Alain. (1992). *Education in Asia: A Comparative Study of Cost and Financing*. World Bank Regional and Sectoral Studies. Washington:

The World Bank.

Jiang Shanye (1988). "A Basic Problem in the Overall Structure of the Secondary School Curriculum." Paper presented at the symposium on curriculum development and continuing teacher education. University of Hong Kong. December (in Chinese).

Jing Kening (1987). "The Present State of Education in China is Very Serious." *Journal of Shenxi Teacher's College*, 1, 16–18 (in Chinese).

Johnson, C. (1987). "Political Institutions and Economic Performance: The Government-Business Relationship in Japan, South Korea, and Taiwan." In: Deyo, F. (ed.) *The Political Economy of the New Asian Industrialism*. Ithaca: Cornell University Press, 136–164.

Johnson, C. (1982). *MITI and the Japanese Miracle*. Stanford, Calif.: Stanford University Press.

Jones, P.W. (1992). *World Bank Financing of Education*. London: Routledge.

Jowett, J. (1990). "People: Demographic Patterns and Policies." In: Cannon, T. and Jenkins, A. (eds.) *The Geography of Contemporary China*. London: Routledge.

Kamens, D.H. (1988). "Education and Democracy: A Comparative Institutional Analysis." *Sociology of Education* 61, 114–127.

KEDI (Korean Educational Development Institute) (1993). *Educational Indicators in Korea*. Seoul: KEDI.

Keswick, J. et al. (1952). *Report on Higher Education*. Hong Kong: Government Printer.

Kim, J.B. et al. (1979). "The Role of Education in Socio-Political Development." *Research Report #92*. Seoul: Korean Educational Development Institute (KEDI), December.

Kim, K.S. and Park, J.K. (1985). *Sources of Economic Growth in Korea, 1963–1982*. Seoul: Korean Development Institute (KDI).

Kim, S. (1987). *In-Service Training in Korea*. Kyung Hee University: GIPS.

Kim, Y.C. et al. (1981). "Toward Normalization of School Education by Eliminating Private Tutoring." *Research Report #132*. Seoul: Korean Educational Development Institute (KEDI).

Kim, Y.H. (1990). "The Evolution of the College Enrollment Quota Policy." Paper presented at the Conference on the State and Development in the East Asian Pacific Rim. University of California, Santa Barbara, March.

Kitamura, K. (1979). "Mass Higher Education." In: Cummings, W.K., Amano, I. and Kitamura, K. (eds.) *Changes in Japanese University: A Comparative Perspective*. New York: Praeger.

Kobayashi, Tetsuya (1986). *Society, Schools, and Progress in Japan*. Oxford: Pergamon Press.

Kohlberg, Lawrence (1976). "Moral Stages and Moralization: The Cognitive-Developmental Approach." In: Lickona, T. (ed.) *Moral Development and Behaviour: Theory, Research and Social Issues*. New York: Holt, Rinehart & Winston.

Kojima, Kiyoshi (1977). *Japan and a New World Economic Order*. London: Croom Helm.

——— (1983). "Japanese Direct Foreign Investment in Asian Developing Countries." In: Fodella, Gianni (ed.) *Japan's Economy in a Comparative Perspective*. Kent: Paul Norbury Publications.

Kostecki, M. (1985). "The Economic Functions of Schooling." *Compare*, 15, 1, 5–18.

Krause, L.B., Koh Ai Tee and Lee (Tsao) Yuan (1987). *The Singapore Economy Reconsidered*. Singapore: Institute of Southeast Asian Studies.

Kua Kia Soong. "Malaysian Ethnic Relations: Divisive Factors in Education." Undated mimeograph.

Kumon, Shumpei (1986). "Designs for a New Industrial Society," *Japan Echo*, 13, 2–4.

Kuo, Eddie C.Y. (1980). "The Sociolinguistic Situation in Singapore: Unity in Diversity." In: Afendras, E.A. and Kuo, Eddie C.Y. (eds.) *Language and Society in Singapore*. Singapore: Singapore University Press.

Kuo, S.W.Y., Ranis, G. and Fei, J. (1981). *The Taiwan Success Story: Rapid Growth with Improved Distribution in the Republic of China, 1952–1979*. Boulder, Colo.: Westview Press.

Kwak, B.S. (1990). *The Impact of Industrialization on Cultural and Educational Development in Korea—Recommendations for Education Policy*. June.

——— (1992). "Korea." In: Wielemans, W. and Choi, P.C. (eds.) *Education and Culture in Industrializing Asia*. Leuven: Leuven University Press.

Kwong, P.C.K. (1993). "Internationalization of Population and Globalization of Families." In: Choi, P.K. and Ho, L.S. (eds.) *The Other Hong Kong Report, 1993*. Hong Kong: Chinese University Press, 147–174.

Kwong, J. (1979). *Chinese Education in Transition*. McGill: Queen's University Press.

Kwong, J. and Rong Xiao (1989). "Educational Equality Among China's Minorities." *Comparative Education*, 25, 2, 229–243.

Lam, T.C. (1991). "Administration and Public Service System in Macau." In: Cremer, R.D. (ed.) *Macau: City of Commerce and Culture* (second edition). Hong Kong: API Press.

Lammers, David (1984). "Science in the Classroom," *Far Eastern Economic Review*, June 14, 67–68.

Landes, J. (1989). "Marxism and the Woman Question." In: Kruks, S., Rapp, R. and Young, M. (eds.) *Promissory Notes: Women in the Transition to Socialism*. New York: Monthly Review Press.

Langness, L.L. (1987). *The Study of Culture*. Novato, Calif.: Chandler & Sharp Publishers.

Lau, L.J. (ed.) (1990). *Models of Development: A Comparative Study of Economic Growth in South Korea and Taiwan*. San Francisco: ICS Press.

Lau, S.K. (1982). *Society and Politics in Hong Kong*. Hong Kong: Chinese University Press.

Lauglo, J. and Lillis, K. (eds.) (1988). *Vocationalising Education: An International Perspective*. Oxford: Pergamon Press.

Lee, C.S. and Yang, Y. (1987). "Higher Education and Equal Opportunity" (in Chinese). Unpublished manuscript.

Lee Kiong Hock (1980). "Education, Earnings and Occupational Status in Malaysia, 1978." Unpublished Ph.D. thesis, London School of Economics and Political Science, University of London.

Lee, K.J. et al. (1983). "An Estimate of Export Effects on the Economy," *Monthly Bulletin*. Seoul: Bank of Korea, August.

Lee Kuan Yew (1959). Speech reported in *The Straits Times*, Dec 9, 1959.

——— (1972). "Traditional Values and National Identity." *The Mirror*, Nov. 20, 1972, 8, 47.

——— (1993). Speech reported in *The Straits Times*, August 13, 1993.

Lee Mei Fah, Frances (1987). "National Identity Characterised by the Effects of Chinese Schooling and Second Language Attainment: A Case Study." Unpublished thesis, University of London.

Lee Tsao Yuan (ed.) (1992). *Singapore: The Year in Review 1991*. Singapore: Times Academic Press.

Legislative Assembly (1956). *All Party Report on Chinese Education*. Singapore: Government Printer.

Leong Yin Ching (1981). "The Objectives and Process of Schooling: Perceptions of Secondary School Leavers, Teachers, Principals and Parents of Kuala Langat District, Selangor in Malaysia." Unpublished Ph.D. thesis, University of London.

Leong, C.C. (1978). *Youth in the Army*. Singapore: Federal Publications.

Leung, Y.M. (1991). "Curriculum Development in the People's Republic of China." In: Marsh, C. and Morris, P. (eds.) *Curriculum Development in East Asia*. Lon-

don: Falmer Press.
——— (1992a). "China's Search for a Relevant Curriculum for Basic Education: Provincial Attempts versus Central Control." In: *Proceedings of Chinese Education for the 21st Century Conference*, University of Virginia, School of Education, 48–51.
——— (1992b). "Education in Dapu County." Unpublished report submitted to the Tin Ka Ping Foundation, Hong Kong (in Chinese).
LeVine, R.A. and White, M. (1986). *Human Conditions: The Cultural Basis for Educational Development*. New York: Routledge & Kegan Paul.
Lewin, K. (1981). "Curriculum Research and Examination Reform: A Case Study from Malaysia." Bulletin 11, 2, Institute of Development Studies, University of Sussex.
Li Habwing (1991). "The Problem of Female Education in Economically Undeveloped Regions." *People's Education (Renmin Jiaoyu)*, 6, 23–25 (in Chinese).
Li Shaoyuan (1989). *Economics of Education*. Heilongjiang Education Press (in Chinese).
Li Shouxin (1988a). "Eleven Major Issues in Chinese Education." In: Li Shouxin et al. (eds.) *Problems of Education Development in China*. Beijing: China Planning Press, 7–51 (in Chinese).
——— (1988b). "The Cultural Quality of Peasants and Economic Benefits in Agriculture." In: Li Shouxin et al. (eds.) *Problems of Education Development in China*. Beijing: China Planning Press, 229–238 (in Chinese).
Li Teying (1989). "Promote Education with a Thriving Spirit." Speech at the work conference of the State Education Commission, February 2, 1989. In: State Education Commission Policy Office (1992) *Important Education Documents since the Third Plenary Session of the Eleventh Party Congress*. Beijing: Education Science Press (in Chinese).
Li Yining (1981). "On the Economic Effects of Intellectual Investment." *Chinese Social Sciences (Zhongguo Shehui Kexue)*, 4, 417–461 (in Chinese).
Li Yuanhun (1990). "Review of China's Economic Development Strategies." In: National Center for Education Development Research (ed.) *The Current Situation and Prospects on Educational Development in China in the Context of Economic and Social Development*. China Excellence Publishing Corporation (in Chinese).
Li Yunkun (1983). "My Humble Opinion on the Issue of Educational Investment." *Financial Study (Caizheng Yanjiu)*, 6, 37–41 (in Chinese).
Li, K.T. (1988). *The Evolution of Policy behind Taiwan's Development Success*. New Haven: Yale University Press.
Lim Chong Yah (1983). "Singapore's Economic Development: Retrospect and Prospect." In: Chan, Peter (ed.) *Singapore Development Policies and Trends*. Singapore: Oxford University Press.
——— (1989). "From High Growth Rates to Recession." In: Sandhu, K.S. and Wheatley, P. (eds.) *Management of Success: The Moulding of Modern Singapore*. Singapore: Institute of South-East Asian Studies.
Lin, J. (1992). *Education in Post-Mao China*. London: Praeger.
Lipset, S.M. (1981). *Political Man* (expanded and updated edition). Baltimore: Johns Hopkins University Press.
Liu Hanzhang (1988). "The Labour Market Should Be More Competitive." *Journal of the Guangzhou College of Education*, 3, 12–15 (in Chinese).
Lloyd George, R. (1992). *The East-West Pendulum*. Cambridge: Woodhead and Faulkner.
Lo Bunong (1985). "Education and Regional Economic Development." *Financial Research (Caizheng Yanjiu)*, 9, 10 (in Chinese).
Lo, L. (1991). "Higher Education and Professional Manpower." In: Huan, H.C. and Brosseau, M. (eds.) *China Review*. Chinese University Press, 1–20.

Lofstedt, J. (1980). "Enrollment Developments in China." Institute of International Education, Stockholm University.

——— (1990). "Human Resources in Chinese Development: Needs and Supply of Competencies." IIEP Research Report No. 80. Paris: IIEP.

Long, S. (1991). *Taiwan: China's Last Frontier*. New York: St. Martin's Press.

*Look Japan* (1986). "Softnomics: A New Path for the Postindustrial Age." May 10, p. 10.

Low, Linda et al. (1991). *Economics of Education and Manpower Development in Singapore*. Singapore: McGraw-Hill.

Lu Xueyi and Lin Peilin (eds.) (1991). *Comprehensive Report of China's Social Development*. Liaoning People's Publishing House (in Chinese).

Lu Zuji (1990). "A Splendid Decade in Shenzhen's Education, 1980–1990." Shenzhen Education Bureau (in Chinese).

Luk, Bernard Hung Kay (1990). "Privatization and Meritocracy: The Real Issue of the Direct Subsidy Scheme." In: Sweeting, A. (ed.) *Differences and Identities: Educational Argument in Late Twentieth Century Hong Kong*. Hong Kong: Faculty of Education Paper 9, 47–55.

——— (1991). "Chinese Culture in the Hong Kong Curriculum." *Comparative Education Review*, 35, 650–668.

——— (1992). "Hong Kong." In: Wielemans, W. and Chan, P.C.P. (eds.) *Education and Culture in Industrializing Asia*. Leuven: Leuven University Press.

Ma, H. (1988) Examining Indicators of National Development (in Chinese). *Chungchi University Bulletin* 58, 229–272.

Macau, Government of (1993). *Quarterly Economic Bulletin*, 36, first quarter.

Macau, Governo de (1988). Anuario Estatístico. Macau: Direcção dos Serviços de Estatística e Censos.

——— (1989a). *Inquérito ao Ensino 1987/1988*. Macau: Direcção dos Serviços de Estatística e Censos.

——— (1989b). *Macau: A Educação em Numéros*. Macau: Gabinete de Estudos e Planeamento da Acção Educativa, Direcção dos Serviços de Educação.

——— (1990). *Proposta de Lei-Quadro do Sistema Educativo de Macau: Anteprojecto*. Macau: Gabinete do Secretário-Adjunto para a Educação e Adminstração Pública.

——— (1991a). *Macau Censos '91: Resultados Preliminares*. Macau: Direcção de Serviços de Estatística e Censos.

——— (1991b). *Macau em Numéros*. Macau: Direcção dos Serviços de Estatística e Censos.

——— (1991c). *Anuario Estatístico*. Macau: Direcção dos Serviços de Estatística e Censos.

——— (1991d). "Sistema Educativo de Macau." Decreto-Lei no.11/91/M, *Boletim Oficial de Macau*. Supplement to No. 34.

Mah Hui Lim (1985). "Affirmative Action, Ethnicity and Integration: The Case of Malaysia." *Ethnic and Racial Studies*, 8, 2, April.

Mahathir Mohamad (1991). *Malaysia: The Way Forward*. Kuala Lumpur: Centre for Economic Research and Services, Malaysian Business Council.

Maimunah, S. and Lewin, K. (1991). "Curriculum Development in Malaysia." In: Marsh, C. and Morris, P. (eds.) *Curriculum Development in East Asia*. London: Falmer Press.

Makino, Shigeru (1986). "Japan's Education System and Its Social Implications." *Japan Education Journal*, no. 27, 1–7.

Malaya (1956). *A Plan of Development for Malaya, 1956–60*. Kuala Lumpur: Government Printers.

——— (1961). *Second Malaya Plan, 1961–1965*. Kuala Lumpur: Government Printers.

Malaysia (1966). *First Malaysia Plan, 1966–1970*. Kuala Lumpur: Government Print-

ers.
——— (1970). *Second Malaysia Plan, 1971–1975*. Kuala Lumpur: Government Printers.
——— (1976). *Third Malaysia Plan, 1976–1980*. Kuala Lumpur: Government Printers.
——— (1979). *Cabinet Committee Report on the Review of the Implementation of the National Education Policy*. Kuala Lumpur: Government Printers.
——— (1981). *Fourth Malaysia Plan, 1981–1985*. Kuala Lumpur: National Printing Department.
——— (1986a). *Fifth Malaysia Plan, 1986–1990*. Kuala Lumpur: National Printing Department.
——— (1986). *Medium and Long-Term Industrial Master Plan, 1986–95*. Kuala Lumpur: Malaysian Industrial Development Authority (MIDA) and United Nations Industrial Development Organisation (UNIDO). 3 (5) Manpower and Training.
——— (1991). *Sixth Malaysia Plan 1991–1995*. Kuala Lumpur: National Printing Department.
Mao Zedong (1965). *On the Correct Handling of People's Contradictions*. Selected Works of Mao Zedong, Vol. 4. Beijing: Beijing Foreign Language Press.
Marsh, C. and Morris, P. (eds.) (1991). *Curriculum Development in East Asia*. London: Falmer Press.
Martin, R. (1982). "The Socialization of Children in China and on Taiwan: An Analysis of Elementary School Textbooks." In: Altbach, P.G., Arnove, R.F. and Kelly, G.P. (eds.) *Comparative Education*. New York: Macmillan, 137–157.
Maruya, T. (1992). "Guangdong as a Model of National Economic Development for China." In: Chen, E. and Maruya, T. (eds.) *A Decade of "Open Door" Economic Development in China, 1979–1989*. Centre of Asian Studies Occasional Papers and Monographs No. 104 (in Chinese).
Masuda, Shigeo (1986). "Technology in the Advanced Society." *Japan Echo*, 13, 5–8.
Maxwell, N. (ed.) (1979). *China's Road to Development* (second edition). Oxford: Pergamon.
McClelland, D.C. (1961). *The Achieving Society*. New York: Free Press.
Mehmet, Oza (1988). *Development in Malaysia: Poverty, Wealth and Trusteeship*. Kuala Lumpur: INSAN, Institute of Social Analysis.
Mellor, Bernard (1988). *The University of East Asia: Origin and Outlook*. Hong Kong: University of East Asia Press.
Miners, N.J. (1993). "Constitution and Administration." In: Choi, P.K. and Ho, L.S. (eds.) *The Other Hong Kong Report, 1993*. Hong Kong: Chinese University Press, 1–22.
Ministry of Education, Japan (1963). *Japan's Growth and Education: Educational Development in Relation to Socio-Economic Growth*. 1962 White Paper on Education. Tokyo: Ministry of Education.
——— (1965). *Higher Education in Postwar Japan: The Ministry of Education's 1964 White Paper*, ed. & trans. J.E. Blewett. Tokyo: Sophia University Press.
——— (1969). *Education in Japan: A Graphic Presentation*. Tokyo: The Ministry.
——— (1983). *Education in Japan: A Graphic Presentation*. Tokyo: The Ministry.
——— (1992). *Development of Education in Japan, 1990–1992*. Tokyo: Ministry of Education.
Ministry of Education, Korea (1987). *Statistical Yearbook of Education*, 1965–1986. Seoul: Ministry of Education.
——— (1993). *Statistical Yearbook of Education*, 1975–1992. Seoul: Ministry of Education.
Ministry of Education, Malaya (1964). *Comprehensive Education*. Kuala Lumpur: Government Printers.
Ministry of Education, Malaysia (1986). *Educational Statistics of Malaysia 1980–1985*.

Kuala Lumpur: Educational Planning and Research Division, Ministry of Education, Malaysia.
——— (1991). *Educational Statistics of Malaysia, 1989*. Kuala Lumpur: Educational Planning and Research Division, Ministry of Education, Malaysia.
Ministry of Education, Singapore (Various years). *Key Education Statistics*. Singapore: Ministry of Education.
——— (1960). *Report on Vocational and Technical Education*. Singapore: Government of Singapore.
——— (1978). *Report on the Ministry of Education*. Singapore: Government of Singapore.
——— (1979). *Report of the Committee on Moral Education*. Singapore: Government of Singapore.
——— (1991). *Improving Primary School Education*. Singapore: Government of Singapore.
Ministry of Education, Taiwan (1975). *Curriculum Guidelines for Primary Schools* (in Chinese). Taipei: Cheng-Chong Publisher.
——— (1985). *Curriculum Guidelines for Junior High Schools* (in Chinese). Taipei: Cheng-Chong Publisher.
——— (1991). *Indices of Educational Statistics of the Republic of China*. Taipei: Ministry of Education.
——— (1992). *Educational Statistics of the Republic of China, 1992*. Taipei: Ministry of Education.
Ministry of Trade & Industry (1986). *The Singapore Economy: New Directions*. Singapore: Ministry of Trade and Industry.
Mokhzani, B.A.R. (1965). "The Study of Social Stratification and Social Mobility in Malaysia." *East Asian Cultural Studies*, 4, 1–4, March.
Morishima, M. (1982). *Why Has Japan "Succeeded?" Western Technology and the Japanese Ethos*. New York: Cambridge University Press.
Morley, J.W. (1974). "The Futurist Vision." In James, J.W. (ed.) *Prologue to the Future: The United States and Japan in the Postindustrial Age*. Lexington, Mass.: D.C. Heath, 3–17.
Morris, P. (1995). *The Hong Kong School Curriculum: Development, Policies and Issues*. Hong Kong: University of Hong Kong Press.
——— (1988). "The Effect on the School Curriculum of Hong Kong's Return to Chinese Sovereignty in 1997." *Journal of Curriculum Studies*, 20, 509–520.
Morris, P., McClelland, J.A.G. and Leung, Y.M. (1994). "Higher Education in Hong Kong: The Context of and Rationale for Rapid Expansion." *Higher Education*, 27, 125–140.
Morris, P. and Sweeting, A. (1991). "Education and Politics: The Case of Hong Kong from an Historical Perspective." *Oxford Review of Education*, 17, 3, 249–267.
Mudzaffar, Chandra (1984). "Has the Communal Situation Worsened over the Last Decade? Some Preliminary Thoughts." In: Ali, S. Husin (ed.) *Ethnicity, Class and Development, Malaysia*. Kuala Lumpur: Persatuan Sains Sosial Malaysia.
Mukherjee, Hena. (1983). "Moral Education in a Plural Society: Malaysia." *Journal of Moral Education*, 12, 2, 125–30.
Mukherjee, Hena and Ahmad, Khairiah (1988). "The Quest for National Unity: Language Textbooks in Malaysia." In: Altbach, Philip G. and Kelly, Gail P. (eds.) *Textbooks in the Third World: Policy, Content and Context*. New York: Garland Publishing.
Mukherjee, Hena and Jasbir Sarjit Singh (1985). "Education and Social Policy: The Malaysian Case." *Prospects*, 15, 2, 289–300.
Mukherjee, Hena, Ahmad, Khairiah et al. (1984). *The Malaysia Secondary School Curriculum and National Unity*. Department of National Unity, Prime Minister's Department, Malaysia.
Murad bin Mohd Nor (1973). *Laporan Jawatankuasa di atas Kajian Pendapat*

*Pelajaran dan Masyarakat (Dropout Report)*. Kuala Lumpur: Government Printers.

Murray, T. (ed.) (1992). *Education's Role in National Development Plans: Ten Country Cases*. New York: Praeger.

Myers, R.H. (1980). *The Chinese Economy, Past and Present*. California: Wadsworth.

——— (1990). "The Economic Development of the Republic of China on Taiwan, 1965–1981." In: Lau, L. (ed.) *Models of Development: A Comparative Study of Economic Growth in South Korea and Taiwan*. San Francisco: ICS Press, 17–63.

Myrdal, G. (1968). *Asian Drama*. London: Allen Lane.

Nairai, Osamu (1983). *Structural Changes in Japan's Economy.* Tokyo: Foreign Press Centre.

National Center for Education Development Research (ed.) (1990). *The Current Stituation and Prospects on Educational Development in China in the Context of Economic and Social Development*. China Excellence Publishing Corporation (in Chinese).

National Council on Educational Reform (1986). *Summary of Second Report on Educational Reform*. Tokyo: The Council.

Nolan, P. (1990). "Background to the Chinese Reforms of the 1980s." In: Nolan, P. and Dong, F. (eds.) *The Chinese Economy and Its Future*. Cambridge: Politic Press.

Nolan, P. and Dong, F. (eds.) (1990). *The Chinese Economy and Its Future*. Cambridge: Polity Press.

Ohashi, Yutaka (1975). "Evaluating Curriculum Change in Japan." In: Adey, Philip (ed.) *Innovation in Science Education.* Proceedings of the Second UK/Japan Science Education Seminar held at Chelsea College, University of London, September 8–12. London: British Council.

Pan Mouyuan (1986). *Traditional Teaching Methods and Reforms*. Shanghai: East China Normal University Press (in Chinese).

Pan Zhongming (1992). "An Abridged Report on the Investigation Study for Setting Teaching Plans for Senior Secondary Education." *Selection of Research Results of the Central Institute of Educational Studies*. Educational Science Press (in Chinese).

Pang, E.F. and Lim, Linda (1979). "The School System and Social Structure in Singapore." In: *Singapore Undergrad*, Special Issue.

Park, S. (1984). "Causes and the Process of Change in Earnings Differentials by Education." In: Park, F. and Park, S. (eds.) *Wage Structures in Korea*. Seoul: Korea Development Institute.

Parkins, Geoffrey (1985). "Japanese Youth 'too pampered.'" *The Times Higher Education Supplement*, February 8.

Passin, Herbert (1965). *Society and Education in Japan*. New York: Teachers College, Columbia University.

Patrick, Hugh (ed.) (1976). *Japanese Industrialization and Its Social Consequences.* Berkeley: University of California Press.

Peck, James (1971). "The Roots of Rhetoric: The Professional Ideology of America's China Watchers." In: Friedmann, E. and Selden, M. (eds.) *America's Asia: Dissenting Essays on Asian-American Relations*. New York: Vintage Books.

Perkins, D.H. (1975). *China's Modern Economy in Historical Perspective*. Stanford, Calif.: Stanford University Press.

——— (1988). *China, Asia's Next Economic Giant?* Seattle: University of Washington Press.

Peters, R.S. (1981). *Moral Development and Moral Education*. London: George Allen and Unwin.

Philips, D.R. and Yeh. A, (1990). "Foreign Investment and Trade: Impact on Spatial Structure of the Economy." In: Cannon, T. and Jenkins, A. (eds.) *The Geog-*

*raphy of Contemporary China*. Cambridge: Routledge.
Pires, B.V. (1991). "Origins and Early History of Macau." In: Cremer, R.D. (ed.) *Macau: City of Commerce and Culture* (second edition). Hong Kong: API Press.
Post, D. (1993). "Educational Attainment and the Role of the State in Hong Kong." *Comparative Education Review*, 37, 3, 240–262.
Postiglione, G. (1992). "China's National Minorities and Educational Change." *Journal of Contemporary Asia*, 22, 1, 20–44.
Premfors, R. (1980). "How Much Higher Education Is Enough?" *Comparative Education Review* 24, 302–322.
Provisional Council on Educational Reform (1985). *First Report on Educational Reform*. Tokyo: The Council.
Psacharopoulos, G. (1973). *Returns to Education: An International Comparison*. San Francisco: Jossey-Bass.
——— (1981). "Returns to Education: An Updated International Comparison." *Comparative Education*, 17, 3.
——— (1988). "Critical Issues in Education: A World Agenda." In: *International Journal of Educational Development*, 8, 1–7.
Psacharopoulos, G. & Loxley, W. (1985). *Diversified Secondary Education and Development*. Baltimore: Johns Hopkins University Press.
Qian Jiaju (1983). "Investment in Intelligence is the Top Priority of Financial Expenditure." *Social Sciences (Shehui Kexue)*, 5, 8–12 (in Chinese).
——— (1986) Speech at the People's Political Consultative Congress, reported in *Ta Kung Pao*, Hong Kong, May 19.
Qin Xin (1987). "Examine Curricular Structure and Reform Teaching Materials in Middle Schools." *Curriculum, Teaching Materials and Teaching Methods (Keching, Jiaocai & Jiaofa)*, 8, 24–27 (in Chinese).
Quah, Jon S.T. (ed.) (1990). *In Search of Singapore's National Values*. Singapore: Times Academic Press.
Rabieyah Mat (1986). "Educational Opportunity, Social Mobility and Poverty Reduction in Peninsular Malaysia, 1972–1982." Unpublished Ph.D. thesis, University of Science, Penang, Malaysia.
Rangel, J.A.H. (1991). "Prospects and Directions for Education." In: Cremer, R.D. (ed.) *Macau: City of Commerce and Culture*. Hong Kong: API Press.
Ranis, G. (1979). "Industrial Development." In: Galenson, W. (ed.) *Economic Growth and Structural Change in Taiwan: The Postwar Experience of the Republic of China*, 206–263. Ithaca: Cornell University Press.
Rassis, G. and Malmrood, S.A. (1992). *The Political Economy of Development Policy Change*. Cambridge: Blackwell.
Reid, Linda J. (1988). *The Politics of Education in Malaysia*. Monograph Series, Political Science Department, University of Tasmania.
Reischauer, Edwin O. (1977). *The Japanese*. Tokyo: Belknap Press.
——— (1988). *The Japanese Today: Change and Continuity*. Tokyo: Belknap Press.
Research Committee on National Development (1973). "A Study on the Financial Issues of the Nine-Year National Education" (in Chinese). *Cultural Study Report No. 13*. Taipei: Research Committee on National Development.
Richardson, B.M. (1974). *The Political Culture of Japan*. Berkeley: University of California Press.
Robinson, T.W. (ed.) (1991). *Democracy and Development in East Asia*. Washington, D.C.: AEI Press.
Rosa, Alexandre (1990). "Macau Education in the Period of Transition: An Overview and Prospects." Paper presented at the UNESCO International Congress on Planning and Management of Educational Development, Mexico City.
——— (1992). "Educaçaõ em Mudanca." *Macau*, second series, 2, 63–67.
Rozman, G. (ed.) (1991). *The East Asian Region: Confucian Heritage and Its Mod-*

*ern Adaptation*. Princeton: Princeton University Press.
Rudner, M. (1975). *Nationalism, Planning and Economic Modernization in Malaysia: The Politics of Beginning Development.* London: Sage Publications.
Sanyal, Bikas C. (1983). "Economic Growth and the Training System in the Asian Countries." (Typescript), IIEP. Paris: UNESCO.
Sautman, B. (1991). "Politicization, Hyperpoliticization and Depoliticization of Chinese Education." *Comparative Education Review*, 35, 4, 669–689.
Schlossstein, Steven (1991). *Asia's New Little Dragons: The Dynamic Emergence of Indonesia, Thailand and Malaysia*. Chicago: Contemporary Books.
Schultz, T. (1961). *Investment in Human Beings*. Chicago, Ill.: University of Chicago Press.
——— (1965). "Investment in Human Capital." *American Economic Review,* 51, 1–17.
Scott, I. (1989). *Political Change and the Crisis of Legitimacy in Hong Kong*. Hong Kong: Oxford University Press.
SEAMEO (1971). *Report on Education in Malaysia in Connection with Third Regional Conference of Ministers of Education and Those Responsible for Economic Planning in Asia.* Kuala Lumpur: SEAMEO.
Shee Poon Kim (1985). "The Evolution of the Political System." In: Quah, Jon S. T., Chan Heng Chee and Seah Chee Meow (eds.) *Government and Politics of Singapore*. Singapore: Oxford University Press.
Shen Fuchuo (1993). "Implementation of Curriculum for 9-Year Basic Education in Zhejiang Province." Paper presented at the conference on comparative analysis of the curriculum for 9-year basic education in Zhejiang province, Hong Kong and Taiwan. Hanzhou, June (in Chinese).
Shenzhen Education Bureau (1991). *A Spendid Decade in Shenzhen's Education, 1980–1990*. Shenzhen: Shenzhen Education Bureau Press (in Chinese).
Shenzhen Educational Science Research Institute (ed.) (1991). *A Study of the Strategies of Educational Development in Shenzhen.* Guangzhou: Guangdong Education Press.
Shenzhen Statistics Bureau (1991). *Annual Summary of Statistics*. Shenzhen Statistical Bureau Press (in Chinese).
Shibagaki, Kazuo (1987). "Japan's Development Aid Policy as Motor for Asia-Pacific Cooperation." In: *East Asia: International Review of Economic, Political and Social Development*. Boulder, Colo.: Westview Press.
Shimahara, Nobuo K. (1979). *Adaptation and Education in Japan*. New York: Praeger.
SIHRD (Shanghai Institute of Human Resource Development) (1991a). *Basic Education and National Development: Forty Years of Chinese Experience*. Beijing: People's Education Press (in Chinese).
——— (1991b). *Report on Education Expenditure in China, 1991*. Beijing: Higher Education Press (in Chinese).
——— (1992). *Report on Education Expenditure in China, 1992*. Beijing: Higher Education Press (in Chinese).
Singh, Jasbir Sarjit (1973). "Education and Social Mobility in Malaysia: A Case Study of Petaling Jaya." Unpublished Ph.D. thesis, University of Malaya, Kuala Lumpur.
——— (1989). "Scientific Personnel, Research Environment, and Higher Education in Malaysia." In: Altbach, Philip G. et al. (eds.) *Scientific Development and Higher Education: The Case of Newly Industralizing Nations*. New York: Praeger.
——— (1991a). "Higher Education and Development: The Experience of Four Newly Industrializing Countries in Asia." *Prospects* 21, 3, 386–400.
——— (1991b). "Multicultural Education, Social Equity and National Unity in Malaysia." In: Ibrahim, Alladin M. and Bacchus, M. Kazim (eds.) *Education, Politics and State in Multicultural Societies*. Needham Heights, Mass.: Ginn Press.

Singleton, John (1990). "Gambaru: A Japanese Cultural Theory of Learning." In: Shields, James J., Jr. (ed.) *Japanese Schooling: Patterns of Socialization, Equality and Political Control.* University Park: Pennsylvania State University Press, pp. 8–15.

Sit, V.F.S., Cremer, R.D. and Wong, S.L. (1991). *Entrepreneurs and Enterprises in Macau: A Study of Industrial Development.* Hong Kong.

Skolnik, R.L. (1976). *The Nation Wide Learning System in Singapore.* Singapore: Institute of Southeast Asian Studies.

Smith, D.C. (ed.) (1991). *The Confucian Continuum: Educational Modernization in Taiwan.* New York: Praeger.

Smith, Michael (1985). "Japan." In: Smith, M. et al., *Asia's New Industrial World.* London: Methuen, 5-36.

Snodgrass, Donald (1980). *Inequality and Economic Development in Malaysia.* Kuala Lumpur: Oxford University Press.

So, D.W.C. (1992). "Language-Based Bifurcation of Secondary Education in Hong Kong: Past, Present, and Future." In: Kwong, L.K.K. (ed.) *Into the Twenty First Century: Issues of Language in Education in Hong Kong.* Hong Kong: Linguistic Society of Hong Kong.

Sobel, I. (1978). "The Human Capital Revolution in Economic Development: Its Current History and Status." *Comparative Education Review,* 22, 2, 278–304.

"Softnomics: A New Path for the Post-industrial Age." (1986). *Look Japan,* May 10, p. 10.

Sohn, I. (1971). *Modern History of Korean Education.* Yonsei University, June.

Soon Teck Wong (1992). *Development of Human Resources and Technological Capability in Singapore.* Washington, D.C.: ED1 (World Bank) Working Papers.

State Education Commission (1992a). *Statistical Yearbook of China.* Beijing: State Education Commission (in Chinese).

——— (1992b). *Development Report of China.* Beijing: State Education Commission (in Chinese).

State Education Planning Office (1984). *Achievement of Education in China, 1949–1983.* Beijing: People's Education Press (in Chinese).

——— (1992). Summary of Educational Statistics. Beijing: People's Education Press (in Chinese).

State Statistics Bureau (1992a). *Statistical Yearbook of China.* Beijing: State Statistics Bureau Press (in Chinese).

——— (1992b). *State Development Report.* Beijing: State Statistics Bureau Press (in Chinese).

*Statistical Survey of Japan's Economy, 1982* (1982). Tokyo: Economic and Foreign Affairs Research Association.

Statistics Bureau (various years). *Statistical Handbook of Japan.* Tokyo: Japan Statistical Association.

Stephens, Michael D. (1991). *Japan and Education.* London: Macmillan.

Sun, C. (1987). "A Perspective of the Republic of China Educational Development in the 21st Century." Keynote Speech to the International Seminar on Toward the 21st Century's Education: Prospects for Higher and Adult Education, Taipei, May 25.

Sun Jinlan (1988). "Speed up the Reform of the Structure of Secondary Education, Raise the Economic and Social Benefits of Education." In: Li Shouxin et al. (eds.) *Problems of Education Development in China.* Beijing: China Planning Press (in Chinese).

Sung, Y.W. (1991). *China–Hong Kong Connection: The Key to China's Open Door Policy.* Cambridge: Cambridge University Press.

Sweeting, A. (1983). "Hong Kong." In: Thomas, R.M. and Postlethewaite, T.N. (eds.) *Schooling in East Asia: Forces of Change.* Oxford: Pergamon, 272–297.

——— (1989). "The Reconstruction of Education in Post-War Hong Kong, 1945–

1954: Variations in the Process of Policy Making." Ph.D. thesis, University of Hong Kong.
——— (1990a). *Education in Hong Kong Pre-1841 to 1941: Fact and Opinion.* Hong Kong: Hong Kong University Press.
——— (1990b). "The Significance of June 4, 1989 for Education in Hong Kong." In: Sweeting, A. (ed.) *Differences and Identities: Educational Argument in Late Twentieth Century Hong Kong.* Hong Kong: Faculty of Education, 13–28.
——— (1991a). "Politics and the Art of Teaching History in Hong Kong." *Teaching History*, 64, 30–37.
——— (1991b). "Hong Kong Education within Historical Processes." In: Postiglione, G.A.P. and Leung, Y.M. (eds.) *Education and Society in Hong Kong: Toward One Country and Two Systems.* New York: M.E. Sharpe, 39–81.
——— (1993). *A Phoenix Transformed: The Reconstruction of Education in Post-War Hong Kong.* Hong Kong: Oxford University Press.
——— (1995). "Educational Policy in a Time of Transition: The Case of Hong Kong." *Research Papers in Education*, 10, 1, 101–129.
Sweeting, A. and Morris, P. (1993). "Educational Reform in Post-War Hong Kong: Planning and Crisis Intervention." *International Journal of Educational Development*, 13, 3, 201–216.
Sze, W.T. (1990). "The Cat and the Pigeons: Relations between the Hong Kong Government and the Universities." In: Sweeting, A. (ed.) *Differences and Identities: Educational Argument in Late Twentieth Century Hong Kong.* Hong Kong: Faculty of Education, 127–159.
——— (1993). "The Cat, Pigeons, Hawks, and Headless Chicks: ECR5 and Aspects of Teacher Professionalism." In: Tsoi, A.B.M. and Johnson, I. (eds). *Teacher Education and Development.* Hong Kong: Faculty of Education, 1993, 134–147.
Tai, H. C. (1989). *Confucianism and Economic Development: An Oriental Alternative?* Washington, D.C.: Washington Institute Press.
Takei, Y., Bock, J.C., and Saunders, B. (1973). *Educational Sponsorship by Ethnicity: A Preliminary Assessment of the West Malaysian Experience.* Athens: Ohio University.
Tan, K.J. (1993). "History of the History Curriculum under Colonialism and Decolonisation: A Comparison of Hong Kong and Macau." M.Ed. dissertation, University of Hong Kong.
Tan, Gerald (1992). *The Newly Industralizing Countries of Asia.* Singapore: Times Academic Press.
Tang, K.C. (1991). "Secondary Schools' Mathematics Curricula in Macau and a Comparison with the Mathematics Curriculum in Hong Kong." M.Ed. dissertation, University of Hong Kong.
Tawara, J. (1968). "Education and Training: the Background in Japan." In: Lauwerys, J.A. and Scanlon, D.G. (eds.) *Education within Industry.* The World Yearbook of Education 1968. London: Evans Brothers.
Taylor, A.J.P. (1982). *The Course of German History.* London: Methuen.
Teixeira, Manuel (1982). *A Educaçaõ em Macau.* Macau: Direcção dos Serviços de Educaçaõ e Cultura.
——— (1991). "The Church in Macau." In: Cremer, R.D. (ed.) *Macau: City of Commerce and Culture* (second edition). Hong Kong: API Press.
Teng Weizao (1982). "Socialist Modernisation and the Pattern of Foreign Trade." In: Xu Dixin et al. (eds.) *China's Search for Economic Growth.* Beijing: New World Press (in Chinese).
Tham Seong Chee (1977). *Malays and Modernization.* Singapore: Singapore University Press.
——— (1980). "Schools and Value Development in Singapore." Paper presented at the DSE-RIHED Conference on Cultural Heritage versus Technological Develop-

ment: Challenges to Education. Singapore, September 23–27, 1980.
Thomas, R. Murray (1983). "Malaysia: Cooperation versus Competition—National Unity versus Favored Access to Education." In: Thomas, R. Murray (ed.) *Politics and Education: Cases from Eleven Nations.* Oxford: Pergamon Press.
——— (1991). "Curriculum Development in Indonesia." In: Marsh, C. and Morris, P. (eds.) *Curriculum Development in East Asia.* London: Falmer Press.
To, C.Y. (1965). "The Development of Higher Education in Hong Kong." *Comparative Education Review*, 11, 1, 74–80.
Todaro, M. (1989). *Economic Development in the Third World* (fourth edition). New York: Longman.
Torney, J.V., Oppenhein, A.N. and Russell, F.F. (1975). *Civic Education in Ten Countries.* Stockholm: Almquist and Wiksell.
Tsang, S.Y.S. (1988). *Democracy Shelved: Great Britain, China, and Attempts at Constitutional Reform in Hong Kong.* Hong Kong: Oxford University Press, 1988.
Tsurumi, E.P. (1977). *Japanese Colonial Education in Taiwan, 1895–1945.* Cambridge, Mass.: Harvard University Press.
Tu Weiming (1991). "Core Values in Economic Culture: The Confucian Hypothesis." Paper presented at the workshop on "The Cultural Dimensions of the Pacific Era." Hawaii, January 24-26, 1991.
Tu Weiming, Hejtmanek, M., and Wachman, A. (eds.) (1991). *The Confucian World Observed: A Contemporary Discussion of Confucian Humanism in East Asia.* Honolulu: The East West Centre.
Tyack, D. (1967). *Turning Points in American Educational History.* Massachusetts: Blaisdell.
UNDP (1991). *Human Development Report.* New York: Oxford University Press.
UNESCO (1972). *Literacy 1969–1971: Progress Achieved in Literacy Throughout the World.* Paris: UNESCO.
——— (1990). *Basic Education and Literacy: World Statistical Indicators.* Paris: UNESCO Office of Statistics.
——— (1993). *World Education Report.* Paris: UNESCO.
UNESCO/APIED, NIER (1981). *Moral Education in Asia.* Report of a Joint Study on Moral Education in Asian Countries. Research Bulletin of the National Institute of Educational Research, Tokyo, Japan.
United Nations (1964). *Technology and Development*, VI, New York: United Nations.
Universiti Teknologi Malaysia (1989). *Tracer Study on Graduates of Polytechnics, Technical and Vocational Schools.* Eighth World Bank Loan, Kuala Lumpur, Malaysia.
Valery, N. (1986). "High Technology: Clash and Titans." *The Economist*, August 23.
Visiting Panel (1982). *A Perspective on Education in Hong Kong.* Hong Kong: Government Printer.
Vogel, Ezra F. (1979). *Japan as Number One: Lessons for America.* New York: Harper & Row.
——— (1987). *The Impact of Japan on a Changing World.* Hong Kong: The Chinese University Press.
——— (1988). *The Japanese Today.* Tokyo: Tuttle.
——— (1991). *The Four Little Dragons.* Cambridge, Mass., and London, England: Harvard University Press.
Von Kopp, Boltho (1985). "Technological Development, 'Technological Mind' and School: A Comparative Analysis with Special Reference to Japan." *Compare*, 15, 2, 121–128.
Wade, R. (1990). *Governing the Market: Economic Theory and the Role of Government in East Asian Industrialization.* Princeton: Princeton University Press.
Walters, P.B. (1981). "Educational Change and National Economic Development." *Harvard Educational Review*, 51, 1.
Wan Li (1985). "The Work of Teachers Greatly Determines the Future of the Coun-

try." Speech at the Beijing Teacher Festival, September 10, 1985. In: State Education Commission Policy Office (1992) (ed.) *Important Education Documents since the Third Plenary Session of the Eleventh Party Congress*. Beijing: Education Science Press (in Chinese).

Wang Bingqian (1989). "Report on the Implementation of the State Budget for 1988 and on the Draft State Budget for 1989," *Beijing Review*, 32, 18 (in Chinese).

Wang Fulang (1988). "Several Problems of the Construction of a Teaching Force for Compulsory Education." *Education Forum (Jiaoyu Luncong)*, 2, 16, 19 (in Chinese).

Wang Shangmai (1986). "A Historical Analysis of the Percentage of Educational Investment in the National Economy." In: *The Future and Development of Higher Education*, 1, 28–29 (in Chinese).

Wang Shenghong (1990). "Speech at the Inaugural Conference of the Shanghai Primary and Secondary Schools Curriculum and Teaching Material Reform Committee." In: *Reform of the Primary and Secondary School Curriculum in Shanghai*. Shanghai: Shanghai Educational Press (in Chinese).

Wang Shouan et al. (1981). *Economics of Worker Education*. Jilin People's Press (in Chinese).

Wang Xiaochang & Bai Nanfeng (1986). *An Economic Field Study of China's Backward Regions*. Chendu: Szechuan People's Press (in Chinese).

Wang Zhenjie (1992). Study on the Policy and Contents of Primary Education in Mainland China. Taiwan National Normal University Education Research Centre (in Chinese).

Ward, F.C. (ed.) (1974). *Education and Development Reconsidered*. London: Praeger.

Waterhouse, Brian (1989). "Japanese Giants Roll Across Asia." *Asian Business*, 25, 10.

Weber, M. (1952). *The Protestant Ethic and the Spirit of Capitalism*. Allen and Unwin: London (first published 1904).

West, E.G. (1975). *Education and the Industrial Revolution*. London: Batsford.

White, Merry (1987). *The Japanese Educational Challenge: A Commitment to Children*. New York: Free Press.

Wielemans, W. and Chan, P.C.P. (eds.) (1992). *Education and Culture in Industrializing Asia*. Leuven: Leuven University Press.

Wilkinson, P. (1969). *Political Elites*. London: Routledge, Kegan and Paul.

Wilson, H.E. (1978). *Social Engineering in Singapore*. Singapore: Singapore University Press.

Wilson, R. (1970). *Learning to Be Chinese: The Political Socialization of Children in Taiwan*. Cambridge, Mass.: MIT Press.

Winckler, E.A. (1988). "Contending Approaches to East Asian Development." In: Winckler, E. A. and Greenhalgh, S. (eds.) *Contending Approaches to the Political Economy of Taiwan*. 20–37. Armonk, N.Y.: M.E. Sharpe.

Wolf, C. (1988) *Markets or Governments: Choosing Between Imperfect Alternatives*. Cambridge, Mass.: MIT Press.

Wong Poh Kam and Ng Chee Yuen (1992). "Singapore: Coping with a Maturing Economy." In: *Southeast Asian Affairs*. Singapore: Institute of Southeast Asian Studies.

Wong, P.M. (1992). "The Evolution of a Secondary School Subject in Hong Kong: The Case of Social Studies." Ph.D. thesis, University of Hong Kong.

Wong, S.L. (1988). *Emigrant Entrepreneurs: Shanghai Industrialists in Hong Kong*. Hong Kong: Oxford University Press.

Woo, J.H. (1991). "Educational and Economic Growth in Taiwan: A Case of Successful Planning." *World Development*, 19, 1029–44.

World Bank (1980a). *Education Sector Policy Paper*. Washington, D.C.: World Bank.

——— (1980b). *World Development Report 1980*. Washington, D.C.: World Bank.

——— (1985). *China: Long Term Development Issues and Options*. Baltimore, Md.:

Johns Hopkins University Press.
——— (1986). *China: Long Term Development Issues and Options.* Washington. D.C.: World Bank.
——— (1988). *World Development Report 1988.* New York: Oxford University Press.
——— (1989). *World Development Report 1989.* New York: Oxford University Press.
——— (1991a). *Vocational and Technical Education and Training: A World Bank Policy Paper.* Washington, D.C.: World Bank.
——— (1991b). *World Development Report.* Washington, D.C.: World Bank.
——— (1993). *The East Asian Miracle: Economic Growth and Public Policy.* Washington, D.C.: World Bank.
Wright, Mary C. (1957). *The Last Stand of Chinese Conservatism.* Stanford: Stanford University Press.
Wu Guangpu (1991). "Basic Education of the Pearl River Delta Region in the 1990s." *Academic Research (Xuexu Yanjiu)*, 3, 39–44 (in Chinese).
Xu Mingdi (1992). *Educational Strategy for the Pearl River Delta.* Guangzhou: Guangdong Higher Education Press (in Chinese).
Yang Zehong (1986). "Summary of the Symposium on Primary and Middle School Teaching Plans Jointly Held by the State Education Commission and the Central Institute of Educational Research." *Curriculum, Teaching Materials and Teaching Methods (Kecheng, Jiaocai and Jiaofu)* 3, 2–4 (in Chinese).
Yano Tsuneta Kinenkai (ed.) (1991). *Niho Kokusei Zue 1991 [Illustrated Book of Facts and Figures on Japan 1991].* Tokyo: Kokuseisha.
Yeo Kim Wah (1973). *Political development in Singapore 1945–1955.* Singapore: Singapore University Press.
Yew Yeok Kim (1982). "Education, National Identity and National Integration: A Survey of Secondary School Students of Chinese Origin in Urban Peninsular Malaysia." Stanford, Calif.: Ph.D. dissertation, Stanford University.
Yip, John (1982). "The Role of the Principal in a Decentralised System of Education Management." In: *Seminar Proceedings: Principalship in a Decentralised System of Education Management.* Singapore: Ministry of Education, Singapore.
You Lin and Wu Qianquo (eds.) (1991). *Socialism in China.* Hongi Press (in Chinese).
Young, Y.R. (1990). "Development through Education: Myth or Reality." *International Journal of Educational Development* 10, 227–30.
——— (1992). "Taiwan." In: Wielemans, W. and Chan, P.C.P. (eds.) *Education and Culture in Industrializing Asia*, 327–378. Leuven: Leuven University Press.
Zepp, R.A. (1991). "Interface of Chinese and Portuguese Cultures." In: Cremer, R.D. (ed.) *Macau: City of Commerce and Culture*, second edition. Hong Kong: API Press.
Zhejiang Education Commission (1991). *Curriculum Guide of 9-Year Basic Education.* Zhejiang: Zhejiang People's Education Press (in Chinese).
Zhongguo Jiaoyubao (1991). "The Teaching Outline for Full-Time Primary and Junior Secondary Schools (trial version)." *Zhongguo Jiaoyubao (Chinese Education Daily)*, November 7 (in Chinese).
Zhou Beilung (ed.) (1990a). *Chinese Education Towards the 21st Century.* Beijing: Higher Education Press (in Chinese).
——— (1990b). "On Some Issues Concerning the Implementation of Compulsory Education." *Education Research (Jiaoyu Yanjiu)*, 2, 14–19 (in Chinese).
Zhou Nanjiao (1992). "Important Issues and Solutions in China's Education Reforms." Paper presented at the Symposium on Education, Social Change and Regional Development, University of Hong Kong Faculty of Education and Centre of Asian Studies, Hong Kong. June (in Chinese).
Zhou Yuliang (ed.) (1990). *Education in Contemporary China.* Hunan: Hunan Education Publishing House.

# Contributors

Mark Bray is a Reader in the Department of Education at the University of Hong Kong.

Saravanan Gopinathan is an Associate Professor in the National Institute of Education, Singapore.

Chon Sun Ihm is a Professor in the Department of Education, King Sejong University, South Korea.

Wing On Lee is a Lecturer in the Department of Education at the University of Hong Kong.

Yat Ming Leung is the Director of the Curriculum Development Institute in Hong Kong.

Paul Morris is a Reader in the Department of Curriculum Studies at the University of Hong Kong.

Hena Mukherjee is an Education Specialist in the Poverty, Population, and Human Resources Division of the China and Mongolia Department of the World Bank.

Jasbir Sarjit Singh is the Chief Program Officer (Higher Education Cooperation) in the Education Department of the Human Resource Development Division of the Commonwealth Secretariat in London.

Anthony Sweeting is a Reader in the Department of Curriculum Studies at the University of Hong Kong.

Yi Rong Young is an Associate Professor in the Graduate Institute of Social Education at the National Taiwan Normal University.

# Index

# Reference Books in International Education

Edward R. Beauchamp, *Series Editor*

Education in the People's Republic of China, Past and Present
*An Annotated Bibliography*
by Franklin Parker
and Betty June Parker

Education in South Asia
*A Select Annotated Bibliography*
by Philip G. Altbach, Denzil Saldanha, and Jeanne Weiler

Textbooks in the Third World
*Policy, Content and Context*
by Philip G. Altbach
and Gail P. Kelly

Education in Israel
*A Source Book*
by Yaacov Iram

Minority Status and Schooling
by Margaret A. Gibson
and John V. Ogbu

Teachers and Teaching in the Developing World
by Val D. Rust and Per Dalin

Russian and Soviet Education, 1731–1989
*A Multilingual Annotated Bibliography*
by William W. Brickman
and John T. Zepper

Education in Sub-Saharan Africa
*A Source Book*
by George E.F. Urch

Education and Cultural Differences
*New Perspectives*
by Douglas Ray
and Deo H. Poonwassie

Contemporary Perspectives in Comparative Education
edited by Robin J. Burns
and Anthony R. Welch

Education in the Arab Gulf States and the Arab World
*An Annotated Bibliographic Guide*
by Nagat El-Sanabary

International and Historical Roots of American Higher Education
by W.H. Cowley
and Don Williams

Education in England and Wales
*An Annotated Bibliography*
by Franklin Parker
and Betty June Parker

Chinese Education
*Problems, Policies, and Prospects*
edited, with an introduction
by Irving Epstein

Early Childhood Education in Asia and the Pacific
*A Source Book*
edited by Stephanie Feeney

Understanding Educational Reform in Global Context
*Economy, Ideology, and the State*
edited by Mark B. Ginsburg

Education and Social Change in Korea
by Don Adams
and Esther E. Gottlieb

EDUCATION AND DISABILITY IN CROSS-CULTURAL PERSPECTIVE
edited by Susan J. Peters

RUSSIAN EDUCATION
*Tradition and Transition*
by Brian Holmes, Gerald H. Read, and Natalya Voskresenskaya

THE UNIFICATION OF GERMAN EDUCATION
by Val D. Rust and Diane Rust

THREE DECADES OF PEACE EDUCATION AROUND THE WORLD
*An Anthology*
edited by Robin J. Burns and Robert Aspeslagh

EDUCATION AND DEVELOPMENT IN EAST ASIA
edited by Paul Morris and Anthony Sweeting

TEACHER EDUCATION IN INDUSTRIALIZED NATIONS
*Issues in Changing Social Contexts*
edited by Nobuo K. Shimahara and Ivan Z. Holowinsky

LEARNING TO TEACH IN TWO CULTURES
*Japan and the United States*
by Nobuo K. Shimahara and Akira Sakai